RESTRICTED

COPY

AIR PUBLICATION 3231

THE SECOND WORLD WAR
1939–1945
ROYAL AIR FORCE

AIRBORNE FORCES

THIS VOLUME MUST NOT BE REPRODUCED IN WHOLE
OR IN PART WITHOUT THE PRIOR AUTHORITY OF
THE AIR MINISTRY

ISSUED BY THE AIR MINISTRY (A.H.B.)
1951

RESTRICTED

The Naval & Military Press Ltd

Published by

The Naval & Military Press Ltd
Unit 10 Ridgewood Industrial Park,
Uckfield, East Sussex,
TN22 5QE England

Tel: +44 (0) 1825 749494
Fax: +44 (0) 1825 765701

www.naval-military-press.com
www.nmarchive.com

In reprinting in facsimile from the original, any imperfections are inevitably reproduced and the quality may fall short of modern type and cartographic standards.

Contents

Page

PART I. THE PROBLEMS OF FORMING AN AIRBORNE FORCE. June 1940 to November 1941.

Chapter 1. Policy and Basic Decisions:

The Central Landing School 2

Initial Policy—The General War Situation—The more urgent needs of other Commands—The First Commitment—Delay regarding Glider production and Glider pilot training—Stop gap Glider pilot training scheme—Duties of the trained Glider pilot—Production of a paper for the Chiefs of Staff—Prime Minister's intervention and the German assault on Crete, May 1941—The Chiefs of Staff Requirement of May 1941—The Chief of Air Staff on Army/Air support.

Air Ministry action after July 1941 12

Gliders—Glider pilots—Paratroops—Aircraft.

War Office action after May 1941 16

Chapter 2. Development, Training and Initial Operation:

The Parachute Training Centre 19

Expansion into the Central landing Establishment.

The Initial Operation: Colossus, February 1941 . . . 25

The Lessons of Operation Colossus.

Parachute Training: February to November 1941 . . . 29

Training of Lambs and Polish troops—Balloon descents and 'Stick' jumping—Further Expansion: October 1941—Training of aircrews for parachute dropping: 1941.

Glider Pilot training: September 1940 to November 1941 . . . 32

The need for combined training facilities.

PART II. EXPANSION INTO AN OPERATIONAL FORCE. November 1941 to October 1943.

Chapter 3. Expansion Policy: November 1941 to April 1943 . . 37

The Army Organisation: November to December 1941—Expansion of the Air components: November 1941 to April 1942—The essential difference between 'individual' and 'collective' training—Formation of the Exercise squadrons and No. 38 Wing Headquarters: January to April 1942—The Airborne Forces Committee—Difficulties regarding shortage of aircraft and the proposal for a 'nucleus force': May 1942—American aircraft and paratroops: May 1942—Decision to form nucleus force and effect on Bomber Command: May 1942—Consequent Expansion of air components: May to October 1942—Increased demands by War Office entailing diversion of bomber effort: July to September 1942—Disagreement at Chief of Staff level regarding comparative priority of Airborne Forces and Bomber Command: October 1942 to November 1943—Prime Minister's decision and Air Ministry/War Office reactions: November 1942—Effect of decision on No. 38 Wing: November 1942 to April 1943—Joint General/Air Staff plans for reduction of Airborne effort: January 1943—The Chief of the Imperial General Staff's continued demands for a large scale force: January to February 1943—The Chief of Air Staff's opposition to any increase of requirement: February to March 1943—Decision to plan for increased Glider pilot training pending results of operation Husky: April 1943.

Chapter 4. Training Development and Minor Operations: November 1941 to October 1943.

Parachute Training 53
Parachute Training at the individual stages: November 1941 to October 1943.

Parachute Operations: November 1941 to November 1942. . . 56
The Bruneval Raid: February 1942—Operation by 1st Parachute Brigade and U.S.A.A.F. in North Africa: November 1942—Commentary.

Glider Training and Operations 64
Glider production—Glider pilot training at the individual stages: November 1941 to October 1943—Glider Pilot training at the ' collective ' stage—Glider operation Freshman: November 1942.

Chapter 5. General Developments and Further Operations . . . 75
The Organisation of No. 38 Wing and its work: 1942 to 1943—The formation and early work of Nos. 296 and 297 Squadrons—No. 38 Wing during the ' nucleus force ' expansion—No. 38 Wing: October 1942 to April 1943—Airborne Exercises—Parachute exercises—Glider exercises—Flying practice for Glider pilots—Parachute training: Middle East 1942 to 1943—Iraq Levies.

The Operation in Sicily: Husky 85
Planning—Final Planning—Preparation and Training—Operation Beggar—The Operations—Operation Elaborate—Experience gained from Husky—Conclusions.

PART III. FULL SCALE USE OF AIRBORNE FORCES. October 1943 to August 1945.

Chapter 6. Airborne Forces in preparation for Overlord . . . 101
Formation of Headquarters, Major-General Airborne Forces—Charter for Major-General Airborne Forces—Formation of Sixth Airborne Division—Formation of No. 38 Group—Operational Organisation—Formation and Role of No. 46 Group—Other functions of No. 46 Group—Casualty Air Evacuation—Anson flights—Large Scale Exercises—Nickel operations.

Chapter 7. Operation Neptune (Overlord):

General Situation 115
The Cover Plan—Diversionary Aids and Cover Support—The Titanic Operations—The Airborne Plan (Operation Neptune)—Joint Planning—Briefing—Routeing—Aids to Navigation—Air/Sea Rescue—Providing the Lift—Available British forces—The Final Plan—Tonga—The Air Plan—The Special Glider Operation.

The Events of 5/6 June 1944 125
Operation Tonga: First Stage—Second Stage: Subsidiary Glider and Main Paratroop Landings—Main Paratroop Landings—3rd Parachute Brigade: Zones ' V ' and ' K '—5th Parachute Brigade: Zone ' N '—Third Stage: Landing of Main Glider Force—The Glider operation against the Merville battery—Operation Tonga: Summary of Results—Operation Mallard—The Re-supply Operations—Rob Roy I—Rob Roy II, III, IV and V—Conclusions—Special Duty Operations—Special Air Service Operations—S.A.S. in relation to Overlord—The American Airborne Operations.

Invasion of Southern France 140
Operation Dragoon—Anvil.

Chapter 8. Development and Policy: June to September 1944.

   Formation of the First Allied Airborne Army 141

   Combined Air Transport Operations Room 145

   Operations Planned and Cancelled during the Period 13 June to 10 September 1944 146
   Swordhilt—Hands Up—Beneficiary—Lucky Strike/Transfigure—Linnet I and II—Comet—Lessons.

   Extension of No. 38 Group Responsibility 149

   Policy and Planning for Operation Market 150
   General Military situation—Object of British Second Army Plan—Main Plan—The Terrain—Intelligence—The Time—Air Forces Available—Order of Battle and Chain of Command—The Landing and Dropping Zones—The Flight Plan—Routes for the Airborne Forces—Navigational Aids—Air Support—Briefing.

Chapter 9. Operation Market:

   The First Lift: 17 September, 1944 161
   Landing Zones 'S', 'Z', 'X' and 'N'—The American Operations—The Ground Situation—Arnhem—Nimegen/Eindhoven.

   The Second Lift: 18 September, 1944 165
   Landing Zones 'X', 'S', 'L' and 'Y'—The Ground Situation Arnhem Sector—Nimegen/Eindhoven Sector.

   The Third Lift: 19 September, 1944 167
   Landing/Dropping Zone 'L'—Landing Zone 'X'—Supply Dropping Point 'V'.

   The Fourth Lift (D+3): 20 September, 1944 168
   Dropping Zone 'Z'—Supply Dropping Point 691785.

   The Fifth Lift (D+4): 21 September, 1944 169
   Supply Dropping Point 693785.

   The Sixth Lift (D+6): 23 September, 1944 170
   The Drop.

   The Seventh Lift (D+7): 24 September, 1944 171

   The Eighth Lift (D+8): 25 September, 1944 171

   Operation Market: Air Movement Summary (R.A.F.) . . . 172
   Conclusions.

   German Reaction to Operation Market 178

Chapter 10. Further Operations in Europe:

   Developments prior to Operation Varsity 179
   Control of No. 46 Group—Naples II—No. 38 Group moves to new location—Training—Pre-crew training for S.A.S./S.O.E. Operations—Training prior to May 1945—No. 1665 Heavy Conversion Unit—Operational Training Units—Exercise Token.

   Crossing the Rhine: Operation Varsity 182
   General situation—Airborne Planning—Providing aircraft and crews for the Lift—Order of Battle (Air Forces)—Supporting Air Effort—Air Defence of the Dropping Zones—The Flight Plan—The Lift of the 6th Airborne Division—The Final Stages of Preparation—The Operation—The Airborne Operation—The Paratroop Lift—The Glider Lift—Re-supply—Enemy Opposition—Glider Loading and Unloading—Casualties—R.A.F. No. 46 Group—Conclusions.

   Minor Airborne Operations 199
   Amherst and Keystone—Conclusions—Operation Schnapps and Doomsday—Conclusion.

	Page
Chapter 11. Dominion and Allied Airborne Forces:	205

Australia—Canada—New Zealand—South Africa—United States of America—Other Allied Airborne Forces.

Chapter 12. Airborne Forces in India and Far East:

Development 209
Visit of Major-General Airborne Forces to India—Parachutes—Glider training—Formation of No. 238 Group—The purposes of No. 238 Group.

Operations 221
The Capture of Rangoon—Operation Dracula.

Chapter 13. Enemy Airborne Forces:

German Airborne Forces 225
Inception—First Use of Airborne Forces—Planned Operation for Sudetenland—Command—Tactics—Polish Campaign—The Western Campaign—Operations in Holland—Proposed attack on England—The Operations in Crete—Training—Aircraft—Gliders—Proposed Operations —New German Airborne Formations—Operations in Italy—Expansion of Paratroop Forces—The Final Phase—The Ardennes Offensive.

Japanese Airborne Forces 235
Gliders—Operations.

Italian Airborne Forces 237

Chapter 14. Conclusions 239
Air Superiority—Moral Effect on the Enemy—The 'freezing' of transport aircraft—Command—Planning—Training—Intelligence and Briefing—Day or night—Navigation—Type of Aircraft—Tow Ropes—Launching an airborne operation—Gliders and Glider Pilots—Air Support for Airborne Operations—Communications—Re-supply—Dropping/Landing Zones.

APPENDICES

1. The Glider
2. The Parachute
3. Standard Operating Procedure for Airborne and Troop Carrier Units
4. The Aircraft
5. Victoria Cross Citation
6. Glider Recovery
7. Supply Dropping from Medium Levels
8. Radar Homing Devices
9. Equipment for Dropping Stores from Aircraft
10. Operations Planned and Cancelled 1945
11. Diagram of Communications No. 1 Airborne Corps
12. Diagram First Allied Airborne Army. Plan of Command

MAPS AND DIAGRAMS

1. Operation Husky. South-East Sicily		91
2. Operation Neptune (Normandy). Route Flight Diagram	facing	118
3. Operation Neptune (Normandy). Dropping/Landing Zones	facing	124
4. Operation Tonga (Normandy). Caen Canal and River Orne		127
5. Operation Mallard (Normandy). Gliders on Zone 'N'		133
6. Operation Market (Arnhem). Dropping/Landing Zones	facing	156
7. Operation Market (Arnhem). Route Flight Diagram	facing	158
8. Operation Market (Arnhem). Gliders on Zones 'S' and 'Z'		163
9. Operation Market (Arnhem). Paratroops on Zone 'X'		164
10. Operation Varsity (Rhine). Route Flight Diagram	facing	184
11. Operation Varsity (Rhine). Dropping/Landing Zones	facing	188
12. Operation Varsity (Rhine). German Children Watching Dakotas		194
13. Operation Varsity (Rhine). Gliders in Tow		195
14. The Invasion of Crete	facing	230
15. The Halifax Aircraft		288
16. The Albemarle Aircraft		289
17. The Stirling Aircraft		290
18. The Whitley Aircraft		291
19. The Dakota Aircraft		292
20. Glider Marshalling at Woodbridge		293
21. The Horsa Glider		294
22. The Hamilcar Glider		295

PART I

THE PROBLEMS OF FORMING AN AIRBORNE FORCE JUNE 1940 TO NOVEMBER 1941

PART I

THE PROBLEMS OF FORMING AN AIRBORNE FORCE JUNE 1940 TO NOVEMBER 1941

CHAPTER 1

POLICY AND BASIC DECISIONS

Although the movement of small numbers of troops by air had previously been undertaken by the Royal Air Force it is true to say that the idea of transporting a whole army by air originated in Russia in the early nineteen thirties. Faced always by an internal security problem caused by vast territories and poor communications, the Russians looked to air transport for a solution. From the carriage and landing of men and equipment by powered aircraft[1], they soon proceeded to the novel idea of landing troops by parachute. Every official encouragement was given by the Russians to parachuting and glider flying in an endeavour to make them national pastimes, a reminder of the English attitude towards the longbow in the 14th and 15th centuries.

In 1936, a British Military Mission, led by General, later Field Marshal Lord Wavell, attended large scale Red Army manoeuvres near Minsk and witnessed the dropping of some 1,500 troops by parachute. In their report the Mission remarked that although this demonstration was a most spectacular performance the use of parachutes was of doubtful tactical value. Nevertheless, in 1937, the Committee of Imperial Defence took note of the possibility of airborne raids being made on this country in time of war but thought that the danger of such raids on any considerable scale was, at that time, negligible[2].

By 1939, however, it had become known that the Germans were experimenting with the towing of glider trains, and at the request of the Deputy Chiefs of Staff investigations had been carried out at the Inter-Services Training and Development Centre. As a result of these investigations it was considered proven that under favourable conditions troops could be dropped successfully, although doubts were expressed as to whether the losses incurred in the face of heavy opposition would be warranted by the results likely to be achieved. One sentence of the report is particularly ominous in view of after events:

" . . . and it is for consideration as to whether the present is the time to divert effort to the production of a weapon which may never be used."

This diversion of effort towards an unproven cause was the main objection to the raising of the force, not only in 1939 but also during the first four years of war[3].

Since the Germans and Russians were known to possess airborne units however, it was felt that something should be done. Our allies, the French, had formed two companies of *"Infanterie de l'Air"* with an estimated total strength of about 300 men, and the suggestion was that two British officers

---

[1] In 1935 they evolved a system of carrying a tank slung between the undercarriage of an aircraft.
[2] Report on visit to U.S.S.R. Red Army manoeuvres in the White Russian Military District—Minsk: September 1936. Minutes of the 280th Meeting of the Committee of Imperial Defence. 25 February 1937.
[3] File A.M. 1081 " The dropping of troops by parachute ": Sub-Committee of Inter-Services training Encl. 1A.

should visit these units and study their technique. The visit never took place. Arrangements, initiated in April 1939, proceeded at such a leisurely pace that they were still incomplete when war was declared, and in October 1939, the visit was cancelled entirely[1].

The subject was not raised again until June 1940, by which time France had been overrun and German troops were in occupation. It was then the Prime Minister, Mr. Winston Churchill, who re-opened the subject with a minute which he wrote on 6 June for the attention of the War Office.

" We ought to have a corps of at least 5,000 parachute troops, including a proportion of Australians, New Zealanders and Canadians together with some trustworthy people from Norway and France. . . . I hear something is already being done to form such a corps but only I believe on a very small scale. Advantage must be taken of the summer to train these troops, who can none the less, play their part meanwhile as shock troops in home defence. Pray let me have a note from the War Office on the subject[2]."

The Central Landing School

On receipt of the minute from the Prime Minister, discussions took place between the Air and General Staffs regarding the setting up of the necessary training organisation. Immediately innumerable problems presented themselves: the provision of suitable aircraft, of parachutes, of instructors, of an aerodrome; the allocation of responsibility, not only within each service but between them; the development of special equipment; the degree to which synthetic training could be used. It was clear that time was needed to examine these questions in detail, but the Prime Minister had stressed his view that training should begin at once[3]. Pending further consideration of the whole subject it was decided on 19 June 1940, to set up a training centre to be known as the Central Landing School. Ringway, the civil airport of Manchester, was selected as the location of the school and six Whitley aircraft and 1,000 R.A.F. training type parachutes were dispatched there. To command the School, which was to be staffed by both Army and R.A.F. personnel, the Air Ministry selected Squadron Leader L. A. Strange, D.S.O., M.C., D.F.C., who arrived at Ringway on 20 June 1940. Major John Rock, R.E., who was to be the senior Army officer at the School, had preceded him by a few hours and together they commenced their rather vaguely defined task. Their staff, like themselves, had little or no experience of parachuting, although one or two of the R.A.F. parachute packers had made descents and later a few professional " stunt " jumpers were found and posted to the unit. But in the early days enthusiasm rather than experience was the keynote of the School[4].

The Whitley had been selected as the aircraft to be used because it was the only type which was available in numbers for operations as well as for training and owing to the varying techniques of exit it was necessary that the paratroop operated from the aircraft on which he was trained.

---

[1] A.M. File 1081 : Encl. 2A.
[2] A.M. File C.S. 6229: Airborne Forces, Provision of—Policy. Encl. 1A.
[3] A.M. File, C.S. 5086, Development of Parachute troops—Air Requirements. Encls. and Minutes 1–9.
[4] O.R.B. of the C.L.S. July–Sept. 1940.

Exit from the Whitley had to be made from a hole in the floor of the fuselage, not an easy task for the beginner. The Bombay which was fitted with a side door, would have been much more suitable but there were only 21 in the country and only three of those had engines[1]. So the first jumps were made from the Whitley using a platform which replaced the rear turret. The R.A.F. training type parachute was used. This was soon superseded by a statichute of American design, but the latter had an inherent fault in that if the user made a bad exit the rigging lines tended to become twisted and prevented the canopy from developing[2]. Such a case occurred at Ringway on 25 July 1940, with fatal results. It was at this time, however, that a new type of British statichute was undergoing trials and the " G.Q." proved so successful that it immediately became the standard design for all British paratroops. Training, which had begun on 8 July 1940 and had ceased following the fatal accident, recommenced with the new type on 8 August and by 5 September 1940 six troops each of 3 officers and 50 other ranks had all completed the course, each man having carried out three descents[3].

A more detailed account of the work of the Central Landing School will be found in Chapter 2. The above summary of the activities at Ringway during June, July and August of 1940 is included in order to emphasise that while policy discussions were in progress something practical was being done also, even though on a small scale.

Initial Policy

The necessary action having been taken regarding the setting up of the Central Landing School, the Air and General Staffs began to examine more closely the possibilities of Airborne Forces. As soon as the Prime Minister's 5,000 paratroops requirement became known the counter suggestion was made that the glider was a better form of transportation than the parachute. This for various reasons: the troops landed in a compact group instead of a scattered line; they were able to take more and heavier equipment; and they carried it with them. In addition the Directorate of Plans at Air Ministry who were dealing with the matter had other ideas for the glider. They felt that it might have possibilities of a purely R.A.F. nature such as the refuelling of heavy aircraft in the air or even the carriage of an additional load of bombs. Designs were therefore made for various types of gliders and production of prototypes begun, and when, on 10 August 1940, the Prime Minister enquired about the progress made with the training of the 5,000 paratroops the opportunity was taken to put the case for gliders before him[4].

It was explained[5] that a major difficulty regarding the paratroop force was operational aircraft. To drop only 600 or 700 paratroops would absorb all the aircraft of the Whitley Group (No. 4 Group). Owing to the shortage of aircraft and aircrew we could not afford to have squadrons of aircraft

---
[1] A.M. File C.S. 6229: Encl. 1c.
[2] Appendix K to 38 Group Paper " Airborne Assault Operations "; O.R.B. of the C.L.S. July–August 1940.
[3] Progress report for August 1940 contained in O.R.B. of the C.L.S.
[4] A.M. File C.S. 6229: Encl. Paras. 6 and 7.
[5] In a minute to the Prime Minister from Gen. Sir Hastings Ismay dated 31 August 1940. A.M. File C.S. 6229: Encls. 2B and 4D.

solely for dropping paratroops and therefore No. 4 Group would have to be withdrawn from its primary role of bombing for any such operations. It would also have to spend about a fortnight in training while the aircrews were taught the technique of dropping. To train a force of 5,000 therefore seemed pointless—especially if the glider trials showed it to be a better form of transport. The Prime Minister was not particularly impressed. He felt that we were in danger of losing a proven policy in favour of a doubtful and experimental one. " Of course," he wrote[1], " if the Glider scheme is better than parachutes, we should pursue it, but is it being seriously taken up?"

He was informed that it was[2]. Development was proceeding on both man-carrying and tank-carrying gliders. Twelve 8-seater gliders were actually under construction on 9 September 1940, and plans for larger ones were on the drawing boards. The Central Landing School (now renamed the Central Landing Establishment) was expanding, provision being made for Glider Training and Tactical Development Sections in addition to the original Parachute Training School. The War Office, Air Ministry and Combined Operations had agreed upon a requirement for three forces of 10,000 men each and the training schemes for these were being worked out. The Prime Minister was convinced. On 12 September he endorsed the minute reporting this progress with a marginal note " Press on ", and with the expanded C.L.E., where enthusiasm abounded, " pressing on " to the best of their ability, the planning staffs at War Office and Air Ministry settled down to the task of formulating a joint policy.

The General War Situation

Overshadowing all discussions on such a joint policy was the general war situation as it stood during the last six months of 1940. Briefly the facts were these. On 10 June, eight days after the completion of the evacuation of the B.E.F. from Dunkirk, the Italians declared war on Britain and France. Although the Strait of Gibraltar and the Suez Canal were, in accordance with traditional British policy, still open, the through passage of the Mediterranean was closed in the narrow seas between Sicily and Tunisia by enemy land based aircraft. Supplies to and from India and the Far East had to make the long Cape voyage; as did the reinforcements so urgently needed by General Wavell in Egypt, now facing an Italian Army of considerable numerical superiority. Until these reinforcements could arrive the British forces in Africa had no option but to withdraw. In the Western Desert we were fighting to hold Sidi Barrani: it was impossible to maintain the frontiers of Somaliland, Kenya and the Sudan: and when in October the Italians attacked Greece a detachment of the all too small British air forces in Africa had to be sent to that country in accordance with our obligations there.

At home the whole weight of the Luftwaffe was thrown against English aerodromes, towns and cities, first by day and later by night. Our land forces —augmented by the Home Guard—were hastily preparing for a German invasion by sea and air. And still further west attacks by U-boats and aircraft were causing heavy losses to supplies on the way from America.

---

[1] Minute dated 1 September 1940.
[2] Minute 13, Gen. Sir Hastings Ismay to P.M. dated 9 September 1940. A.M. File C.S. 6229: Encl. 11B.

A large part of the defence against this many sided attack, particularly at home and over the Atlantic, was an Air Force responsibility, and the demands of R.A.F. operational commands received a high degree of priority. Moreover, the only force able to fight back in an offensive role was Bomber Command, which was consequently given the highest priority of all.

Thus when the first discussions upon the raising of a large airborne force took place two points of view were advanced. One school of thought argued that bombing alone would not win the war and in the long run, as always, battles must be fought and won on land. For this an Airborne Force would be needed, and since to train such a force would take time and would need aircraft and crews, these must be made available at once, even at the expense of the bomber force. The other school of thought replied bluntly that the use of an airborne army was at the best a slightly Wellsian dream of the somewhat distant future, whereas the bombing policy was one possible of immediate attainment. Until a plan involving a major airborne force was adopted the provision of airborne forces in England should be limited to the development of equipment and technique for parachutists and gliders, and the training of a nucleus of paratroops and glider pilots sufficient for minor operations such as raids, and for instructional duties[1]. In other words Airborne Forces must make do with whatever equipment, particularly aircraft, other Air Force Commands could spare or did not want. This second was the view which triumphed. Until 1943, when the supply position improved considerably, the limited number of aircraft available had to be sent wherever the need was greatest. It was the divergence of opinion on the degree of priority warranted by the Airborne Forces project which caused the frequent, and often violent, changes of policy on the subject until this time.

Thus when reading of these changes of policy and the delays caused by them it is important to remember these two points. Firstly that the Airborne Forces requirement, while in the long run no less necessary than many of its rivals in the scramble for supplies, was probably a less urgent and certainly a less obvious need. Secondly that from July 1940 onwards the work of training and developing the force was going forward at Ringway so that, even although the production of the operation force was delayed, the foundations were firmly established when the time for expansion eventually came.

The first detailed estimates of the number of men needed were made by the Directorate of Combined Operations in September 1940. It was considered that the principal operation for which the airborne forces should be prepared was as the spearhead for a large operation in which they would be supported by land forces, and that preparation for this would embrace the requirements for various types of minor operations such as raids. The force needed for any such operation which could at that time be foreseen was about 1,000 men and in view of the possibility of such a force being lost during the first operation three such forces should be raised[2].

---

[1] A.M. File C.S. 8502: Encl. 1A.
[2] A.M. File C.S. 6229: Encl. 9A. Paras. 3A and 4A.

On 5 September 1940, at a meeting between the Vice Chief of Air Staff and the Vice Chief of the Imperial General Staff[1], the target date for the raising of this force was set at the spring of 1941. Of the 1,000 men in each force only 100 were to be parachutists the remaining 900 to be glider borne troops and their pilots. The parachutists would be used as pathfinders for the gliders and would be largely concerned with local reconnaissance duties. In view of their value as saboteurs however all parachutists would be trained in this role and 200 would be trained for this sole purpose. The commitment thus became:—

500 parachutists, and

2,700 glider troops of whom it was estimated 360 would need to be pilots.

These 3,200 men would be provided by the Army, the R.A.F.'s responsibility being to train them and to provide aircraft (gliders, statichutes) and aircrews for operations as and when necessary.

Of this commitment only one part was met, the training of 500 parachutists. This presented no difficulties as by the end of September the training organisation at Ringway was already running smoothly and there were plenty of volunteers for the job[2]. Since it was decided that any normal infantry formation could be used as glider borne troops without special training no action was needed on this point until about a fortnight prior to any operation. This principle was also applied to the aircraft and aircrews although early in 1941 arrangements were made for one crew from each bomber squadron of No. 4 Group to visit Ringway for training. On return these crews were to pass on the knowledge so gained to the other members of the squadron. This was an unsatisfactory scheme because the wastage rate in Bomber Command was high and the personnel of the squadrons continually changing. The few crews who did visit Ringway did not remain with their units permanently but on completion of their bombing "tour" were posted to other duties so that at no time could it be claimed that even one squadron had all its crews trained in dropping paratroops. There was considerable delay also in modifying aircraft and as late as 24 June 1941 only seven were fully modified and 18 partly so[3]. Nevertheless, on the one occasion during this period when the R.A.F. were called upon to provide a very small number of aircraft and crews for operations of this kind they did so within the time stipulated, namely a fortnight[4]. This was on the occasion of a raid on an aqueduct in Southern Italy, and the full story of this operation, known as Colossus, is contained in Chapter 2.

The real reason for the failure to provide the force in the spring of 1941, was delay in producing both the gliders and the pilots to fly them. In October 1940 an order had been placed with the Ministry of Aircraft Production for 400 eight seater gliders. In January 1941 the future production of these was estimated at only 50 by May 1941 and it was not until much

---

[1] Among others present were: Lt. Gen. A. G. Bourne (D.C.O.); Maj. Gen. C. C. Malden (D.M.T.); Air Marshal Sir Philip Joubert (A.C.A.S.R.); Air Vice-Marshal Blount (A.O.C. 22 Group); Air Commodore R. Saundby (A.C.A.S.T.); Air Commodore J. C. Slessor (D. of Plans); Air Commodore A. J. Capel (D.T.O.); Air Commodore A. Durston (D.N.O.).—A.M. File C.S. 6229 Encl. 9A.
[2] A.M. File C.S. 6229: Encl. 22A Para. 1.
[3] The necessary modifications were being manufactured but were not generally fitted.
[4] A.M. File C.S. 8513: Encl. 1A. A.M. File C.S. 8502 Encl. 36A.

later in the year that steps were taken to speed up production[1]. The same applied to the 25-seater of which it was stated in January 1941 that two would be ready for flight trials in August and no more until November when 50 should be available. These gliders were made of wood and as their manufacture was undertaken by the furniture trade there was no question of them affecting production of powered aircraft. At this stage claims of the Mosquito and other wooden aircraft had not arisen and there seemed to be no reason for the delay except the lack of a definite instruction for the construction of the gliders to be carried out rapidly and in large numbers. It was later stated by Ministry of Aircraft Production that the hold up was partially due to the size of the initial order which was so small as to prohibit the production of jigs on any but the minimum scale. It also arose from the fact that a final decision on the type to be used for operations was held up pending flight trials. During late 1940, four types of glider were being investigated[2]. They were:—

An 8-seater—later named the Hotspur and used for training only.

A 25-seater—later named the Horsa and modified to carry equipment, used in a general purpose role as the major operational type.

A 15-seater—later named the Hengist. Designed as an insurance against the Horsa proving unsuitable this type was not proceeded with after the first prototype trials due to the success of the Horsa.

A tank carrying type—later named the Hamilcar.

Thus it was not until August 1941, when the Horsa prototype first flew, that this vital question was finally settled, and even after that date had an operation requiring gliders been planned Hotspurs would have had to be used since so few of the larger type were available[3]. As already mentioned the delay was partly due to the small numbers of gliders ordered: the R.A.F. did not feel justified in increasing this order until definite plans were drawn up for an operation in which they would be used. And no such plans were drawn up because unless there were gliders ready such planning was pointless[4].

The lack of gliders reacted upon plans for training pilots to fly them for until flight trials had been made the degree of skill necessary to fly a glider was unknown. Various guesses were made but they differed so widely[5] that it was impossible to produce a permanent scheme for glider pilot training

---

[1] A.M. File C.S. 8502: Encls. 27A and 4A.
[2] A.M. File C.S. 6229: Encl. 2A. A.M. File C.S. 8503 Pt. I Encl. 87A. A.M. File C.S. 6229: Encl. 4B.
[3] A.M. File C.S. 8503 Pt. I: Encl. 113A.
[4] A.M. File C.S. 8503 Pt. I: Encl. 114A.
[5] Although it later became a trainer the Hotspur was originally intended for operational use and for this a month's course on light aircraft was considered sufficient basic training. But by December opinion had swung in favour of using the Horsa for operations and the Deputy Chief of Air Staff remarked: "The idea that semi-skilled, unpicked personnel (infantry corporals have I believe even been suggested) could with a minimum of training be entrusted with the piloting of these troop carriers is fantastic. Their operation is equivalent to forced landing the largest sized aircraft without engine aid—than which there is no higher test of piloting skill." A.M. File C.S. 6229; Encl. 22A Para. 2A. A.M. File C.S. 6229: Encl. 54A.

until the gliders had flown. In spite of this difficulty it was felt that something should be done towards training glider pilots and as a temporary measure a number of Army volunteers with a little flying experience were found from the Commandos. These men were attached to Army Co-operation squadrons where they flew light type aircraft and received a certain amount of instruction. Although it was the best arrangement which could at that time be made it was not a very satisfactory one, for the squadrons had their normal duties to carry out and naturally these had to take priority over the training. Moreover few, if any, of the squadron pilots were qualified by experience, training, or temperament to act as instructors at Elementary Flying Training School level and the majority of the Commandos had no more than 20 hours flying experience[1]. But with all its faults the scheme proved worth while for between November 1940 and April 1941, 37 of these pupils did receive training and when, early in April 1941, the Glider Training Section of the Central Landing Establishment moved to Haddenham, 24 of these were posted there to commence glider flying. In fact it was not glider flying proper for only one Hotspur was available, but they flew such sailplanes and civilian gliders as the R.A.F. had been able to locate and requisition[2]. On 23 April 1941 the unit moved to Thame and here the remaining 13 pupils arrived and it was these men, together with their R.A.F. instructors, who worked out a basic procedure for glider flying and glider flying organisation[3].

From the first this method of training was a temporary measure. But as soon as improvements were suggested more difficulties arose, the greatest of which was the status of the glider pilot after training. The glider pilot was a dual personality for not only had he to be a pilot but also a " total soldier ", able on landing to take his place beside his passengers in the battle. After training he was a very valuable man and neither the Army nor the Air Force viewed with favour the prospect of using him for no more than one or two operations a year. In 1940 and 1941 the R.A.F. training organisation was stretched to the limit providing R.A.F. pilots, and the Air Ministry view was that anyone who passed through even a part of that organisation must become available for normal R.A.F. duties. They were willing to accept Army personnel for training as glider pilots but reserved the right to train them to operational standard and use them on operations as required. For this purpose they demanded that officer glider pilots should be seconded and other ranks transferred to the R.A.F. In effect this meant that glider flying was to be a part time job: a certain number of R.A.F. pilots would be trained to fly gliders as well as powered aircraft and these would be withdrawn from normal duties as and when glider operations required: it meant that some of the best manpower of the Army would be diverted to augment the supply of R.A.F. crews (this in fact later became an accepted policy): and it meant that the " total soldier " principle would have to be abandoned[4].

---

[1] A.M. File C.S. 6229: Encl. 23 Paras. 15–20.
[2] A.M. File C.S. 7424 Pt. I: Encl. 8D.
[3] S/Ldr. H. E. Hervey was in command of the Glider Training Squadron. Prior to the war he was Secretary of the London Gliding Club and the majority of his staff were instructors of the club or had been trained by them. A.M. File C.S. 7424 Pt. I: Encl. 9B.
[4] A.M. File C.S. 7424 Pt. I: Encl. 8c, Para. 11. A.M. File C.S. 6229: Encl. 50A, Para. 18.

The Army hoped that it would be found possible for the pupils to complete the normal Elementary and Senior Flying courses and then branch off the main stream of pilots and do a conversion course on to gliders. They would then remain glider pilots and would not be used on ordinary R.A.F. duties. In practice both schemes were used, in varying measure, according to the manpower position of either service at a given time[1]. This question of glider pilots was however, in 1940 and early 1941, but a part of the larger problem of Airborne Forces, which in turn was included in the wider field of Army/Air support. As the training of glider pilots was likely to have more effect on the R.A.F.'s plans for expansion than any other part of the Airborne requirements no action other than the stop gap scheme was taken pending a ruling on this wider issue.

It was decided early in December 1940 that a joint Air Ministry/War Office paper dealing with the Airborne Forces aspect of the subject should be prepared. But great difficulty was encountered in reaching agreement on the form and contents of the paper and it was not until May 1941 that it was eventually completed. In the meantime draft after draft was prepared and put up by each staff only to be turned down or amended out of all recognition by the other[2].

The Air Ministry wanted the Chiefs of Staff's approval on three main principles:—[3]

(i) That until an operational plan had been adopted in which airborne forces were required any preparation for such a force was to be regarded as a subsidiary issue and reduced to the most economical basis.

(ii) That owing to the shortage of pilots all pilots of the airborne force were to be members of the R.A.F. and remain in it, whatever their origins.

(iii) That the commitment of September 1940 could not be met and should be replaced by a general requirement that the raising of the Force should proceed as rapidly as the low order of priority indicated in (i) permitted.

This did not accord with the War Office proposals: their paper was based on a definite Army requirement of two Airborne Brigade Groups of 5,000 men each. One of these would be a Middle East Force, the other based on the U.K. This would entail a total Air Force commitment of approximately 800 25-seater and 36 tank-carrying gliders, and the necessary pilots and tug aircraft. Moreover, if this commitment received the Chiefs of Staff's approval it would have to be met, even at the expense of other commands[4]. With two such widely divergent proposals the only solution would have been a compromise. No satisfactory compromise was suggested and by February 1941 the situation had reached a deadlock. A proposal to refer the whole problem to the Joint Planning Committee was turned down by the Directorate of

---

[1] A.M. File C.S. 6229: Encl. 50A Para. 1.
[2] A.M. File C.S. 6229: Minute 69.
[3] A.M. File C.S. 8502: Encl. 1A.
[4] A.M. File C.S. 8502: Encl. 4B.

Plans at the Air Ministry on the ground that "it would be a pity to have a difference of opinion at C.O.S.[1] level on a matter which had so little bearing on any immediate plan for the prosecution of the war"[2].

On 19 February 1941 the question was raised at a meeting on general army co-operation matters between the Chief of Air Staff and the Vice Chief of the Imperial General Staff. The War Office requirement was accepted to the extent of an order being placed with the Ministry of Aircraft Production for the number of gliders needed. The Air and General Staffs were to prepare a paper for the Chiefs of Staff Committee and discussions between them for this purpose were to be based upon the War Office requirements[3]. After this some progress was made. In addition to the 400 Hotspurs an order was placed for 800 Horsas, 400 to be made in U.K. and 400, if possible, in India for use there or in the Middle East. Early in April the Treasury queried the need for the gliders ordered in February, the total cost of which was estimated to be in the neighbourhood of eight million pounds. Since the project had not received the approval of the Chiefs of Staff this attitude on the part of the Treasury was justified and their objection at least served the purpose of indicating the urgency of preparing the recommendations[4].

But still the staffs were unable to agree upon the paper for the Chiefs of Staff. A typical example of the delay occurred in May 1941. In one draft the Army relegated certain important air considerations to an Appendix, together with the remark that the provision of an organisation to train and develop Airborne Forces must unavoidably cause some diminution in the expansion of the Royal Air Force operational commands, especially Bomber Command. Air Ministry rewrote the draft incorporating the remarks into the body of the paper and returned it to the War Office for approval[5].

The shuttlecock action over the C.O.S. paper was still in full progress when on 26 April 1941, the Prime Minister paid a visit to the Central Landing Establishment at Ringway to see how things were progressing. The demonstration consisted of the dropping of 24 parachutists, a formation landing by sailplanes, and a fly past by one Hotspur. Mr. Churchill was much impressed by what he saw and much depressed by the slowness in development of gliders and the small numbers of parachutists then trained. On his return from Ringway he made enquiries about the proposals for increasing the parachute and Glider Force[6]. In a reply giving a brief summary of the position General Sir Hastings Ismay, his Military Secretary, stated that discussions had been going on between Air Ministry and War Office and the proposal was that two Airborne Brigade Groups should be formed, one in this country and one in the Middle East. The lack of aircraft and crews was again emphasised. "As I see it, the fundamental obstacle to going large on airborne troops is that we cannot at present afford to divert either bomber pilots, or large numbers of bomber aircraft whether for towing gliders or for dropping parachutists) from their primary role". This was dated 30 April 1941[7].

---

[1] Chiefs of Staff.
[2] A.M. File C.S. 6229: Minute 75.
[3] A.M. File C.S. 6229: Encl. 89A, Para. 7.
[4] A.M. File C.S. 8502: Encls. 14A and 20A.
[5] A.M. File C.S. 8502: Minute 29.
[6] A.M. File C.S. 8502: Encls. 23A and 24.
[7] A.M. File C.S. 8502: Encl. 239.

Throughout May the Germans were assembling an Airborne Army in Greece. On the 20th they struck at Crete. On 1 June the last of the British forces were evacuated leaving the island in German hands. The attack on Crete had been made entirely from the air, the one German sea convoy involved being destroyed by the Royal Navy before reaching the island. In Whitehall the first reaction came from the Prime Minister. On 26 May 1941 he attached a minute to the progress report drawn up for him after his visit to the C.L.E. " This is a sad story . . . the gliders have been produced on the smallest possible scale, and so we have practically now neither the parachutists nor the gliders. Thus we are always found behind-hand by the enemy. We ought to have 5,000 parachutists and an Airborne Division on the German model, with any improvements which might suggest themselves from experience. These will all be necessary in the Mediterranean fighting of 1942 or earlier if possible. . . . A whole year has been lost, and proposals must now be made for trying, so far as is possible, to repair the misfortune[1]."

Fortunately the long delayed paper was nearing completion when the invasion of Crete took place. In response to the Prime Minister's minute the final touches were hurriedly added. On 30 May 1941 it was put before the Chiefs of Staff who agreed with Mr. Churchill that by the summer of 1942 the strategic situation might be such that an airborne force would prove valuable. They accordingly authorised the raising of a force equivalent to a Brigade by that date, and they mentioned that a second similar force might be required later in that year[2].

A month later, in July 1941, further high level discussions took place on a subject wider than Airborne Forces, but in which the latter were involved —the whole subject of Army/Air Support. The Chief of the Imperial General Staff had put forward a request for the allocation to the Army of an Air Component of various specialised types of aircraft, and in a memorandum to the Chiefs of Staff Sir Charles Portal, the Chief of Air Staff, analysed these requests in detail[3]. He stated the impossibility of meeting them in full, explaining that the Air Component suggested involved a total of 3,888 aircraft, a number which exceeded by some 300 the front line strength of the Royal Air Force at that time. To build up such a force would entail a reduction in the R.A.F.'s planned expansion programme of 215 squadrons of which 130 would be of the heavy bomber type. Such reduction would mean the sacrifice of air power, " yet one of the essential preliminaries to the landing of an army on the Continent is the defeat of German air power. When that has been achieved the whole weight of the Royal Air Force can be employed to assist the Army to land in France, to march towards, and to occupy Germany ".

There existed between the Chiefs of staff, however, complete understanding of each other's difficulties. The Chief of the Imperial General Staff stipulated that the Army's requirements should be met with the least possible interference with the growing power of the Royal Air Force for strategic action, and a modified programme for the expansion of Army/Air Support Forces was

---
[1] A.M. File C.S. 8503 Pt. I: Encl. 49B.
[2] C.O.S. (41) 90 (O) dated 30 May 1941.
[3] A.M. File C.S. 8502: Encl. 43B and embodied in C.O.S. (41) 119 (O).

agreed upon. In the case of the Airborne Force this programme required the R.A.F. to provide sufficient gliders to lift two Brigade Groups, one at home and one in the Middle East: to provide modified "tug" aircraft to tow these gliders in two waves: and to provide modified aircraft sufficient to carry and drop a force of 2,500 paratroops. The R.A.F. also undertook the training of the additional 2,000 paratroops needed to make up this number as soon as the Army could supply the men. And the Chief of the Air Staff agreed to push ahead with this programme as rapidly as possible. This emphasised two points. First that the R.A.F. were still not able to divert as large an effort as they would wish towards fulfilling the Army needs; and secondly that the Chief of Air Staff was determined to do all in his power to implement the modified programme, which in the case of Airborne Forces meant fulfilling the commitment of May 1941[1].

Air Ministry Action after July 1941

Gliders

No major changes of organisation took place until September 1941. Then on the 1st of that month, as a prelude to the breaking away of the glider organisation, the Central Landing Establishment was abolished, its place being taken by the Airborne Forces Establishment. The latter remained at Ringway and was, in effect the C.L.E. minus the Glider Training and Exercise Flights. The task of the A.F.E. became " to investigate problems of technical development, to establish the principles of glider and parachute training, and to form the first units carrying out this training, in due course developing them to a standard of stability where they could be absorbed as normal units into the R.A.F.[2]"

The first of these units broke away from A.F.E. on 4 November 1941, when No. 1 Glider Training School formed at Thame around the old Glider Exercise Squadron which had been detached there from Ringway throughout the summer of 1941. The second break-away came on 15 February 1942, when the Parachute Training Section became No. 1 Parachute Training School, a self-contained unit which remained at Ringway as a lodger unit. On 16 February 1942, the remainder of the A.F.E., that is the Headquarters, the Technical Development Section and the Experimental Flight merged into a new formation, the Airborne Forces Experimental Establishment. The new unit, A.F.E.E., was " to carry on the Technical Development programme in connection with the R.A.F. side of airborne warfare ". It too remained at Ringway for a time until on 1 July 1942, it moved to Sherburn-in-Elmet, near Leeds.

For administrative purposes A.F.E.E. was placed under No. 70 Group Army Co-operation Command and although it worked under the direct control of the Ministry of Aircraft Production in technical matters, the Commanding Officer (Group Captain L. G. Harvey) was given authority to conduct such exploratory trials as he considered desirable at the direct request of the Airborne Forces or any R.A.F. command concerned in the training and equipment of an airborne force.

---

[1] A.M. File C.S. 8503 Pt. I: Encl. 79B Para. 2.
[2] O.R.B.s of the C.L.E. the A.F.E. and the A.F.E.E. November 1941–February 1942.

The first step to be taken was an enquiry into glider production. Deliveries of Hotspurs were far behind schedule[1] and the Horsa prototype was not due to make its flight trials until later in August. Moreover the Ministry of Aircraft Production informed Air Ministry on 27 July 1941 that delivery of the 400 Horsas being built in the United Kingdom could not be expected until February 1943. It will be remembered that when the use of gliders was first suggested the possibility of using them as bomb carriers had been mentioned. In February, when the Chief of Air Staff and the Vice Chief of the Imperial General Staff had authorised the construction of 400 troop-carrying Horsas, the Air Ministry had placed an order for an extra 200 Horsas for the bomb-carrying role. Later, in the summer, this latter order was cancelled and it was this cancellation which caused M.A.P. to postpone the delivery date. On 27 July 1941 the Director General of Aircraft Production discussed this matter with Mr. Herman Lebus of Messrs. Harris Lebus Ltd., the manufacturers of the Horsa, and they agreed upon the following programme[2]:

1942									1943	
March	April	May	June	July	August	Sept.	Oct.	Nov.	Dec.	Jan.	Feb.
1	9	20	30	40	50	50	50	50	50	50	20

In a letter to the Director of Operational Requirements at Air Ministry the Deputy Director of Aircraft Production explained that any greater deliveries would involve an increased jigging programme out of all proportion to the size of the total order. Neither M.A.P. nor the manufacturers felt justified in expending the capital necessary for rapid production unless they could be assured that the production capacity so created would be warranted by further orders at some future date[3].

This assurance the Air Ministry were unable to give. In the first place they wanted to wait until prototype flight trials had confirmed the suitability of the Horsa for its task. Secondly their original objection to placing orders for more gliders than were required by existing plans was still valid. But the 400 which were ordered they wanted very quickly—in fact rapid delivery was essential if the Chiefs of Staff's requirement was to be met. Consequently a compromise was effected. At the request of Air Ministry the Ministry of Aircraft Production stated that there was a possibility of delivering 300 Horsas by 31 July 1942 providing the order was restored to the original figure of 600. This the Air Ministry agreed to do on condition that M.A.P. would increase Hotspur production so that the smaller, and now trainer type could, if necessary, be used in an operation to overcome the deficiency of Horsas. To make this possible the existing order of 390 was raised to 990 of which M.A.P. estimated they could produce 625 by 31 July[4].

Such were the arrangements for home glider production. The Chiefs of Staff had also stated that a similar force should be available for use in the Middle East. In view of the seriousness of the shipping situation at that time the Chief of Air Staff had directed that if possible these gliders should be built in India. The Treasury had previously sanctioned expenditure up to £10,000 by Messrs. Tata Ltd., an Indian firm, for the purpose of developing their organisation and planning for glider production, and a representative

---
[1] Only 15 had been delivered by 15 August.
[2] A.M. File C.S. 8503 Pt. I: Encl. 106B.
[3] A.M. File C.S. 10545 Pt. I: Encl. 36A.
[4] A.M. File C.S. 10545: Pt. I. Encl. 36A.

of the firm was in England to collect the necessary designs and specifications. Consequently when the home order was raised to 600 Horsas plus 990 Hotspurs an order was also placed with Tata for 400 Indian built Horsas, an order which in November was, at the Chiefs of Staff's request, raised to 800, the target date for the new figure being July 1943[1].

Glider Pilots

Under this new scheme it seemed that there was a good chance of having the necessary gliders to carry at least the home-based Brigade by the summer of 1942. But the envisaged use of Hotspurs to repair the deficiency of Horsas entailed an increase of pilots to fly them. The difficulty was partially, although by no means wholly, offset by the fact that Hotspur trials had indicated that the degree of pilot skill required of glider pilots would not be unduly high. On 22 August 1941 a meeting was held at the Air Ministry at which the problem of providing glider pilots was discussed[2]. Until this date the Air Ministry policy had always been that the gliders should be flown by fully trained R.A.F. pilots who would be withdrawn from normal duties especially for the glider operation. This policy, which owing to the lack of glider pilots had never been put into effect, was now reversed. The meeting recommended that glider pilots should be Army volunteers, trained by the R.A.F. but remaining in the Army after training, and that they would not be employed on any flying duties other than glider flying. The reasons given for this change of policy were the advantages of glider pilots being capable of taking their place on landing as fighting soldiers in the Airborne Brigade, this being made possible by the lesser degree of pilot skill now considered necessary. Furthermore it was unlikely that the R.A.F. would be able to spare the numbers of trained pilots now likely to be required. The War Office had always been in favour of this "total soldier" principle so that the new policy was universally popular. The Army had already made provision for the transfer of a maximum of 15,000 men to the R.A.F. for aircrew duties[3] and the War Office asked that in view of the manpower shortage with which they were faced, the 600 men needed for glider pilot duties should be selected from these volunteers. The Air Ministry reluctantly agreed to this and detailed planning for the training of the glider pilots was at last possible[4]. For this purpose a further meeting[5] was held at Air Ministry on 26 September 1941 and the training organisation planned at this meeting remained in force throughout the war, although modifications were introduced periodically according to the source of trainees.

---

[1] A.M. File C.S. 10545 Pt. I: Encls. 39A and 90B.
[2] Present at this meeting were: Air Commodore Dickson (D. of Plans) (chairman); Air Commodore Cole Hamilton (70 Group: Representing C.-in-C., A.C. Command); Air Commodore Breen (D. of P.); Air Commodore Goodwin (D.T.O.); G/Capt. Ellwood (D.D.B. Ops.); G/Capt. Hardman (D.D.M.C.); W/Cdr. Troop (T.O. 3); S/Ldr. MacPherson (70 Group); S/Ldr. Colebrook (M.C. 3); W/Cdr. Earle (Plans 2). A.M. File C.S. 8503 Pt. I: Encl. 106D, Paras. 7, 8 and 9. A.M. File C.S. 7424 Pt. I: Encls. 17A, 18A, 19A, 20A, and 35A,
[3] Under the conditions of Army Council Instruction No. 1520 of 1940.
[4] A.M. File C.S. 8503 Pt. I: Encls. 121A, 125 and 128A.
[5] Present at this meeting were: Air Commodore E. S. Goodwin (D.T.O.) (chairman); Group Captain L. G. Harvey (C.L.E.); Wing Commander R. C. Jones (T.F.1); Wing Commander E. W. Clifton (D.P.2); Major R. A. Fyffe (A.C. Command); Squadron Leader H. E. Hervey (G.T.D.); Squadron Leader W. D. MacPherson (70 Group); Flight Lieutenant G. W. Blake (T.F.1); Wing Commander C. L. Troop (T.O.3).—A.M. File C.S. 8503 Pt. I: Encl. 129A.

The standards of intelligence and physical fitness required of glider pilots were to be similar to those in force for R.A.F. aircrews. Volunteers were to be interviewed by R.A.F. selection boards on which the Army would have one representative. Their first course would be an Elementary Flying Training Course of some 60 flying hours on light powered aircraft. Superimposed on this would be a modified Initial Training Course of ground instruction in such subjects as elementary navigation, map reading, and the theory of flight. One of the existing R.A.F. Elementary Flying Training Schools—No. 16 located at Meir, was eventually chosen—was to be set aside for the exclusive use of glider trainees. This course would be of approximately 12 weeks duration, and would be followed by two glider flying courses, one at a Glider Training School where initial Hotspur flying would be the primary concern, and one at a Glider Operational Training Unit where more advanced Hotspur and later Horsa flying would be taught. To meet the increased need for experienced instructors it was proposed to call for volunteers at C.F.S. and to select 19 men which, with the seven qualified instructors at Thame, meant that 26 would be available.

The first of these schools to operate was No. 1 Glider Training School which opened at Thame on 4 November 1941. This was formed from the old Glider Exercise Flight, the unit to which the 36 Army Co-operation trained commando ex-pilots had been posted. A second School, No. 2 G.T.S., was opened at Weston-on-the-Green on 1 December[1]. No. 16 E.F.T.S. at Meir was not due to turn over to glider pilot training until 31 December 1941 consequently Army personnel from this school would not be available until the end of March 1942. It so happened however that, in November 1941, there were a number of R.A.F. pilots, trained to Service Flying Training School level, who were surplus to R.A.F. requirements at that time. Since sufficient Army personnel would obviously not be trained by 31 July 1942 these R.A.F. pilots were, as a temporary measure, posted to the two Glider Training Schools. As soon as the supply of Army pilots permitted they were to be withdrawn from glider flying and to return to normal R.A.F. duties. In fact when the time came the majority of these men remained with the Schools as tug pilots, their glider flying experience proving most valuable to them in this role. The first two Glider Operational Training Units opened at Netheravon and Kidlington on 1 January 1942 and 1 February 1942 respectively[2]. Thus 4 November 1941, the opening of No. 1 G.T.S. at Thame, can be said to mark the commencement of glider pilot training under any permanent scheme.

Paratroops

Once again the paratroop section of the commitment proved the easiest part to meet. During the summer of 1941, there had been a lull in individual training at Ringway but the organisation there had been kept " ticking over " by the training of replacements for No. 11 Special Air Service Battalion. Also a number of exercises were carried out at various places in the United Kingdom which, although mainly designed to enable the Army to devise defensive tactics against Airborne Forces, very often had the effect of impressing Army Commanders with the values of possessing such a force themselves.

---

[1] D.M.C. Monthly Progress Report, December 1941.
[2] D.M.C. Monthly Progress Report, September 1941.

The only other work carried out had been the training of a number of special agents and a few Polish Army Officers—the Poles were enthusiastic about paratroops from the first and later formed a Polish Independent Parachute Brigade. In August 1941 when the Chief of the Imperial General Staff decided to raise immediately two further parachute battalions, the Parachute Training School were able to state that they anticipated no difficulty in building up their output of trained personnel to 100 a week. By November 1941 this figure had been attained and although the aircraft available were not as new as could be desired the output was maintained[1].

Aircraft

The aircraft used at Ringway were Whitley Mk. IIs and Mk. IIIs. During the autumn of 1941 one Mk. V was delivered but the priority of the School was low, as was to be expected in the case of a training establishment, and no more arrived until the following year[2]. In any case paratroop dropping imposed little strain on an aircraft and the older Marks were maintained at a sufficiently high level of serviceability to carry out the programme.

Very different was the case of the Glider Training Schools. Here the Hotspurs were being towed by Hectors. All of these had seen long service before they reached the Glider Training School and were in no condition to undergo the rigorous life of a tug aircraft. As with all obsolescent types, spares were difficult and replacements impossible to obtain. Consequently the time spent in the hangars was out of all proportion to that spent in the air. Trials were under way with the Lysander and the Swordfish but even when cleared the supply position with these types was not likely to be good. In the meantime the Schools had to make the best of a bad situation and accept the loss of flying time as inevitable[3].

The technical development section of the Central Landing Establishment had by now increased in size and during late 1941 was carrying out investigations on all types of aircraft to ascertain their possibilities in either tug or paratroop dropping roles. Particular attention was paid to the heavy bomber types and where necessary modifications were made to suitable types during production. It was not until 1943 when aircraft could at last be spared from the bomber effort that the full benefit of this work was felt. Then, when the aircraft were suddenly needed in an Airborne role, they were available in large numbers and the time spent on conversion for the new role was cut to a minimum.

War Office action after May 1941

The War Office were, at this stage, concerned with only one shortage—manpower. Whereas the Air Ministry had to overcome shortage of aircrews, aerodromes, and most of all aircraft including glider production before devoting large efforts to the Airborne project, the Army, providing they could find the men, could begin their effort at once. In his original minute of June 1940 Mr. Churchill had remarked of the paratroops that even during training " they can, none the less, play their part meanwhile as shock troops in home defence[4] ".

---

[1] No. 1 O.R.B. of P.T.S., Ringway.
[2] Whitley Mark V had Merlin engine.
[3] D.M.C. Monthly Progress Reports.
[4] War Office Narrative " Airborne Forces ", Chapter III.

Just prior to this original requirement for 5,000 paratroops the decision had been taken to raise an irregular force known as Commandos, the Directorate of Combined Operations being set up for this purpose. In the view of Staff officers at that time the idea of a soldier entering the battlefield in a vertical instead of a horizontal direction was highly irregular. The first trained paratroops accordingly became No. 2 Commando. In September 1940 however, the decision was taken to train 500 troops for general parachuting duties, for pathfinder and sabotage work as well as for the raiding and assault parties originally envisaged. Consequently in October 1940 the Commando was merged into a new formation, No. 11 Special Air Service Battalion, whose duties embodied all of these tasks. By the early summer of 1941, the Battalion was up to strength.

Immediately following the Chiefs of Staff's decision of 30 May 1941 the Chief of the Imperial General Staff ordered the raising in the United Kingdom of a parachute brigade of about 2,400 men. These men would be required either as a component of a gliderborne force, or as an independent body for field operations, or for sabotage. It was realised that, owing to the shortage of aircraft, it might prove impossible to drop the whole brigade in one lift but in spite of this the brigade should be trained and ready for operations within a year. Brigade Headquarters, two more parachute battalions and an airtroop R.E. were to be raised at once; the raising of a fourth battalion and other special units such as Artillery, Signals, Medical and Supply, and possibly Light tank detachments, were approved but were not to be raised until later.

The whole question of paratroop service was now reviewed, consideration being given to the advisability of turning over selected units en masse to parachuting duties. Such a policy had obvious advantages, mainly because it was a quicker way of producing a training unit, but also because the unit *esprit de corps* was maintained and because administration was so much easier. Nevertheless parachuting being an individual act required considerable determination and great physical fitness: if a unit were turned over en masse a high proportion of the men in it would be found to be unfit for the task either physically or psychologically, many of them being too old.

As no difficulty was anticipated in training the new battalions by the summer of 1942 the decision was made in favour of keeping to the " volunteers only " principle. After consideration of the rates of pay for comparable duties in the other services, submarine service in the Royal Navy and flying pay in the Royal Air Force, a new rate of parachute pay was fixed at 4s. per day for officers and 2s. for other ranks. An age limit of 22-32 years and a top weight limit of 196 lbs. were also introduced[1].

These were the terms of service offered when on 28 August 1941 United Kingdom Commands were notified of the decision to form two new battalions and volunteers up to a maximum of ten from each unit[2] were called for. Headquarters No. 1 Parachute Brigade and Nos. 1, 2 and 3 Parachute Battalions formed in September 1941 under the command of Brigadier R. N. Gale. No. 11 S.A.S. Battalion became No. 1 Parachute Battalion under Lt.-Col. E. E. Down, and Lt.-Col. Flavell and Lt.-Col. Hope-Thompson commanded Nos. 2 and 3 Battalions respectively[3].

---

[1] War Office Narrative " Airborne Forces ", Chapter III.
[2] This maximum was designed to prevent units being unduly depleted by the loss of too many of their better men.
[3] A.M. File 10582, Part I: Encl. 18B. War Office Narrative " Airborne Forces ", Chapter III.

Thus for the first time the paratroop formation had an Army commander who was not immediately concerned with the raising and training of his own unit. Brigadier Gale was able to devote his attention to questions of detailed policy and could begin to co-ordinate the parachuting requirements of units other than infantry. He was authorised to deal direct with the War Office on all matters of policy, to effect liaison with C.L.E. and No. 70 Group R.A.F.[1] for technical and domestic training purposes, and to utilize the normal Army Command channels for routine matters. At first he undertook general responsibility for the glider side of Airborne Forces but the War Office soon realised that he would be fully occupied with his parachuting task and on 10 October 1941 the 1st Airlanding Brigade Group was formed. The name " Airlanding " was chosen instead of " Gliderborne " since this Brigade was to prepare itself to travel in powered aircraft as well as in gliders. The 31st Independent Brigade Group, a regular formation recently returned home from India, was selected for this role and placed under the command of Brigadier Hopkinson, whose powers were similar to those granted to Brigadier Gale. War Office instructions were that the Brigade Group were to " carry out the initial investigations into the problems of organisation, equipment and training of an Air Landing Formation ". Particularly they were to bear in mind the possibility of attacks in the rear of the enemy's main force and consequently were to be prepared to be self contained for a period of at least three days. In certain circumstances they might be isolated for longer periods and might have to depend upon supply by air for their maintenance. They were likely to be required to operate in an area of up to 500 miles of their base[2].

Such instructions are of interest here because they demonstrate the line of thought then being adopted by the War Office. In September 1940 the role of an Airborne Force had been envisaged as the spearhead for a large operation with minor operations such as raids and sabotage as subsidiary tasks. In October 1941 attention was being concentrated upon their value in a tactical role, the role in which they were to be used for the first time more than three years later. [Operation Varsity.]

Stimulated by the Chiefs of Staff's requirement of 30 May 1941 rapid progress was now being made. An organisation had been set up through which individuals could be trained. Army formations of trained individuals had grown from one " Commando " to two brigades. The next step was to provide a means of training not individually but collectively. Inter-unit, inter-battalion, inter-brigade and finally inter-service training would all be needed. To meet this need the War Office decided, on 29 October 1941 to appoint Major General R. A. M. Browning, D.S.O., to command the 1st Airborne Division, and to form at once a Divisional Headquarters to assist him in his task.

This appointment of a senior officer with the sole task of co-ordinating the whole development and training of the Army side of Airborne Forces was a milestone along the road of Airborne progress. Having reached that milestone it is convenient to pause and examine in more detail the story of the training and experimental organisations from their inception in June 1940 until that stage.

---

[1] Ringway had been transferred from No. 22 Group to No. 70 Group for administrative purposes on 1 December 1940. O.R.B. of the C.L.E., December 1940.
[2] ACC/S76/Air Encl. 89A. A.M. File 11076, Part I: Encl. 8A.

CHAPTER 2

DEVELOPMENT, TRAINING AND INITIAL OPERATION

The Parachute Training Centre

In June 1940, when the investigation into paratroop dropping was begun, a certain amount of information was available at Air Ministry regarding the German methods of organisation and training. The German Parachute Troops had their Headquarters in Berlin, and were controlled by the Seventh Fliegerdivision (Air Division). They were organised on a Regimental Basis, three Battalions to a Regiment, three Companies to a Battalion, 200 men to a Company. The Directorate of Intelligence at Air Ministry estimated that three such regiments, a total strength of over 5,000 men, were available[1]. Each Battalion carried one 2.95 in. mountain gun, one 3.16 in. mortar, twelve heavy machine-guns, 54 light machine-guns and 54 machine-pistols in addition to the personal arms and individual equipment carried by officers and men. Some troops carried light anti-tank rifles; some W/T or telephone apparatus; about one man in ten was equipped with a folding bicycle; all carried rations for two or three days.

The enemy were expanding the force rapidly at this time and the training course had been considerably curtailed. Originally it had occupied as long as twelve months, a six months' disciplinary course followed by six months at a Parachute School. Four types of training were included; the usual infantry training (including use of weapons, general tactics, assembly and dispersal at given points, and a particularly intensive map-course on large scale maps); physical training, with special exercises to aid jumping; actual parachute descents from heights varying between 800 and 250 feet carried out in six stages, first from platforms and later from aircraft; and training in demolition and sabotage work. The troops were also instructed in the care and maintenance, and in the packing of their parachutes.

The aircraft employed were Junkers Ju.52s, of which plenty were available. The enemy had built up a large fleet of these aircraft prior to 1938 which though ostensibly for passenger carrying had been visualised from the first as a bomber. After the Munich agreement however, when all attempts at secrecy regarding re-armament were abandoned, the Junkers 52 was rapidly replaced in the Luftwaffe by more modern bomber types and became instead a very valuable troop carrier. Large sliding doors fitted in the side of the fuselage made an ideal paratroop exit, and the aircraft could carry fifteen men. The parachutes used were approximately 21 feet in diameter and were attached to the aircraft by a light rope which, before being disconnected, caused the parachute to open immediately after the man had jumped. Although during the attack on the Low Countries the Germans had landed most of their paratroops on airfields they did not consider it essential to do so. Any open and flat ground of 600 yards by 600 yards was suitable and they aimed at landing each Company in an area 170 by 400 yards.

---

[1] A.M. File C.S. 5085: Encl. 3A.

With these facts as a basis of discussion a conference was held at Air Ministry on 10 June 1940, and the decision to establish and organise a Parachute Training Centre as soon as possible was reached[1]. The training type parachute then in use by the R.A.F. was selected as that most likely to be suitable for the purpose, the service type being too small to carry a fully-equipped man. The training type with its diameter of 28 feet was larger than that used by the Germans and by fitting a static cord it was hoped to use it from as low as 500 feet. One thousand of this type were ordered immediately. To provide a similar aircraft to the Ju.52 was not so easy for we had very few civil aircraft in the country. But the Whitley bomber with its long square fuselage was capable of carrying perhaps twelve men, and six Mark Is were also demanded. Ringway, the civil airport of Manchester, had been selected as the location of the school and arrangements were made for the Whitleys and the parachutes to be delivered there with all possible speed.

The station was at that time occupied by No. 110 Wing under the command of Wing Commander Sir Nigel Norman, Bart., who from the outset took a keen interest in the work of the school and who was within a few weeks posted to the new unit. Fifteen volunteers were found for instructional duties, nine from the R.A.F. and six from the Army. Between June and October a few ex-professional parachutists were found and posted to the unit, but among the first instructors experience was very limited[2]. Five of those from the R.A.F. had in the past made parachute descents in pull-off style[3] from the wings of Vickers Virginia aircraft during Empire Air Displays at Hendon, but the Army volunteers had no knowledge of parachutes whatsoever; in fact until they arrived at Ringway they were sublimely ignorant of the nature of their duties except that they had been told that they were of a secret and special nature. But on arrival they all set to work immediately and, while waiting for the Whitleys to undergo the necessary modifications, they managed with much ingenuity and improvisation to construct a number of platforms and swings for preliminary ground training. As sufficient space and tables were not available in the parachute section the packing of the newly arrived parachutes was carried out on the dining tables in the Airmen's Mess. The rear turrets of the Whitleys were removed and a circular aperture cut in the floor of the fuselage and fitted with hinged doors. A suitable dropping zone was found nearby at Tatton Park, and this was requisitioned early in July. On 9 July 1940 the first pupils, Army volunteers, arrived. They were given air experience in the Whitleys and spent much of their time in physical training, special attention being paid to leg and ankle strengthening exercises[4].

The first live jumps[5] took place on 13 July 1940 when the R.A.F. instructors staged a demonstration at Tatton Park consisting of two " pull-offs " from the open tail and six aperture descents from the modified Whitleys. On the following day further descents were made using American type statichutes which, it had been decided, were an improvement on the training type.

---
[1] A.M. File, C.S. 5085: Encl. 4A.
[2] O.R.B. of the P.T.S., June–October 1940.
[3] In this type of descent the rip cord of the parachute is pulled before leaving the aircraft, so that the canopy develops in the slipstream pulling the parachutists clear as it does so.— Appendix K of No. 38 Group Paper entitled " Airborne Assault Operations ".
[4] O.R.B. of the P.T.S., July 1940.
[5] Numerous trials with dummies had previously been carried out. O.R.B. of the P.T.S., July 1940.

The first pupils to jump did so on 22 July 1940, one or two of the descents being made in the pull-off style but this was shortly afterwards discontinued and all exits were made through the aperture.

On 25 July a fatal accident occurred when a pupil, Driver Evans, jumped using an American type statichute. It was an inherent fault of this type that in the case of a bad exit the wearer could turn and entangle himself in the emerging parachute thus causing a premature breakaway of the static line. This had occurred in Driver Evans's case and all jumping was cancelled pending a full investigation into the problem. On 30 July, however, the first tests were made on a new type of statichute designed by Mr. Quilter of the G. Q. Parachute Co. of Woking. The success of the new type was such that the Air Ministry decided that it should entirely replace the American type. Five hundred trial descents with dummies were immediately carried out and on 8 August, nine days after the initial test, the first live descents took place with the " G.Q." statichute[1].

The design of the " G.Q." embodied a revolutionary characteristic. Hitherto both parachutes and statichutes had been so packed that the canopy emerged first followed by the rigging lines. With the " G.Q." this sequence was reversed, the effect being similar to the method used during the war of 1914-1918 when the parachute was packed in a cone attached to the side of the cockpit. The downward velocity of the falling body is thus transmitted smoothly through the rigging lines to the canopy causing it to fill with air more quickly, but less suddenly than by the old system. The comparative absence of shock load, i.e. the " jerk " as the canopy opens and the rigging lines suddenly become taut, was most noticeable with the " G.Q. " type of statichute and all the instructors who carried out tests on 8 August 1940 remarked upon this fact.

As was to be expected the " G.Q." brought with it various teething troubles each of which was carefully investigated as it became apparent and all were eventually overcome. An example was the danger of the canopy fouling the non-retractable tailwheel of the Whitley. Such a case did in fact occur during the trials with the dummies and a temporary solution was found by dropping only while the aircraft was flying in a shallow glide. Later the fitting of " spats " covering the tailwheels was found to be a more satisfactory safeguard.

The Central Landing School was three months old when the Central Landing Establishment was officially opened on 19 September. During that time 961 live jumps were made, and 342 pupils had received instruction. Of these 290 had successfully completed the course, although they had to return later for more advanced training such as stick jumping. Of the remaining 52, 30 men had refused to jump; seven had been returned to their unit for disciplinary reasons; 13 had received minor injuries such as sprains and were temporarily unable to continue training; and two had been killed. Of the 30 who refused 17 did so before their first jump, although many of them got as far as sitting over the hole. Eight refused after their first jump, two after their second and one after his fourth. One or two in every dozen were reported to have no apparent nervous reaction at all and indeed appeared

---

[1] O.R.B. of the P.T.S., July 1940.

to like jumping out. But for the majority the operation entailed great nervous strain, and in a few cases men left the aircraft in a state of collapse having forced themselves to jump by sheer will power[1].

At this time the School was using an old " Bombay " for jumping as well as the " Whitleys ", and it is interesting to note that although over 200 jumps were made from the " Bombay " there were no refusals. Those from the Whitley were attributed to three reasons. Firstly the dark, gloomy, depressing interior of the Whitley fuselage ; secondly the unpleasant sight of other men disappearing through the hole in the floor—the refusals almost invariably occurred among the last few men to jump ; and thirdly a number of men finding the exit difficult scraped their faces on the side of the hole as they went out. Very little could be done in the first two cases but for the third a windshield fitted below the fuselage and forward of the hole made for a much easier exit, the full effect of the slip stream not being felt until the man was almost clear of the aircraft. Another factor which also contributed to refusals to jump was the delay prior to take off. On occasions the men would have to stand by for quite long periods waiting for the weather to improve sufficiently for dropping to take place. Sometimes when they were actually in the aircraft, and even over the dropping zone, a sudden change in the wind strength would cause a cancellation. Such delays were unavoidable but their adverse effect upon morale could have been mitigated by providing crew rooms for the troops, where they could wait in warmth and comparative comfort.

But the work of the C.L.S. had not been confined to parachute training[2]. In August a small flight of very light civil gliders which had previously been located at Christchurch aerodrome, near Bournemouth, moved to Ringway. This, together with the increasing amount of research work being carried out by the school[3], heralded the expansion which officially took place in the following month.

Expansion into the Central Landing Establishment

The authorisation for and instructions regarding the expansion of the C.L.S. originated at a meeting held at the Air Ministry on 5 September 1940[4]. The Prime Minister's consent had been obtained to an alteration of policy whereby the paratroop commitment would be severly curtailed, emphasis being instead placed on gliderborne troops[5]. The meeting therefore decided that the Central Landing School should be replaced by a new organisation to be called the Central Landing Establisment, of which the parachute training school would be but a part.

Under the new arrangement three sections were set up, a Development Section, a Parachute Training School, and a Glider Training Squadron. In the course of time each of the first two grew into completely self-contained

---

[1] C.L.S. Progress Report dated 21 September 1940, and contained in a folder entitled " Letters and Documents extracted from the files of P.T.S." held by No. 38 Group H.Q.
[2] No. 22 Group letter 22G/S1091/Org. dated 20 July 1940.
[3] This research was during August, largely concerned with the development of Quilter's statichute and also with experiments regarding the rotachute, a one-man cradle suspended beneath a propeller which during descent, behaves in a similar manner to a falling leaf.— O.R.B. of P.T.S. entry, 7 August 1940.
[4] A.M. File C.S. 6229: Encl. 10A.
[5] Minute of 1 September 1940, subsequently confirmed by another Note of 12 September 1940. A.M. File, C.S. 6229, Encls. 4D and 11B.

units, the Parachute Training School remaining at Ringway as No. 1 Parachute Training School, and the Development Section becoming the Airborne Forces Experimental Establishment located first at Ringway, then at Sherburn-in-Elmet, and later at Beaulieu, near Southampton[1]. From the Glider Training Squadron was formed, in November 1941, No. 1 Glider Training School, the first school to be established under the glider pilot training scheme.

The change from C.L.S. to C.L.E. officially took place on 19 September 1940[2]. On that date Group Captain L. G. Harvey was posted from Air Ministry to Ringway to command the C.L.E. Wing Commander Sir Nigel Norman was appointed Air I. (Staff), C.L.E. and was empowered to deal direct with Air Ministry on matters of technical development. A local purchase order up to a limit of £150 per month was also granted to assist the work of the Development section. The Air Officer Commanding No. 22 Group, who was responsible for the Establishment, was empowered to short circuit official channels and to deal direct with the War Office on all except policy matters[3]. The station remained under the control of No. 22 Group until 1 December 1940 when it was transferred to No. 70 Group[4].

The Development Section under Wing Commander G. M. Buxton, consisted of some 120 officers, N.C.O.s and airmen, and was augmented by a number of civilian specialists. They were soon at work on the many problems, major and minor, which came to light. Close contact was established and maintained with the Royal Aircraft establishment at Farnborough, where R.A.F. experimental work was normally carried out, and also with the Ministry of Aircraft Production. Examination of various types of aircraft in order to ascertain the likelihood of their being used in an Airborne role occupied much time, but did not result in a substitute for the Whitley being found. Arrangements were made however, for paratroop apertures to be incorporated in future Marks of the Halifax and the Stirling, although the priority of Bomber Command prohibited the immediate use of these types for training. Development of special equipment for the paratroops was an important and urgent matter too. Successful designs of equipment containers and methods of dropping cargoes varying from carrier pigeons to mortar base plates were evolved[5].

The Glider Training Squadron had a strength of about 200 officers and men who, in the absence of the service gliders the designs of which had only recently been approved, maintained and flew an assortment of civil gliders mostly " Kirby Kites " and " Vikings " about 20 of which had been located and requisitioned by the R.A.F. Hectors were used to tow the larger of these craft but for the others—some of them were sailplanes rather than gliders—Tiger Moths could be, and were, used[6].

But Ringway was not a very satisfactory location for a glider towing unit. The renowned bad weather of the Manchester area affected glider towing even more than normal flying. Also the continual dropping of

---
[1] Both No. 1 P.T.S. and A.F.E.E. formed on 15 February 1942.
[2] 22 Group Signal P733 dated 11 September 1940.
[3] A.C.A.S.(R) folder " Formation of the Central Landing School " Minutes of meeting, 19 August 1940.
[4] O.R.B. of the C.L.E., December 1940.
[5] O.R.B. of the C.L.E. Weekly Progress Reports of C.L.S. contained in folder " Extracts from Documents and Files of P.T.S." held by No. 38 Group H.Q.
[6] Appendix K of No. 38 Group paper " Airborne Assault Operations " and O.R.B. or G.T.S.

paratroops on the Tatton Park D.Z.[1] restricted glider flying near the aerodrome. In any case it was realised that when the Hotspur, and more particularly the Horsa, came into use a bigger airfield would be necessary. In November preparations were made for the Glider Section to move to Side Hill aerodrome near Newmarket, but Bomber Command intervened and the allocation of the aerodrome was cancelled[2]. Later attempts to find a new home for the Section, first at Rearsby then at Ratcliffe, were foiled by the occupation of those landing grounds by M.A.P.[3].

Towards the end of 1940 the problem seemed more urgent than later events proved for it was anticipated that the Section would be required to convert the ex-Commandos to glider flying. In fact the number of these men, who received Tiger Moth instruction at Army Co-operation Squadrons, was so small and the production delays over the Hotspur were so prolonged, that another airfield was not essential until November 1941. C.L.E.'s demands made during December 1940 did serve however to emphasise the need for preparing aerodromes for use by the heavy gliders. Shobden, Herefordshire, was chosen as a suitable site and work commenced on concrete runways, and by the time the first Horsas were delivered it was ready for use.

During the autumn and winter of 1940-41 by far the greatest activity at Ringway was going on within the Parachute Training Section. During November the first "stick" jumps were carried out by instructors, eight men jumping from one aircraft. For this a new system of strong points was evolved by the Development Section, two strong points only being used. These were both just forward of the aperture, one on each side of the fuselage. Canvas panels fitted with press studs and attached to the sides of the fuselage kept the straps safely clear of the men waiting to drop. So successful was this arrangement that with a little practice eight men could leave the aircraft in as many seconds, thus reducing length of the stick to 300 yards. Further experience proved that the number of men in a stick could be increased to ten, which henceforth became the standard number[4]. On 7 December 1940 the first stick jump with containers took place. Metal containers fitted with a parachute at one end and a primitive shock absorber at the other were carried in the bomb cells of the Whitley, the release switch being operated by the first member of the stick immediately before jumping[5].

A simple, but efficient system of warning lights had also been installed in all the aircraft. The success of this system was so great that it was one of the few points of dropping procedure which remained unchanged. Two small lights, one red, one green, were located in the fuselage close to the parachute aperture. On being warned over the intercommunication system that the aircraft was approaching the D.Z. the stick would take up their positions for the jump. Approximately five seconds before reaching the correct spot either the pilot or the navigator switched on the red light from a control in the cockpit. When he switched the light from red to green the first man jumped followed as rapidly as possible by the remainder of the stick. The system was, by virtue of its simplicity, so reliable that the need for change never arose.

---

[1] D.Z.: dropping zone.
[2] O.R.B. of the C.L.E., November 1940. A.M. File C.S. 6229: Encl. 36B.
[3] Ministry of Aircraft Production.
[4] O.R.B. of the P.T.S., November 1940.
[5] O.R.B. of the P.T.S., December 1940.

During December 1940 a number of exercises were carried out by the paratroops, most of them at Ringway or Tatton Park. Such exercises as these were arranged locally between Lieut.-Colonel Down, the Commander of No. 11 S.A.S. battalion, and Group Captain Harvey. On 2 December however, a small party was detached to Old Sarum aerodrome near Salisbury and on the following day two Whitleys dropped 32 men in sticks of eight during an exercise on Salisbury Plain. This effort, small though it was, was a great success. It also served the purpose of drawing attention to the fact that no establishment existed at C.L.E. for an exercise flight, which was by now needed in order that training by companies could be undertaken. Although the training programme had been intertered with but little by the withdrawal of the two Whitleys for this exercise it was obvious that any exercises on a larger scale would cause considerable interference unless more aircraft were available. In January such an interruption did in fact occur, but the cause was something far more exciting than an exercise[1].

The Initial Operation—Colossus : February, 1941[2]

Within a few days of Italy's entry into the war the Air Ministry received two letters, both from civilians with first-hand knowledge of the country, suggesting an operation against a certain aqueduct in Southern Italy, and by December 1940 it had been decided that such an attack might usefully be carried out. The three ports of Taranto, Brindisi, and Bari all relied for their supply of drinking water on the great system known as the Acquedetto Pugliese, which carried water across the Apennine Mountains to the arid province of Apulia. At the end of 1940 these ports were being used as departure bases for troops on their way to Albania and North Africa; the proposal was to cut the water supply by a raid on one of the aqueducts. But attacks on the Acquedetto Pugliese by bomber aircraft were considered impracticable and the only vital and vulnerable points were too far from the coast for a seaborne raid to be successful. It was therefore suggested by Admiral Sir Roger Keyes, then Director of Combined Operations, that paratroops of No. 11 Special Air Service Battalion should be employed on the task, and this suggestion was approved by the Chiefs of Staff and the Prime Minister. The Acquedetto Pugliese was fed from one river, the Sele which flows into the Tyrrhenian Sea south of Salerno. The water was drawn from this river at its source, in very mountainous country near Calatri, and carried over the natural bed of the river by the Traqino Aqueduct. This aqueduct, at the very fountain head of the system, was selected as the most suitable target, and detailed planning for an attack against it began.

The only available base for the attack was Malta[3] which was a distance of some 400 miles from the target. The choice of aircraft lay between Bombays—of which four were now available—and Whitleys. The Whitleys and crews had to be drawn from Bomber Command and the Air Officer Commanding-in-Chief was reluctant to detach some of his best crews for as long as a month—the time estimated as necessary for the preparation and

---
[1] O.R.B. of the P.T.S. and Appendices, December 1940.
[2] A.M File C.S. 7951: Operation Colossus.
[3] Athens was considered but was deemed to be unsatisfactory for security reasons.

execution of the operation. The operation was thus originally planned to use only five Whitleys augmented by the Bombays. But Group Captain Harvey of the C.L.E. and Wing Commander J. B. Tait, D.F.C., who was to command the Whitley detachment, immediately pointed out the immensely increased difficulties of maintenance involved in such a scheme. At the request of the Deputy Chief of Air Staff, the A.O.C. eventually agreed to supply eight Whitleys and experienced crews from No. 78 Squadron so that only one type of aircraft would be used. Even so no Whitley spares were available at Malta and both spares and ground crews had to be flown to the island in advance of the main party. For this purpose a Sunderland Flying Boat was supplied by Coastal Command.

Much had to be done before leaving for Malta and the whole of the preparations for the operation took place at Ringway. The Whitleys were modified for paratroop dropping by C.L.E. ground crews; the Development Section were busy improving the rather primitive containers; the Bomber Command aircrews were trained for troop dropping; the thirty-seven selected troops from No. 11 S.A.S. Battalion made their first night descents; a scale model of the target was constructed from the photographs and information available and " X " Troops spent much time studying this; a " cover story " telling of a proposed attack on a bridge in Abyssinia was built up; and an urgent signal was sent to Malta requesting that further photographs of the aqueduct be obtained. All of these preparations took place between 12 January and 7 February 1941. In charge of them was the " Operation Controller ", Wing Commander Sir Nigel Norman; the " Attack Commander-Air " was Wing Commander Tait, and the " Attack Commander-Ground ", Major T. A. G. Pritchard.

On 5 February, having been held up for over a week by bad weather, the Sunderland carrying the spares and the ground crews left for Malta. Lt. A. J. Deane Drummond, one of the officers of " X " Troop, also flew in this aircraft carrying with him copies of the Operation Instructions for the Air Officer Commanding, Malta, and for the A.O.C.-in-C., Middle East. Two days later the Whitleys, each carrying their own troops and parachutes followed: they reached Malta at 0800 hours on 8 February.

The operation was timed to take place on the first good-weather night after 9 February, the full moon period being 9-16 February. Many reconnaissance flights had been made by Glenn Martin aircraft of No. 69 (G.R.) Squadron from Malta in an attempt to obtain new photographs of the target but it was not until the 9th that one was successful. On examination of the hurriedly produced prints it was found that a second aqueduct spanning a tributary of the River Sele was situated about 300 yards from the original structure. Some doubt was expressed as to which of these two was the intended target and it was eventually decided that the more easterly one of the two was to be attacked. There was no time to obtain further photographs for the weather of the night of 10-11 February proved favourable and at 1740 hours Wing Commander Tait took off in the first aircraft.

Although time did not permit test drops of containers, testing of fittings or any last minute combined drill for crews it was decided that risk of failure was less than would have resulted from delaying the operation. Two of the aircraft carried bombs only and were to make diversionary attacks against Foggia. The remaining six all carried troops, containers, and one bomb each. No opposition was encountered except some slight flak over the Sicilian coast, and by 2330 all six aircraft had reached the D.Z. and had dropped their troops. Two of the aircraft however were unable to release their containers. The packing and loading of containers was a delicate business if the centre of gravity was to be so adjusted that the container would leave the bomb rack easily. Prior to Colossus this had not been fully realised and the troops themselves had been responsible for both tasks. Following the failure on this occasion a standard method of packing was evolved and the loading onto the aircraft became the responsibility of the navigator of the aircraft, who by his bomb-aimer training was better able to appreciate the niceties of this rather delicate task.

It was unfortunate that one set of containers which "hung-up" was that in the aircraft "J for Johnie". This aircraft had had trouble at Malta where engine trouble delayed take-off for almost half an hour; then a bad landfall on the Italian coast further complicated matters. Eventually the stick was dropped, but two miles away from the correct D.Z. in a neighbouring but wrong valley. Finally the pilot found himself unable to clear his containers. What was still more unfortunate was that the troops carried in this aircraft were all Engineers. Consequently when "X" troop assembled Major Pritchard found himself short of his senior R.E. officer, Captain G. F. K. Daly, five of his sappers, and a considerable proportion of his explosives. The troop nevertheless made their way to the aqueduct and set to work with what explosives they had. They found that the centre pier was of reinforced concrete instead of masonry as had been expected and was consequently too strong to be destroyed; but the end pier and the second smaller aqueduct were of masonry, and both of these could be attacked with the explosives available. The remaining Engineers under Lt. G. R. Patterson placed the dynamite under these two structures and at 0030 hours on 11 February the charges were fired. Both aqueducts collapsed and the water flooded down into the ravine. The operation was at least partially successful.

Major Pritchard now organised his party into three sections and gave orders for them to make their way independently to the mouth of the River Sele where they were to be picked up by a submarine, H.M.S. *Triumph*, on the night of the 15th/16th. But their efforts to reach the rendezvous were unsuccessful and by 12 February all had been taken prisoner, with the exception of Captain Daly and his men, who were captured on the 15th when only 12 miles from the mouth of the river.

After dropping the troops the Whitleys went on to bomb various minor objectives in the area before returning to Malta. On the return journey one of the diversionary aircraft "R for Roger", in which Wing Commander Norman was flying as passenger, flew over the D.Z. and saw the troops assembling. The other, "S for Sugar", developed engine trouble and had to force land in Italy. The point is mentioned here because a series of coincidences was thereby started which worried the authorities at Malta not a little. The pilot of "S for Sugar" sent a W.T. message in Syko code to Malta that he would land as near as possible to the mouth of the River Sele in the hope that the crew could be picked up. It was purely by chance that he selected this point for until after the drop no one apart from Major Pritchard, his officers and a few of the naval staff at Malta knew of the evacuation plans. But the question now arose whether or not H.M.S. *Triumph* should risk going to the rendezvous, and after consultations with the Admiralty in London it was decided that she should not. In fact, of course, had she done so her voyage would have been in vain for the troops were, by that time all in enemy hands.

Soon after their capture " X " Troop received a visit from the American Military Attache. They told him that local Italians, being under the impression that they were German troops, helped them first to locate the containers, and then to carry the explosives up to the objectives. The prisoners, said the Attache, were in high spirits; their morale was " terrific " and they intended to escape at the first opportunity. Lt. Deane-Drummond did in fact do so shortly afterwards; after a series of amazing adventures he returned to England in time to join the 1st Airborne Division in their attack on Arnhem, where he was again captured and yet again escaped.

The hindrance caused to the Italian war effort by Colossus was not as great as had been hoped. The fact that the end instead of the centre pier had been damaged shortened the time needed for repairs to be carried out, and the reserves of water in the local reservoirs lasted for almost the whole of this period. Nevertheless the attack was sufficiently successful to shake Italian self-confidence and to cause some waste of effort on unnecessary defence measures. But its greatest value was the experience gained of the organisation and equipment necessary to stage an airborne operation, and on his return to Ringway, Wing Commander Sir Nigel Norman in conjunction with Group Captain Harvey immediately prepared a paper setting out the lessons learned from the operation and making suggestions for action to be taken.

The Lessons of Operation Colossus

Firstly the need for up-to-date intelligence supported by air photographs at the time of planning the operation was emphasised. The last minute discovery that the target area for Colossus contained two aqueducts instead of one had clearly shown the need for this. Even so the model of the area which had been constructed at Ringway had proved most valuable, and the paper strongly recommended that similar models be prepared for any future operations.

Secondly the aircrews chosen for such a task should be carefully selected and regard paid to their powers of " organisation, adaptability and tolerance, in addition to the qualities of enthusiasm and courage ". This because the necessity of maintaining the closest possible contact with the paratroops, especially when using an advanced base, had been shown.

Thirdly it was considered proven that the landing of paratroops in bright moonlight was practically as easy as in daylight, and that trained men could be dropped in close country, even with moderate winds, without suffering casualties[1]. A long flight did not necessarily have a bad effect on the paratroops whose morale and enthusiasm was very high. But the Army personnel should be given opportunities to become completely familiar with the aircraft used, particularly with the container dropping system, and should have more air experience under operational conditions than was possible in the case

---

[1] Although it was known when the report was written only one man of " X " Troop had been injured at all. He had sprained an ankle on landing.

of Colossus. This point reaffirmed the necessity of providing an Exercise Flight at C.L.E. so that more unit training as distinct from individual training could be given[1].

Only three weeks, and that in wintry unsuitable weather, were available at Ringway for training, aircraft modifications and all the necessary preparations for the flight to Malta. This was by no means sufficient. It was considered that the appointment of a unified command would obviate many of the organisation and administrative difficulties which occurred during Colossus. The advance party did not arrive in Malta until a very short time before the main force resulting in preliminary arrangements being incomplete when they arrived.

Finally the arrangement for container release was not satisfactory. An alteration of procedure whereby the navigator would release the containers after the men had left the aircraft would probably improve this. But an investigation into the whole problem was needed and both the release system and the design of the containers would need revision in order to overcome the danger of "hang-ups". Such an investigation was at once undertaken by the Development Section of the C.L.E. who, by the time the next operation took place, had at least partially overcome the difficulty[2].

Parachute Training : February—November 1941

Training of " Lambs " and Polish troops

Besides training replacements for No. 11 S.A.S. Battalion the Parachute Training School was giving instruction to two other classes of pupil, the Poles and the "Lambs". The "Lambs" were secret agents: their training was elementary and brief. Often they would travel up to Manchester overnight, spend one day at Ringway, and return to London by the evening train. Two hours in the morning on the swings, jumping platforms and dummy fuselage followed by two or three jumps with portable radio or sabotage equipment in the afternoon was often all they were able to spare time for. And, of course, their training was always of top priority. As the number of these pupils increased it became clear that special arrangements for them were necessary. A flight, originally called "E" Syndicate, but later renamed No. 51 Special Training School, was therefore formed with its own quarters, aircraft and instructors. This not only ensured that the urgency of "Lamb" training would not interfere with the normal work of the Section, but also provided an additional security guard, for this work was naturally of a most secret nature.

Although it did not become an important part of the C.L.E. duties until 1941, "Lamb" training had been going on in a small way since the inception of the School. Courses for Polish troops did not begin, however, until April 1941. From the very first the Poles had been enthusiastic about paratrooping and had asked for permission to set up their own training school. But lack of resources had prevented this, so that when the P.T.S. had fulfilled the 11 S.A.S. Battalion commitment the Poles were delighted to fill the gap by supplying pupils. During the summer, until the training of the 2nd and 3rd Parachute Battalions commenced, Polish officers and men were being trained at the rate of about 100 a month. This number by no means satisfied

---

[1] A.M. File C.S. 7951. [2] A.M. File C.S. 16084.

the ambitions of the Poles but it was not until 1942 that facilities were available for them to recommence training and so build up the Independent (Polish) Parachute Brigade[1].

Balloon descents and "Stick" Jumping

As early as August 1940 C.L.S. instructors had visited Cardington and had carried out trials with dummies from a captive balloon there. In December further investigations took place and live jumps were made: in April 1941 the world's largest barrage balloon—promptly christened "Bessie"—was delivered to C.L.E.[2]. A balloon car was constructed, fitted and tested by dropping dummies. This being satisfactory, the syllabus was henceforth amended to include two balloon drops prior to the five aircraft jumps normally carried out. Jumping from a balloon provided an extra thrill for the parachutists for, owing to the lack of slipstream the statichute took 2.7 seconds to open instead of the usual 1.7 seconds. Nevertheless that same absence of slipstream prohibited the danger of twisted rigging lines and allowed the pupil to practise controlling his exit-position. Therein lay the great virtue of balloon drops[3].

Balloon jumping was an innovation: the other major change in the training syllabus was not an innovation but an expansion. The first "stick" jumps had been carried out in December 1940, first by instructors, then by selected pupils. As one by one more aircraft were allotted to the C.L.E. it became possible to extend this important part of the course to all pupils. Officially it was not incorporated into the course until the syllabus was completely revised in October 1941, but in fact many pupils made their final training jump as a member of a stick of two, three or four men. Moreover the lesson of Colossus regarding the need for unit exercises had been well learned. Troops from No. 11 S.A.S. gained "stick jumping" experience during normal Army manoeuvres in all parts of the country and also in Scotland and Northern Ireland. The numbers involved were on each occasion small but for the troops the experience gained was invaluable. Increasing interest was being shown too by a number of influential persons. Not a month passed during 1941 but at least one V.I.P. paid a visit to the Station. And on each occasion demonstration drops were carried out which, leaving apart any favourable impression made on the visitor, provided excellent experience for all concerned in the careful planning needed to "lay on" a successful operation.

This then was the situation at the P.T.S. when, in October, the Army decided to form the 1st Parachute Brigade. No. 11 S.A.S. Battalion had reached its established strength of 500 but was finding difficulty in maintaining it due to the very high wastage rate: P.T.S. were training replacements for No. 11 S.A.S., Polish officers and men, and had established "E Syndicate" to train the "Lambs": the standard of training had been improved by the introduction of initial jumps from the balloon and by stick-jumping and by exercises: the total output of trained personnel, including the "Lambs", was about 200 per month.

The Chief of the Imperial General Staff had asked for an output of 100 a week in order to train the 2nd and 3rd Parachute Battalions as quickly as possible. Wing Commander M. A. Newnham, D.F.C. (who had taken

---

[1] Appendix K to 38 Group paper "Airborne Assault Operations".
[2] The balloon was officially known as the Mk. XI. It had a capacity of 41,900 cubic feet so that, although similar in shape, it was much larger than a normal barrage balloon.
[3] O.R.B. of P.T.S., August 1940 and December 1940.

over the P.T.S. from S/Ldr. Strange on 11 July 1941), considered that this figure could be met without difficulty provided the necessary increase of equipment and personnel was granted. The essential alterations in the establishment were made and during September the staff were busy preparing the School for its new commitment. The title of Central Landing Establishment was changed on 1 September 1941 to " Airborne Forces Establishment " and in anticipation of the commencement of the Glider Pilot Training Organisation establishment for a glider flight was withdrawn thus leaving two sections only, the P.T.S. and the Development Unit. The aircraft establishment, which was still officially only four I.E. plus two I.R. Whitleys, was doubled and one I.E. plus one I.R. Ansons added: plans for a new hutted camp to accommodate 250 men were approved: a new syllabus, entailing six jumps, two from the balloon, two individually and two in sticks, was prepared: the R.A.F. provided the whole of the instructional staff who were drawn on a volunteer basis from R.A.F. Physical Training instructors[1].

On 1 November 1941, the R.A.F. officially assumed full responsibility for the training of parachute troops. No. 1 Course arrived on 3 November and the instructors, 35 of whom had themselves completed their course only a few days previously, began the task of training 100 men per week. The Army had instituted a synthetic training course (the advanced Airborne School and Depot) through which the pupils passed prior to arriving at the P.T.S. At the Advanced Airborne School, situated at Hardwick, Chesterfield, the pupils were taught much of the P.T. and synthetic training which had previously been included in the course at Ringway. Moreover the new conditions of service and system of volunteering were quickly reflected in the type of pupil. On the first course of 18 officers and 237 other ranks there were only seven injuries and two refusals[2].

Training of aircrews for parachute dropping : 1941

During 1941 much attention was paid to the question of providing aircrews to fly the paratroop aircraft. The policy was for bomber crews to be withdrawn from their normal duties at short notice, and this had in fact been done for Colossus. Such a measure would not be possible in the case of a large-scale operation however, and it was felt that some sort of " part-time " training should be given to bomber crews. Discussions on these lines between No. 4 Group Bomber Command (the Whitley Group) and the C.L.E. commenced as early as March 1941[3]. At this time such training as was undertaken was carried out on the squadrons during air tests. C.L.E. supplied squadron commanders with the details of the procedure used for dropping and notified them of any change. In May, however, an improvement on this was effected, arrangements being made for observers to attend a short five-day course in paratroop dropping at Ringway between leaving their O.T.U. and joining their new squadron. Flight Commanders from No. 4 Group squadrons would also attend the course if possible. This arrangement was put into practice, although rather intermittently, until September 1941, when it was replaced by a new scheme under which the complete crew were to attend the course at Ringway[4].

---

[1] A.M. File 10582, Pt. I: Encl. 23A. O.R.B. of the A.F.E., 1 September 1940.
[2] War Office Narrative " Airborne Forces ", Chapter III. Appendix K to 38 Group paper " Airborne Assault Operations '.
[3] A.M. File 8513.
[4] D.M.C. Monthly Progress Report, October 1941.

One crew from each squadron was to attend the course and on return to the squadron they would pass on the knowledge gained to their fellows. That there were great snags to this arrangement was clear from the first: Bomber Command claimed that crews withdrawn from operations during their tour were apt to " lose their edge ", with consequent effect on the bomber effort: the crews did not remain with the squadrons for more than a few months: the amount of practice possible at Ringway in so short a time was very small, in fact the crews often did not even carry out a live drop: finally the overall priority of their bombing role prohibited them from continuing practice drops on return to their squadrons—even if modified aircraft were available, which was seldom.

Moreover the aircrews, like the paratroops, would need practice at flying and dropping large numbers of men and dropping in formation. Obviously Bomber Command could spare neither the aircraft, crews, nor time for such exercises on any but the smallest scale. On two occasions, once at the end of September and again during November, crews and aircraft were provided by operational squadrons for troop dropping during Army manoeuvres. But the rapid expansion of the paratroops force into the 1st Parachute Brigade soon made demands for exercises on a scale which would very seriously have impeded the bombing effort. The only solution was to provide special squadrons for the task and in December 1941, this was done.

Glider Pilot Training : September 1940—November 1941

When in September 1940 the Glider Training Section was set up at the C.L.E. the production of gliders had hardly begun. The Hotspur was the only type which had progressed further than the drawing boards, and deliveries of these could not be expected until the new year at the earliest. But the policy regarding the supply of glider pilots was already causing numerous headaches: that policy has already been discussed in Chapter 1[1].

In spite of the originally optimistic forecasts by the War Office no further volunteers could be found: Army Co-operation Command had continually pointed out the difficulties of training the men in addition to carrying out normal squadron duties, and in fact the impossibility of training them satisfactorily[2]: the Air Ministry were claiming that any of the trainees who were suitable should be transferred to the R.A.F. for normal operational duties: some of the trainees themselves stated that unless this was done they did not wish to continue training. Finally there were still no Hotspurs available. One was in fact, delivered by 26 April 1940 in time to take part in the demonstration for Mr. Churchill at Ringway: but apart from this the glider demonstration consisted of a formation landing of five sailplanes[3]. During the summer however the position did improve, and Hotspur conversion was going on at Thame[4]. But the pilot strength of the Exercise Flight dwindled steadily as one by one the pilots were, for various reasons, posted away from the unit without replacements being available. By 1 September 1941 only 19 remained on flying duties at Thame although the total on strength was 29. But at least the hope that the establishment of the Glider Training

---
[1] A.M. 7424: and O.R.B. of the Glider Training Squadron.
[2] ACC/S76/Air: Encl. 86A: and O.R.B. of the G.T.S.
[3] O.R.B.s of the C.L.E. and of the G.T.S., April 1941.
[4] O.O.C./S76/Air: Encl. 86A.

Squadron would provide 36 fully trained glider pilots had been fulfilled, for if the original 18 R.A.F. instructors were included the number available was 37. Thus with all its faults the scheme had at least produced some pilots. In fact all of the 19 had been trained, not only as glider but also as tug pilots and during the summer it was possible to carry out a number of exercises.

Like the paratroop exercises these were on a very small scale, six Hotspurs being the maximum number employed. In the main they consisted of landings on the aerodrome at Ringway, followed by mock attacks on the hangars and other station buildings. The passengers carried were usually men from No. 11 S.A.S. Battalion, although members of the R.A.F. Regiment from Ringway also flew on occasions. Co-operation exercises with Fighter Command at Duxford resulted in the evolution of fighter tactics to be used against gliders. Later a detachment from Thame visited stations in Nos. 10, 11 and 12 Groups to enable squadrons to practise these attacks. The great virtue of these early small scale exercises was that a basic procedure for glider flying was evolved. The connecting of tow ropes; signals for take-off; circuit procedure before casting off and landing; the dropping of tow ropes by tug aircraft; all these involved difficulties which, though small in themselves, were of great cumulative effect. Air Commodore Harvey, Lt.-Col. Rock and Flying Officer P. B. N. Davis, Harvey's second-in-Command, were able during the summer of 1941, to study these problems and to produce a paper defining the best solutions. Thus by October, when a plan for glider pilot training was finally settled, the glider flying procedure to be used at the schools had been worked out.

For the training scheme however, more instructors were needed, for only seven of the original 18 were considered suitable. Volunteers for glider flying were found from the Central Flying School and during October 19 of them were posted to Thame thus making a total of 28 instructors[1]. Like the parachute instructors at Ringway, the 19 completed their own course only a few days before the first intake of pupils arrived. But at Thame not only were the instructors qualified instructors and experienced pilots, but their first pupils were the R.A.F. pupils who had already reached Service Flying Training School level on powered aircraft. The commencement of glider pilot training was therefore a comparatively easy matter, the innumerable difficulties, both real and imaginary, which had so impeded the policy decisions being suddenly swept away. The first course at No. 1 G.T.S. began on 4 November 1941 and ended on 6 January 1942[2].

As with the paratroops the need now arose for combined exercises as distinct from individual training. Not only would the glider pilots require practice in flying and landing in formation but the 1st Airlanding Brigade would have to have facilities for glider flights and exercises on a large scale. Even if Bomber Command could supply the bulk of the R.A.F. effort in an operation it was impossible to divert bomber aircraft and crews for the training of the Airborne Force. The newly formed Airborne Division needed its own R.A.F. organisation and it was to meet this need that No. 38 Wing was formed. The policy decisions which resulted in its formation and which governed its work during 1942 and 1943 are now considered in Chapter 3.

---

[1] O.R.B. of the G.T.S.
[2] A.M. File C.S. 7424: Encls. 22B and 25A.

PART II

EXPANSION INTO AN OPERATIONAL FORCE NOVEMBER 1941 TO OCTOBER 1943

CHAPTER 3

EXPANSION POLICY: NOVEMBER 1941—APRIL 1943

The Army Organisation: November—December 1941

The Army requirement for the home based Airborne Forces which existed in November 1941, involved a total of 10,000 men; 5,000 paratroops and 5,000 airlanding troops. In addition the glider pilots, although an R.A.F. responsibility while training, reverted to the Army on completion of their course and would so need their own special organisation[1]. The actual strength of the force was of course far below these figures, for only the 1st Battalion of the Parachute Brigade was in existence, this being the former No. 11 S.A.S. Battalion. The 2nd and 3rd Battalions and the Air Troop R.E. were still in embryo although by November men from each were under training at Ringway. The Airlanding Brigade Group was, however, at full strength since it was an existing formation and had merely to change its role. (When the decision to make it the Airlanding Brigade was taken the 31st Independent Brigade Group, as it had previously been called, was stationed in South Wales and was training for mountain warfare.) The case of the glider pilots resembled that of the paratroops in that only a small number were at that time under training[2].

Nevertheless, since the hope was that by the summer of 1942 the whole force would be fully trained the need for a commander and headquarters staff was obvious. There was some doubt regarding the correct title as it was still undecided whether or not the force would ever operate at more than Brigade strength. But General Sir Alan Brooke, Commander-in-Chief, Home Forces, advanced the use of the titles of "Divisional Commander" and "Divisional H.Q." from the first, since, apart from reasons of morale and convenience at home, it also served to impress the enemy[3]. Brigadier F. A. H. Browning, D.S.O., formerly commanding the 24th Guards Brigade Group was appointed G.O.C. the Airborne Division and, together with a nucleus of staff officers, reported to G.H.Q. Home Forces for his new duties on 3 November 1941. Initially his staff was small[4] and included only Army officers, although it was soon augmented by Sir Nigel Norman from Ringway, who acted as adviser on all air aspects[5].

Expansion of the air components: November 1941—April 1942

General Browning's primary task was to co-ordinate the whole development and training of the Airborne Force and the initial establishment of his headquarters was designed to provide for the supervision of training

---

[1] The details of this special organisation, which was named the Glider Pilot Regiment, were not actually approved until December 1941, that is to say after the establishment of the Divisional H.Q.
[2] War Office Narrative " Airborne Forces ", Chapter III.
[3] " Division " is a very elastic term which may in some circumstances be used for a force of as many as 40,000 men. Although by no means unknown a force of 10,000 was small to be given this title.
[4] 1 G.S.O. 1: 1 G.S.O. 2: 1 G.S.C. 3: 1 D.A.Q.M.C.: and 1 A.D.M.S., although within a month it was increased to include also 1 A.A. and G.M.G.: 1 D.A.A.G.: 1 Chaplain: 1 A.D.O.S.: 1 D.A.D.O.S. (O.M.E.): and 1 Camp Commandant.
[5] W.D. Loose Minute 20/Misc./2061 (A.G.1A) dated 2 December 1941.

and for the investigation of the many problems of organisation and equipment which were continually appearing. Consequently his first action on assuming his new command was to visit Air Marshal Sir Arthur Barrett, who as Commander-in-Chief Army Co-operation Command, was the Senior Air Force Officer most concerned with the development of Airborne Forces[1]. During their discussions the two Commanders became convinced that the immediate need was twofold: firstly, the provision of special R.A.F. exercise squadrons in order that the troops could carry out combined as distinct from individual training: and secondly, the concentration of the whole force, paratroops, airlanding troops and exercise squadrons within one area[2] so that such training could be carried out without undue waste of time. After consideration of various localities they decided that Salisbury Plain alone possessed the attributes demanded, namely suitability for all stages of training in land warfare; the frequent landing with some degree of freedom of both gliders and paratroops; and the easy retrieval of gliders and their return to their parent aerodromes. After further and more detailed investigation of the air aspects Sir Arthur Barrett submitted these proposals to the Air Ministry. In this letter, which was dated 10 November 1941 he advocated the formation of two special squadrons, one for parachute dropping and one for glider towing, and he suggested that, in view of the advantages of concentration upon Salisbury Plain, the two aerodromes at Netheravon and Shrewton should be made available for these two squadrons[3].

These suggestions were accepted by the Air Staff and were embodied in the scheme for the expansion of the Airborne Forces organisation which was then being drawn up[4]. Official notification of the new organisation was promulgated on 28 November 1941 the list of units concerned being:—

One E.F.T.S.[5] Two Glider Training Schools Two Glider O.T.U.s.	For individual training of Glider Pilots.
One Parachute Training School	For individual parachute training
A Technical Development Section One Parachute Exercise Squadron One Glider Exercise Squadron	For collective training

For administrative purposes the first three of these, that is the five schools concerned with individual glider pilot training, were placed under Flying Training Command: the remainder being the concern of Army Co-operation Command. Of the nine units four were already in existence, the E.F.T.S. (No. 16 at Meir): one of the G.T.S.'s (No. 1 at Thame); the P.T.S. (at Ringway); and the Technical Development Section (also at Ringway). The

---

[1] The training organisation at Ringway had always been a part of A.C.C. and was destined to remain so. And although the E.F.T.S. and the Glider Training Schools of the Glider Pilot Training Scheme were to become the responsibility of Flying Training Command it was assumed that operational training for the Airborne Force would be an Army Co-operation concern.
[2] The location of the schools concerned with individual training was not of great importance in this connection.
[3] ACC/S76/Air: Encl. 21A.
[4] A.M.: L.M. 356/D. of O. dated 28 November 1941.
[5] Elementary Flying Training School.

remainder commenced to form immediately upon the issue of this authorisation and by March 1942 the expansion was complete, the location of the new units being:—

No. 2 G.T.S. at Weston-on-the-Green;

Nos. 101 and 102 G.O.T.U's at Kidlington;

Nos. 296 and 297 Squadrons (The Exercise Squadrons) at Netheravon.

The essential difference between "individual" and "collective" training

At this point it is well to emphasise once again the difference between "individual" and "collective" training. The two specialised groups of men peculiar to airborne forces, the paratroops and the glider pilots, both need a considerable amount of "individual" training. Until numbers of them have completed this the force can hardly be called an Airborne Force. But there are large numbers of other personnel, the glider-borne troops and the aircrews in particular, without whom the Airborne Force would not be a force at all. These latter, however, do not need individual training—or need very little—to transfer them from any other to the Airborne role. But the whole force, paratroops, glider pilots, glider-borne formations and aircrews alike, all need "collective" or "combined" training. The key to success in airborne operations has always been recognised to be concentration of the force both in the air and on the ground, and to achieve concentration constant practice with the whole force taking part is absolutely necessary, and wherever possible full scale rehearsals should be carried out.

During 1940 and the early part of 1941 those responsible for raising an Airborne Force had devoted their efforts to training at the "individual" stages—successfully in the case of the paratroops; not so successfully in the case of the glider pilots. The policy governing individual training had been reviewed during July, August and September 1941, following the Chief of Staff's approval of the Army proposals made during May. The new policy which arose from the revision resulted in an expansion of paratroop training at Ringway and the setting up of the Glider Pilot training organisation, which is described at the end of Chapter 1 and in the paragraph immediately above. It so happened that this new policy for individual training was put into effect at the same time that policy regarding collective training began to be discussed in detail. A clear picture of the events of November 1941-April 1942 will not be obtained unless we continually bear in mind the essential difference between the two. The glider pilot training organisation was set up under a policy decided in May 1941 and was based on plans evolved by discussions lasting over a period of three months: the "collective" training organisation (i.e. the exercise squadrons) was set up immediately following recommendations by the Commander-in-Chief, Army Co-operation Command and the G.O.C. the Airborne Division. That the formation of units for both organisations was promulgated in one notice did a lot to confuse the issue and to obscure the fact that the glider pilot training organisation did not exist until a firm policy had been evolved, laid down, and implemented, whereas the exercise squadrons were in existence for some months before high level discussions on policy regarding them began.

Policy regarding the "individual" training organisation remained firm throughout 1942, and indeed through the war. Chapter 1 contains the story of its birth pang and of the final plans concerning it. We have noted above that between November 1941 and March 1943 these plans were put into effect. And there for the moment we may leave policy as it affected the "individual" and turn instead to the "collective" training organisation for it is with that type of training that this chapter is mainly concerned.

Formation of the Exercise Squadrons and No. 38 Wing Headquarters January—April 1942.

The two exercise squadrons formed at Netheravon during January 1942 the initial establishments being :—

No. 296 (Glider Exercise Squadron) :
    8 + 3 Light tugs (Hectors).
    20 + 6 Heavy tugs (Whitleys).
    30 + 10 Horsa gliders.
    16 + 14 Hotspur gliders.

No. 297. (Parachute Exercise Squadron) : 12 + 4 Whitleys.

Although aircrews were immediately available there was a delay regarding aircraft deliveries, and it was not until the end of March that both Squadrons were up to establishment. In the meantime, on 15 January 1942, 38 Wing Headquarters was formed to "co-ordinate" the operation and training of the Parachute Exercise and the Glider Exercise Squadrons. Sir Nigel Norman, promoted to the rank of Group Captain, was given command of the Wing, his headquarters being situated together with the H.Q. of the Airborne Division, at Syrencote House, a commandeered country house in a small village roughly equidistant from Netheravon and Bulford Camp. Very shortly after the formation of the Wing, Sir Nigel Norman and his staff were called upon to plan and carry out the second parachute raid against the European mainland, the Bruneval Raid, which took place on the night of 27-28 February 1942. The full story of the raid is contained in Chapter 4. Its importance here is that it caused the first change of policy regarding the Exercise Squadrons. In his original proposals Sir Arthur Barratt had pressed for the Squadrons to be made operational at once. But Air Ministry had overruled this and had designated them non-operational. When the Bruneval raid took place neither Squadron was equipped with aircraft so that their use during the operation was not possible, and No. 51 Squadron of Bomber Command was again called upon to provide the aircraft and crews. But the operation drew attention to the folly of having two specialist squadrons who were prohibited from taking part on operational sorties and the Air Ministry ruling was reversed. Any future small scale operations would be undertaken by the No. 38 Wing Squadrons who would only call upon Bomber Command for reinforcements if they were themselves unable to supply the numbers of aircraft required. It is worthy of mention here that although no such raids were carried out by the Squadrons until as late as 1943 a number were planned, cancellation sometimes taking place at the very last minute. This was the case in August 1942 when the Dieppe raid took place, and the paratroops were in fact enplaned in the aircraft before plans for their part in the action were cancelled.

After the successful execution of the operation at Bruneval Sir Nigel Norman and his staff were free to devote the whole of their attention to the day-to-day exercises of the two Squadrons. Aircraft arrived steadily during March and by April, when the Prime Minister announced his intention of visiting the Division, it was possible to lay on a combined exercise involving 12 paratroop Whitleys and 9 Hector-Hotspur combinations. The visit took place on 16 April 1942 and is particularly important since from it arose high level discussion regarding the size of No. 38 Wing[1]. During his visit Mr. Churchill suggested that the size of the demonstration was small compared with the existing strength of the Airborne Division. General Browning explained that with only two squadrons at their disposal it was impossible to carry out training of either paratroops or gliderborne troops on more than a company basis. The Prime Minister evidently considered this to be insufficient for he stated that he would personally investigate the matter on his return to London.

The Airborne Forces Committee

One other event of some importance concerning Airborne Forces which occurred during April 1942 was the appointment of the Airborne Forces Committee under the chairmanship of Sir Robert Renwick. The Committee was established at the instigation of Colonel J. J. Llewellin, then Minister of Aircraft Production. Consultation with the Minister for Air (Sir Archibald Sinclair) and the Minister of War resulted in the terms of reference being defined as follows:—

> " to co-ordinate arrangements for the development, production, supply, transport, and storage of all equipment for the Airborne Forces, and to secure rapid decisions ".

Sir Archibald Sinclair expressed the view that the phrase " to secure rapid decisions " implied that the committee were free to concern themselves with policy as well as with production, but after an assurance from Colonel Llewellin that these would not occur the definition of responsibility was allowed to stand[2].

The committee was composed of the following members:—

For the Air Ministry—Air Vice-Marshal R. S. Sorley (A.C.A.S. (T)), Group Captain J. D. I. Hardman (D.M.C.).

For the War Office—Major General D. G. Watson (D.S.D.), Major General F. A. M. Browning (G.O.C. the Airborne Division).

For the Ministry of Aircraft Production—Mr. M. Rosenburg (Technical), Mr. S. V. Connolly (Production).

As pointed out by Sir Archibald Sinclair, its work was concerned only with production so that very little mention of it will occur in this chapter, which is devoted to operational and administrative policy. But the setting up of the committee illustrates the growing importance attached to the development of the force by the Ministries concerned, particularly the Ministry of Aircraft Production. It is for that reason, and also to preserve chronological sequence, that it is mentioned here, even at the expense of interrupting the narrative of Mr. Churchill's enquiry into the aircraft situation.

---

[1] D.M.C. Monthly Progress Reports, March and April 1942. O.R.B. of No. 38 Wing H.Q., April 1942.
[2] C.A.S. Folder 864: Encl. 26.

Difficulties regarding shortage of aircraft and the proposal for a "nucleus force" May 1942

On his return from Netheravon Mr. Churchill began his investigation into the possibility of providing the Division with more aircraft by writing a minute to the Chief of Air Staff.

> "Please make me proposals for increasing the number of discarded bombers which can be placed rapidly at the disposal of the Airborne Corps. At least 100 should be found within the next three months. We cannot go on with 10,000 keen men and only three aircraft at their disposal[1]."

Unfortunately the problem was not so simple for there were no bombers which could be described as discarded. All as they became obsolete, were urgently required by the Bomber Command Operational Training Units where the demand far exceeded the supply, and already the planned expansion of Bomber Command had been delayed by the urgent calls for aircraft from the overseas theatres and by the Battle of the Atlantic.

The subject was fully discussed at a meeting of the Chiefs of Staff on 6 May 1942 the Prime Minister himself presiding[2]. Mr. Churchill again stressed that unless the troops received an adequate supply of aircraft they would lose heart; and Sir Charles Portal again replied that any addition to the training facilities for the force would entail a loss of bombing effort. The Air Staff, he said, were fully prepared to provide the aircraft necessary for any specific operation, even if it meant striking them off the bomber role for as much as five weeks prior to the actual operation: but for training purposes they suggested that one further exercise squadron was the most that could be spared, and this not until Whitley airscrews of which there was an acute shortage, became available[3]. The real solution to the problem was agreed to lie in increased supplies of transport aircraft from America.

During the course of the discussion however, General Browning mentioned a suggestion made by Group Captain Sir Nigel Norman regarding a "nucleus force". Briefly the suggestion, which had been put before the Air Officer Commanding-in-Chief, Army Co-operation Command in the form of a memorandum, was for the formation of a self-contained force of four squadrons, a total of 96 aircraft, whose primary task would be to train and operate the Airborne Division[4]. The plan entailed a change of policy for it had previously been held that all operations would be undertaken by Bomber Command, but the difficulties of maintaining a supply of Bomber Crews trained in the Airborne role had been all too clearly demonstrated in the past by the unsatisfactory "short courses" at Ringway. Apart from overcoming this wastage of trained Airborne crews and the flying hours expended on their training the proposal had the advantage in providing a more efficient air component which would be able to operate a maximum force with a

---

[1] Annex 3 to C.O.S. (42) 250.
[2] In addition to the Chiefs of Staff the following were also present: Col. The Rt. Hon. J. J. Llewellin (Minister of Aircraft Production); Sir Robert Renwick (Chairman of the Airborne Forces Committee); Air Commodore Hardman (D.M.C.); Maj. Gen. Sir Hastings Ismay; Maj. Gen. F. A. M. Browning; Brig. Gale. C.O.S. (42) Minutes of 142nd Meeting.
[3] At this time 109 Whitleys were unserviceable at A.S.U.s due to lack of airscrews.
[4] ACC/S76/Air: Encl. 96A.

maximum of surprise and with a minimum of delay. It was also noted that should the need arise the four squadrons could at any time be used to reinforce the bombing effort[1]. Finally, by providing the necessary O.T.U. facilities for the supply of aircrews to the force the proposal aimed at avoiding entirely any future demands upon Bomber Command resources. This last consideration in particular was welcomed by the Chief of Air Staff and in fact the whole scheme was favourably received by the meeting. The Air Staff were invited to investigate the possibility and implications of providing such a force and their recommendations, which were laid before the Chiefs of Staff on 31 May 1942 followed closely the lines of Sir Nigel Norman's proposals.

In the meantime the Prime Minister cabled to Mr. Roosevelt explaining the position and asking for an immediate stepping up of the allocation of transport aircraft, even at the expense of deliveries due later in the year. He also took the opportunity to express to the President his hope that American Airborne troops would be able to come to the United Kingdom and train alongside their British counterparts[2]. This invitation was cordially welcomed by the President and arrangements were made in America for a battalion of parachutists to sail for Europe in June.

The President's reply to the request for aircraft was a promise of indirect help only. It was impossible to supply transport aircraft to the British owing to the tremendous demands of the American Forces but he promised that four transport groups of the American Army Air Force would sail for England as soon as possible, two arriving in June 1942, the other two a month later. These four groups would be equipped with a total of 208 aircraft and by November 1942 it was hoped that the arrival of further similar groups would increase this total to 416 aircraft. On reaching England all of these transport groups were to be available to assist the British forces both in operations and in training.

In the meantime the Air Staff had been investigating the implications of meeting General Browning's request for 96 aircraft[3]. Their conclusions and proposals which closely followed those of Sir Nigel Norman were summarised in a memorandum by the Chief of Air Staff which was approved by the Chiefs of Staff Committee and by the Prime Minister on 19 June 1942. Sir Charles Portal explained that the medium bomber aircraft needed by No. 38 Wing could only be found at the expense of either Bomber or Coastal Commands. He had decided that they should be drawn from the former. Ten Whitleys would be delivered in May, 10 in June, 20 in July, 23 in August and 23 in September, making a total of 86 aircraft. Whitleys had, by now, been withdrawn from all operational squadrons of Bomber Command but were in use at O.T.U.s by crews under training to fly Halifaxes. The loss of these 86 aircraft would entail a drop of 120 trained bomber crews by the end of 1942. As the Whitleys were not powerful enough to tow the Hamilcars, the first of which was expected to be delivered in July, five Halifax aircraft would also be assigned to No. 38 Wing during August. By

---

[1] On the occasion of the first 1,000 bomber raid No. 297 Squadron had stood by at Snailswell but had been withdrawn before the attack took place.
[2] Prime Minister's personal telegram Serial No. T 714/2 dated 8 May 1942.
[3] C.O.S. (42) 285, dated 31 May 1942.

September, when eight Hamilcars were due this number would be increased to ten. This diversion of heavy aircraft would delay the re-equipment of a medium bomber squadron by three weeks. The request that Operational Training Unit facilities be granted to No. 38 Wing was also conceded on condition that, apart from the initial instructional staff, no further calls were made on Bomber Command to supply pilots and aircrews for No. 38 Wing. The whole of these proposals, particularly the latter stipulation, were in accordance with the Chief of Air Staff's stated opinion that the Airborne project should as far as possible be kept entirely clear of Bomber Command.

Consequent expansion of air component May—October 1942

The general principles of what may be called " the nucleus force scheme " having received Chief of Staff approval detailed plans were drawn up by Army Co-operation Command for putting the scheme into effect. One point which was generally agreed was that in future the idea of differentiation between the paradropping and tugging roles must be abolished. One of the main advantages of the scheme was that it would avoid the possibility of calling upon Bomber Command to supply aircraft for any but large scale operations, and if this advantage were to be gained without loss of operational efficiency the air component must be able to undertake both parachute and glider work. Consequently arrangements would be needed to establish at each of the No. 38 Wing stations a glider flight of some 30 Horsas. But the final selection of aerodromes for the expanded force had not yet been made so that when the organisation memorandum authorised the formation of two new squadrons and the revision of establishment of the two existing ones a temporary arrangement had to be made to apply during the expansion period[1]. This was as follows:—

- No. 295 Squadron: This was one of the new squadrons and would be equipped with 24 + 6 Whitley aircraft. It would be formed around a nucleus drawn from No. 296 Squadron and would commence to form at Netheravon on 3 August 1942. It should be complete by 21 October 1942 by which time it would have moved to its permanent location.

- No. 298 Squadron: This was to be the other new squadron and when complete would have 16 + 4 Whitley and 8 + 2 Halifax aircraft. Forming on 10 August 1942 from a nucleus flight drawn from No. 297 Squadron it would initially be located at Thruxton, near Andover, when eight Whitleys would be available. Delivery of the Halifaxes would take place during September and by 21 October the squadron would be up to strength. Its permanent location would, it was hoped be at Lasham aerodrome.

- Nos. 296 and 297 Squadrons: Both of these had moved from Netheravon to Hurn, near Bournemouth, in May 1942. Each would throw off a flight of experienced crews who would go to the two new squadrons, but replacement crews would be found and by 21 October they should again be up to strength. Each would have an establishment of 24 + 6 Whitley aircraft.

---

[1] A.M.: L.M.1603/D. of O. dated 16 July 1942. ACC/S1070/11/Org. dated 25 July 1942.

The proposal for a non-operational Glider Exercise Squadron, equipped with Whitleys and Horsas was not approved by Air Ministry on the grounds that such training could be carried out by the operational squadrons. The formation of a G.E.U. at Netheravon equipped with light tugs and Hotspurs was, however, approved on 1 August 1942[1] as was the allocation of 43 Horsas plus five Hamilcars to Hurn and 48 Horsas to Lasham, when the latter was opened.

During August and September the expansion went ahead as planned except that no aircraft arrived for No. 298 Squadron. On 19 October 1942, No. 295 Squadron at Netheravon had two flights, both at full personnel strength and 21 aircraft; at Hurn both Nos. 296 and 297 Squadrons were at full strength regarding aircrews and the latter also had its full complement of aircraft; No. 296 Squadron had 21 Whitleys on this date. The nucleus flight from No. 297 Squadron had arrived at Thruxton, on 14 September 1942, but the formation of No. 298 Squadron had not progressed further, owing to lack of aircraft[2]. This was the situation when, on 19 October, two days before the planned expansion was due to be complete, notification was received from Air Ministry that until further notice no more aircraft or personnel would be posted into Airborne Forces Units[3]. This standstill order was the result of Chiefs of Staff discussion which had been going on during August and September. In October it became clear that the conflicting views of the Chief of Air Staff and the Chief of the Imperial General Staff were incompatible and it was agreed that the problem should be placed before Mr. Churchill in his capacity of Minister of Defence. Pending his decision the Air Staff ordered that the expansion of No. 38 Wing was to cease.

Increased demands by War Office entailing diversion of bomber effort: July—September 1942

This review of high policy had originated in War Office plans for still further expansion. On 20 July 1942 the Chiefs of Staff considered a memorandum by Commander-in-Chief, Home Forces, in which Lt.-General Paget had stated that he would like two Airborne Divisions for the North African operations which were then being planned and that were it not for the acute shortage of aircraft the War Office would be pressing for airborne forces on a much larger scale than then existed[4]. As it was, the General and Air Staffs had considered the matter and had recommended that a second division should not be formed: instead they suggested the formation of two independent parachute brigades. General Paget said that it was clearly not worth pressing ahead with this suggestion unless aircraft would be available to exercise the brigades. He requested that the Air Staff be invited to consider the implications of the proposal.

---

[1] A glider flight known as No. 296B Squadron had remained at Netheravon when the rest of the unit No. 296A Squadron, which had adopted the dual role (parachute dropping as well as glider towing), had moved to Hurn. It was from this flight (296B Squadron) that the Glider Exercise Unit was formed. On 12 August Master II's replaced the old Hectors which were becoming impossible to maintain. ACC/S76/Air: Encl. 39A.
[2] O.R.B.s of Nos. 295, 296 and 297 Sqdns. O.R.B. No. 38 Group H.Q. September 1942.
[3] A.M.: L.M. 2806/D. of O. dated 19 October 1942.
[4] Minutes of 212th Meeting of C.O.S. dated 20 July 1942.

A month later another proposal, this time from the Vice Chief of the Imperial General Staff, confirmed the Air Staff view that further expansion would infringe upon the bomber effort. The V.C.I.G.S. considered that the time was ripe for Bomber Command to assume full responsibility for the Airborne Force, "since the policy is that Bomber Command will operate the Airborne Division, even if not all of the Division is used[1]". There was a limit to the number of gliders which could be operated from each aerodrome, and eight aerodromes would be needed to operate one brigade group. He was of the opinion that arrangements should be made now for the gliders to be stored at the units where they would be needed and that the staff organisation necessary for an operation should be set up at these units. "I recommend that the Commander-in-Chief, Bomber Command, be asked to report to the Chiefs of Staff upon the implications of the assistance which will be required from Bomber Command, and in particular upon the effects he considers the necessary preliminary training and subsequent operation of the Division, or of a Brigade Group, would have on the bomber effort."

In the view of the Air Staff one of the great virtues of the "nucleus force" scheme had been that it relieved Bomber Command of the responsibility of providing the Airborne Force with aircraft and crews for any except large scale operations, such as an invasion. The new proposals indicated that the War Office were not satisfied with this scheme and the resources which it placed at their disposal and were again attempting to increase these resources at the expense of the bomber effort. Generally the feeling at Air Ministry was that having been given an inch the War Office were trying to take an ell, and the Air Staff were determined to do all in their power to prevent this and the further reduction in the striking power of Bomber Command which it would entail. Their view was shared to the full by Sir Arthur Harris, who had been unfavourably inclined towards the project from the beginning. In his report he made no attempt to conceal his opinion that the Airborne Force was causing unnecessary diversion of effort, and much of his memorandum was devoted to questioning the potential value of Airborne operations compared with the value of bombing operations against Germany[2].

In his comments on the memorandum the Chief of Air Staff remarked that "the A.O.C.-in-C. was not asked for this, but I think it very natural that he should put his views forward when asked to state the implications of a project which he considers would result in the cessation of bombing." This was a reference to the first of the Commander-in-Chief's three major conclusions concerning the effect upon the bomber effort of operating the Airborne Division. These conclusions were:—

(i) that bombing would cease entirely;

(ii) that only one parachute brigade could be carried at a time;

(iii) that the operation would be inefficient and liable to incur heavy losses because the aircraft were not really suitable and the opposition would be too strong.

---

[1] This statement was, of course, in direct opposition to the Chief of Air Staff's view; the divergence probably arose owing to the difference in the size of the force visualised, C.A.S. having in mind only small operations and V.C.I.G.S. thinking of large-scale attacks and particularly the invasion of the continent.—C.O.S. (42) 376 dated 16 August 1942.

[2] C.O.S. (42) 398.

Sir Charles Portal agreed with the two latter conclusions but considered that bombing would not entirely cease although it would be curtailed by as much as 50-75 per cent. He then went on to state in some detail his own view of the subject with particular reference to the Commander-in-Chief, Bomber Command's report.

" I regard the bombing of German industry ", he said, " as an incomparably greater contribution to the war than the training and constant availability of the Airborne Division and as the two things at present seriously conflict I would certainly accord priority to bombing. I have nevertheless, always undertaken to back the Army's invasion of the continent with the whole of the available M.A.F., and if such an invasion is undertaken while the Airborne Force is dependent upon Bomber Command it will be for consideration two or three months in advance whether better support will be given by carrying bombs or troops."

It was difficult to say whether the aircraft being used for airborne training would be better employed in the bombing role because no authoritative appreciation existed of the value of Airborne Forces against such opposition as they were likely to encounter. On the other hand the damage likely to be caused by a given number of bombers over a given period could be assessed and that damage did not increase only in direct proportion to the numbers of aircraft used. By doubling the force used the damage inflicted might be as much as four or five times and the damage per aircraft two or three times greater than before.

" I certainly do not think that a case has been made out for the use of Airborne Forces for a full scale invasion of the Continent. We are all agreed that this will not succeed until German resistance has started to crack, and once this stage has been reached better to allow the process to continue under growing pressure from the condition which caused it than to incur heavy losses by a premature invasion. Moreover, if by doing without Airborne Forces we could for two years add appreciably to the Bomber strength we might well be in occupation with land forces earlier and not later than if we maintained the Airborne Division to facilitate the initial cross channel operation."

The Chief of Air Staff was in favour of maintaining a parachute force for raiding and minor operations but he suggested that the present ideas were too ambitious in view of the evident limitations: the resources employed in equipping and maintaining the Division could be used to increase substantially the size of the attack on Germany. He consequently proposed a revision of policy as follows[1]: —

" (i) A reduction in the size of the force: —

>   From: Four Parachute Brigades of 2,000 men each and one Air Landing Brigade of 7,000 men ; to: two Parachute Brigades and a small Glider Force.

(ii) Since gliders would only be required to carry the heavier weapons needed by the paratroops only 200 would be needed instead of 760."

---

[1] C.O.S. (42) 398.

The advantages to be gained by such a revision of policy were summarised thus: —

(i) Keeping the target date for the first operation at 1 April 1943, aircraft saving would be:

302 light trainers.
148 advanced trainers.
92 Whitleys.
4 Halifaxes.

(ii) Important economies of labour, personnel and material involved in the production of gliders and storage space.

(iii) By using the Whitleys at O.T.U.s Wellingtons would be released to supplement the first line bomber strength.

The Chief of the Imperial General Staff was quick to reply to this memorandum. He drafted a reply, which was subsequently circulated to the Chiefs of Staff, reiterating his view of the value of the force emphasising particularly its strategic mobility and the dispersal of enemy defence forces caused by its very existence. " We are all agreed that for the defeat of Germany it will sooner or later be necessary for our armies to invade the Continent. To do this we shall first be confronted with the attack of strongly defended beaches. The employment of the Airborne Division in the rear may offer the only means of obtaining a footing on these beaches." Sir Alan Brooke claimed that the establishment of land based fighters at the earliest possible stage, and the prevention of enemy reserves reaching the beaches would be the two vital factors when consolidating the initial footholds, and he considered that strong airborne forces, including gliderborne supporting arms, would be needed for these tasks.

At the Chiefs of Staff meeting which considered these two conflicting memoranda, these opposing views were re-stated and it became clear that no compromise agreement would be reached. Consequently it was agreed to refer the whole problem to the Minister of Defence (Mr. Winston Churchill) for decision[1]. Thus on 23 October 1942, the Chiefs of Staff submitted to the Minister of Defence a report on the whole Airborne situation. The report contained in full the memoranda by the Chief of Air Staff, the Chief of the Imperial General Staff, the Commander-in-Chief, Bomber Command, together with the appendices to these statements[2]. It so happened that four days previously, on 6 October 1942, the Production Committee of the War Cabinet had met and had discussed methods which might be adopted to eliminate waste during production programmes generally, and among the points mentioned was that of the glider building programme. Conclusion (vi) of the minutes of the meeting was as follows: —

" The Chiefs of Staff were asked to examine the planned provision of gliders and to report whether any reduction could be made[3]."

On 1 November 1942, Mr. Churchill gave his decision[4]:

" This is all a question of balance and emphasis. I have, as you know, always been anxious to have a well found airborne division but there is no prospect in the near future of our being able to provide the necessary aircraft for a force of the size contemplated by the War Office.

---

[1] C.O.S. (42) Minutes of 288th Meeting dated 14 October 1942.
[2] C.O.S. (42) 434 dated 23 October 1942.
[3] Extract from W.M. (42) 133rd Meeting held 6 October 1942.
[4] C.O.S. (42) 398 (O) dated 18 November 1942.

Moreover I am worried by the excessive construction of gliders and the difficulty of storing these wooden machines. We might look very foolish if we had a lot of these things standing about out in the rain spoiling when no opportunity for their offensive use occurred. We should find out at once how many C.47s we may expect to get from the U.S.A. as we cannot accept a heavy drain on our bomber offensive. In any event I am sure that the Horsa programme will have to be drastically curtailed.

Our immediate target should be the creation of a force of the dimensions recommended by the Chief of Air Staff in para. 10 of his note, i.e., two parachute brigades plus a small gliderborne force to lift the heavier supporting weapons and vehicles which cannot be dropped by parachute. Let the details be worked out forthwith between the War Office and the Air Ministry and a report made. A stand-still order for gliders should be issued at once.

The position should be re-examined in about six months' time—say 1 June.   W.S.C.

1.11.42."

Effect of decision on No. 38 Wing: November 1942—April 1943

In the meantime the standstill order regarding No. 38 Wing was still in force. The crews of No. 297 Squadron who had been posted to No. 298 Squadron were reposted and on 26 October 1942, the whole unit moved to Thruxton. Two days later, No. 296 Squadron moved to Andover, but the airfield there was unsuitable for Horsa towing and on 22 December they returned to Hurn[1]. No. 295 Squadron which had succeeded in forming before the standstill order was issued remained at Netheravon and was soon trained to the same level as the others. Between October 1942 and April 1943, all three squadrons spent much of their time on exercises, both with paratroops and with gliders. In addition they flew a number of operational sorties over enemy occupied countries. In the main their cargoes were pamphlets— much to the disgust of the crews—so that when in 1943 they bombed two small power stations in France the operations were regarded as "plums" and the competition to be selected for the task was great. The morale of the aircrews was, at this time, a continual source of worry to the Air Officer Commanding No. 38 Wing. Thus nickel operations had the double advantage of relieving Bomber Command from the less important part of its commitments; it helped to maintain the keenness and morale of the crews and also served as "flak inoculation" for them.

On 10 January 1943, the Joint General/Air Staff memorandum on the reduction of the Airborne Force was presented to the Chiefs of Staff. In accordance with Mr. Churchill's decision the glider production programme had already been cut, the Horsa order being reduced from 2,400 to 1,250[2], deliveries were due to be complete by June 1943[3] and after that production was

---

[1] These movements were in any case not intended to be permanent, they were made because Hurn had to be evacuated by 38 Wing in order to meet other operational requirements, e.g. Torch.
[2] The Chiefs of Staff at their 61st meeting of 1942 (23 February 1942) had approved a suggestion by V.C.I.G.S. that the order for Horsas be raised to a total of 1,975, 1,375 to be delivered by 1 May 1943 and a further 600 by 1 June 1943. This figure was increased by Air Ministry to 2,345, the extra 370 to allow for "tailing off" production.
[3] 388 had been delivered by 31 October 1942.

to tail off at a delivery rate of 20 per month until the end of 1944. As Hamilcar production was behind schedule[1] the order of 200 (160 during 1943 and 40 during 1944) was unchanged pending further review in June 1943.

The Air and General Staff proposals were therefore more concerned with the organisation of the force than with production. Their recommendations fell under three general headings as follows: —

(i) Air Force Units:

The Parachute Training School to remain as then established.

The three existing No. 38 Wing squadrons to be retained at an establishment of 24+6 Whitleys each. But the proposal to form a fourth squadron, partly equipped with heavy aircraft to be abandoned.

(ii) American Gliders:

W.A.C.O. Gliders were now becoming available from the United States and twenty each would be made available for trials to British Forces in the United Kingdom and India as soon as possible. If suitable it was proposed to supply a further 30 to India and 130 to the Middle East.

(iii) Glider Pilots:

1,150 glider pilots were already under training: wastage would probably reduce this number to 1,000 and it was considered advisable to continue and complete the training of this number in case the June review demanded an increased output of pilots. When trained however 360 of the pilots would be returned to military units and would cease to fly, being given a short refresher course when they were again required for pilot duties; of the remainder 370 would become first pilots and 270 second pilots, the former figure allowing a reserve of 100 of the more highly skilled men. The new programme having made possible a supply of two pilots per glider this was accepted as firm policy[2].

Sir Alan Brooke immediately challenged these proposals[3]. On the day following their presentation to the Chiefs of Staff he submitted a note stating that he wished to draw attention to the fact that he was uneasy concerning the implications of curtailing glider production and considered that the position should be reviewed at once instead of waiting until June. He reiterated the values of an Airborne Force, again expressed his conviction that at least one Airborne Division would be needed for the invasion of the Continent and referred to the planning of the invasion of Sicily " in which the need for a strong and well-balanced airborne force is consistently apparent ". He requested that the cuts in glider production be rescinded: that America be asked to supply as many W.A.C.O. gliders as we needed: and that the provision of transport aircraft be accelerated by all means possible.

---
[1] None had been delivered by 31 October 1942.
[2] Previously the advantages of having two pilots had been recognised but had been outweighed by the lack of training facilities.
[3] Annex to C.O.S. (43) 17, 11 January 1943.

On 24 February 1943 he followed this up with a further memorandum which stated that it had been decided at Casablanca[1], that Anglo-American Strategy against Germany in 1943 should be based on offensive action against the Axis forces in the Mediterranean after North Africa had been cleared. Should the opportunity occur re-entry into north-western Europe would also be made in 1943. Sir Alan Brooke considered that in either or both of these contingencies the employment of an adequate Airborne Force would be an essential factor for success. He went on to quote outline plan for operation Husky[2], in which the Joint Planning Committee visualised using three British and two American Airborne Brigades. For this operation and for the re-entry into north-western Europe he considered that two forces would be needed, one based in North Africa—the other in the United Kingdom, each consisting of a Division containing two Parachute Brigades, one Air Landing Brigade, and Divisional troops including artillery and engineer units.

Sir Charles Portal was unable to agree with either of these papers. He did not feel that there was justification for recommending a review of the position at once instead of in June as existing strategy had already been agreed when in November the requirements of the force had been authorised. He quoted figures to show that the Chief of the Imperial General Staff's proposals would seriously handicap the Bomber effort[3]. The position regarding operation Husky was as follows:—

(i) Gliders: The W.A.C.O.s allotted to North Africa during the first quarter of 1943 would prove sufficient.

(ii) Provision of Glider Pilots and Paratroops presented no difficulties.

(iii) Transport aircraft: A cable had been sent to the United States requesting them to provide the balance needed to make 200 transport aircraft available.

" I remain strongly of the opinion that the large drain on our resources which would result from the C.I.G.S.'s proposals cannot be justified by the results likely to be obtained. This was the conclusion reached by the Prime Minister in November as a result of an exhaustive survey of the whole problem. I can point to no new factors which have emerged in recent months which would serve to modify that conclusion.

" In regarding my opinion in this sense I am very far from denying all value to Airborne Forces . . . but they can only be operated at a cost to other air activity not only at the time the force is used but also during the training period beforehand. This cost may or may not be worth paying. As I see the matter the problem is, in the words of the Prime Minister, essentially one of balance and emphasis. We must avoid on the one hand underestimating the value of Airborne Forces, and on the other of devoting more

---

[1] The Conference at Casablanca between the Prime Minister and the President had taken place in January 1943.—C.O.S. (43) 810, 24 February 1943. Memorandum by C.I.G.S. entitled " Airborne Forces in U.K. and North Africa ".
[2] The invasion of Sicily.—J.P. (43) 7 (Final).
[3] They involved 1,750 aircraft, 15,000 personnel and 20 aerodromes for glider pilot training alone; C.I.G.S. had suggested that a diversion of 7 per cent. of Bomber effort would meet Airborne needs. This would amount to the loss of 16,000 tons of bombs on Germany.—C.O.S. (43) 46.

resources to this commitment than our strategy as a whole justifies. I believe this to be achieved in the agreed recommendations submitted to the Chiefs of Staff in C.O.S. (43) 12 and I accordingly recommend that they be reaffirmed subject to such minor adjustments as are necessary to bring them up to date."

During further discussions on these two memoranda it became clear that the figures quoted by the Chief of Air Staff regarding the implications of the C.I.G.S.'s proposals had been based on the assumption that an Air Landing Brigade Group contained four battalions whereas in fact it only contained two. The Air Staff were therefore instructed to re-examine the implication of the proposals[1]. To form such an estimate takes time and it was 21 April 1943 before it was complete[2]. It was then presented to the Chiefs of Staff as a note by the Combined Air and General Staffs and it embodied the following four points:—

(i) The number of gliders considered necessary to lift a full Airborne Division was reduced from 760 to 630. But it was considered an operational necessity that a 2nd pilot be carried in each glider.

(ii) The requirement for Glider Pilots was accordingly reassessed at 1,800 for two British Airborne Divisions.

(iii) Under the existing arrangements 1,000 of these would be available by October 1943, although 300 would not be trained to full operational standards.

(iv) An assessment had been made of the resources needed to train the extra 800 pilots and the most economical target date for the completion of their training was July 1944.

Sir Charles Portal consequently agreed[3] that if the General Staff were convinced of the necessity of a complete Airborne Division by 1944 the Air Staff would make arrangements for the training of the extra 800 pilots. But he emphasised that the Royal Air Force could not undertake to provide the aircraft to lift the four Airborne Divisions which would then be available[4], even with American assistance to cope with the United States contingent. "But the first real test of Allied Airborne Forces is shortly to be made. I suggest that, although preparations are made for training the 800 pilots, the final decision be postponed to await the result of operation Husky. The delay entailed will not be more than one month in the complete training programme which will then commence in July/August 1943, and will be complete by August 1944."

The Chiefs of Staff willingly agreed to this proposal. Accordingly, pending the results of operation Husky the existing arrangements for glider pilot training were maintained: the plans for expanding the output were laid but were not put into effect: and the No. 38 Wing organisation which had resulted from the short lived expansion policy of 1942 was left unchanged.

---

[1] Minutes of C.O.S. (43) 57th Meeting, 5 March 1943.
[2] C.O.S. (43) 206 (O) dated 21 April 1943, "Airborne Forces in North Africa and United Kingdom".
[3] C.O.S. (43) 37th Meeting, 28 April 1943.
[4] These Divisions would be: One British in the U.K.; one British in the Middle East, and two American in the U.K.

CHAPTER 4

TRAINING DEVELOPMENT AND MINOR OPERATIONS NOVEMBER 1941—OCTOBER 1943

This chapter is concerned with the growth of the home based Airborne Force during the years 1942 and 1943. The word "development" is used in a wide sense and includes development of organisation, administration, operational use and procedure, and production, both of equipment and trained manpower[1].

The expansion which took place during the autumn of 1941 was caused by three major factors. Firstly the Chiefs of Staffs' requirement of May 1941 which had authorised the raising and training of a force of brigade strength by the summer of 1942. This had resulted in the planning of the "individual" training organisation, planning which began to become effective in November 1941. Secondly the gliders which had been ordered in 1940 were beginning to appear. By the end of November 1941 60 Hotspurs had been delivered and during that month the first Horsa prototype had been making its test flights. Thirdly the increase in the size of the Army component which took place between June and October 1941 resulted, in November, in the formation of the Airborne Division ; a parallel expansion of the air component thus became necessary in order to maintain the balance of the force. Parachute troops had to be trained and exercised ; similarly glider pilots. The glider-borne troops having been selected (the 1st Air Landing Brigade) it would be necessary for them to be given air experience. The formation of the Airborne Division emphasized the need for combined training facilities ; it also brought with it a demand for a considerable extension of the " individual " training organisation.

Parachute Training

The first step in the setting up of the expanded individual training organisation had been taken on 1 September 1941, when the Central Landing Establishment became the Airborne Forces Establishment[2]. It was laid down that the new unit was "to investigate problems of technical development ; to establish the principles of parachute and glider training ; and to form the first units carrying out this training, in due course developing them to a standard of stability where they can be absorbed as normal units of the R.A.F." With this object in view the A.F.E. had been organised in sections, the Technical Development Section, the Parachute Training Section, the Glider Training Squadron, and the Glider Exercise Unit. The first three of these had, in effect, already been established under the old C.L.E.: the Glider Exercise Unit was the only innovation and this was formed in September 1941 under the command of F/Lt. P. B. N. Davis from Thame.

---

[1] It is not possible to include lengthy accounts of technical development as this would upset the whole balance of the narrative and would overwhelm the policy story with a vast quantity of detail. Some reference to specific items, e.g., the introduction of a blind towing device, are included but in general tne original reports of the development unit concerned (usually the R.A.E. or A.F.E.E.) should be consulted together with the relevant Air Publications published during the period.
[2] O.R.B. of the A.F.E.

It was equipped with five Hectors and three Hotspurs and its task was to relieve the Glider Training Squadron of fighter affiliation and other exercises, so leaving the latter free to concentrate upon expansion into No. 1 Glider Training School.

Chronologically the two glider Sections were the first to become self-contained units, the G.T.S. on 4 November 1941 (No. 1 Glider Training School) and the G.E.U. on 1 January 1942 (No. 296 Glider Exercise Squadron). But in order that the story of the glider organisation, which continued to change and grow throughout 1942 may be told without a break it is convenient to write first of parachute training.

Paratroop training presented no major difficulties. As has been described in Chapter 2 the expansion of the Parachute Training Section which took place in the autumn of 1941 was brought about by the Army requirement for two further battalions which, with the one already trained, another yet to form, and certain H.Q. troops would form the 1st Parachute Brigade[1]. To meet this requirement the establishment at Ringway was adjusted so that the output of trained pupils would reach the figure, suggested by the Army, of 100 per week. The expansion began on 1 September 1941, when 34 R.A.F. physical training instructors arrived for training as parachute instructors. They completed their course on 1 November and on that date also the R.A.F. assumed full responsibility for the training of parachute troops, the Army instructors being withdrawn[2]. The first trainees of the 2nd and 3rd Battalions arrived immediately and by 12 December 1941, three courses had been completed and 711 men had qualified as parachutists[3].

After three courses the Commanding Officer felt justified in estimating the risk of injury during an operation to be " not more than 1 per cent. providing that the landing ground chosen is ideal ". It will be noted that there were no fatal accidents on these three courses and in fact this clear record was maintained until 16 February 1942. On that date a fatality was caused by twisted rigging lines and this, and another similar accident which followed two days later, had a serious effect upon the morale of the pupils[4] even although a demonstration descent by the instructors and the Commanding Officer was staged immediately after the second accident. Twisted or tangled rigging lines, usually due to a faulty exit and consequent somersaulting, were, throughout the war, the commonest cause of fatal parachuting accidents. A great deal of thought was given to the problem, by the P.T.S. staff as well as the research and development units. Minor modifications to the method of packing the statichute which were introduced in August 1943 reduced the risk of twisted lines, but did not completely overcome the problem, and the accident rate was not greatly reduced until the introduction of other types of aircraft—the Albemarle, Halifax, Stirling and Dakota—from which exit was less difficult.

On 1 January 1942, a new course, No. 1 Advanced Course, consisting of 103 officers and men from the 1st Battalion and 97 officers and men from the 2nd Battalion commenced operational training at Ringway. During initial training it was the practice to carry an instructor in the aircraft who

---

[1] A.M. File C.S. 10582: Encl. 1A.
[2] A.M.: L.M. 22/D. of O. dated 6 October 1942 in A.M. File C.S. 10582: Encl. 23A.
[3] The detailed figures for these three courses were:—Total intake, 772; Qualified, 711; Sickness and Injury, 39; Refusals, 5; Returned to Unit, 1; Total descents, 5,239.
[4] The 32 failures during this course was the highest figure then recorded.

checked the parachutes and harnesses of the men to ensure correct fitting. This instructor was known as a "dispatcher" since, being in "intercom" touch with the pilot, it was he who told the troops when to jump. These duties were now assumed by the "stick commander", usually the Senior Officer or N.C.O. in the stick, and no instructor was carried in the aircraft. Also jumps were made with full operational paratroop equipment and with fully loaded arms containers: after the drop the troops usually carried out ground exercises and manoeuvres. "Advanced" courses now became a regular feature of the routine at Ringway and the initial training adopted the pre-fix "Preliminary".

By 1 January 1942 both Glider Sections had broken away and the A.F.E. consisted of two sections only, the P.T.S. and the Development Section. On 16 February 1942 the A.F.E. was disbanded, the P.T.S. becoming the No. 1 Parachute Training School, and the Development Section becoming the Airborne Forces Experimental Establishment[1]. Both remained at Ringway until 1 July when the latter moved to Sherburn-in-Elmet in Yorkshire. This move came at an opportune time for all available accommodation at Ringway was then required by the P.T.S. As a result of the Chiefs of Staff's decision of May 1942 the War Office were increasing the parachute element of the Airborne Division from one brigade to two; consequently they requested that the output of trained men from Ringway should be raised to 250 per week. Again no difficulty was experienced in carrying out the necessary expansion: the establishment of instructors and aircraft was raised; more statichutes were allotted, and in August 1942 the monthly output was 1,189 trained men[2]. In addition to British troops men from the Free Forces of Poland[3], Holland, Belgium, Norway and France received instruction, the Polish force later growing to Brigade strength.

Throughout 1942 and 1943 requests were continually being made by the P.T.S. for the allotment to them of a Dakota aircraft, or even an old or crashed fuselage, so that door jumping experience[4] could be gained by the instructors. The experiences of the 1st Parachute Brigade in North Africa during November 1942 added weight to this appeal; during their operations the troops were, in most cases, making not only their first operational descent but also their first descent from this type of aircraft. Casualties due to the latter reasons were high—and the fact that the American aircrews who were flying the aircraft had no experience of parachute dropping increased the casualty rate. But the P.T.S. request could not be granted until September 1943: until then the few Dakotas available were urgently needed for transport work, and the transport pilots did their work so well that not even a crashed fuselage became available![5]

The Dakota was required in order that the instructional staff might increase their already extensive knowledge and experience of parachute jumping. As

---

[1] O.R.B. of the A.F.E., February 1942.
[2] O.R.B. of the A.F.E.E., July 1942. A.M. File C.S. 10852: Encl. 97A dated 27 May 1942 and C.O.S. (42) 285 and Minutes of C.O.S. 212th Meeting, 20 July 1942 refer. A.M.: L.M. 3145/01 dated 22 May 1942 at A.M. File C.S. 10582: Encl. 121A.
[3] The Poles had re-commenced training on 16 January 1942.
[4] Exit from the Dakota is made through a door in the side of the fuselage, a very different procedure from jumping through a hole in the floor.
[5] A.M. File C.S. 10582: Encl. 170A.

it was they had made descents from all British aircraft which might conceivably prove suitable for the job. It is worthy of record here that the enthusiasm and determination to know thoroughly the peculiarities of parachuting was not limited to the instructors. Many of the administrative and special duty officers on the staff of the school became qualified parachutists: the descents into water were made by Sir Nigel Norman, Wing Commander Newman and Flight Lieutenant Winfield, the Medical Officer of the School[1]. The two first named officers, together with Squadron Leader Strange established firmly the tradition that the senior officers connected with the School should have expert knowledge of parachuting and should themselves carry out trial and demonstration jumps whenever possible. In conclusion an amusing story regarding this enthusiasm of the staff for their job is contained in the Operations Record Book of the Unit which records that on 27 September 1942 40 instructors of the P.T.S. who were to visit the Army Airborne Depot at Hardwick decided "to prove that parachuting is the modern method of travel" and literally descended upon their hosts, arriving by means of Whitley aircraft and "X" type parachutes.

So the overall picture of parachute training at the individual stages during the period 1942-43 is one of steady progress in technique and growth in size, two major expansions being outstanding, that of November 1941 and that of July 1942 the final important feature being the introduction of courses for considerable numbers of Allied, as well as British troops. The ease with which the output of trained pupils could be expanded or reduced according to the needs of the moment made for a stable organisation which contrasted strongly with the constantly changing organisation concerned with the production of glider pilots. It must, of course, be remembered that to train a glider pilot took nearly six months: to train a paratroop in jumping only three weeks. But whatever the causes, the fact remained that, during 1942-43, the training of parachutists was carried out smoothly, steadily, and efficiently, and the demands made by policy were met immediately and without difficulty.

Parachute Operations November 1941—November 1942

In February 1942 the second parachute raid against the European mainland took place. A small force of men from the 2nd Parachute Battalion, augmented by radiolocation experts of the R.A.F., carried out an attack on a German radar station on the French coast at Bruneval, north of Le Havre. The air plan of the attack followed the lines of that used in Operation Colossus and was, in fact, prepared by Sir Nigel Norman and the experts lately posted with him to form the Headquarters of No. 38 Wing. Owing to lack of aircraft the newly formed No. 297 (Parachute Exercise) Squadron, was unable to take part in the operation and No. 51 Squadron of Bomber Command had again to be called in. The other parachute operations during the period although on a much larger scale were undertaken entirely without R.A.F. support. These operations occurred during the campaign in North Africa during November 1942, the troops being men of the 1st Parachute Brigade—the aircraft and crews being supplied by the U.S.A.A.F.

---

[1] O.R.B. of No. 1 P.T.S., 26 August 1942.

The Bruneval Raid : February 1942[1]

Towards the end of 1941 the Air Ministry received information that the Germans had a new type of radar equipment which was playing an important part in the control of German " flak ", and probably in the control of searchlights. It was a serious menace to our aircraft. Counter measures to give adequate protection to our aircraft were being investigated but these were hampered by the lack of information about the enemy apparatus. An object presumed to be one of these sets was reported to be situated at Theuville, on the French coast, a little north of Le Havre. This station was well protected against assault from the sea, both by military defences and by the nature of the cliffs upon which it stood. A Commando raid against it was likely to prove expensive in casualties and to be too slow to capture any of the equipment before it could be destroyed by the guards. The Commodore, Combined Operations (Commodore Lord Louis Mountbatten) therefore suggested, after consultation with General Browning, that parachute troops should be employed in an attempt to capture this radar apparatus. This suggestion received the approval of the Chiefs of Staffs Committee on 21 January 1942 who gave instructions for one operational Whitley squadron of Bomber Command, one company of parachute troops, and sufficient light naval craft to evacuate the force by sea, to be made available.

The Commander of the 1st Parachute Brigade wished to keep the 1st Parachute Battalion intact for an operation when called for and he consequently selected Major J. D. Frost and " C " Company of the 2nd Battalion to carry out the raid. No. 51 Squadron of Bomber Command were again called upon to supply the aircraft and aircrews ; and Assault Landing Craft under the command of Commander F. N. Cook, operating from H.M.S. *Prince Albert* provided the evacuation party. Two specialist personnel to drop with the troops were provided through H.Q., Combined Operations : F/Sgt. Cox, R.A.F., an R.D.F. Specialist ; and Private Nagle, No. 93 Pioneer Coy., a German fighting against Hitler who was taken to act as interpreter. Both of these men were given a hurried course of parachuting at Ringway before taking part in the operation. One other specialist took part in the raid, F/Lt. Priest, who was given a temporary commission in the R.A.F. in order that he could accompany the expedition. The risk of his capture by the enemy prohibited his being dropped by parachute but he accompanied the force in one of the A.L.Cs.

All information about the radar station, the enemy's dispositions and defences, and all photographs and models of the ground and buildings were provided through H.Q. Combined Operations, who also obtained as much as possible of the special weapons, ammunition and equipment needed for the raid. One of the lessons learned was that H.Q. Combined Operations should be empowered to demand the provision of such equipment without question because demands made through the usual channels could not always be quoted as operational requirements and numerous questions and difficulties raised by inquisitive staff officers had to be parried. This was, in fact, the gravest threat to the security of the operation: another was the necessity of clearing beaches in Southern Command of mines, scaffolding and so on, in order that " C " Company could carry out training: finally the " cover story ", that the

---

[1] Report on Operation " Biting " by G.O.C., the Airborne Division.

object of the preparation was to carry out training in a new phase of combined operations, was not used fully enough either by G.H.Q. Home Forces or, in isolated cases, by the troops themselves. Even so the success of the operation proved that on the whole security had been well preserved and that there had been no leakage of information to the Germans.

Training for "C" Company occupied five weeks. They moved from the Airborne Depot at Hardwick to Tilshead on 24 January 1942, and were to spend a little over a fortnight on further parachute and ground training on Salisbury Plain. But the weather, with heavy falls of snow and intense cold, interrupted this programme and when on 9 February the Company moved to Inveraray for preliminary training with the Royal Navy they had not been able to do any drops at all and only a minimum of ground training. At Inveraray some elementary combined training was carried out and inter-services signal codes were arranged. On return to Tilshead in February, the men were able to carry out one drop as a company from aircraft of No. 51 Squadron, at that time at the advance base at Thruxton aerodrome. More specialised practices were made in conjunction with A.L.Cs on south coast beaches near Weymouth: other exercises designed to simulate conditions after the drop were carried out on the South Marlborough Downs. These two locations were chosen for their similarity with the area in France on which the attack was to be made. Naturally there were some discrepancies and after the operation General Browning emphasized in his report that training areas should be chosen to simulate distances as nearly as possible, other factors such as gradients being of lesser importance. During this phase of training, as during the first, the weather was unkind, and no less than four unsuccessful attempts were made before a practice evacuation with M.G.Bs and A.L.Cs of the Royal Navy could be carried out. The weather also caused some postponement of the raid itself: but the forecast for the night of 27/28 February 1942 indicated favourable conditions for both air and sea operations and the Commander-in-Chief, Portsmouth (Admiral Sir W. M. James) who was the Supreme Commander for the operation gave the order "Carry out operations Biting tonight 27 February".

The naval force, under the command of Commander F. N. Cook sailed during the afternoon: at 9.30 p.m. in the evening "C" Company emplaned at Thruxton and at 9.45 p.m. the first aircraft flown by Wing Commander P. C. Pickard, took off. As on the occasion of the raid on Italy, the R.A.F. Force Commander was Group Captain Sir Nigel Norman, who had been responsible for the planning of the air side of the operation. The flight to the target went exactly according to plan. Some flak was met on crossing the French coast in the area of St. Jouin which caused slight damage to some of the aircraft but no personnel were injured. Two aircraft dropped their men in the wrong area, a distance of about two miles from the correct dropping zone: all other aircraft located the correct zone and dropped their troops accurately. All the containers were dropped correctly and found quickly. The operation was entirely successful—the radar experts obtaining all that was required from the set. The evacuation was carried out according to plan and including seven men missing the total casualties for the whole operation were 15 (one killed and seven wounded).

Operation by 1st Parachute Brigade and U.S.A.F. in North Africa: November 1942[1]

In response to Mr. Churchill's invitation of May 1942 the 2nd Battalion of the 503rd American Parachute Regiment arrived in the United Kingdom in June 1942. The Battalion was placed under the operational command of the British Airborne Division. Towards the end of September General Mark Clark of the United States Army informed Major General Browning[2] that these American parachute troops would be required to take part in the campaign planned to take place in North Africa in November. Major General Browning immediately suggested that the proposed campaign, conducted over great distances in suitable country and with probably comparatively light opposition, offered tremendous possibilities for the use of airborne troops on much more than battalion scale. The approval of the Commander-in-Chief, Home Forces, and of the War Office having been obtained, the British 1st Parachute Brigade was accordingly added to the force allotted for the campaign.

In order to complete the 1st Parachute Brigade to war establishment it was necessary to take many personnel and much equipment from the remainder of the Airborne Division. But cross-posting between the three brigades and some improvisation regarding equipment enabled the 1st Parachute Brigade to leave England at the beginning of November on their way to take part in the first large scale Allied parachute operation[3]. On the air side difficulties had been greater. The priority of bombing commitments prohibited the employment of R.A.F. aircraft in the operation[4]: consequently No. 60 Group of the American 51st Wing U.S.A.A.F. were called in, bringing with them Dakota aircraft and all the difficulties attendant with operating parachute troops from an entirely strange type of aircraft. On 9 October 1942 a practice drop was carried out in the United Kingdom by 250 of the British troops: in spite of the exertions of a group of No. 38 Wing instructors, who had been giving as much elementary instruction in door jumping as possible, the method of exit from the side, instead of the floor, of an aircraft was not fully understood by the British troops, three of whom were fatally injured. It was suggested that the real cause of the accidents was that the American flying technique for dropping paratroops from the Dakota was not suitable for British equipment. The Americans released in a pull-out from a shallow dive, whereas the equipment demanded straight and level flight. The consequent delay in carrying out further practice drops (while investigations into the causes of the faulty exits were in progress and remedies being devised) resulted in a large number of personnel of the 1st Parachute Brigade departing from the U.K. without ever having jumped from a Dakota aircraft. As strategic troops the Brigade was placed under the command of General Dwight Eisenhower, the Supreme Allied Commander, and were sub-allotted by him to the 1st British Army for specific operations, the Supreme Commander retaining the right to withdraw them for use as strategic troops on any part of the front of the Allied Expeditionary Force as requested.

---

[1] War Office Narrative " Airborne Forces ", Chapter V.
[2] Major General Browning had, by this time, been officially appointed as the British adviser on airborne forces to Commanders-in-Chief in all theatres of war.
[3] Hurn was the despatch centre for the movement of four twin engined H.S. bombers also transport aircraft. This operation Torch was under the direction of a H.S. controller and transported British and U S. personnel and equipment to North Africa.
[4] It should be emphasized that the airborne activities during the invasion of North Africa, valuable though they may have been, were not an essential part of the planned campaign which would have been carried out regardless of the presence or absence of the paratroops. Hence the use of American aircraft, the R.A.F. being already fully occupied with their allotted task of strategic bombing.

The first parachute operation in North Africa was the attempt to capture Tafaraoni airfield near Oran on 8 November 1942[1]. Although (it was an American operation) carried out by 39 C-47 aircraft of U.S.A.A.F. who dropped troops of the 503rd Parachute Infantry Battalion of U.S. Army, it is mentioned here because 25 of the aircraft carried R.A.F. navigators, most of whom had just completed their training. The operation was abortive, the troops being scattered over a wide area. Nevertheless the operation is of interest in that it involved the longest operational flight in which airborne troops took part during the war. The aircraft took off from St. Eval and Predennick in Cornwall and flew non-stop to North Africa.

The general plan of the 1st British Army, following the landings at Algiers, was a swift advance eastwards on Bizerta and Tunis: included in this plan was a requirement for the capture of Bone port and airfield as soon as possible after the initial landings. General K. Anderson, C.B., M.C., Commanding the First British Army decided that one parachute battalion should be employed to seize Bone airfield immediately after the initial Brigade should be held in reserve for opportunity tasks. The 3rd Parachute Battalion, under the command of Lt. Col. Pine Coffin, was selected for the former task and flew to Gibraltar in Dakota aircraft of No. 60 Group, No. 51 Wing, American Transport Command, U.S.A.A.F. on 10 November 1942. The Battalion carried light equipment only and thus had no transport; it was also one company under strength. The main operation at Algiers having gone well the 3rd Battalion were ordered to carry out their prepared plan and seize Bone airfield on 12 November. This they did at 1020 hours, capturing the airfield without opposition: one man was killed during the drop and three more fatal casualties occurred when two aircraft crash landed in the sea. The American aircrews had had little experience of paratroop dropping and the troops were scattered over an area about three miles in length: even so the dropping was, in the face of the negligible opposition, sufficiently accurate, as the number of recovered parachutes and containers, 90 per cent. shows.

The remainder of the 1st Parachute Brigade, commanded by Brigadier E. W. C. Flavell, M.C., had moved to Algiers by sea taking with them an R.A.F. Mobile Parachute Servicing Unit. This unit which had formed at Netheravon during October 1943 for the especial purpose of servicing parachutes during operations overseas, was, according to its stated duties, capable of drying 180 parachutes in 24 hours; of packing 500 during the same time; and when fully equipped with its special transports, of storing 570 " X " type parachutes plus 240 containers and canopies[2]. The unit was quickly tested. The 1st Parachute Brigade (less the 3rd Battalion) landed at Algiers on 12 November 1942. By nightfall their reconnaissance parties were at the airfield of Maison Blanche, some 12 miles from Algiers itself. On 13 November the Brigade moved into billets in that area, Maison Blanche, Maison Carver and Rouiba; on that date also the 2nd Battalion, 503rd American Parachute Infantry was placed under the Brigade's command[3].

---

[1] C.A.S. Folder 1765 Memos, 31 October 1942 and 2 November 1942.
[2] D.M.C. Monthly Progress Report, October 1943.
[3] The American battalion had flown direct from Cornwall to drop in the area of Oran on D-Day in support of General Mark Clark's American 2nd Army.

At 0930 hours on 14 November orders were received from the 1st Army that on the following day, two airborne operations, each of battalion strength should be carried out. In the first one battalion of British troops was to drop at Souk el Arba, to contact French forces stationed at Beja, to hold the cross-roads at Souk el Arba, and to patrol eastwards and harass the enemy, resorting to guerrilla warfare if necessary[1]. In the second operation the American battalion was to drop at and seize the airfields of Tebesca and Youks les Bains. Lack of transport hindered the preparations for both operations, for the 1st Army had been unable to allot shipping space for the Brigade's own transport. But by using the operational troops themselves for the work all the equipment and parachutes were unloaded from the ships and moved to Maison Blanche airfield. It was now that the small R.A.F. Mobile Parachute Servicing Unit[2], under the command of F/Lt. W. Hire distinguished itself. Using improvised packing tables made from the parachute crates they inspected every parachute and container prior to it being issued or loaded onto the aircraft[3]. The final load of stores arrived at the airfield at 1630 hours on 14 November: at 0730 hours on 15 November the 1st Parachute Battalion took off in 32 Dakota aircraft of the U.S.A.A.F. for the operation. As it happened the rush had been in vain for thick cloud on the route caused the aircraft to turn back, the operation being postponed until the next day. The American battalion was more fortunate: they too took off at 0730 hours on 15 November and their drop was successfully completed. They were employed in the Tebessa area for some time and were consequently removed from the command of the 1st Parachute Brigade.

At 1100 hours on 16 November the 1st Parachute Battalion took off again, under the same arrangements. Their task was now altered to the extent that they were to establish their battalion H.Q. at Beja and push out patrols to contact the enemy thus securing the Souk el Khemis-Souk el Arba plain for use by the R.A.F. Owing to the lack of reconnaissance photographs the dropping zone had to be selected from the air by the battalion commander (Lt. Col. S. J. L. Hill) immediately prior to jumping: he travelled in the leading aircraft and the battalion were dropped on a "follow-my-leader" principle, satisfactory enough in this case as neither ground nor air opposition was encountered, but less likely to prove so under normal operational circumstances. These troops were the first Allied forces to meet the enemy in the Tunisian campaign: they raised the French in the area and carried out the prepared plan. When enemy opposition stiffened they withdrew to a defensive position at Oued Zerga (halfway between Medjez and Beja) which they held until reinforced by ground troops. The 1st Battalion then came under the orders of "Bladerforce", the ground force command.

Between 17 November and 29 November 1942, orders, counter orders and cancellations were received with monotonous regularity by the remainder of the 1st Parachute Brigade who were still standing by for operations at Maison Blanche. On the 19th the 3rd Battalion, who had carried out the operation at Bone, arrived at Maison Blanche and took over the billets

---

[1] War Office Narrative "Airborne Forces", Chapter V.
[2] Formed at Netheravon, 3 October 1942.
[3] During October, at the urgent request of the War Office, 4,300 "X" type parachutes, 2,294 canopies, and 1,500 containers had been operationally packed, each parachute in a watertight greased paper envelope and had been crated for shipment, twelve parachutes to a plywood case. The cases were lined with balloon fabric.

vacated by the 1st Battalion a few days previously. During the nights of 20/21 and 21/22 November enemy aircraft bombed the airfield with some success, a number of aircraft and the store of parachute containers for one company being destroyed.

At 1130 hours on 29 November, after many counter orders and changes of plan the 2nd Battalion took off in 44 aircraft of the American 62nd and 64th Groups to drop at Deprenne airfield. This had been the objective of one of the cancelled operations, but the enemy had now withdrawn after destroying as much of the station as possible and ploughing up the flying ground. The new objective was to be Oudna aerodrome, the task being to destroy enemy aircraft and stores. Confusion reigned just before and during the take-off, the number of aircraft available being suddenly revised, some aircraft arriving later and with unexpected numbering (chalk numbers were used to indicate which men and containers were to be carried in a certain aircraft), and a heavy fall of rain turning the airfield into thick mud. However, all except one aircraft, which was bogged in the mud, were eventually off by 1245 hours.

Again the dropping zone had to be selected from the air and for the second time absence of enemy opposition was fortunate to say the least. After making arrangements for the salvage of parachutes and containers the battalion moved off, using commandeered mule carts as transport, at 0015 hours on 30 November. By 1600 hours the objective, Oudna airfield, had been reached and, after an engagement with the enemy, occupied and consolidated. But the enemy were no longer using the airfield: the whole object of the operation had been to destroy aircraft and stores—and there were no aircraft or stores in the area. Lt. Col. Frost therefore decided to move west, aiming to join up with the troops of the British First Army who were, according to the original plan, to make an armoured thrust towards Tunis. During the night a wireless message was received: the 1st Army thrust on Tunis had been postponed. For the next three days the battalion withdrew westwards over difficult hilly country and was continually attacked by tanks, infantry and aircraft.

On 3 December 1942, the leading elements reached the Allied lines at Medjaz: small parties, isolated in the withdrawal continued to arrive until 5 December. On the latter date the strength of the battalion was about 150 all ranks, some 260 personnel being killed, missing or wounded. A week later—the battalion remained in the area until 11 December—some 100 of the missing had rejoined having fought their way individually to the Allied lines. The operation had been based on faulty information and inadequate arrangements for co-ordination with the advance of the main ground forces on Tunis had resulted in a heavy casualty rate.

This operation by the 2nd Battalion was the last airborne operation carried out during the North African campaign. The 1st Parachute Brigade remained in the theatre and fought as infantry until April 1943 when they rejoined the 1st Airborne Division for training, re-organisation and re-equipping prior to taking part in operation Husky. An account of their work during these months is included in the Army history but is not relevant to this narrative of Airborne Forces which is concerned only with the air aspects. A report on the air aspects of the parachute operations was made by General Browning and Group Captain Sir Nigel Norman in December 1942 after a visit to North Africa. The report stated that the attacks by the 1st and 2nd Parachute Battalions had been severely handicapped by the complete lack of air photographs, by a shortage of maps, and by the fact that Nos. 62 and 64 Groups, U.S.A.A.F. had little or no experience of dropping parachutists using British equipment.

The lack of British aircraft and aircrews trained with the men they would carry into action was felt in a concrete operational form for the first time. In spite of the gallant efforts of the American aircrews the drops had been inaccurate and dispersed, facts which had been offset by the lack of enemy opposition: but had this not been the case the effects of such dropping might well have been disastrous. The only American Group, No. 60, which had been trained in England with British troops, had no container racks available in the theatre and consequently could not be employed for troop dropping. Furthermore, none of the American Groups had been trained in dropping by night so that fighter escort had had to be provided at the expense of other operations for daylight drops. The report drew attention to the need for much closer contact between the H.Q. staffs controlling the whole force and the Airborne specialist advisers. Also the fact that there had been no expert in airborne matters at either Allied Force H.Q. or First British Army H.Q. had resulted in the 1st Parachute Brigade not being used to the full in their airborne capacity and in the arrangements for the operations not being as good as they should and would have been.

The use of the 1st Parachute Brigade—as distinct from the one battalion of American parachute troops—in the campaign was rather in the nature of a last minute experiment. The British airborne enthusiasts grabbed at the chance of using the parachute force operationally and accepted a good deal of improvised organisation in order to do so ; for example they accepted the necessity of using a strange American aircraft, the Dakota, and inexperienced American aircrews ; they accepted the fact that for these American air formations the dropping of the British paratroops was a subsidiary task, secondary to their primary role of American air transport duties ; they accepted the fact that no shipping space could be spared for the Brigade to take its own transport. In effect they were " hangers-on " to the planned operation, which would have taken place regardless of their presence or absence.

The justification for accepting such a role was undoubtedly the opportunity of proving the value of parachute troops in action, and from the Army viewpoint that value was proved. But the role of " hanger-on " had carried with it heavy penalties, for by accepting so much improvisation on the air side the airborne enthusiasts had left themselves open to the charge of complete failure and were themselves forced to admit that only the lack of enemy opposition had saved two of the operations from becoming complete fiascos. Thus the effects of the airborne operations were twofold ; the pro-airborne were more firmly convinced than ever that an adequate and efficient air component was all that was required to make the Airborne Force into a most potent weapon: the anti-airborne were more convinced than ever that airborne operations were, if not a failure, at least not worth the colossal effort and expenditure of the air forces which they involved, since equally satisfactory results could be obtained by more usual methods of warfare.

Glider Training and Operations

To return to the air problems in Airborne Forces during 1942-43. During this period as during the years 1940 and 1941 the part of the force which had involved the greatest difficulties was the glider element. From the outset it had been decided that the greater part of the total force should be glider borne, and this entailed the provision of men to fly the gliders. The hold up in glider pilot training had been caused by the lack of machines to train them: thus two periods of delay were bound to occur, one until the gliders were made and the other between the delivery of the gliders and the completion of the first training courses. The key to the problem and the solution of the difficulties was glider production.

Glider Production

A trickle of Hotspurs, the gliders to be used for training, had begun in the early summer of 1941. But it was not until November 1941 that they began to arrive in large numbers. In that month the deliveries began to assume more satisfactory proportions.

Thus production reached its peak in June 1942. By the end of that year 948 Hotspurs had been delivered: the "tail-off" period which extended until April 1943 provided the additional 42 gliders necessary to complete the total order of 990. With the rising production of November 1941-June 1942 it became possible to establish the glider pilot training organisation and to expand it rapidly[1]. During these months the Hotspur was the only glider available, but during May 1942 the first production model of the heavier and general purpose machine, the Horsa, was flown. The success of the Horsa during trials had been such that the Hotspur was no longer regarded as an operational aircraft: consequently from June 1942, when deliveries of Horsas to the R.A.F. began, instruction at "individual" level on the heavier type of machine was also needed. The arrangement regarding Horsas was that the component parts should be delivered in sets to the A.S.U.s where assembly would take place. The first sets were delivered in May 1942 but it was June before sufficient were assembled to permit training to begin.

But from then, June 1942, onwards there was no shortage of Horsas: rather the reverse for, as the Prime Minister remarked in November 1942, the problem later became the storage of these large machines until such time as they were all needed.

Glider Pilot training at the individual stages: November 1941-October 1943

It was this flow of gliders from the production lines which enabled the glider pilot training organisation to be established in November 1941. The plans for its establishment were made during September and October 1941 and accounts of the various meetings at which the governing policy was decided are contained in Chapter 2. The account which follows deals with the execution of that policy, and it begins once again, with the changes which took place at the Airborne Forces Establishment in November 1941.

---

[1] The construction of the tail unit of the Hotspur was found to be weak, and numbers of the gliders were damaged when landing with a full load. Modifications were immediately designed but owing to the difficulties of incorporating them into the production line it was some months before the satisfactory Mark became available in numbers. This weakness in the earlier models was the major cause of the fact that by July 1943 as many as 130 of the 990 Hotspurs had been written off.

On 4 November 1941 the Glider Training Squadron of the Airborne Forces Establishment, which had been located at Thame throughout the Summer of 1941, became an independent unit, No. 1 Glider Training School. During the previous month nineteen C.F.S. instructors had been training so that, with the seven qualified instructors already there, twenty-six glider instructors were available. The school was to have a pupil population of 64, the course lasting six weeks, and an intake of 32 pupils being made every three weeks. A similar G.T.S. No. 2 was to be set up as soon as possible, but lack of light tug aircraft and difficulties regarding aerodrome accommodation delayed this until December. Then the second school formed at Weston-on-the-Green, a number of experienced personnel being posted from No. 1 G.T.S. to form the nucleus.

These schools were designed to train Army Glider pilots, and the Army agreed to provide 400 plus a reserve of 50 per cent. But these men had to complete a thirteen-week course on light powered aircraft before they arrived at the G.T.S. No. 16 E.F.T.S. at Derby had been allotted for this purpose and the Air Ministry offered to begin Army training there on 1 December 1941, so that the first pupils would reach G.T.S. by the beginning of March 1942. The War Office were unable, however, to complete the arrangements for the selection and posting of the personnel until 31 December and it was on 1 January 1942 that the first Army pupils commenced Glider Pilot Training proper. Bad weather held up their E.F.T.S. training during the early months of 1942 so that it was April before they first flew gliders, even of the training type[1].

In the meantime R.A.F. personnel were being trained as glider pilots. The commitment was to lift a force of Brigade strength by the summer of 1942 and it was obvious that the Army pupils would not be available by that time. Consequently the Air Ministry suggested (at the meeting of 26 September 1941), that a number of R.A.F. pilots, who had reached S.F.T.S. standard but who were surplus to normal R.A.F. requirements, should be used to help fill the gap. This scheme was approved on 4 October 1941, since the Chief of Air Staff had directed that everything possible should be done to train sufficient pilots to match glider production up to the approved first line limit of brigade strength. But it was emphasised that it was a temporary scheme, and that the R.A.F. pilots were to be withdrawn as soon as Army pilots became available to replace them. The first course at No. 1 G.T.S. commenced on 4 November 1941 and at No. 2 G.T.S. during January 1942[2]. At first there were complaints from R.A.F. pilots, particularly when Army Battle Training was introduced during the courses. Nevertheless they proved to be good glider pilot material, and in comparison with them the lower standard of airmanship, due to lack of experience, of the Army pupils who followed them was very noticeable. When the flow of Army pupils began a number of the R.A.F. personnel were transferred to tug pilot duties at the schools, their glider experience proving most valuable in this role[3], and when in the Spring of 1943 some of the schools were closed down many of them were released and achieved their ambition of a posting to an operational unit.

---

[1] A.M. File C.S. 7424 Pt. I: Encls. 28A, 45A and 50A, and O.R.B. of No. 16 E.F.T.S.
[2] A.M. File C.S. 7424, Pt. I, Encl. 26A.
[3] As the A.O.C.-in-C. Army Co-operation Command remarked " During glider training it is essential to have an experienced pilot on one end of the rope ".

After completing the G.T.S. course glider pilots spent weeks at a Glider Operational Training Unit, where more advanced Hotspur flying was taught. Two G.O.T.U.s were established, both at Kidlington, No. 101 in January and No. 107 in February 1942. The course included night flying and full load flying, although the latter had to be modified owing to the structural faults of the earlier Hotspurs when landing with a full load. Nearly all the pupils who completed the G.O.T.U. course were R.A.F. personnel, some of them the ex-S.F.T.S. pilots, others instructors or staff pilots who were in need of more flying hours on the Hotspur or who needed a refresher course. The first Army pupils did not arrive until the end of May 1942 and a month later a re-organisation took place, the G.O.T.U.s being abolished[1].

It had been agreed during the planning of the glider pilot training organisation that Flying Training Command should be responsible for glider pilot training at the initial stages. The E.F.T.S.s were already in this command, and Nos. 1 and 2 G.T.S.s were transferred on 3 December 1941 respectively[2]. In May 1942 a proposal was made that the two G.O.T.U.s should be abolished, or rather should become Glider Training Schools. The War Office estimates of the numbers of pilots required by the end of the year was continually changing, but it was clear that an insufficient number would be produced under existing arrangements. Also experience had shown that the night and full load flying could be incorporated quite satisfactorily into the G.T.S. course. Advanced training would be covered by the conversion course on to Horsas, which were just becoming available. This unit, the Heavy Glider Conversion Unit, formed at Shrewton on 29 June 1942, and was, like the G.O.T.U.s, in Army Co-operation Command. Early in July, however, the re-organisation of the glider training scheme was approved and became effective. To meet the Army requirements[3] it was agreed to allocate eighteen E.F.T.S. flights for glider pilot training, and the extra flights were provided by Nos. 3, 21 and 27 E.F.T.S.s. Five Glider Training Schools would deal with Hotspur training, Nos. 1 and 2, No. 3 (the latter was formed at Stoke Orchard on 21 July 1942), and Nos. 4 and 5, these two being formed from the two G.O.T.U.s which were to be closed. The Heavy Glider Conversion Unit, which accepted its first intake of pupils during July, moved to Brize Norton which, having runways and a good grass surface, was more suitable than Shebden, the original selection[4]. All of these units were now placed under the jurisdiction of Flying Training Command who, as the experts in flying training at "individual" level, were better suited for the task than Army Co-operation Command. No. 1 G.T.S. was moved from Thame to Croughton, thus leaving the former free for glider instructors school which opened there on 25 August 1942. This unit had a short life, but by 13 January 1943 when it closed it had trained sufficient instructors to meet the needs of the glider training organisation.

---

[1] O.R.B.s of Nos. 101 and 107 G.O.T.Us.
[2] A.M. L.M. 379/D. of O. dated 3 December 1941.
[3] The War Office requirements were constantly changing as new estimates were made of the amount of equipment needed to be carried during an operation and of the number of gliders needed to carry it. On 8 April, 1942 D.M.C. at Air Ministry summed up the situation by saying " The target should be to train many glider pilots as we can as quickly as possible—the aim being to lift the Air Landing Brigade by December 1942 ".
[4] The runway at Shebden had been built in order that the aerodrome would be used by Horsas: but in July 1942 the newly sown grass was in no condition to stand up to the continued wear of heavy glider flying and the attendant tractor traffic, although it was used by Hotspurs.

From now on the scheme worked smoothly. Volunteers, having been selected, joined the Glider Pilot Regiment Depot[1] where they attended lectures in mathematics, airmanship, map reading, navigation and similar subjects. This short course was the equivalent of the R.A.F. pilots Initial Training Wing course: originally it had been superimposed upon the E.F.T.S. Course but as the pool of selected men formed it was possible for this ground instruction to be dealt with while waiting for vacancies on the flying courses.

The E.F.T.S. was, of course, the first of these, and the embryo glider pilot underwent an experience very similar to that of his R.A.F. counterpart. The Army pupils were reported to be very keen, and the number of failures was not high. Eighteen E.F.T.S. flights were now available; (after July 1942) three whole E.F.T.S.s and a part of a fourth: these and the five G.T.S.s were run on standard Flying Training Command lines, a smooth flow of pupils through the schools being maintained at all times. The sudden expansion of elementary training facilities caught the Army unawares and during August 1942 it seemed that an early breakdown of the scheme would be caused by a shortage of Army pupils from the pre-E.F.T.S. course. But by a hasty recruiting drive and by temporarily shortening the pre-E.F.T.S. course the crisis was averted: and a crisis it was, for the Flying Training Command system was like a factory production line, and a gap or stoppage at any point could result in a hold-up of the finished product out of all proportion to the original cause. As it was the flow of pupils was maintained, and truth to tell the success of the Flying Training Command organisation was such that the glider pilot problem ceased to be "how to get them" and became "what to do with them[2]".

There was, however, an intermediate stage. During the autumn of 1942, as the pool of fully trained glider pilots grew steadily, the War Office began to consider the quality rather than the quantity of these men. This is not to say that there was any slackening of the pressure on the Air Ministry to produce glider pilots as quickly as possible, but discussions took place concerning the standard of flying required of the men which resulted in the Army accepting a reduction in the output of trained pilots providing a higher level of training could thus be reached[3].

The new syllabus had hardly come into operation when the "standstill" order relating to all Airborne Forces units was issued. This, it will be remembered, was a Chief of Air Staff instruction pending a decision by the Prime Minister on the question of Airborne effort. This greatly increased the difficulties which Flying Training Command had been experiencing for some time at the H.G.C.U. where Whitley unserviceability and shortage of hangar space in which to effect major repairs and inspections were the great problems. Early in 1943 the H.G.C.U. was released from the standstill order, and in view of the urgency of training at this stage instructions were given for the replacement of the Whitleys there by Albemarles. But before this could be done the operational demands of No. 296 Squadron, who were re-equipping with Albemarles in preparation for Operation Husky

---

[1] The G.P.R. had been established during November 1941.
[2] A.M. File C.S. 7424, Pt. II, Encls. 153A, 159A and 160A.
[3] A.M. File C.S. 7424, Pt. II, Encls. 197A and 247A.

arose, and the H.G.C.U. were informed that they must continue to make the best of the older aircraft. The standstill order had a less immediate effect upon the rest of the training organisation, although the shortage of skilled ground personnel became noticeable as postings " out " continued and postings " in " ceased[1].

Even the Prime Minister's decision of 15 November 1942 had very little immediate effect upon the work of the E.F.T.S.s and G.T.S.s. For although that decision had been against a large scale glider force it was pointless to stop the training of the men already at and just about to enter the schools. The selection and intake of further volunteers ceased, but even so the supply of pupils was sufficient to keep the organisation going until the Spring of 1943. Then, during March and April, the E.F.T.S.s (with the exception of one flight at No. 3 at Booker) returned to their normal role of grading schools for R.A.F. aircrews, and Nos. 1, 2 and 4 G.T.S.s were closed, their accommodation, equipment and personnel being largely combined to form No. 20 (P) A.F.U., a normal Flying Training Command Unit. The other two glider schools, Nos. 3 and 5, remained and were used to provide refresher courses, and were also, incidentally, an insurance in the event of glider pilot training being suddenly resumed[2].

When the schools closed some 700 Army Glider pilots had been trained to fly Hotspurs. The H.G.C.U. was, of course, kept in existence, and was in fact expanded, in order to carry out conversion on the operation type[3].

Glider Pilot training at the " collective " stage

The reader will have noticed how the emphasis of glider pilot training was continually shifting. Initially the bottleneck was production of gliders: then the emphasis moved to the individual training of the pilots at the elementary stages ; then difficulties arose at the H.G.C.U. stage as the flow of pupils from the schools exceeded the limited capacity of the conversion unit. Now, in the Spring and Summer of 1943 the overwhelming need became facilities for exercising the fully trained pilots, who required a certain minimum of flying hours each month[4] in order to maintain their newly acquired skill. As early as November 1942 General Browning had expressed his concern regarding this lack of flying ; but the standstill order had prohibited any large increase in the amount of flying which could be carried out by the squadrons, who were responsible for this work. Also the three squadrons available, Nos. 295, 296 and 297 had, during the winter of 1942-43 been undertaking two other tasks, the dropping of leaflets on enemy occupied

---

[1] It is interesting to note that the O.R.B. of No. 2 G.T.S. for November and December 1942 makes special reference to this, and emphasises the value of W.A.A.F. tradeswomen, who were just beginning to arrive at the unit in large numbers.

[2] This possibility was very present in the minds of both Air Ministry and Flying Training Command. It explains largely why the three schools which were closed (Nos. 1, 2 and 4) were kept as centralised as possible and were not disbanded entirely.

[3] Full output figures for " Hotspur only " pilots for the period April 1942 to May 1943 were:—

	1942							
April	May	June	July	Aug.	Sept.	Oct.	Nov.	Dec.
60	50	30	30	78	103	87	82	99
				1943				
		Jan.	Feb.	Mar.	April	May		
		66	76	50	30	26		

[4] Estimates varied but 5 hours per month per pilot was considered essential and 8 desirable.

countries, particularly France, and the movement by air of squadrons within the United Kingdom. The latter task was not entirely a loss to the glider pilots, for the moves were made by glider and the pilots thus obtained full load flying practice. But even so the tactical practice and value of such flying was negligible[1].

The Chief of the Imperial General Staff's memorandum of 24 February 1943 which envisaged the use of a glider force during the invasions of Sicily and North-Western Europe, caused more attention to be given to this necessity of exercising the glider pilots, and the problem was recognised as being one of some urgency[2]. During March 1943 discussions were held between representatives of Army Co-operation Command, the Airborne Division and No. 38 Wing and these resulted in a policy being formulated which in due course received Air Ministry and War Office approval[3]. It had already been decided (in December 1942) that two pilots were needed to fly the Horsa during most training and all operational flights. It was agreed that there should be two distinctive gradings, first pilot and second pilot. The more experienced and capable of the pilots already trained were graded as first pilots and were "crewed up" with a less experienced man. Flights were then formed with crews per flight and each flight was attached to one of the squadron flights for a period of one month at a time. At the end of the one month the glider pilots were replaced by new flights and left the squadrons for two months after which they returned for more training. By this system each squadron aircrew had attached to it three glider crews, and in fact they were encouraged to regard themselves as one crew of six men—four aircrew and two glider pilots—and as far as possible they always flew together.

During the two months "rest" period the glider pilots were kept occupied in various ways according to the facilities available. As many as possible were sent to the Glider Pilot Exercise Unit where they carried out Hotspur refresher training: others returned to the G.P.R. Depot for military and tactical courses of various types: and, as they became sufficiently experienced, the second pilots were sent to the H.G.C.U. for their own advanced Horsa flying and first pilot's courses.

As far as it went this scheme proved admirable: but the necessary flying hours were still not forthcoming. By April 1943 the problem was being discussed at Air Ministry level, and the Director of Operational Training, expressed strongly the view that the three No. 38 Wing Squadrons should be relieved of their leaflet dropping commitment in order that they could devote their entire effort to glider training[4]. It was an unpopular suggestion: the Foreign Office were insistent upon the value of the work, emphasising that if the No. 38 Wing Squadrons were withdrawn they would have to request that other squadrons, probably from Bomber Command, were found to replace them. Army Co-Operation Command and No. 38 Wing H.Q. supported the leaflet raids on the grounds that they served as "flak inoculation" for the aircrews and maintained their morale. Nevertheless the primary role of these squadrons was the training and operation of the Airborne

---

[1] A.M. File C.S. 7424, Pt. II, Encls. 257A, 227A and 229A.
[2] C.O.S. (43) 81 (O).
[3] A.M. File C.S. 7424, Pt. II, Encls. 55A and 31A.
[4] A.M. File C.S. 7424, Pt. III, Encls. 83A and 84A.

Division, and on 15 May 1943 an order was issued by Air Ministry stating that their entire effort was to be devoted to this end. The decisive factor in favour of stopping leaflet dropping and similar subsidiary tasks was the withdrawal from the training programme of No. 296 Squadron, who were to be detached to North Africa for Operation Husky.

Re-equipment of this squadron with Albermarles began in February and was completed in May 1943. The establishment was increased from two flights to three ; and inter-posting with No. 297 Squadron resulted in the most experienced aircrews in the Wing (many of them the original crews) joining No. 296. Thus from February these preparations caused the squadron to be progressively withdrawn from the training programme and in May they moved to their advanced base in North Africa. This left Nos. 295 and 297 Squadrons to carry out the increased glider flying commitment demanded in order to keep the glider pilots in practice. Both were depleted: No. 297 by the withdrawal of most of its experienced crews: No. 295 by the formation within the squadron of a Halifax flight which, as it was responsible for the towing of the Horsas to North Africa (for Husky) had complete priority over all other squadron demands. Furthermore, in July No. 297 Squadron began to re-equip with Albemarles: a third flight was formed and a number of trained and experienced Coastal Command crews were posted in: also the flow of crews from No. 42 O.T.U. increased. But to offset this there was a constant drain on the Squadron in the form of reinforcement crews for No. 296 Squadron, still in Tunisia awaiting recall to the U.K.: also the new crews, even those from Coastal Command, had to be trained in the Airborne role and the few experienced pilots and navigators became Air Force instructors instead of being available for constant glider towing themselves[1].

So in spite of all efforts and instructions, and the cancellation of the leaflet dropping commitments[2] the amount of flying carried out by the Army glider pilots during the summer of 1943 was not large. In the meantime the number of such men, trained to H.G.C.U. level was rising rapidly, and by 30 September 1943 about 885 were available[3]. Of this number some were in the Mediterranean area after taking part in Husky: others were attached to flying units in the U.K. squadrons, the G.P.E.U. or at H.G.C.U. for their captains course ; the remainder were at the G.P.R. Depot or similar army units.

The gliders which they were to fly were also very conspicuous by their presence. As Mr. Churchill had foreseen the difficulty became to find storage space for them: a meeting held as early as July 1942 had decided that the Horsas should be stored at Bomber Command stations in the South of England : the plan was to store them partially assembled (60 per cent. without, 40 per cent. with main planes fitted: all with tail units not fitted): they were to be stored in hangars, although these could be up to one mile from the station : 700 Horsas and 60 Hamilcars, were to be so stored. By March 1943, 648 of the 700 Horsas had arrived, 27 to each of

---

[1] O.R.Bs. of Nos. 295, 296 and 297 Squadrons.
[2] The leaflet raids were resumed for a short period during August 1943 by Albemarle crews of No. 297 Squadron in order to provide operational experience prior to the journey to North Africa as reinforcements for No. 296 Squadron.
[3] On 1 May 1943, the number had been about 650.

24 Bomber Command stations. The lack of hangar space, and the slowness with which new buildings were being erected made it impossible however to store the machines under cover, and they were left in the open. Responsibility for these gliders was assumed by a new unit, set up specifically for the purpose, No. 2 Heavy Glider Maintenance Unit which was formed in July 1943. It consisted of 24 Glider Maintenance Sections one of which was attached to each of the Bomber Command Stations, the Station Engineer Officer being in charge of each section. In May 1943 a long list of instructions had been issued which set out in detail the duties of R.A.F. Station Engineer Officers relating to glider maintenance.

Glider Operation—Freshman : November 1942[1]

Before leaving the subject of gliders and describing the work of the No. 38 Wing Squadrons during 1942 and 1943 mention must be made of the one glider operation which took place in the period. It was, in fact, the first glider operation ever undertaken by the British Airborne Force. Quite early in the war it became known that the Germans were experimenting in the production of an atomic bomb. A compound known as "heavy water" played an essential part in these experiments and this was being produced at German research installations, the most important of which was at the Norak Hydro Plant at Vermork in Norway. In order to dislocate the experiments and delay the production of the bomb it was vital that both the stocks of "heavy water" and the means of production should be destroyed. The compound was extremely difficult to produce and a successful attack on the plant at Vermork would have long lasting effects upon the work there.

Vermork is a village some two and a half miles to the west of Rjukan, about 60 miles due west of Oslo, and about 60 miles inland. Rjukan itself is a very isolated town situated in a deep valley, the thickly forested sides of which rise steeply from a narrow river bed to a height of 3,000 feet. The valley is overlooked by Gaustal Fjell, a mountain, 5,400 feet high. The "heavy water" plant itself was built on a broad shelf of rock which rose sheer from the river bed to a height of 1,000 feet, the climb above being dangerously steep through a thick pine forest. It was thus a most difficult area to attack by any means. The first method attempted was by use of bomber aircraft but this was only partially successful and was not again attempted owing to the difficulty of both locating and attacking the pinpoint target and the danger to the civilian population, who were exceptionally friendly to the Allied cause. The alternatives were to attack from the ground by airborne troops or by Norwegian saboteurs. It was the latter method which eventually succeeded : but it was the former which was first chosen and attempted.

Headquarters Combined operations were in charge of all such attacks and in the middle of October 1942 they instructed Major General Browning and Group Captain Sir Nigel Norman to plan an operation against the installation. A suggestion that troops should be landed on Lake Tinnajon, some 15 miles from the objective was considered impracticable owing to the steepness of the surrounding mountain slopes. The use of paratroops

---

[1] War Office Narrative "Airborne Forces", Chapter V. 1st A.B. Division Report, 38W/MS 10/15/Air.

entailed drawbacks because of the risk of too great dispersion when dropping in such country and because of the limitation of equipment: the destruction of the installation would demand a considerable quantity of explosive—and a high degree of technical knowledge on the part of the attacking party.

In view of all this it was decided to make use of gliders for the first time in an operation: the troops were, nevertheless, to be fully trained parachutists, in case a last minute change of plan became necessary. The units available were limited as the 1st Parachute Squadron R.E. was already committed to the North African campaign and the 9th Field Company R.E. (Airborne) and 261 Field Park Company (Airborne) were called upon to provide volunteer parachutists for the task. Two parties of 16 men each were selected, one commanded by Lieut. A. C. Allen, R.E., and the other by Lieut. D. A. Metheren, G.M., R.E. (who replaced 2nd Lieut. M. D. Green, R.E., when the latter was injured three days before the operation was due). Lieut.-Colonel N. C. A. Henniker, M.C., R.E., was in charge of the Army side of planning for the operation.

For No. 38 Wing, Group Captain Cooper, D.F.C., commanded the small detachment which was formed especially for the operation. This consisted of three Halifax aircraft—these being the only type capable of towing a Horsa glider over the required distance—and two aircrews, specially selected to include an element of Dominion personnel. The glider pilots were very experienced, and all four had been among those who were with the Glider Detachment of the C.L.E. at Thame during the summer of 1941. Two of them, Staff Sergeant M. F. C. Strathdee and Sergeant P. Doig were members of the Glider Pilot Regiment: the other two Pilot Officer Davies and Sergeant Fraser were both of the Royal Australian Air Force. Squadron Leader Wilkinson, R.A.F., captained the first tug aircraft and Flight Lieutenant Parkinson, Royal Canadian Air Force the second. Thus there were in reality two separate parties each of which was capable of carrying out the operation individually. Both would be used in the operation, duplication being considered advisable in view of the hazards of each, a long tow over such difficult country, and also in view of the importance of the operation.

Training for both the Army and Air Force elements was comprehensive and concentrated: for the former it included technical specialist training, the use of snowboots and snow equipment, and hard physical exercises; for the latter practice long distance tows with laden gliders gave both the pilots and crews valuable experience and confirmed the assumption that the use of gliders was a practical proposition. The aircraft were fitted with the new Rebecca-Eureka radar homing device, the Rebecca set being the one fitted in the aircraft. Eureka, the ground set, had to be delivered to Norwegian agents prior to the operation and this was done by H.Q. Combined Operations. The agents were informed of the landing zone and would erect the Eureka set, which was small and portable, and start it working on instructions from H.Q. Combined operations. Arrangements were also made for Norwegian guides to assist the attacking parties both to reach their objectives and to make their way to the Swedish frontier after the attack.

On 17 November 1942 the whole force moved to Skitten, a satellite of Wick aerodrome, in Scotland, the operation being scheduled for the night of 19-20 November or the first suitable night following during the moon period.

As the R.A.F. commander of the force the final decision regarding weather conditions lay with Group Captain Cooper, who had to assist him a meteorological expert on Norway and also the latest reports from agents in that country. The forecast for the night of 19-20 November was reasonable, though not ideal, and with the possibility of a deterioration in the weather for the remainder of the moon period it was decided to mount the operation that night. All was ready and morale was very high.

The first aircraft took off at 1750 hours and the second at 1810 hours, and each set course individually across the North Sea: the first news to reach the base airfield was a signal received at 2341 hours from the second aircraft (F/Lt. Parkinson) asking for a course to fly to return to base. R.D.F. bearings plotted this aircraft's position as over the North Sea: from then on nothing more was heard from this aircraft. At 2355 hours however a signal was received from the other aircraft (S/Ldr. Wilkinson and G/C. Cooper) saying " my glider released in sea " but an R.D.F. plot indicated that the aircraft was, in fact, over the mountains of Southern Norway, and this was later confirmed by a careful navigation check when the aircraft returned. The glider had been released just over the coast but nowhere near the target.

The actual course of events, as far as can be ascertained (even with post-war reports available) was as follows. The first aircraft (S/Ldr. Wilkinson) completed the sea crossing successfully, made a landfall on the coast and flew on towards the target: just before crossing the coast the Rebecca set had become unserviceable so that the run-up to the landing zone from the coast had to be made, through patchy cloud, on map reading alone. On the second attempt to locate the landing zone the aircraft flew into thick cloud when about 40 miles north-west of Rjukan, and was unable to climb out of it: moreover the petrol reserve, which was not large, was rapidly being used up: icing on both tug and glider caused the combination to lose height and the effect of the ice on the tow rope was equally dangerous. The combination was still losing height rapidly when, just north of Stavanger on the Norwegian coast, the rope iced-up completely and snapped: the aircraft returned to base and landed just before its petrol was exhausted. The glider crash landed at Fylesdalen, on top of snow-covered mountains overlooking Lysefjord: the weather was extremely bad and snow was falling: of the 17 men in the glider eight (including Lieut. Methuen, Staff Sergeant Strathdee and Sergeant Doig) were killed immediately, four were severely injured, and five were uninjured. The four injured were poisoned later by a German doctor on the order of the Gestapo, and the five uninjured were shot by the Gestapo, on 18 January 1943, all having been captured before they could get away from the scene of the crash. The Norwegian agents on the landing ground had heard this aircraft flying almost directly above them on what must have been its first run in: the failure of the Rebecca set in this aircraft had caused the failure of the operation.

The second aircraft (F/Lt. Parkinson) and its glider both crashed immediately after crossing the Norwegian coast, landfall was made near Egersund and the combination headed towards Rjukan. For some reason still unknown, the glider crash-landed in the mountains just north of Helleland and the tug, after just clearing the mountains landed in another range of hills to the south. In the glider three men were killed immediately and the remainder were captured and shot within a few hours under the terms of a general order issued by Hitler. In the tug all of the crew were killed immediately. The Norwegians in the locality buried the dead and tended their graves throughout the war. In May 1945, when the 1st Airborne Division moved into Norway, the bodies were re-buried at Egenes (Stavanger) and Oslo with full military honours. Effective action was also taken to bring to trial the Germans responsible for the murders.

Operation Freshman was a failure, and the task of destroying the " heavy water " installation remained for Norwegian agents to attempt successfully later. Freshman had been a most hazardous task from the beginning: a sea crossing of 340 miles and a landing in difficult and unknown country, both by night, was an extreme test for this, the first glider operation ever to be undertaken by British forces.

CHAPTER 5

GENERAL DEVELOPMENTS AND FURTHER OPERATIONS

The Organisation of No. 38 Wing and its work, 1942-43

Before considering the formation and work of No. 38 Wing, the collective training organisation, it is well to mention the events and factors leading to its formation. In November 1941 the Army had expanded its Airborne organisation into a Division of some 10,000 men, Major General F. A. M. Browning, D.S.O., being appointed G.O.C. on 4 November 1941. Moreover the increasing supply of Hotspur gliders enabled great expansion in the glider pilot training organisation to be put in hand: finally the Chiefs of Staff's decision of May 1941 that a force of brigade strength should be available by the summer of 1942 necessitated the formation of a collective training organisation in order that the men who had completed their individual training could practise their operational tactics under simulated operational conditions. During November 1941 General Browning visited Air Marshal Sir Arthur Barratt and as a result of that meeting the Commander-in-Chief of Army Co-operation Command evolved proposals which, on being approved by the Air Ministry, were put into effect during the closing weeks of 1941.

Two squadrons, originally designated Glider Exercise and Parachute Exercise Squadron soon became Nos. 296 and 297 Squadrons respectively. The Glider Exercise Squadron was formed from the Glider Exercise Flight of the A.F.E., which in the previous October had been formed at Ringway to relieve the Glider Training Squadron of its demonstration and exercise commitments[1]. The new squadron formed at Netheravon on 1 January 1942 and was originally equipped with Hectors and Hotspurs only, although its official aircraft establishment was 8 + 3 light tugs (Hectors), 16 + 14 Hotspurs, 20 + 6 heavy tugs (Whitleys), and 30 + 10 Horsas. Later in the year when this establishment was complete the squadron split into two, the light tugs and gliders becoming the Glider Pilot Exercise Unit and the Whitley element becoming No. 296 Squadron[2]: until that time a distinction was made by referring to the two sections as Nos. 296A and 296B Squadrons.

The glider pilots of the squadron were, initially, the R.A.F. pilots from the first courses to pass through the recently established No. 1 G.T.S., at Thame: tug pilots were provided from the Glider Exercise Flight and later, when replacement glider pilots began to arrive, from the R.A.F. glider pilots themselves. The squadron was commanded by S/Ldr. P. B. N. Davis, whose work and experience in the glider field has already been mentioned in this narrative.

Hotspur flying began at Netheravon as soon as the Squadron was established there, although the weakness of the Hotspur tail unit when landing with a full load, and the lack of and difficulties of servicing the Hectors

---
[1] W.O. File War/AC/116A.
[2] The Horsa element was never formed and deliveries of these gliders did not commence until after the split had occurred: when the Horsa did become available they were established on the station concerned as separate glider flights and were not attached to Squadrons.

limited the number of hours which could be flown. Nevertheless by March 1942 flights with troops of the Air Landing Brigade as passengers were being undertaken regularly and 900 such troops were given air exercise during that month. By 15 May 1942 the Squadron had received 19 of the 26 Whitleys and at the end of that month the split between the two sections became effective although not officially recognised until August: the Whitley section adopting the dual purpose airborne role of both parachute dropping and glider towing, moved to Hurn; the light glider section remaining at Netheravon[1].

No equivalent unit had existed in the old Airborne organisation which could supply a nucleus for the squadron. The P.T.S. at Ringway was small in numbers, indeed it was the drain on its limited resources caused by the demands of Army Exercises which had shown so clearly the need for the Squadron. Consequently when No. 297 Squadron formed at Netheravon on 1 January 1942 only one pilot experienced in parachute dropping could be spared from Ringway[2]. The remainder of the pilots were drawn from varied sources, some having considerable operational experience, others being straight from Operational Training Units; the other aircrews were all newly trained personnel posted direct from their training courses without even passing through O.T.U.s[3]. Later, however, the Squadron received reinforcements of complete crews both from No. 42 O.T.U. (which had been allotted to supply the Airborne Squadrons) and from Nos. 13 and 104 Squadrons of Army Co-operation Command. The Squadron had an establishment of 12 + 6 Whitleys, but as these did not begin to arrive until late in February a number of Tiger Moths were found and used to give the pilots and navigators practice in low level map reading, a vital subject for crews engaged in dropping parachutists in small areas from a height of 500 feet or below. During March and April, however, Whitleys arrived steadily and the squadron reached full strength.

A dropping zone, which became known as the "Divisional D.Z." was located on Netheravon North aerodrome, and the aircrews began to learn their new task, first dropping containers, then single or pairs of paratroops of the 1st Parachute Battalion, and finally full sticks of ten men. By the end of May a number of combined exercises had been carried out, each usually consisting of some 12 or 13 parachute dropping aircraft flying in close line astern formation[4] the exercises sometimes being augmented by Hotspur gliders of No. 296 Squadron and smoke cover provided by Blenheims of Nos. 13 and 104 Squadrons. It was such an exercise that was witnessed by Mr. Churchill on 16 April 1942, the result of which was his enquiry into Airborne resources and the decision to expand the air component[5].

During May a similar demonstration was given before their Majesties the King and Queen, and on this occasion the prototype of the large tank-carrying Hamilcar glider also took part. Netheravon aerodrome was not ideal for heavy aircraft flying; however, when the squadrons had first

---

[1] D.M.C. Monthly Progress Report, March 1942.
[2] Squadron Leader McMonnies, who commanded "B" Flight, No. 297 Squadron and later in 1943 became Squadron Commander of No. 296 Squadron.
[3] At this stage the Squadron was non-operational.
[4] 100 yards interval was the aim.
[5] D.M.C.'s Monthly Progress Reports, C.S. 10786, O.R.B. No. 38 Wing.

formed it was occupied by an S.F.T.S. training Fleet Air Arm pilots on Master aircraft: the Admiralty had agreed to move this unit as soon as the existing courses had completed training, but bad weather delayed this until the end of March 1942 and in the intervening period the flying field and circuit were very congested, the variety of aircraft, Masters, Tiger Moths, Whitleys, Hectors and Hotspur gliders, adding to the confusion. Even after the S.F.T.S. had moved, the undulating surface of the aerodrome—a Whitley in one of the " valleys " was often invisible from other parts of the aerodrome—and the short take-off run in certain directions made the use of the aerodrome for night flying by heavy aircraft impossible. For night flying the Whitleys had to use Thruxton, a neighbouring airfield and satellite to Andover. By the end of May it had been decided that the Whitley Squadrons would both be dual purpose, and would carry out Horsa towing as well as troop dropping: as the prospect of Horsa deliveries grew brighter the need for a more suitable flying field than Netheravon became clear: consequently when Hurn, a new aerodrome near Bournemouth with concrete runways and full night flying facilities, became available in May 1942 both Whitley Squadrons were instructed to move there. This they did during the first week of June 1942.

Parachute exercises on an ever increasing scale, both by day and night, were carried out during the summer by the two Squadrons. Preparations for a number of operations were also made[1] but for various reasons these were all cancelled. These included the Dieppe raid for which parachutists were originally to be used only to be withdrawn at the last minute owing to the increased limitation which their use imposed on the suitable weather conditions. On one occasion, a planned raid on the Isle of Ushant, the paratroops were actually in the aircraft, the first of which was on the runway with engines running prior to taking off, when the operation was cancelled. The two Squadrons—including the light glider element of No. 296 which was still at Netheravon—were under the control of No. 38 Wing Headquarters, which had been established in a country house near Netheravon during January, and which was commanded by Group Captain Sir Nigel Norman.

No. 38 Wing during the " nucleus force " expansion

Following the high level decision of May 1942[2] to expand the Wing into a " nucleus force " Sir Nigel Norman and his staff, in conjunction with the Headquarters staff of Army Co-operation Command worked out details for the expansion. The light glider element of No. 296 became a separate unit, the Glider Pilot Exercise Unit, with effect from 12 August 1942. The transfer to Flying Training Command of all glider pilot training schools had left Army Co-operation Command without a unit at which tactical exercise could be carried out with Hotspurs as a preliminary to exercises with the larger Horsa, and the establishment of the G.P.E.U. remedied this. In addition it provided valuable air experience flights to troops of the Air Landing Brigade.

---

[1] Mention of the change of policy, subsequent to the Bruneval raid, whereby the Squadrons became operational has already been made in Chapter 3.
[2] P.M./C.A.S., May 1942.

The two other new units planned under the "nucleus force" schemes were Nos. 295 and 298 Squadrons[1]. The former, with an establishment of 24 + 6 Whitleys began to form at Netheravon on 3 August 1942 and was to be of a similar nature to Nos. 296 and 297 Squadrons (both of which now had establishments of 24 + 6 Whitleys) from which a nucleus of experienced aircrews was drawn to form the new squadron: the light glider flight of No. 296 Squadron had retained on its strength one or two Whitleys and these, and their crews, were also now transferred to No. 295 Squadron. The plan was for this Squadron to remain at Netheravon until 21 October 1942 by which date it should be at full strength: it would then move to a more suitable aerodrome to be allotted meanwhile.

The second Squadron, No. 298, was to form at Thruxton with an establishment of 16 + 4 Whitleys and 8 + 2 Halifax aircraft, the latter being allotted as tugs for the Hamilcar gliders which would in due course, be coming into use. The usual nucleus of aircrews were selected from the other squadrons and posted to No. 298 Squadron at Thruxton at the end of August 1942. When they arrived there, no aircraft were available, and almost immediately the experienced crews were detached back to their old squadrons in order to stand by for the Dieppe raid. When the airborne effort in that operation was cancelled the crews returned to Thruxton only to be reposted back to their former Squadrons within a few days: the aircraft allotment to No. 298 Squadron had been postponed: on 19 October 1942 the standstill order relating to all Airborne Forces units was issued: No. 298 Squadron, which had only ever existed on paper, was disbanded[2].

Thus the planned expansion had only become effective in part, and from 19 October 1942 two days before it should, under the original plan, have become complete not only reinforcements but replacements also ceased, and a re-organisation became necessary. No. 38 Wing now consisted of three dual purpose Squadrons, Nos. 295, 296 and 297, each with 24 + 6 Whitley aircraft: the G.P.E.U. with Hotspurs and Masters which had replaced the old Hectors as tugs: the P.T.S. at Ringway: and No. 42 O.T.U. which had been placed within the Wing at the beginning of the expansion period in order to supply the necessary aircrews and to avoid drawing upon Bomber Command sources. The three Squadrons were all engaged on parachute exercises and also upon glider towing and exercises. Hotspur tows had begun in July and during August the first Horsas had arrived at stations in the Wing and were promptly used in exercises.

During July a regular weekly glider service to Northern Ireland was instituted to carry Irish personnel of the Airborne Division proceeding to and from leave: originally towed by Whitleys of the No. 206 Light Glider Flight (the G.P.E.U.) the Hotspurs provided by the G.P.E.U. were later towed by aircraft of each of the Squadrons in turn, thus providing the aircrews with experience of long distance tows. Also the Wing had, early in October, been given a commitment to drop leaflets on enemy occupied countries, particularly France. This work, which was regarded as being of some importance by the Foreign Office, had been carried out by Bomber Command aircraft and crews who were now released for bombing operations over Germany. For No. 38 Wing the commitment had the double advantage of

---

[1] O.R.B. Nos. 295 and 298 Squadrons.
[2] No. 38 Wing O.R.B.

providing "flak inoculation" for the aircrews who had not already flown operationally and also of improving the morale of the Squadrons which was deteriorating due to lack of operational activity.

When the standstill order was issued the squadrons were employed more fully then they had ever been, the leaflet raids, the appearance of the Horsas, and the continually increasing flow of personnel from the individual training organisation who needed more advanced training, all making heavy demands upon their flying capacity. Moreover the allocation of bigger and better aerodromes, which had been promised during the expansion period, was now cancelled: and as Hurn was required for operational purposes by other Commands the two Squadrons there had to be moved. No. 42 O.T.U. was moved to Ashbourne in Derbyshire, and No. 296 Squadron went to Andover, the move taking place on 26 October 1942: two days previously No. 297 Squadron had moved to Thruxton: No. 295 Squadron were condemned to remain at Netheravon and used Thruxton for all night flying. No. 296 Squadron were hardly better off at Andover for the flying field there had no concrete runways and the field was sometimes waterlogged: there was also the now unusual snag of take-off runs which were too short for heavy glider towing. Fortunately by the middle of December accommodation for one Squadron again became available at Hurn and No. 296 Squadron returned there. On this occasion the move was carried out to a large degree by air, much of the Squadron's equipment being carried in Horsas. In fact a similar task had been undertaken by this Squadron a month previously when No. 168 Squadron had been moved by air. These "Pickford" tasks now became a normal part of the routine of the No. 38 Wing Squadrons, units of varying types, operational Squadrons, O.T.U.s, and training units, all being assisted in their moves from one aerodrome to another[1].

During April 1943 an outstanding lift of this description was undertaken when an engine was flown in a Horsa to the Isle of Man for a Bomber Command Stirling which had forced landed there during the previous night: the delivery of the replacement engine by air instead of by sea enabled the aircraft to be repaired with a saving of time amounting to days. The advantages of moving units by glider were especially applicable to operational Squadrons for essential personnel and equipment arrived at the new aerodrome at the same time as their aircraft—who, of course, flew there independently—so that the work of servicing and maintenance went on without a break. Non-essential personnel and very heavy equipment could be sent on ahead by road to prepare for the arrival of the air party: the essential personnel and stores remained at the aerodrome and were able to continue work until the last moment, and if bad weather delayed the move of the aircraft they were still available to carry out daily inspections and routine duties. Such moves were undertaken by the Wing until June 1943 after which the increasing demands of tactical glider exercises caused them to cease. Nevertheless they remained the standard method of removal for the Wing Squadrons themselves, one Station Commander (Group Captain T. M. Abraham, D.F.C.) going so far as to have the officers' mess bar so constructed that it could be dismantled and carried in a Horsa from station to station[2].

---

[1] O.R.B. No. 38 Wing and Nos. 295, 296 and 297 Squadrons.
[2] A boast that it would be "the first British bar to land in Tokyo" was not, unfortunately, to be fulfilled.

Thus during the winter of 1942-43 the three squadrons, Nos. 295, 296, and 297 were engaged on all three types of work, leaflet raids, removals by air, and airborne exercises of both parachute and glider borne troops. The last was, in theory, the primary role of the squadrons, but a combination of circumstances, the employment of the 1st Parachute Brigade outside the U.K., the standstill order, and the natural enthusiasm of the squadrons for the more active work of the leaflet raids, all tended to lessen the emphasis on the airborne role so far as the personnel at squadron level were concerned. At the higher levels this was not so, however, and already the problem of keeping the rapidly increasing number of trained glider pilots in flying practice was receiving consideration[1].

A note concerning the organisation of a typical airborne exercise is of interest here, for on such exercises was based the detailed plan for the operation against Sicily. H.Q. Airborne Division having decided the general Army plan for the exercise, a conference was called between the Division Staff and the Staff of No. 38 Wing, representatives of both the Army and R.A.F. formations taking part (e.g. Battalion and Squadron Commanders) being present. At this conference the plan would be explained in detail, a suitable dropping or landing zone[2] selected (usually on the advice of the senior R.A.F. navigation officer), the allocation of certain troops to certain squadrons made and details regarding the air routes to be followed and the timing of the drops discussed. Following the conference a detailed brief was prepared by the navigation staff of No. 38 Wing working in conjunction with the Army officers attached to that H.Q. This brief having been approved by the senior Army and R.A.F. officers concerned it was circulated to the commanders of the units taking part. In the case of the R.A.F. units this brief was next considered by the Station and/or Squadron Commanders and navigation officers who planned their units task in even greater detail.

Paratroop exercises of this nature had been going on since early in 1942 and in that twelve months much had been learnt. Each aircraft was given a specific time at which the paratroops were to be dropped, the interval between each aircraft being usually 30 seconds. In effect, so far as daylight drops were concerned, this meant that the old method of flying in close line astern formation was still used: for night drops each aircraft flew individually and by flying very exact airspeeds, by extremely exact navigation, and by continued pin pointing and wind checks, the pilot and navigator had to arrive over a *field* at a time stated in half minutes after a flight of usually two to three hours. This was, of course, the reason for the unusually careful time check which has always been a part of the standard briefing procedure for airborne aircrews. Only by constant practice could such exactness be achieved and maintained and as operations later showed, those crews who had been with the squadrons since their formation had benefited immensely from these constant exercises.

Probably the most exact drop ever carried out was made during a daylight exercise in which crews of Nos. 295 and 297 Squadrons were taking part[3]. Fifteen aircraft carrying paratroops of the 9th Parachute Battalion left Thruxton at 1000 hours on the morning of 9 August 1943 to take part in a

---
[1] O.R.B. Nos. 295, 296 and 297 Squadrons.
[2] D.Z. for paratroops: L.Z. for gliders, this usually being an aerodrome to facilitate retrieval of the gliders.
[3] No. 296 Squadron was at this time in North Africa.

demonstration drop before high ranking officers of all services: the dropping zone, some 700 by 1,500 yards in area, was in a valley roughly 15 miles south of Kinloss in Scotland, a flight of some five hours: a smoke candle was placed on the zone at the point on which the first paratroop should land, and an officer of the Airborne Division was on the ground to give a running commentary over loudspeakers explaining to the audience what was happening: the drop was timed for 1500 hours. At ten seconds past that time the first paratroop, Brigadier Hill, left the leading aircraft, the navigator of which was F/Sgt. L. Miller of No. 297 Squadron. To the amazement of the crowd, the delight of the commentator, and the surprise of the Brigadier himself, he landed right on the smoke candle. Such exactness is, of course, to a great extent a matter of luck. Nevertheless it was becoming unusual for troops to be dropped either outside the dropping zone or at the wrong time[1].

The glider exercises provided rather different problems although the emphasis was still on the now time honoured formula " Correct place: correct time: correct height ". During the actual flight to the objective the same technique was used, the line astern formation being general although formation of " Vics " were occasionally flown. But the slipstream difficulty was increased when towing gliders, especially as the Whitleys could rarely fly at more than 105-110 m.p.h. when tugging a laden Horsa: the unfortunate aircraft at the end of the line had a constant battle with the eddies and air pockets caused by the earlier members of the formation. To overcome this " stepping-up " was usually adopted, a remedy which entailed a difference in height of perhaps as much as 500 feet between the first aircraft and the last.

Paratroops were dropped from 450-800 feet, gliders released (usually) from 1,000-2,500 feet, so that the difference of 500 feet was proportionately considerable. For paratroop dropping it was essential that the pilot lost this extra height before dropping, and with a solo aircraft this was possible; it was more difficult when towing a Horsa to lose the height without increasing air speed and so breaking formation: of necessity therefore the remedy was often the responsibility of the glider pilot who, by judging his release carefully, could adjust his position in relation to the landing zone and land on the correct spot in spite of the extra height. The question of deciding the exact spot at which to release was, of course, a delicate one, and eventually it was found best to select a definite release point before take-off, basing the calculation on the forecasted wind speed and direction for the area at the time of release. A little before casting off the navigator of the tug aircraft informed the glider pilot of the wind speed and direction which he calculated was actually effective at that moment: thus, firstly by slight adjustment of position by the tug, and later, after release, by adjusting the rate of descent of the glider, the two pilots could so position their aircraft and enable the glider to land in the correct area.

The greatest difficulty relating to large scale glider exercises was found to be the take-off. By the time the tug aircraft had taxied onto the runway[2], the glider towed on by a tractor, and the tow rope been connected at both

---
[1] O.R.B. Nos. 295 and 297 Squadrons. War Office Narrative " Airborne Forces ," Chapter IX.
[2] This difficulty is, of course, less acute when a grass aerodrome with a wide and long take-off run is being used.

ends, valuable minutes were lost which, if the exercise or operation was large and involved perhaps 30 or 40 combinations, amounted to quite a considerable period. Many devices were tried in order to reduce this time lag, which meant that the first aircraft off had to fly a time wasting run to allow the remainder to take-off and to assume formation.

Where possible all the gliders were marshalled onto the runway before take-off and were staggered, two abreast, the tugs being fed onto the runway from alternate sides[1]. By this method the even numbers took off on one side of the runway and the odd numbers from the other, which involved the additional advantage of easing the take-off difficulties caused by the slipstream of the former aircraft: but it also had the disadvantage of causing complications if either tug, glider or tow ropes became unserviceable at the last moment, for the very detailed planning and timing and briefing, required that a specific glider be towed by a specific tug. It also had the far greater disadvantage of shortening the available take-off run of the first aircraft by sometimes as much as 300 yards: and that run was already shortened by the length of the tow rope. Even so this became the standard method, especially when the more powerful aircraft, such as the Stirling, became available and when better aerodromes with longer runways were used. It was, of course, impossible on aerodromes where the grass surface was too soft to permit even the taxying of aircraft. In such cases the tugs and gliders had to be marshalled on the perimeter track on either side of the runway and fed in as their turn came for take-off: under these circumstances unserviceable tugs or gliders had usually to be cleared off the perimeter track on to the grass even at the expense of the surface and getting the aircraft bogged[2].

The final great difficulty regarding mass glider take-off was the wind direction. Most aerodromes had three concrete runways giving six available take-off directions: of these only one runway or two directions was usually of such a length to permit laden gliders to be taken off with ease, and in many cases the pilots preferred to use this long runway even despite a cross wind provided it was not more than 12-15 m.p.h. But if the wind strength was high this was a dangerous business and with a tug glider combination a take-off dead into wind was even more desirable than with a solo aircraft. The complicated system of marshalling needed for both tugs and gliders demanded that the decision regarding take-off direction be taken as early as possible, and a change of wind direction entailing complete re-marshalling could play havoc with the planned timing of take-off. These were some of the problems of technique which the exercises carried out by the three squadrons during 1942 and 1943 were solving. Only by experience and practice could the best methods of planning and executing an operation with either paratroops, gliders or both be established, and this was one of the main objects of the exercises.

Owing to the comparative ease with which a paratroop drop could be arranged it was not difficult to keep the parachutists at a reasonably high standard of proficiency. The problems of glider exercises, and the rapidity with which glider pilots were being trained in the closing months of 1942 and early 1943, however, made the need for glider exercises more urgent.

---

[1] See Appendix 3.
[2] No. 38 Group Report, Section III, Appendix A, 38 G/S.10/46/Air.

As early as 21 October 1942 Major General Browning had foreseen that the future difficulty would be, not to train glider pilots, but to keep them in flying practice after they had completed training. By the end of February 1943 this problem had become acute and on 1 March the Director of Air at the War Office wrote to the Air Ministry pointing out that[1] "It is estimated that there are some 550 glider pilots now with the Airborne Division who require extensive exercising if they are to be ready for operations as envisaged[2]. In the opinion of the G.O.C., Airborne Division these pilots will require a further 100 hours flying practice before they are fit for operations". From this time onwards the problem overshadowed all others.

On 29 March 1943 the Air Ministry cancelled the standstill order relating to Airborne Forces and instructed that aircraft and personnel be allocated to the units affected in order to bring them up to establishment[3]. But even so the task of exercising the glider pilots now available was not being fulfilled. No. 296 Squadron, which had begun to re-equip with Albemarle aircraft in February had been selected as the R.A.F. formation to carry out the airborne attack on Sicily and during March and April was preparing for this operation, with consequent loss of flying time on exercises. Moreover, in order to provide the most experienced crews of the Wing for the coming operation No. 297 Squadron had been stripped of the majority of its experienced crews who were posted to No. 296, leaving only a nucleus of experienced men to train the replacement crews.

In view of the urgency of glider pilot exercising, D.T.O. at Air Ministry suggested on 19 April 1943 that the No. 38 Wing Squadrons should stop all such diversionary effort as leaflet dropping and concentrate entirely on their primary role of training the Airborne Force. This proposal met with strenuous opposition, from the Squadrons, with whom the task was very popular being their only operational effort: from the Wing, who considered the operational experience of value to the crews; and from the A.C.A.S. (A) who pointed out that the Foreign Office attached great importance to these operations which had previously caused some diversion of the bombing effort. But the fact remained that the exercising of the Airborne Force was the primary role of the squadrons and on 13 May 1943 an instruction was issued by the Director of Military Co-operation at Air Ministry stating that "in view of the loan of No. 296 Squadron and one flight of No. 295 Squadron to North Africa every endeavour must be made to produce the maximum training effort available from the remainder of the Wing. In order to devote maximum flying hours to training it has been decided that Nickel Operations and minor bombing raids by No. 38 Wing shall be suspended until further notice "[4].

---

[1] A.M. File C.S. 7424, Pt. II, Encl. 257A.
[2] This paper on the planned invasion of Sicily included mention of the use of Airborne Forces.
[3] A.M. File C.S. 7424, Pt. III, Encl. 69B. L.M. 854/D. of O. dated 29 March 1943.
[4] The " flight of No. 295 Squadron on loan to North Africa " was a special flight of Halifax aircraft which began to form in February 1943 for the express purpose of towing the Horsa gliders needed for Husky to Africa, the Halifax being the only aircraft capable of such a task. The work and organisation of No. 295 Squadron proper was not affected by the attachment of this flight. " Minor bombing raids " refers to two small operations undertaken during February in which two French transformer stations were attacked, the pin point nature of both targets causing them to be considered good practice for the No. 38 Wing crews. A.M. File C.S. 7424, Pt. III, Encls. 83A, 84A, 87B and 103A.

Thus at the end of May 1943, when No. 296 Squadron moved to their advanced base in North Africa the two remaining Squadrons began a heavy programme of exercises. In No. 297 Squadron, particularly, to this was added the task of training the aircrews from No. 42 O.T.U., who had replaced the crews withdrawn to form "C" flight of No. 295 Squadron. The number of glider towing hours needed prohibited them from being flown during exercises and many of them had to be obtained by cross country flights made by individual combinations.

Parachute Training. Middle East 1942-43[1]

The origin of parachuting in the Middle East can be traced to the formation of an airborne detachment (L) of the Special Air Service Regiment on 28 August 1941, but owing to the scarcity of qualified instructors and equipment it was not until 3 May 1942 that an official parachute training school was opened. No. 4 Middle East Training School came into being at Kabrit, Palestine with only the barest skeleton of an establishment. At first Bombay aircraft were used with early type statichutes and containers and the ground equipment was rather primitive, being locally improvised[2]. Training continued spasmodically throughout the summer except for an interval during August when the units were so far below strength that work was not possible. In fact the unit was merged with No. 2 M.E.T.S. for ferry purposes and it was not until September 1942, that the training establishment became really organised. However, in August one parachute operation did take place and as it was the first of its kind in the Middle East it is worthy of mention.

On the night of 16-17 August 1942, immediately prior to General Auchinleck's summer offensive on 18 August an operation was carried out with the intention of destroying aircraft on the ground and harassing communications in the area of the aerodromes at Gazala and Timini. This operation was not successful owing to heavy rain and high wind (30-35 m.p.h. ground). Thirty-two of the 52 men operating were lost and although an unconfirmed report claimed that 19 aircraft were destroyed at Timini the result was not encouraging.

When training re-commenced in September 1942, there were only three Wellington aircraft and one of those was not modified for parachuting but, due to the strenuous endeavours of the tiny staff, courses began to pass through. The majority of the pupils came from S.A.S., M.O.4 and I.S.L.D., and in the period January—August 1942 about 100 men had been trained. By the end of November when 156 Battalion of the 4th Parachute Brigade came from India for training the unit had five aircraft—two Hudsons having arrived and been modified for door-dropping. Trouble was experienced with Hudson serviceability due probably to the removal of the bomb-doors which resulted in more power being required from the engines than usual.

Kabrit was not a suitable site for No. 4 M.E.T.S., for a variety of reasons which became apparent as the volume of training and exercises increased. Aerodrome facilities were inadequate—a bomber squadron was stationed there in addition to No. 4 M.E.T.S.; the D.Z. at Kabrit was too hard for initial training; the weather conditions—wind—sandstorms and periodical great heat—were unfavourable; and the terrain was not of the type required

---
[1] File Ramat David, R.D./S.54/8/Air T.R.G.
[2] For example, jumping backwards off a three-ton lorry.

by No. 4 Parachute Brigade to train them for European operations. On 13 March 1943, No. 4 M.E.T.S., moved from Kabrit to Ramat David in Northern Palestine and from thence onwards conditions were easier once the problems of settling in had been overcome. Serviceability improved; there was an adequate staff of pilots and instructors and much extra training equipment had been provided. There were two Wellingtons and six Hudsons available. The main difficulty was a shortage of parachutes both for initial training and exercises which caused the packers considerable work, but despite the increased pressure upon them no accidents occurred due to faulty packing.

During March No. 7 Troop Carrier Squadron, U.S.A.A.F. arrived at the unit to carry out exercises in conjunction with No. 4 Parachute Brigade and stayed until the end of May, 1943. Serviceability was good and exercises involving often 11 out of a total of 13 aircraft were arranged. The courses were extended to 14-15 days and pupils made eight jumps (two at night) as well as container jumps. They received a very thorough training in all phases of their work. During the ten months September 1942-June 1943 nearly 17,000 jumps were made and considerably less than 1 per cent. sustained any injury. During the summer of 1943, exercises continued and occasionally were of a large scale bearing in mind the limited number of aircraft. On 23 July Exercise Jerbon II was carried out involving the use of 35 aircraft and 483 troops of 10th British Parachute Regiment were dropped by night, successfully. This was the first time a Company had ever dropped as such by night[1].

Iraq Levies

It is of interest that in 1942 Air Marshal H. V. C. de Crespigny called for volunteers from the R.A.F. Iraq Levies to form a parachute company. In order that the right type be attracted no special privileges as regards pay or promotion were offered. Although there were only 150 vacancies nearly 1,000 men volunteered. Of those selected 80 per cent. were Assyrian and 20 per cent. Kurds. The company was commanded by a British Army Officer (from No. 156 Parachute Battalion Middle East) and trained mostly by British N.C.O.s several of whom had been at Ringway. The only aircraft available for this training were four Valencias. During the whole period there was only one fatal casualty and no refusals to jump. When the German threat to Iraq lessened the company was offered to the Middle East and attached to No. 11 Parachute Battalion of the 4th Parachute Brigade. In August 1943 they operated successfully near Corfu on the Adriatic coast. One British officer and 14 Iraquis were killed.

The Operation in Sicily. Husky

In January 1943 President Roosevelt, Mr. Churchill and the Chiefs of Staff met at the Casablanca Conference to determine the strategy for 1943. The most urgent problem before the Conference was to decide on the step following the successful conclusion of the North African Campaign. Something had to be done to relieve the strain on Russia and the issue eventually lay between invading Sicily or Sardinia[2].

---

[1] File Ramat David, R.D./S.54/2/Air T.R.G.
[2] A.M. File C. 32153/46, C.O.S. (43) 81 (O).

Finally, on 19 January it was decided to undertake the conquest of Sicily with the object of:—

  (a) Securing lines of communication in the Mediterranean;

  (b) Diverting as much German strength from the Russian front as possible; and

  (c) Increasing the pressure on Italy.

It was considered that the employment of adequate airborne forces would contribute to the success of the operation. The date suggested for the landing of this operation was the favourable moon period of July 1943—acting on the assumption that North Africa would be cleared by 30 April. But the exact date of invasion was not settled until 13 April. Prior to this the Joint Planning Staff of the War Cabinet had prepared an outline plan for the conquest of Sicily and had given August as the earliest date. The reason for this was that they did not consider it likely that the necessary trained British forces would be available before the end of July.

The overall plan for the invasion of Sicily consisted of two main attacks by both British and American forces.

  (i) The British were to assault in the S.E. corner of the island with three divisions to secure airfields and the ports of Syracuse and Augusta.

  (ii) One British division would be launched against Catania on D+3 to capture the port and neighbouring airfields.

  (iii) On D Day strong U.S. forces were to land at three points on the south coast to capture airfields.

As for the airborne forces, this original plan provided for the use of five airborne brigades—three British and two American. Their tasks were as follows:—

  (i) On the night of D−1/D two parachute battalions were to land, one on the North and one on the South of the toe of Italy, to block road and rail communications.

  (ii) On D Day one parachute brigade (less one battalion) was to be dropped to assist in the capture of the airfield at Comiso. Another similar brigade was to do likewise at Ponte Olive.

  (iii) On D+3 three brigades were to be landed in the area of Gerbini to assist in the capture of airfields.

Detailed planning was not easy because of the wide distribution of the various Headquarters in the Mediterranean area. However intelligence officers were attached to the following headquarters, Allied Force and Force 141 at Algiers—8th Army at Cairo—5th American Army at Oran and XIII Corps who would be in command of the 1st Airborne Division. High level planning was then started in March, 1943[1].

In the same month Air Commodore Sir Nigel Norman visited North Africa with Brigadier General Hopkinson, Commanding the Airlanding Brigade, to investigate and discuss the part that the Airborne Division could play in the

---

[1] G.P. File (43) 7. 141F/R.A.F./252/Air (P). 141F/R.A.F./236/5/Air (P).

operation[1]. They found that there was a definite requirement for airborne troops, but realised at once that the operation was more complicated and ambitious than anything hitherto undertaken. It involved a 350 mile flight across the sea in a semi-tropical climate using aircraft and gliders different from those in which the men had trained. It was also evident that there would not be sufficient time to train thoroughly all units. There were doubts as to the ability of the American aircrews to reach the necessarily high standard of night flying and navigation in time for the operation.

Also in March Major General Browning handed over command of the Airborne Division to Brigadier Hopkinson and became Airborne Adviser to Generals Eisenhower and Alexander. (He was in charge of all inter-service co-ordination) and began the preliminary overall planning for all the airborne operations as well as preparing for the arrival of the Airborne Division in North Africa. At first it was decided to abandon the original plan and carry out a divisional assault on the coast defences but owing to the shortage of available aircraft this was not practicable. On 10 May 1943 the plans which were eventually carried out were formulated and provided for three successive brigade assaults against objectives ahead of the advance of XIII Corps.

The objectives allotted to the 1st Airborne Division were the Ponte Grande bridge South of Syracuse and the Western outskirts of the town; the bridge and high ground West of Augusta and the Ponte di Primasole bridge over the river Simeto. In addition to these British operations the 82nd American Airborne Division under the command of U.S. 7th Army would also carry out attacks on D night and D+1 night, to cover the landings of the American 5th Army in S.W. Sicily. Any aircraft remaining would be used to replace casualties in the 1st Airborne Division[2].

It was not until mid-June that it was decided to use gliders in the first operation near Syracuse; by then it was known that sufficient gliders and pilots would be available and also that there were adequate landing places near the target area. It was recommended that the number of airborne troops to be lifted be restricted to 500 aircraft. Airlanding troops were considered more suitable than parachute troops because more armour could be carried which increased their fighting potential so No. 1 Airlanding Brigade was allocated to the operation near Syracuse. No. 2 Parachute Brigade was allotted to the Augusta operation and No. 1 Parachute Brigade to the Primasole bridge. No. 4 Parachute Brigade was retained in reserve[3].

One of the primary considerations in planning this operation was the routeing of aircraft to avoid flying over friendly shipping near the beaches, even if it considerably lengthened the distances to be flown. Either this had to be done or A.A. fire restricted completely when the aircraft were due to pass over the shipping[4].

The allotment of aircraft and gliders was decided by Fifteenth Army Group and Mediterranean Air Command. The allocation of Wings to Divisions and the details of control and training were carried out by Troop Carrier Command

---

[1] 1st Airborne Division Report.
[2] Report by Major-General, Airborne Forces. OO/216/Appendix D.
[3] C.O.S. (43) 81 (O).
[4] T.A.F. File 53/1/Air.

under the direction of the North West African Air Force. The responsibility of launching all airborne operations was that of the Air Commander-in-Chief or the Senior Air Officer at the Air H.Q. controlling the operations concerned.

The Waco gliders which provided most of the lift for the airlanding troops were sent direct to North Africa by sea but the Waco could not carry all the loads required by 1st A.B. Division so the problem of moving the Horsa gliders arose. They could not be shipped by sea so after long distance trails had been carried out in England, the Air Ministry, who at first refused to sanction the attempt, finally allowed No. 38 Wing to tow them to North Africa—a difficult and hazardous undertaking the ultimate success of which was a tribute to the skill and courage of the crews[1].

Operation Beggar[2]

On 23 April 1943 No. 295 Halifax Squadron were ordered to ferry 36 Horsas to Sale in French Morocco by the end of June[3]. The difficulties involved in this flight of 1,400 miles were considerable—the Halifaxes were not fully modified and training was held up while waiting for these to be carried out—also there was a shortage of crews; either they were qualified on Halifaxes and had not experience of airborne work or vice versa, and trained navigators had to be obtained from Coastal Command.

Over a period of about six weeks 30 Horsas left the advanced base at Portreath and by 7 July 1943, 27 had reached North Africa. Of these only 19 had arrived at Kairouan; three landed in the sea, three force landed in inaccessible parts of North Africa and four crashed near Sale. The tow was by no means easy—the Halifaxes were at full load and none of the petrol was jettisonable making any forced landing extremely dangerous. Gliders had not previously been towed at this full load. For this trip the undercarriage was jettisoned and a spare one carried. The recommended speed which was 130-135 m.p.h. did not allow much margin of error above stalling speed. Much time was wasted in waiting for favourable weather as the combinations had to avoid cloud; for this reason too the flight was carried out by daylight. Despite these precautions several pilots had to fly through cloud which caused one glider to ditch in the Bay of Biscay due to a broken tow rope. The pilot was picked up by a destroyer.

The later stages of the journey from Sale to Froha and thence to Kairouan, totalling almost another 1,000 miles, had their difficulties too. Low cloud often delayed the take-off from Sale and between Froha and Kairouan mountains up to 7,000 ft. made conditions extremely bumpy and tiring for the pilots. The first glider reached Kairouan on 28 June 1943. Several conclusions were drawn from this operation:—

(a) On all long distance ferry tows glider to jettison undercarriage.

(b) If blind flying instruments were used in gliders, trips could be done by night thus safer from enemy action.

(c) Ferrying gliders over long distances was practical but not simple or quick. Considerable ground organisation and adequate inspection facilities were required at each stage.

---

[1] O.R.B. No. 38 Wing. War Office Narrative "Airborne Forces", Chapter IX.
[2] No. 38 Group Report, Appendix E, Section III.
[3] O.R.B. No. 295 Squadron.

The 1st Airborne Division arrived in North Africa in two main convoys —2nd Parachute Brigade on 26 April 1943, and 1st Airlanding Brigade on 26 May, and began intensive training, also collecting from the various ports equipment which had been sent from the United Kingdom. Much of this training was done at Mascara and an operational base was set up at Kairouan near Sousse in Tunis and gradually the division established itself there. The move, a distance of over 600 miles, started on 19 June 1943, and ended on 5 July. The Airlanding Brigade, some 1,200 men, were transported in 84 Waco gliders followed by more Wacos and by 8 July there were 140 Wacos and 19 Horsas at Kairouan. Throughout this period training continued. There were six airfields at Kairouan each merely having one runway strip and these were shared by 51st Wing U.S. Army Air Force and No. 38 Wing detachment.

The Glider Pilot Regiment was out of training and the majority of these pilots had to be converted to the American Hadrian (Waco C.G.-4A) glider. The main difficulty in this conversion concerned the tug aircraft. When being towed by an Albemarle it was difficult to keep the speed down to 150 m.p.h. Only three weeks were available for night training—scarcely long enough—but 1,800 night lifts were made without serious casualty[1].

Parachutes and their containers presented a problem at this juncture. No. 1 Mobile Parachute Servicing Unit was attached to each Brigade and subsequently events justified this to be a correct allocation. In one period of six weeks prior to 18 June some 12,700 parachutes were used and repacked. One M.P.S.U. could pack a maximum of 250 parachutes per day. The parachute containers were held by units of the 1st Airborne Division on a scale sufficient for one drop and a large reserve was held by various Army units. The R.E.M.E. were responsible for modifications and maintenance, i.e., painting containers white for night recognition, modifying new lighting sets and other small jobs which involved considerable work.

Operation Ladbrooke

The first operation Ladbroke, against Syracuse on the night of D-1/D, 9-10 July, was undertaken by No. 1 Airlanding Brigade, which comprised two battalions, anti-tank guns, Royal Engineers and medical. It was a gliderborne operation and the Brigade had at its disposal a total of 109 Dakota aircraft from Troop Carrier Command with 28 Albermarle and seven Halifax aircraft from Nos. 296 and 297 Squadrons of No. 38 Wing. This provided tugs for 144 gliders, though eventually the number was reduced to 137 (127 Wacos and 10 Horsas). The normal Waco payload was 3,700 lb. —mostly consisting of 14 men and one handcart, whereas the Horsa, which was towed either by a Halifax or an Albemarle, carried 32 men, a payload of 6,900 lb.[2]

In the early evening of 9 July 137 aircraft, each towing its glider, took off from the six aerodromes at Kairouan. For various mechanical reasons six Waco gliders did not carry out their tasks and cast off or crashed between

---

[1] 1st A.B. Division Report. Glider Pilot Regiment.
[2] Joint memo. by General and Air Staffs, September 1943. 38G/M.S.66/1/Air. File A.O.C./264/10/7/15/8.

the aerodrome and the coast. The timing of the take-off had to be carefully calculated owing to the varying distances and different speeds of the aircraft. They flew individually and not in formation. The route lay via the S.E. corner of Malta to Cap Passero on the S.E. corner of Sicily thence along the E. coast to the landing zone, keeping 3,000 yards out to sea to avoid A.A. fire[1].

Although the pilots had been correctly briefed as to the wind-strength, which had increased during the afternoon to about 30 m.p.h., their navigational experience was limited and they were unused to handling gliders in high winds. Several factors contributed to the inaccuracy of this drop. First it was necessary to judge distance from the shore by moonlight; even experienced pilots tended to underestimate the distance. Secondly, map reading was difficult owing to the run-in being made down moon especially in view of the low altitude of the flight. Thirdly, the low altitude allowed little or no margin to correct any errors in release or to allow for increased wind speed which in fact was the case. Thus it was that there were serious miscalculations in judging the times of release, so much so that 69 gliders landed in the sea and 56 were scattered along the S.E. coast of Sicily. Only 12 reached the correct landing zone, including one Horsa which landed 300 yards from the bridge[2].

The probable cause of so many gliders landing in the sea was the fact that the Americans were unaccustomed to flak, that the C.47 aircraft were not armoured and had no self-sealing tanks and that their navigation was not up to the standard required. Major General Browning commenting on Group Captain Cooper's report which referred to American inexperience of flak conditions stated that No. 38 Wing had aircraft armed and designed to face it. This was not entirely so as the two aircraft used by No. 38 Wing, the Albemarle and Halifax, were not armoured against flak but only against lateral fire. The majority of the gliders that landed on the shore were damaged, with casualties to equipment, but in view of the extremely rough ground this could scarcely be avoided[3]. Despite the fact that only eight officers and 65 O.R.s reached the canal bridge that night, they managed to hold it until 15.30 on 10 July although they were surrounded and driven away from the bridge. However the enemy had not time to destroy it and the situation was relieved by patrols of an infantry brigade who drove them North of the bridge.

The remainder of the force took what offensive action they could in the various places where they landed and succeeded in causing considerable trouble to the Italians. The coastal defence battery which was one of the brigade's objectives was captured after daylight by seven officers and about 10 men; they inflicted 12 casualties on the Italians and took 40 prisoners. Another small party of six, survivors of a glider that landed in the sea, managed to rejoin their battalion but not before they had captured two pill boxes, 21 prisoners and some guns; in fact the confusion caused to the Italians by these scattered parties all of whom accomplished what they could where they could, was sufficient to cause the Italians to think that a much larger force had landed, which naturally assisted the main operation[4].

---

[1] C. 32153/46.
[2] Report by Major-General, Airborne Forces. 00/216/Appendix D. War Office Narrative, Chapter IX. C.O.S. (43) 552 (a).
[3] Report of A.B. Forces Adviser. No. 38 Group Report, Appendix E, paragraph 49.
[4] 1st Airborne Division Report. Husky.

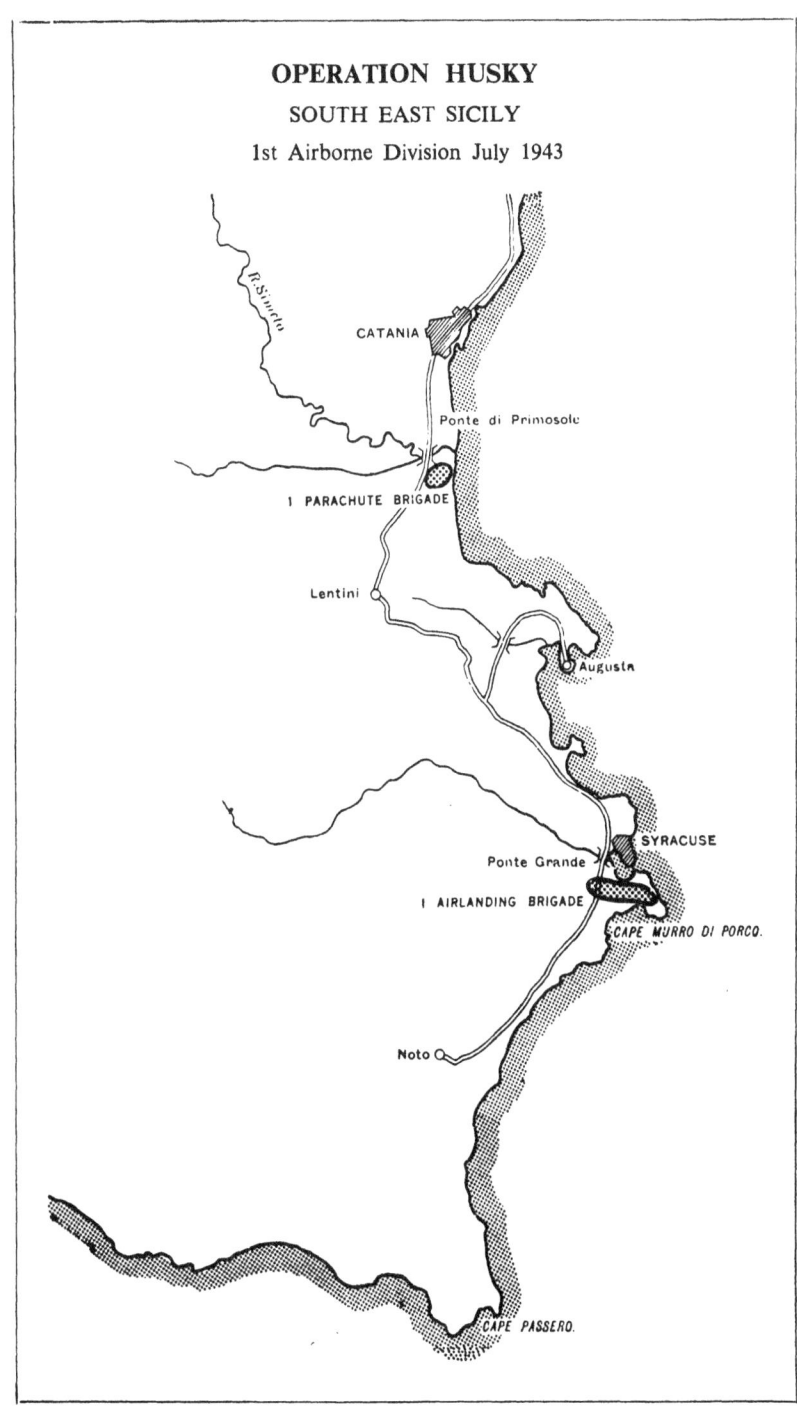

Fig. 1

The cost in gliders and men was considerable although none of the 134 tugs was lost. It was indeed fortunate however that sterner opposition was not encountered. Altogether the operation could be said to have been partially successful if not entirely satisfactory. The American force of 226 C.47s which dropped parachutists of the 82nd Airborne Division were also fortunate only eight failing to return. Bad navigation was responsible for inaccurate dropping but the objectives, high ground and road junctions East of Hela, were captured. There is little doubt that both these airborne operations although they were not carried out according to plan, did very materially assist the landing and advance of the seaborne troops. The Commanders of the Seventh and Eighth Armies both paid high tribute to the effect of the airborne operations on their advances and stated that they were considerably accelerated as the result of them.

On the following night, 10-11 July, an operation against the bridge and high ground West of Augusta was scheduled to be carried out by the 2nd Parachute Brigade. However the speed of advance in Sicily by the 5th Division rendered the operation unnecessary and it was cancelled. Meanwhile the Americans had a disastrous experience. The U.S. IX Troop Carrier Command who had dropped the first lift of the 504th Regimental Combat Team on the night of 9-10 to capture high ground and road junctions six miles East of Gela operated again on the following night. Twenty-three aircraft were lost out of 144, and many others were damaged. This was mainly due to the route being taken too near the coast—the aircraft were subjected to heavy A.A. fire from enemy and friendly sources both from land and sea. This caused much concern to Admiral Cunningham and General Alexander and resulted in strong action being taken to improve Naval fire control and discipline. Although control of Naval gunfire might not always be feasible clearly defined time limits during which fire was totally prohibited should be laid down. Either that or route the convoy away from the Navy[1]. It is interesting to note that on the day previous to this operation Air Chief Marshal Tedder strongly advised its cancellation and stated that he considered it to be " serious misuse ". He was of the opinion that the tasks could have been carried out by ordinary troops[2].

The Chestnut Operations

Minor S.A.S. operations were carried out on night of 12-13 July when two Albemarles of No. 38 Wing dropped two detachments of twelve men each at Randazzo and Enna to harass and disrupt enemy communications in Northern Sicily.

On the following night two Albemarles were to drop 36 re-inforcements but the ground signals were not visible and the aircraft returned to base. Supplies were however successfully dropped on the next night by two Albemarles. One aircraft was lost on the first night[3].

The last of the airborne operations (in the Mediterranean area) Fustian took place on the night of the 13-14 July and the objective was a most important bridge over the River Simeto. This bridge was the only crossing over the obstacle which controlled the exits from the high ground into the

---

[1] R.D./S.54/4/Air/T.R.G. C.A.S. File J.S. 2026, Encl. 31A.
[2] A.C.M. Personal File, 1943.
[3] Report on Husky. R.D.M./29. S.C.O.R.B.4. A.H.B.II. J.S./81. 141F/8013/SF. 29 June 1943. II J.S./86/154.

Catania plain. It was vital that it be kept intact until XIII Corps could reach it. For this task parachute troops and gliders were used and the force, which numbered in all some 1,900 men, consisted of 1st Parachute Brigade (less half a battalion), Gliderborne Anti-Tank Guns, Royal Engineers and one Parachute Field Ambulance. One hundred and seven aircraft, Albemarles and Dakotas did the parachute dropping and the 17 gliders, 11 Horsas and 6 Wacos were towed by Halifaxes and Albemarles[1].

The route via Malta was carefully arranged so that it should not pass too near Sicily—at least five miles off shore was the nearest—and the Navy had been fully warned of the times that friendly aircraft might be expected. A.A. fire was expected to be heavier than previously but was not wholly responsible for fifty-five pilots reporting that they had been fired on, whilst ten miles out to sea. It was fairly obvious that they were much closer to the coast than they realised. It is probable also that an enemy raid on shipping about this time made the Naval gunners more trigger-conscious than they would have been and caused them to fire at all aircraft not immediately identifiable as friendly. Despite further opposition from the ground in the vicinity of the target area 56 aircraft managed to do their dropping in the vicinity of the D.Z.s.

Twenty-seven aircraft failed to drop owing to being lost and 19 returned to base without dropping because of the intensity of the flak which according to observers, was not more than was generally anticipated. This was undoubtedly due to the fact that the Americans had not had the same opportunities of becoming accustomed to flak as the No. 38 Wing pilots. They were mostly transport pilots and could therefore in some measure be excused for their aversion to flying through it. In addition American navigational training emphasised Dead Reckoning and Celestial navigation rather than map reading and usually there was only one navigator per three aircraft. Also the American transport pilots were mostly used to flying on radio beams and beacons. Had operationally experienced pilots been used there is little doubt that the results would have been far better[2].

The remaining 24 aircraft dropped their troops more than half-a-mile from the dropping zones. Ten aircraft were lost. The gliders had a higher proportion of success, 13 landing in the correct area, although one crashed. Of the other four, three were damaged during take-off, one landed in the sea, two were missing. One of the tug aircraft was lost. About 200 parachute troops and five anti-tank guns soon captured the bridge and removed explosive charges from it. Although the ground operations could not proceed as planned owing to the inaccurate dropping the bridge was saved. Enemy counter-attacks by German parachute troops necessitated a withdrawal to the southern bank of the river but they failed to reach the bridge. Early on the morning of 15 July XIII Corps arrived and the object of the operation had been achieved, so much so that both Army Commanders, U.S. Seventh and British Eighth, said that their advances had been greatly accelerated.

It could not be said that the operation was successful from the airborne aspect alone. As on the previous nights there was far too much inaccurate

---

[1] R.A.F./Med.ME. File J.S. 2026, Encls. 22A and 23A. 00/216/Appendix D.
[2] Report by Major-General, Airborne Forces. 00/216/Appendix D.

dropping and far too many unnecessary casualties to men and aircraft. However, valuable lessons were learned in time for the preparations for subsequent and larger scale operations in Europe. Apart from a few small demonstration drops there were no further airborne operations by the British in the Mediterranean area.

The 1st Airborne Division was re-concentrated by 20 July, though there was some delay in obtaining reinforcements from England, and held back in North Africa pending possible future airborne operations; whereas the 82nd American A.B. Division stayed in Sicily and carried out ordinary ground divisional duties. Thus they were ready and available for parachute operations at Anzio[1].

Although this narrative is concerned with airborne operations it is worthy of note that the 1st Airborne Division, acting in their ground capacity captured Taranto on 9 September 1943 and moved on to Foggia where they were halted while other divisions continued the advance. On 1 October 1943 the division was notified of its pending return to England and in November sailed, less 1st Airlanding Light Regiment which rejoined the division three months later. Meanwhile the Halifaxes of No. 295 Squadron had already returned to England for Horsa ferrying but No. 296 Squadron remained in North Africa and Sicily for a further three months and was used for training 51st T.C. Wing[2].

Operation Elaborate

Between 15 August and 7 October 1943 reinforcements were being ferried to North Africa. The requirements were 20 Albemarles, 10 Halifaxes and crews and 25 Horsas. The Halifax-Horsa combinations took off from Portreath for Sale and of 23 gliders which left England 15 reached North Africa; three landed in Portugal, five in the sea due to bad weather and enemy action. Only two of the eight Halifax tugs finished in North Africa; three forced landed in Portugal and one in the sea. The Albemarles of No. 297 Squadron were more successful and 19 arrived safely in North Africa only one being lost en route due to enemy action. The squadron returned to U.K. in October 1943[3].

On 16 July the Chiefs of Staff decided unanimously to cancel all future parachute operations. Their use North of Catania had been discussed but General Alexander agreed that commandos would carry out the task more efficiently[4]. The publication on 28 July 1943 of Group Captain Cooper's[5] report on the operations and the events prior to them, caused a sharp difference of opinion on several points between the Airborne Forces and the R.A.F.

---

[1] 1st Airborne Division Report.
[2] O.Ops/1/509.
[3] O.R.B.s Nos. 295, 296 and 297 Squadrons.
[4] A.R.F./MED.M.E./File J.S. 2026, Encl. 40A.
[5] Group Captain Cooper had succeeded Sir Nigel Norman as Airborne Forces Adviser in North Africa.

The conclusion to be drawn from the controversy was that insufficient liaison existed between the services concerned and that the co-operative spirit which so characterised later operations was to a certain extent lacking[1].

When Air Commodore Norman returned to England from North Africa in May 1943 he had stated that there would be no large-scale glider operations, but Group Captain Cooper after arriving in Algiers on 23 May, found that the first operation was planned to be entirely a glider one. His opinion and that of other experts was that a night glider operation was unsound even for highly trained crews; the crews were not, nor was there time for them to become, highly trained. Two experienced pilots, Squadron Leader Musgrave and Colonel Chatterton had successfully experimented with remote release by moonlight and without a flare path, but they were experts and proficient to a degree not to be expected from the main body. Squadron Leader Musgrave's opinion was that, although the landing zone chosen for the first operation South of Syracuse was satisfactory, there would be considerable difficulty in finding the other two even for experienced No. 38 Wing pilots[2].

Group Captain Cooper presented his reasons in writing for preferring paratroop operation to G.O.C.1 Airborne Division staff on 29 May, but despite this the glider plan was put into operation. The Group Captain also pressed for the use of Barton flares to assist tugs in locating dropping zones, but the Army considered that they would cause confusion on the ground if other fires were burning. The R.A.F. did not consider this to be likely as the flares had been especially constructed to overcome such a contingency. Nevertheless, they were never tried out in North Africa.

In Group Captain Cooper's eventual report on the Husky operations, he suggested that they would have been more successful had the following conditions been observed:—

(i) Glider release should have been made overland and into the moon.

(ii) A rendezvous should have been selected some 10 miles from the release point and the run-in from there done by map reading, or

(iii) Flares, ground aids, etc., put out by the Independent parachute company to assist tugs in finding D.Z.

(iv) The briefing was too hurried. Some crews had to be double briefed. Several days must be allowed for briefing and adequate models, films and other aids provided.

(v) Each individual aircraft should do its own navigation[3].

An examination of results achieved in the two operations in which No. 38 Wing participated showed that they had achieved very creditable results. Out of 134 aircraft taking part in the first operation only 32 belonged to No. 38 Wing and 26 of these released their gliders over the correct zone. In the second operation No. 38 Wing towed all 17 of the gliders and, apart from those shot down, released the rest over the zone.

---

[1] Report by Major-General Browning to Director of Air, 8 August 1943. MGAF/M.S./1003/1/G. Air Commodore Primrose's letter to A.O.C. T.A.F. 38 Wing/MS56/5/Air, 6 August 1943.
[2] No. 38 Group Report, Appendix D, Section 3.
[3] Group Captain Cooper's letter to H.Q. 30 Group. No. 38 Group File TR/272/Air.

Experience gained from Husky[1]

General Eisenhower stated in his report on Sicily that the outstanding tactical lesson of the whole campaign was the potential value of airborne operations[2]. Many lessons were learned from operation Husky and were summarised at the time as follows :—

> (i) All airborne operations are air operations and must therefore be the responsibility of the Air Commander in Chief. This factor was stressed repeatedly but never met with full Army approval.
>
> (ii) There must be better planning and greater co-ordination between the three Services. A high percentage of losses caused by " friendly " A.A. fire was due to faulty co-ordination. Technical experts must be available and adequate time allowed for preparation.
>
> (iii) Very thorough and intensive training is absolutely vital. The assumption that parachute operations can be carried out by crews lacking in operational experience is fallacious. Apart from preliminary operational experience the crews need particular training in low flying, navigation over sea and judging distances by moonlight. Inability in the latter caused many pilots to fly too near the coast during the last Sicilian operation with costly results. The general standard of navigation by both British and American crews was poor throughout; approximately 60 per cent. of the pilots lost their way and only 30 per cent. found their destinations.
>
> (iv) Suitable means of aircraft identification must be provided (I.F.F. and Verey Lights). The onus of identification is always with the aircraft.
>
> (v) Corridors for the airborne force to follow should be made at least five miles wide and marked if possible by naval craft.
>
> (vi) It was considered important to provide path-finder aircraft to lead in the force, which would considerably facilitate finding the Dropping or Landing Zone.
>
> (vii) Routeing was of extreme importance. Wherever possible convoys should be avoided.
>
> (viii) The glider force should be preceded by a parachute party to provide flares, beacons or flare path ; and to provide homing devices, lights or other signals to indicate the release point and landing zones.

---

[1] After the Sicilian Operation H.Q. Major-General Airborne Forces issued a pamphlet containing certain standing Operating Procedures for use by airborne forces based on experience gained up to that time. The Americans, having no Standing Operating Procedure of their own borrowed the British version and adapted it for their own use. Later on a combined British and American version was published by British and American Army and Air Force staff officers and when General Eisenhower's headquarters was established for the control of operations in north-west Europe this Anglo-American Standing Procedure was reproduced by Supreme H.Q. Allied Expeditionary Force as an operational instruction. (See Appendix 3.)

[2] J.S. 2027, Encl. 38A 28 July 1943.

(ix) The dropping zone should be an easily recognisable area rather than a pin-point chosen for tactical reasons.

(x) The Dakota (C.47), although an ideal aircraft for the task must be fitted with self-sealing tanks and protective armour for the pilots[1].

Conclusions

(i) The operation of airborne forces should be so planned that they have a strategic or major tactical effect on the operations in support of which they are launched.

(ii) Airborne forces are vulnerable by day and would therefore be more advantageously used at night which was infinitely less to the enemy's liking.

(iii) They should fly as concentratedly as possible to ensure landing in a short time and in a small area. In training as many as 128 gliders have been landed in a square mile at night.

(iv) As airborne operations were largely dependent on the weather they should be regarded as an aid to the main effort rather than an essential part of it.

Gliderborne troops have a great advantage over parachute troops because they are compact units ready for action. They can carry more equipment—heavier weapons—more ammunition and can more nearly fulfil the ideal of landing in concentration in a short time.

This advantage more than compensates for their drawbacks:—

(i) The operation of gliders is more difficult for the Air Force.

(ii) The number of gliders to be used may be limited by the number of available landing areas.

(iii) Gliders are liable to damage with consequent difficulty in unloading heavy equipment and lastly the operation of gliders is dependent on cloud conditions.

General Eisenhower in a training memo, issued 2 August 1943 from A.F.H.Q. also stressed the foregoing points and directed that a thorough study of the Husky operations be made by all Services and arms in the Mediterranean theatre[2].

The operations in Sicily appeared to show that small numbers of airborne forces could cause as much confusion and chaos to the enemy as a much larger ground force. Subsequent events tended to disprove this statement as, in later operations, the enemy provided sterner and better organised opposition tha nthe Italians. Even if, as in Sicily, the dropping is inaccurate those troops who land miles away create very effective diversions—a lesson already learned in Java in 1942 when small forces of Japanese paratroops had a similar effect[3].

It was realised after Sicily that airborne forces could be used in many ways—in direct support of landings by sea—the capture of forward aerodromes for our own use or to deny the enemy the use of them—an attack

---
[1] File O.Ops. 1/509. D.D.Ops./TAC 12 Joint Memo C.O.S. (43) 38G/MS60/1/Air. File C.O.S. (43) 552 (o).
[2] A.F.H.Q. Training Memo. No. 43. Encl. R.D.S./54/8/Air T.A.G.
[3] Joint War Office/Air Ministry Report on Sicilian Operations.

against the enemy's flanks or rear in conjunction with frontal attack by our own forces—seizing and holding bridgeheads over rivers and valleys—attacking enemy reserves before they can be brought up and intercepting retreating enemy forces[1].

Operations in the Aegean

In August 1943 eight Dakotas of No. 216 Group were diverted to Ramat David to undertake tactical exercises with No. 11 Parachute Battalion and although there was an hiatus while the Dakotas were required for operations the training was completed by 17 October 1943. The operations concerned were those on the island of Cos during September. On the 15th of that month six Dakotas dropped paratroops of the 11th Battalion Parachute Regiment on Cos. The drop was completely successful and three days later 14 Dakotas and three Hudsons dropped supplies. One aircraft landed in the sea but the crew were picked up by a Turkish ship and after a short period of internment returned to base. Four subsequent supply drops took place, two of them by night, until on 25 September the paratroops were taken off the island[2].

Another operation Accolade was planned for September 1943 against the island of Rhodes in the Aegean sea but it was cancelled on 12 September when it became known that the Germans were in complete control of Rhodes. A successful night operation was carried out on the nights of 31 October-1 November and 1-2 November when 200 troops of the Greek Sacred Squadron with little or no experience of parachuting were dropped on Samos. Five Dakotas dropped 100 troops on each night and a sixth aircraft followed up with supplies[3]. Training continued at Ramat David during the winter of 1943-1944. Many supply dropping exercises were carried out in March and April 1944 to give practice to infantry in securing and indicating dropping zones and arranging for the reception and collection of supplies dropped by air. By 31 March 1944 109 courses had completed training at No. 4 M.E.T.S. In May, 1944, the unit was disbanded[4].

---

[1] Minutes of Meeting, C.O.S. (43) 552 (o).
[2] O.R.B. H.Q. Ramat David.
[3] R.D./S.50/2/Airops, 216 Group Report.
[4] Detailed accounts of experimental work in the technical development of No. 4 M.E.T.S., and the exercises, training programmes, etc., can be referred to in Ramat David Files A.H.B. 1.

PART III
FULL SCALE USE OF AIRBORNE FORCES
OCTOBER 1943 TO AUGUST 1945

CHAPTER 6

AIRBORNE FORCES IN PREPARATION FOR OVERLORD

Formation of Headquarters, Major General Airborne Forces

Major General Browning, the commander of 1st Airborne Division had long held the view that a separate Airborne Headquarters was necessary to relieve the staff of 1st Airborne Division of much extra work. He maintained that, in addition to their normal duties as divisional staff officers, they had to deal with the numerous problems of research and experiment connected with airborne forces. From 17 June 1942 onwards Major General Browning stressed this point until on 21 November 1942 in reply to his letter of 19 November, G.H.Q. Home Forces asked the War Office to approve the appointment of a Brigadier and staff in an advisory capacity to deal with all air matters. This did not satisfy Major General Browning who insisted that a specialist staff was essential to deal with airborne problems, but it was not until April 1943 that the War Office finally approved the formation of Headquarters Major General Airborne Forces[1]. Later in 1943 the lessons of Husky made apparent the necessity for a separate H.Q. and the formation of six Airborne Divisions (which started in July 1943) made its inception even more urgent.

Final authority to form the H.Q. was given on 5 May 1943 and Major General Browning was appointed as the first Major General Airborne Forces. On 12 June 1943 a charter was issued setting out the duties of Major General Airborne Forces but after some weeks Major General Browning, having had time to form an opinion on the new lay-out, forwarded a letter to the War Office on 20 August 1943. In it he stated in full his views on the organisation and gave his recommendations for its improvement[2].

Some time elapsed before the War Office put these suggestions into force but on 8 October 1943 a new charter for Major General Airborne Forces was issued[3].

Charter for Major-General, Airborne Forces

1. The Major-General, Airborne Forces, was responsible to the War Office Director of Air.

2. His duties were:—

   (a) To advise the War Office on all airborne matters, including policy, doctrine, planning, organisation, training, equipment, research and development, both tactical and technical.

   (b) To be available for consultation on all airborne matters, including planning by Supreme Commander, Commanders-in-Chief and other interested authorities at home and abroad.

   (c) To keep the War Office informed on all points connected with the training and efficiency for war of all airborne forces. He was empowered to carry out inspections for this purpose.

---

[1] W/O File 20/Gen./5957. 100/Misc./1359 (S.D.1).
[2] W/O File M.G.A.F./M.S/1001/1/G.
[3] W/O File 100/Misc./1359 (S.D.1).

(d) To assist Allied airborne force commanders at home and abroad in co-ordination of their training and equipment.

(e) To co-ordinate in consultation with the R.A.F. the allotment of R.A.F. training capacity for army airborne training.

(f) To command all training, holding, depot and army experimental establishments in connection with airborne forces, except those training in establishments which were the domestic concern of airborne formations as such.

Later in 1943, on the 26 December, Major-General Airborne Forces was disbanded and Headquarters Airborne Troops was formed under the command of Twenty-first Army Group. The rank of the Commander Major General Browning, was raised to that of Lieutenant General.

The Formation of 6th Airborne Division

The story of the formation of 6th Airborne Division really began in the late months of 1942 when there existed some divergence of high level opinion regarding the increase of airborne forces[1]. The Army were convinced that large scale operations would be essential to the successful continuation of the war, principally the invasion of Western Europe. They were encouraged in this view by the increase in supplies of Troop Carrier aircraft from America and later on by the experience of 1st Airborne Division in Sicily. On 21 October 1942 the War Office decided that the Army Order of Battle for 1944 should include one airborne division in Western Europe, one in Britain and one in India. The extent to which the Air Ministry disagreed with this decision and Mr. Churchill's arbitration on the matter has already been discussed in detail[2].

The position was that a final decision regarding the increase of airborne forces be left until the results of operation Husky became known, although planning was to be carried out for the increase of glider pilot training. In April 1943 a Chiefs of Staff Sub-committee, appointed for the purpose, examined the estimates for the increased training and requirements necessary for the formation of a second airborne division[3]. Eight hundred extra glider pilots would be required and the following additional resources for training and practice were essential:—

(a) 18 Elementary Training Flights.

(b) $2\frac{1}{2}$ Glider Training Schools.

(c) $\frac{1}{2}$ a Heavy Glider Conversion Unit.

(d) 473 Light Training Aircraft.

(e) 67 Transport or Medium Bomber aircraft.

(f) 9 Airfields.

(g) 425 officers and 5,360 Airmen and Airwomen.

These increases were very little altered after 1942 except for the greater numbers of aircraft and personnel required and it was expected that they would be completed by July 1944. Meanwhile the War Office issued orders on 23 April 1943 for the formation of 6th Airborne Division on a phased programme. The number 6 was chosen for security reasons. The phased

---

[1] C.O.S. (43), 37th meeting.
[2] See Chapter 3.
[3] A.M. File C.S. 17553, April 1943.

programme allowed for 30 per cent of H.Q. 6th Airborne Division to be formed immediately, 30 per cent. to be formed on 1 July 1943 and the remainder to be reviewed in September 1943. The H.Q. was situated at Syrencote House, near Netheravon, and on 3 May 1943 Major General R. H. Gale was given command[1].

H.Q. 6th Airlanding Brigade was also formed on 3 May 1943 at Amesbury, consisting of 2nd Battalion Oxford and Bucks Light Infantry and 1st Battalion Royal Ulster Rifles. In addition a third battalion (12th Devonshire's) allocated to the division on 18 September 1943 ; this was the result of a lesson learned from Husky that three battalions were necessary for an Airlanding Brigade. The Brigade was under the command of Brigadier H. K. N. Kindesley[2]. A new parachute brigade and two parachute battalions were formed by the 1 June 1943 and the third battalion was composed of the 1st Canadian Parachute battalion which arrived in England on 27 July. A new parachute squadron and parachute field ambulance were also formed. Most of the divisional troops were formed on 1 June 1943 and on 22 September 1943 the remainder of the division was ordered to form, less the second composite company R.A.S.C. which was to form later[3]. During this formation period unit training was being carried out and, despite the unavoidable strain upon all concerned, many exercises were held. On 23 December 1943 the division was ordered to mobilise. This was completed by 1 February 1944, the given date, which was a very creditable achievement as by that time the division was less than a year old[4].

Formation of No. 38 Group

The first suggestion that No. 38 Wing be made into a Group came from Air Commodore Groom, S.A.S.O. of the Special Planning Staff for operation Round-up, in August 1942. He proposed that the group be formed under Bomber Command. The suggestion was rejected[5]. On 13 February 1943 the Air Officer Commanding Army Co-operation Command under whose control No. 38 Wing was at that time forwarded a letter to the Air Ministry. In it he detailed the functions and duties of No. 38 Wing and pointed out that, although the formation was not necessarily a very large one, it had a great deal of planning, operational control and administration requiring considerable judgement and discretion on the part of its Commander[6]. The A.O.C. proposed therefore that the Wing be reconstituted as a Group and the rank of its Commander up-graded to Air status. These proposals were considered by the Establishments Committee who recommended the upgrading in rank of the Commander No. 38 Wing to Air Commodore but turned down the suggestion of raising the Wing to Group status on the grounds that it would be too expensive in personnel[7].

When the lessons of Husky were known, and the recommendations arising out of them had been generally accepted, it became increasingly obvious that No. 38 Wing would have to be considerably expanded and re-organised

---

[1] C.O.S. 11076. A.M. File S.O. 1/C/17A/43, Appendix A.
[2] 20/Gen./6094 S.D.1.
[3] 20/Gen./6094 (Air/2).
[4] War Office Narrative, Chapters VIII and X.
[5] A.E.A.F./M.S/80.
[6] A.M.S.O. File. Encl. ACC/S.1006/149/Org.
[7] L.M. 398 D.D.O. Est. 1.

in order to provide facilities for the training and practice of the airborne forces. It would also be necessary to co-ordinate the various and scattered training establishments under one head[1]. For several months during the summer of 1943 Air Commodore W. H. Primrose, Air Officer Commanding No. 38 Wing since the unfortunate death in a flying accident on 19 May 1943 of his predecessor Air Commodore Sir Nigel Norman, pleaded in vain for the return of his detachment from North Africa. In view of the fact that time was running short for all that had to be done in preparation for the operations in 1944 he recommended that No. 38 Wing be re-equipped with suitable aircraft and be screened from all extraneous commitments[2]. These recommendations were made in detail in a letter written by Air Commodore Primrose to the Air C.-in-C. on 15 September 1943. However on the 6 September 1943 a conference had been held at Headquarters Tactical Air Force under the chairmanship of Air Commodore Hardman D (Ops) Tac. to discuss the expansion and future organisation of the Wing. No. 38 Wing were asked to prepare a plan for the formation and re-equipment of squadrons within the Wing[3].

This plan provided for the return of the North African detachment to Britain; the re-equipping of No. 295 Squadron with Albemarles and No. 297 Squadron with Albemarles and Venturas, the latter to be split off later to form another squadron; the formation of a Halifax squadron from the already existing flight in No. 295 Squadron and the division of No. 296 into two squadrons. The aircraft strength of the Wing would then be 180 and it was estimated that it would be ready for large scale operational exercises by 1 January 1944. As a result of this proposal a meeting was held at the Air Ministry on 28 September 1943 to decide on the *modus operandi* of the expansion of No. 38 Wing. The meeting was attended by the Allied Air C.-in-C.[4], the A.O.C. Tactical Air Force, the A.O.C. No. 38 Wing and the Director of Air from the War Office[5].

It was agreed that No. 38 Wing be expanded to a group and a minute was sent on 11 October containing instructions for the phased expansion of the Wing. Firstly the Wing to be disbanded and H.Q. No. 38 Group formed in the Tactical Air Force, Fighter Command and situated at Netheravon. In view of the increase in size of the group and the extra responsibility entailed the rank of the A.O.C. was upgraded to that of Air Vice-Marshal and on 6 November 1943 Air Vice-Marshal L. N. Hollinghurst was appointed to the position in the place of Air Commodore Primrose. Secondly the new Group was to absorb entirely all stations and units of No. 38 Wing and was authorised to a strength of nine squadrons. These were to comprise four Albemarle squadrons, one Halifax and four Stirling and the target date for their formation was 1 February 1944[6].

The first phase, to be completed by 4 November 1943, involved the re-equipping of Nos. 295, 296 and 297 Squadrons with Albemarles, No. 298 was to be the Halifax squadron and in mid-October the Halifax flight of No. 295 Squadron moved from Hurn to Tarrant Rushton to form the nucleus

---

[1] No. 38 Group Report, Appendix E to Section III.
[2] T.L.M/M.S/150.
[3] 38W/M.S.1/6/Air.
[4] Air Marshal Leigh-Mallory was at this time Allied Air C.-in-C. designate—he was not formally appointed until November 1943.
[5] A.E.A.F./M.S./80.
[6] L.M. 2564/D. of O. A.E.A.F./M.S./80. A.M.S.O. File 3CA/7. D.O. Est. Folder No. 186.

of it. No. 299 Squadron was to have Venturas until it could be converted to Stirlings. This conversion was to take place by 15 February 1944. Nos. 295 and 296 Squadrons were to be located at Hurn, No. 298 at Tarrant Rushton and Nos. 297 and 299 at Stoney Cross. Meanwhile during October No. 42 Operational Training Unit at Ashbourne and Darley Moor (and No. 1 P.T.S. Ringway) were transferred from No. 70 Group Fighter Command to No. 38 Group. Both these units were re-established[1].

On 16 November 1943 the formation at Hurn of No. 570 Squadron was authorised using Albemarles, established at (16 + 4) and the personnel were drawn from Nos. 295 and 296 Squadrons. A week later, as a result of a conference between the C-in-C. Bomber Command and the Air Ministry Nos. 196 and 620 Stirling Squadrons were transferred from No. 93 Group Bomber Command to No. 38 Group[2]. Stirlings were chosen because they could more easily be spared, being obsolete for bombing were large enough and had a lower airspeed, more suitable for airborne work, although Halifaxes would have been more acceptable. This move was effected by 1 December 1943. These two squadrons were equipped with Stirling IIIs, complete with fittings for glider towing[3] and were established to (16 + 4) aircraft. Early in the New Year Air Ministry authorised the formation at Leicester East of No. 190 Squadron (16 + 4 Stirlings) and also the re-equipping of the Ventura Squadron No. 299 to a similar establishment. This completed the nine squadrons in the Group—they were established at 16 + 4 aircraft and were as follows:—

Stirling	Halifax	Albemarle
299	298	295
190		296
196		297
620		570

On 30 December 1943, it was decided at A.E.A.F. to allocate new airfields to No. 38 Group—the four Albemarle squadrons to be at Aldermaston and Greenham Common—the four Stirling squadrons at Fairford and Keevil and the Halifax squadron at Tarrant Rushton. On 1 January 1944, No. 81 O.T.U. at Tilstock was transferred to No. 38 Group and on the 14th R.A.F. Fairford was also transferred from No. 70 Group. These changes completed the programme of centralising control of all airborne training establishments under the Group.

There were many difficulties for the A.O.C. No. 38 Group to face in these vital early months of 1944 principal amongst which was the difficulty in drawing experienced crews from Bomber Command to form a nucleus for the Stirling squadrons. Eventually this problem was referred direct to the Chief of Air Staff[4]. The A.O.C. was also compelled to deal directly with the Ministry of Aircraft Production to ensure getting the necessary aircraft in time. Even then aircraft promised by mid-March were not allotted until

---
[1] 38G/S.201/30/10 Org. L.M. 2638/D. of O.
[2] No. 38 Group O.R.B.
[3] All heavy bombers were produced with fittings for glider towing in order to be readily available for airborne work if required. Re-equipment to Stirling Mark IV took place in the early months of 1944.
[4] A.E.A.F./T.L.M./31.

weeks later. Study of the minutes of the A.E.A.F. Commanders Weekly Conferences shows the extent of the difficulties which had to be overcome in order to provide crews, aircraft and airfields in time for training to be completed for Neptune. The main problem was that of providing crews particularly as the extent of the operational commitments was not decided definitely until the spring, when it was broadly estimated that No. 38 Group would have to be trained up to an equivalent of 248 aircraft by about D+90. The great difficulty always present in planning aircraft operations was the fact that large numbers of men, aircraft and much equipment had to be tied up in expectation of operations that might never take place. This could not be avoided if the essentially high standard of training was to be reached[1].

By 16 March 1944, No. 38 Group had completed their movements to the various stations and the Order of Battle (excluding training units) was as follows[2]:—

Station	Squadrons	Aircraft	Gliders
Brizenorton	296	22 + 4 Albemarle	50 Horsas
	297	22 + 4 Albemarle	50 Horsas
Harwell	295	22 + 4 Albemarle	50 Horsas
	570	22 + 4 Albemarle	50 Horsas
Keevil	196	22 + 4 Stirling	50 Horsas
	299	22 + 4 Stirling	50 Horsas
Fairford	190	22 + 4 Stirling	50 Horsas
	620	22 + 4 Stirling	50 Horsas
Tarrant Rushton	298	18 + 2 Halifax	70 Hamilcars
	644	18 + 2 Halifax	50 Horsas

Meanwhile, as explained in a later section, No. 46 Group had been forming to an establishment of 150 Dakotas plus 25 reserves. The group consisted of five squadrons giving a total of 15 under the operational control of No. 38 Group. The total number of operational aircraft available was therefore 362 + **61**.

Operational Organisation

When No. 38 Wing was formed on the 15 January 1942, it was placed under the control of Army Co-operation Command because its sole function was the operational training of 1st Airborne Division. All the other training organisations—the Whitley flight for training replacement crews—No. 1 P.T.S. at Ringway—the Glider Training School and the Heavy Glider Conversion Unit were controlled by No. 70 Group Fighter Command or Flying Training Command[3]. Such dispersal of control militated against an efficient organisation, especially in view of the probable expansion, and the A.O.C. No. 38 Wing Air Commodore Primrose proposed in a memorandum to the Allied C.-in-C. on 16 May 1943, that a new organisation was needed, in order

---

[1] A.E.A.F./T.L.M./Folder 17.
[2] 38 and 46 Group Joint Report on "Overlord".
[3] L.M. 583/D. of O.

that all the R.A.F. elements of Airborne Forces be placed under one commander[1]. In June 1943 the Air Ministry decided to transfer No. 38 Wing to the control of 2nd Tactical Air Force[2].

When the Headquarters Allied Expeditionary Air Force was formed on the 15 November 1943, under Air Marshal Sir Trafford Leigh-Mallory at Stanmore, No. 38 Group H.Q. and all its units were transferred simultaneously to his command from 2nd T.A.F.[3]. The Air Commander-in-Chief wanted direct control of No. 38 Group because its purpose was largely strategic rather than tactical and he was responsible for all airborne operations. Because of the static nature of the Group—it would not move overseas— it was placed on 10 January 1944, under Air Defence of Great Britain for administrative purposes but remained under A.E.A.F. for control of operations and training. This was not changed until the autumn of 1944 when the Group was incorporated into the 1st Allied Airborne Army.

In order to ensure fullest possible co-ordination between U.S. IX Troop Carrier Command under Brigadier-General Williams, who were to supply the lift for the American Airborne Divisions, and No. 38 Group a Combined Command Post was formed at Eastcote. This Post was convenient to both Uxbridge and Stanmore and from there the British and American Commanders controlled their operations.

Thus the organisation of the commands was as follows:—

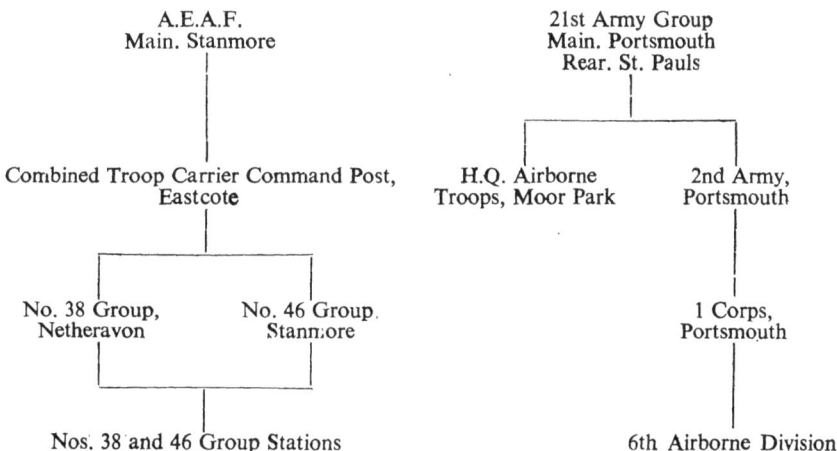

Formation and Role of No. 46 Group

As the time drew near for the detailed air planning for the invasion of Europe one of the major considerations was to ensure an adequate supply of aircraft for the airborne operations and preliminary training. No. 38 Group was obviously not going to be large enough, with only 180 aircraft, to cope with the demands likely to be made upon it and so the formation of a new Group (46) was authorised. This Group was formed on 17 January 1944 within Transport Command; the reason for this was because operational needs, heavy and intensive though they were likely to be, were infrequent and

---

[1] M.S./A.E.A.F./80.
[2] 38G/S.201/42/Org.
[3] S.D./155/1943.

it was neither feasible nor possible to keep large numbers of aircraft idle during the periods between operations. Thus No. 46 Group when not employed on operations or in the training for them, when it would be under the operational control of No. 38 Group was to carry on with normal transport duties[1]. The group was formed with a Unit Equipment of 150 Dakotas at Harrow Wealdstone. Very little space was available there and in February the H.Q. moved to the " Cedars," Uxbridge Road. Air Commodore Fiddament was appointed A.O.C.[2].

It was realised even at this early date that the 150 Dakotas, which were expected to be available from No. 46 Group, would not be sufficient and that probably twice as many aircraft would be required. Despite this it was not intended to withdraw any aircraft from the hard-pressed Bomber Command except perhaps in cases of sheer emergency; Transport Command would be called upon to supply the needs[3]. In view of the very limited time remaining and the fact that scarcely any of the crews were experienced in airborne operations basic training was started immediately by the two original squadrons of the group, No. 271 at Doncaster and No. 512 at Hendon. No. 271 squadron consisted of Harrow/Sparrows and although it began to re-equip with Dakotas in March it was decided to retain a flight of Harrow/Sparrows. These were to be used for casualty evacuation and in fact did remain in service until almost the end of the European war. Harrow/Sparrows were more suitable than Dakotas for landing on some of the temporary airstrips on the continent[4].

Owing to the unsuitable location and weather of the aerodromes at Doncaster and Hendon Nos. 512 and 271 were transferred to new stations which had been allocated to the Group. These three airfields—Broadwell, Down Ampney and Blakehill Farm—were chosen mainly because of their convenience to the other stations which were to be used in the launching of the airborne operations[5]. Apart from their geographical advantages these airfields were at first most unsuitable. They had been intended for use by American Medium bomber squadrons and while the runways—tracks and dispersal points were good the remainder was incomplete and much work was involved erecting and improving accommodation—laying roads, parking places, etc. The airfield nearest completion was Broadwell and No. 512 Squadron moved there, where early in February No. 575 Squadron was also formed by taking a flight from No. 512. No. 271 Squadron moved to Down Ampney and the Group was completed with the transfer, on 1 March 1944 of Nos. 48 and 233 Squadrons (to Down Ampney and Blakehill Farm respectively) from Coastal Command, where they had taken part in the Battle of the Atlantic. With these five squadrons the group began training.

The principal duty of No. 46 Group was to operate under the control of No. 38 Group as part of the British lift for airborne assault—training gliders —dropping parachutists and tactical re-supply by air. The Dakota squadrons were exclusively reserved for the re-supply role. The normal lift was to be

---

[1] M.S. A.E.A.F./80, 14 December 1943.
[2] File L.M./31/Org. 1.
[3] File A.C.A.S. (P) 5604, 1 January 1944. A.M. File C.S. 8503/11/A.C.A.S./Ops.
[4] File 46G/T.S. 4562/1 Org., 26 April 1944.
[5] No. 46 Group O.R.B. Unofficial History, No. 46 Group.

300 tons—the maximum not to exceed 700 tons per day: not that this latter figure was ever reached. On 26 April 1944 the A.O.C. in a letter stated that it would not be possible to lift 600 tons per day without outside assistance[1].

Training during the early months of 1944 consisted of conversion on to Dakotas, basis and squadron training and combined exercises with Army Airborne Units[2]. Although the weather was often unsuitable dropping exercises were planned almost daily and for the most part took place. The training was thorough and before crews were considered to be up to the standard necessary for participation in combined exercises they had to do more than 50 hours in addition to 25 hours' Dakota conversion. This period included glider towing—formation flying—paratroop dropping—navigation and supply dropping. Night vision training centres were opened at Blakehill Farm, Broadwell and Down Ampney—in view of the importance of crews being able to navigate accurately in little light[3].

On 3 February 1944 at a meeting of the "Support" committee (formed within Transport Command 21 January 1944) it was decided to form an advanced H.Q. of No. 46 Group at No. 38 Group H.Q. Netheravon to facilitate the closest possible co-operation between the groups. The advanced H.Q. would be near to the aerodromes in the group and would deal entirely with operational matters leaving Administrative and Personnel questions to be dealt with at H.Q. No. 46 Group. The new H.Q. was formed in time to control the first large operational exercise on 16 March 1944, and remained at Netheravon until 23 July 1944, when it returned to No. 46 Group H.Q[4].

Apart from its role in airborne operations which took priority over all else No. 46 Group played a considerable part in Supply by Air, i.e., fetching and carrying for the forward areas. Every conceivable type of cargo was transported in the period following D day—medical supplies—armament—aircraft spares—vehicles—bombs and personnel. In fact on 20 June the group carried loads totalling more than 100,000 pounds[5].

Following the Normandy operations it seemed as if No. 46 Group would revert to its transport duties but airborne commitments were the first priority and the Group stood by for several operations which were planned and later abandoned. When First Allied Airborne Army Group was formed in August 1944, No. 46 Group came under its control.

Casualty Air Evacuation

Throughout the latter months of 1943 there had been much argument and discussion over the arrangements for evacuation of casualties and it was not until 22 May 1944 that a definite policy was agreed upon, as a result of a War Office conference. It was decided that six Sparrows, from No. 271 Squadron, and 70 Ansons from Flying Training Command were to be available for use in forward areas for casualty evacuation. A casualty rate of 600 per day by D+40 was allowed for and these were to be accepted

---

[1] 46G/Memo. Admin. Plans, 23 February 1944.
[2] The combined exercises are dealt with in more detail in the next section of this narrative entitled "Mass Exercises".
[3] 46G/T.S. 4562/Org., 26 April 1944.
[4] 46G/O.R.B., 21 January 1944.
[5] File 46G/S 235/2/Air.

at 200 per day at Broadwell—Blakehill Farm and Down Ampney. A control H.Q. was set up at Swindon in direct contact with the airfields, hospitals and ambulances. No. 46 Group did its first job of casualty evacuation two weeks after D day when Dakotas flew 23 Army and one R.A.F. casualty from France to Blakehill Farm. By 28 July 10,000 casualties had been transported back to England[1].

Ansons were detailed from Flying Training Command for use in cases of emergency and these were modified to carry freight or casualties. A reserve pool of 50 aircraft was stationed at Watchfield but they were scarcely ever used. Three other Anson flights were authorised to form by the end of March 1944 to provide transport for crews and spares to 2nd T.A.F. Later these flights became Nos. 4 and 5 O.A.D.U.s to serve Nos. 83 and 84 Groups[2]. The remainder of the story of No. 46 Group and the part it played in the great operations in Europe is shown in later chapters.

Large Scale Exercises

Throughout the early months of 1944 training for the invasion of Europe was carried on until with the coming of Spring large scale exercises were held by Nos. 38 and 46 Groups in conjunction with the airborne divisions. On 6 February 1944 the first airborne exercise in which both British and American forces took part was carried out by No. 38 Group in conjunction with a transport group of the U.S.A.A.F. The aim of the exercise was to drop troops of the 3rd Parachute Brigade Group from C.47 aircraft of No. 435 Group U.S.A.A.F. and No. 38 Group R.A.F. on to the dropping zone at Winter-bourne Stoke. Ninety-eight aircraft actually took part in a successful exercise in which good concentrations were made—but mainly owing to bad weather the supply dropping by two Stirlings and the glider exercises were not so successful. In the latter 45 Horsas carrying troops of the 6th Air-landing Brigade took part but owing to poor navigation many of the releases were ill-timed[3].

The first large scale parachute-dropping exercises to be carried out by No. 46 Group took place on 16, 17 and 18 March. Thirty Dakotas were used in each of these and the general result was satisfactory—the dropping being accurate both as to time and position. A week later another parachute and glider exercise, " Bizz II ", took place. Forty-two Dakotas from No. 46 Group squadrons dropped 480 troops of the 7th Parachute Battalion at dusk on the D.Z. at Watchfield. The aircraft took off from Broadwell in $10\frac{1}{4}$ minutes. In addition W.T. container, bicycles and even a dog were dropped[4]. Everything was well within the D.Z. Meanwhile 88 Dakotas of the American 53rd Troop Carrier Command were also engaged in dropping parachute troops. The glider towing involved the use as tugs of Dakotas, Albemarles, Halifaxes and Stirlings, 154 in all, and the exercise was carried out in two

---

[1] It is beyond the scope of this narrative to detail the story leading up to the formation of Casualty Air Evacuation Units. It is dealt with more comprehensively in " Liberation of North-West Europe ", Volume II, Chapter XIV B and in the " Unofficial History of No. 46 Group ".—H.Q. A.E.A.F. O.R.B. P.M.O. Branch, Appendix VIII.
[2] A.E.A.F. File S. 17021, Part II, Encl. 27B.
[3] No. 38 Group Report. No. 38 Group O.R.B. No. 46 Group O.R.B.
[4] One collie dog " Rob " made over 20 operational parachute jumps in North Africa and Italy. He received the Dicken Medal.

lifts. Both these were successfully accomplished and completed the largest single exercise up to that date and the first attempt to simulate a real airborne assault[1].

Apart from actual dropping several navigation exercises both by day and night were planned and carried out. The importance of navigation had been amply illustrated in Sicily and North Africa—in fact good navigation was certainly one of the most vital factors to the success of an airborne operation. Exercise Dreme on the 4 April 1944 was planned as a night navigational test but the results were spoiled by low cloud and deterioration of the weather during the evening. Nevertheless 137 out of 165 tug/glider combinations managed to land safely at Harwell or Brizenorton but naturally the concentration was not good. One Stirling and its glider hit some trees on high ground resulting in the deaths of both crews but the remainder who were unable to find the D.Z. cast off and forced landed without casualties. The 9 April 1944 saw another attempt at a night navigation exercise in " Tour " but the weather was still unkind and many aircraft had to be diverted. This time no paratroops or gliders were used and only four out of 188 aircraft failed to find the D.Z., though the timing was by no means good[2].

Nickel Operations

After a meeting at Norfolk House on 14 April 1944 H.Q., A.E.A.F., agreed that No. 46 Group should take part in Nickel Operations as part of their training but subject only to the following conditions:—

(a) All operations were to be controlled by No. 38 Group Operations Room.

(b) Aircrew should normally be limited to one sortie each.

(c) Targets were to be selected in comparatively safe places.

(d) If casualties resulted then the decision was to be reconsidered.

Following this decision several successful Nickel Operations were carried out before the end of April 1944.

Meanwhile No. 38 Group were gaining experience of flying over enemy territory by carrying out S.A.S. operations at frequent intervals with a very fair proportion of success[3]. During May approximately 200 sorties were flown over France and of these 60 per cent. completed their missions and only two aircraft were lost[4]. It was during this very active period that many training and operational instructions were produced. At the outset there had been very little guidance in the form of publications and it was a question of co-ordinating experience and knowledge gained whilst training was continuing. Orders on glider-marshalling and take-off, also the landing of aircraft in rapid succession and the correct marshalling to enable them to take-off rapidly, were evolved in this manner. A demonstration of a fast take-off resulted in 18 aircraft, which had been marshalled in vics of three at the end of the runway, being airborne in 56 seconds[5].

---
[1] No. 46 Group Unofficial History.
[2] No. 46 Group O.R.B.
[3] The results of these S.A.S. operations enabled a close check to be made on the individual abilities of the aircrew taking part. This was valuable when the time came to select crews for operations.
[4] O.R.B. No. 38 Group.
[5] No. 46 Group Unofficial History.

April 1944 was a busy month for training and culminated in Mush on the 21st, an Airborne Corps exercise which was, as nearly as possible, a dress-rehearsal for Neptune. As such it was by far the largest exercise held and took place over an area stretching from the Severn estuary to the border of Wiltshire and Oxford. Approximately 700 aircraft from Nos. 38 and 46 Groups and U.S.IX Troop Carrier Command took part in glider towing, parachute dropping and re-supply exercises.

Following a discussion between No. 46 Group Training and Ops (3) A.D.G.B. on 13 April 1944, it was decided to undertake exercises involving searchlight co-operation. Very few of the crews in No. 46 Group had flown over enemy defended areas and these exercises were designed to simulate, as nearly as possible, conditions they might have to face on real operations. A series of night cross-country flights were planned similar to Bomber Command "Bullseye" exercises. Several of these took place satisfactorily, during the last days of April; the searchlight co-operation was provided by No. 10 Group and the Royal Observer Corps plotted and analysed the tracks of the aircraft, thus providing a check on the night navigational ability of the crews.

The majority of the crews required for the D-Day operations were ready by the end of April 1944 but training continued throughout May—if not at quite the same tempo as in April. Night parachute dropping exercises took place early in May and were carried out most successfully using the Polish Parachute Brigade, who did not take part in the Normandy operations. Their Majesties the King and Queen and H.R.H. Princess Elizabeth visited Netheravon on 19 May 1944 to watch a demonstration exercise Exeter. Gliders were landed—a tank was unloaded from a Hamilcar that had landed after being towed by a Halifax and parachute troops were dropped.

The last large scale exercise before D-Day was in the form of a concentration practice on 21 May when 74 Horsas landed by night in $12\frac{1}{2}$ minutes on a small landing zone at Netheravon. This excellent result was all the more creditable in view of most unfavourable weather. A repeat exercise the following night resulted in 31 gliders being written off due to landing in the wrong direction.

In addition to the normal parachute and glider exercises special training was necessary for the *coup de main* party which was to land near the bridge at Ranville. A large number of rehearsals were carried out at night, using a small enclosed landing zone on Salisbury Plain, under conditions approximating as closely as possible to those which would prevail in the actual operation. As can be imagined these exercises were difficult and dangerous; there were casualties to gliders and crews. Notwithstanding this both Major General Browning and Air Vice-Marshal Hollinghurst were of the opinion that it was preferable to take risks in training, in order to simulate operational conditions than to send half-trained and inexperienced crews into battle. Events proved their decision to be a wise one.

This account of the training in preparation for D-Day, while giving an overall picture of the principal exercises carried out, would not be complete without mentioning the intensity of the work involved for the ground organisation. The plan for the airborne phase of the operation called for an extremely concentrated lift and drop. The purpose of this was to utilise the surprise element to the full and also to accomplish the tasks before the enemy could organise resistance. In order to obtain this concentration the greatest possible accuracy in the preparations on the ground was essential. Correct take-off times had to be maintained to a matter of seconds involving perfect marshalling arrangements.

In the words of the Air Officer Commanding No. 38 Group, Air Vice Marshal Hollinghurst, who, when discussing the operation later, said, " The interval between take-offs was of paramount importance as we were working with very little margin of range. The use of different types of aircraft, and different types of combinations, complicated matters because of the different speeds and approach periods. All this pointed to the ground crews working to split seconds and to the aircrew doing exactly as they were briefed. One of the biggest jobs of the whole show was the instilling of this appreciation of the time factor. The ground crews responded magnificently." Without perfect co-operation from the ground crews the operation could never have been effectively launched and no appreciation of the success of any airborne operation can ignore the fact that the ground organisation to provide the lift and enable it to take-off according to plan played almost, if not equally, as important a part as the aircrews.

CHAPTER 7

OPERATION NEPTUNE (OVERLORD)

General Situation

For a long time prior to the invasion of Europe the fact that ultimately it was inevitable, failing an unexpected and almost total collapse of German resistance, was realised, but it could not be said that any really practical planning took place until April 1943 when Lt. General F. E. Morgan, Chief of Staff to the Supreme Allied Commander was instructed to plan for the invasion of Europe[1]. On 27 May 1943 a directive was issued which set the requirements for naval, land and air forces which were to be available by 1 May 1944. The plan for Overlord was to be prepared and ready by 1 August 1943. The aim of the proposed invasion was to land large forces of British and American troops somewhere on the coast of Europe so as to make the destruction of the German forces in N.W. Europe strategically possible and eventually to launch an onslaught against Germany itself.

There were two good reasons in support of landing on the Normandy coast. Firstly the bridgehead had to be within fighter range so that the landings might be covered from the air, and secondly France had ports on the Atlantic coast which would be required for the landing of further supplies and troops once the Allies became established on the continent. It was this latter factor which influenced the choice of the Caen area in preference to Calais as a suitable bridgehead. The Germans had somewhat naturally concentrated their defensive measures at the most vulnerable positions such as Calais, Le Havre, Cherbourg and Brest, therefore it was up to the planners to choose an area within fighter range, possessing adequate beaches and yet as lightly defended as possible. The Caen area was also suitable geographically for an early attempt to capture the ports of Cherbourg and Le Havre; it offered suitable sites for the establishment of airfields and finally the ground inland from Caen did not lend itself to counter attack. Thus on 19 June 1943 this area was finally chosen by a meeting of Principal Staff Officers[2].

The military plan for Overlord (as finally settled in 1944) had as its main and immediate objectives the capture of airfields in the Caen area; the construction of airstrips for the landing of supplies and the forward operation of our aircraft as the battle progressed; the capture and opening up of the port of Cherbourg and generally the preparation for the eventual landing of upwards of a million men. Broadly speaking the Cherbourg area was allotted to the Americans and Caen to the British. The main British forces, 2nd Army, who were to land on the beaches between Ashelles-sur-Mer and Ouistrehan at the mouth of the river Orne would have on their left flank the Canal de Caen and would also be overlooked by high ground East of the river Orne. It was therefore essential that the enemy be dispossessed of this high ground as early as possible; if not they would be in a position to cover most of the British assault with artillery fire and considerably jeopardise the success of the operation. The task of safeguarding against this eventuality was given to the 6th Airborne Division; 1st Airborne Division was to remain in England as reserve[3].

---

[1] C.O.S. (43) 214, 26 April 1943.
[2] T.L.M./M.S./136.
[3] C.O.S.S.A.C. (43), 11th meeting. Section III.

Since December 1943 when the first meeting of the Joint Commanders-in-Chief was held, the question of selecting a date and time for the D-Day assault had caused considerable controversy between the three Services[1]. It is outside the scope of this narrative to dwell on the problem except in so far as airborne forces are concerned. The deciding factor in selecting a date was naturally the weather and the following limitations had to be considered with regard to airborne operations:—

(i) For parachute dropping the wind should not exceed 20 miles an hour if at all possible. Thirty miles an hour was the absolute limit and this would almost certainly lead to an increase in casualties.

(ii) For gliders winds of 25-30 miles per hour were strong enough but a steady wind of 40 miles an hour was not impracticable. Finally, there was not to be any risk of fog.

The final decision was based entirely on the weather and starting on 2 June 1944 conferences, attended by Commanders and their Chiefs of Staff, were held at the Supreme Commanders Forward Headquarters at Portsmouth[2] when the meteorological reports were considered. Although 4 June had been chosen as D-Day, a sudden change for the worse in the weather on Saturday 3 June rendered the next day impossible. After two more meetings on Sunday 4 June, when an unexpectedly improved forecast had been received, General Eisenhower gave the order for the invasion to be launched on the night of 5-6 June 1944.

The Cover Plan

The purpose of the cover plan was two-fold. Firstly, to disrupt the enemy radio warning devices thus preventing them receiving early warning of approaching forces and also to prevent the use of radar controlled gunfire against surface forces. Secondly, the airborne operations were to be assisted by producing threats of diversionary attacks with the intention of dividing the enemy fighter forces and delaying movement of enemy reserve ground forces. The most effective method of radio counter measure was to destroy enemy apparatus and installations by air attack, but where this was not possible jamming devices had to be employed. These could either be "physical" (window dropping) or "electronic" (transmitters).

The Titanic Operations

Bomber Command were given the task of jamming the German radar system. Ten aircraft were to drop "window" which would create images on the enemy receiver screens and give the illusion of an airborne assault taking place near the Seine Estuary. These aircraft, seven of which completed their tasks, were sent off in pairs one of each pair carrying 325 lbs. of N. Type "window" and the other with 1,200 lbs. of M. Type (b) "window". Dropping was to start on the outward and finish on the return journeys at a point 60 miles from the French coast. Other aircraft dropped "window" further to the West. There is no doubt that these radio counter measures

---

[1] A.E.A.F. File T.L.M./Folder 18.
[2] T.L.M./M.S. 136/39.

contributed in no small way to the comparative lack of enemy air interference with the airborne operations, resulting in far less casualties than had been anticipated[1].

Intense attacks on radar installations were carried out prior to D-Day by Spitfires and Typhoons with such efficiency that seven of the extra long range stations and at least 15 others were rendered useless. Bomber Command also attacked the most important W/T stations putting most of them out of action. Particular success was achieved on the W/T centre Cherbourg, Urville, Hague, which was completely destroyed. The Oboe pathfinder technique was primarily responsible for the high degree of precision attained on these raids. Several minor operations were planned and carried out during the early hours and evening of D-Day to assist the main tasks and create confusion for the enemy. One hundred Lancasters of Bomber Command were to attack the battery at Merville, dropping 4,000 and 8,000 lb. bombs immediately (10 minutes) before the main body of paratroops were due to begin their attack. Unfortunately, as will be seen later, the bombers completely missed their target[2]. The six tug aircraft towing the gliders for the *coup de main* attack on the bridges at Benouville were each to drop two 500 lb. bombs on a powder factory a short distance South East of Caen. It was hoped that this would mislead the enemy as to the purpose of the aircraft[3].

The Airborne Plan. (Operation Neptune)

Early in 1944 it became apparent that the tasks allotted to the airborne division were definite enough to permit detailed planning to proceed. Broadly the airborne plan then was as follows. The reasons for its amendment are shown later:—

Prior to D-day – 1

S.A.S. missions to be carried out.

D – 1/D. One American Airborne Division to land in the area East of Carentan (Carentan-Ste Mere Eglise). Two British Parachute Brigades to land in the general area East of Caen, apart from a small force detailed to the vicinity of the bridges at Benouville.

D/D + 1. One American Division in the area East of Barneville or in area La Haye Puits-Lessay.

This plan was the result of a meeting between the Planning Committee and the Army C. in C. regarding the employment of airborne forces. A memorandum was issued defining the tactics to be carried out, the forces necessary and their subsequent allotment as well as a general guide to the construction of the plans[4]. HQ. No. 38 Group were ordered to start detailed planning of the British Airborne tasks with the units concerned and IX T.C.C., the American tasks with the U.S. Airborne units concerned.

---

[1] A.E.A.F. File T.L.M./M.S. 136/58/1.
[2] Notes of Preparation and Planning of A.E.A.F. for Overlord, Part V, Section 10.
[3] A more detailed account of the cover plan can be found in " Notes on the planning and preparation of the A.E.A.F. for the invasion of North West France in June 1944, Part V, Section 10."
[4] Minutes, 5th meeting A.B. Planning Committee, Appendix A. A.E.A.F./Ops. 3, 28 February 1944.

Joint Planning

In order that the planning should be as co-ordinated as possible between 6th Airborne Division and No. 38 Group Air Staff a combined planning room was opened in a private house, under conditions of great security, at Milston near Netheravon and 6th Airborne Division planning staff moved there in mid-April. At the same time a War room was opened at Netheravon where the final air planning was completed[1]. Planning for an airborne operation is necessarily rather complex. The first step is to decide upon the dropping and landing zones according to both army and air requirements. Once these have been agreed upon, with allowances made for the air problems of navigation and suitable landing grounds for gliders and the army plan having allotted troops to the various objectives, then the flight plan can be worked out.

The selection of suitable dropping and landing zones for Overlord presented no great difficulty. Since February 1944 very close inspection of the ground had revealed that the Caen area was excellent for airborne landings as the fields for the most part were open, large and level; there were plenty of distinctive features to assist map reading and the general estimate of the opposition from Flak and ground defence was favourable. The only dropping zones, where the terrain was likely to present any problems were those near the bridges at Benouville and the battery at Merville.

The main task of 6th Airborne Division as previously stated was to ensure that the enemy did not retain possession of the high ground East of the river Orne. In order to accomplish this the following subsidiary objectives were allotted. The Division was to capture the area between the rivers Orne and Dives, North of the road Troam-Sannerville-Colombelles. They were also to attack and delay enemy reserves and supplies approaching Caen from the East and South East[2]. The objectives involved in carrying out this latter part of the operation were the bridges over the Canal de Caen and the river Orne at Benouville. These had to be captured and, if possible, maintained intact. The bridges over the river Dives had to be destroyed. Finally, and most important of all, the battery at Merville had to be captured or destroyed. This heavily armoured and defended battery held a commanding position over the beaches near Ouistrehan and was therefore a serious menace to the landing of the seaborne forces.

In addition to the British operations two American airborne divisions were to drop paratroops on the night of D – 1/D. The 101st U.S. Division in the area St. Mere Eglise and the 82nd U.S. Division in the area St. Sauveur le Vicomte. Glider operations in support of these landings involved the landing of 50 in each area by first light of D-Day and not more than 200 in the St. Sauveur le Vicomte area by last light[3].

Briefing

Briefing for Overlord was carried out under conditions of the strictest secrecy and began three days before D-Day after which all units and transit camps were sealed from any contact with the outside world. The principal

---
[1] No. 38 Group Report " Operation Neptune ".
[2] Minutes, 5th meeting A.B. Planning Committee, 25 February 1944. A.E.A.F./M.S. 628/Air Plans.
[3] Appendix A to Minutes of meeting on 29 April 1944. A.E.A.F./T.S. 628 Airborne Plans.

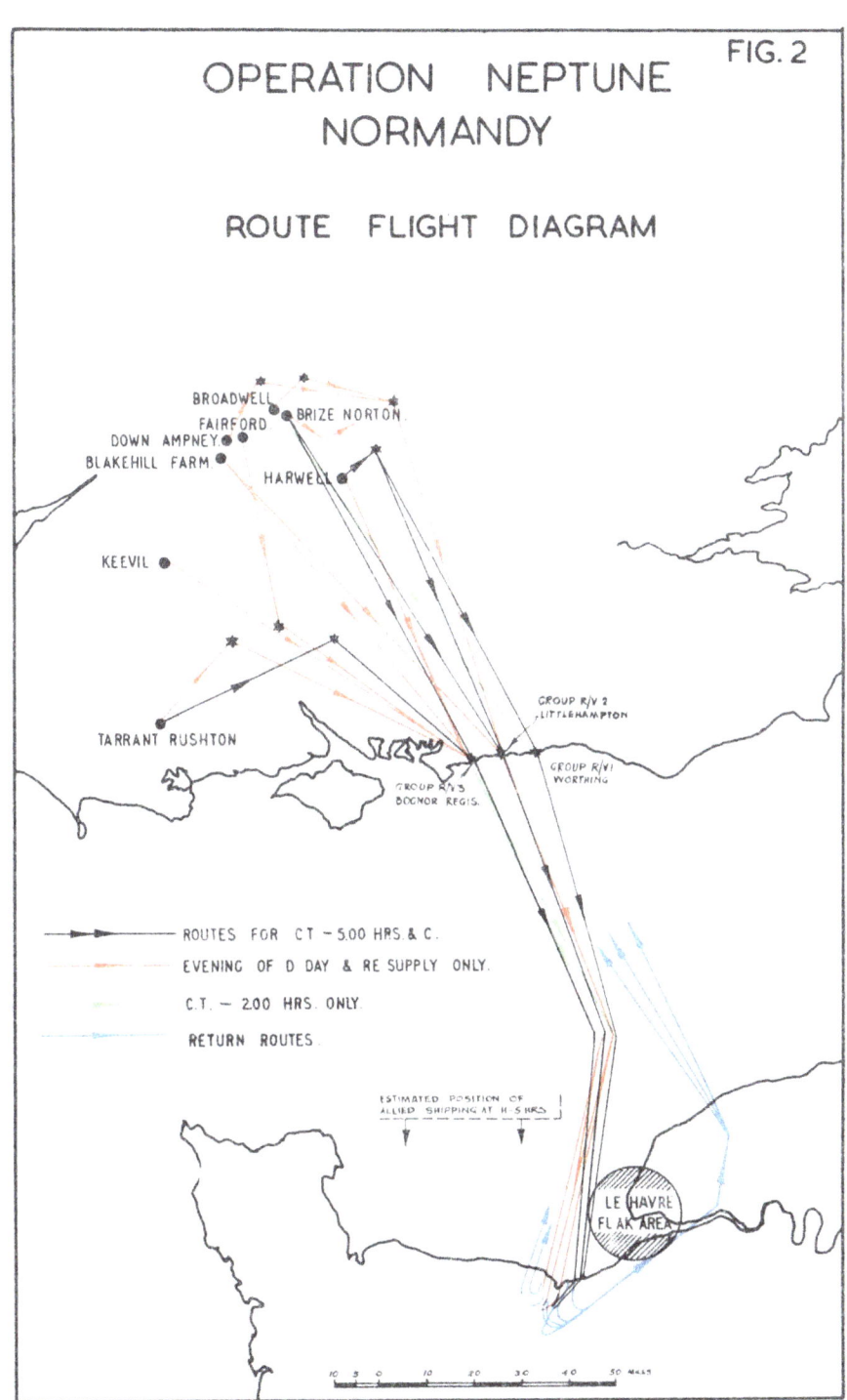

features of the briefing were the aids to ground recognition in the shape of models, particularly the scale model (1:5,000) of the Neptune area erected at Netheravon by the C.I.U. Medmenham from photographic reconnaissance. Owing to the impossibility of providing sufficient models for all aircrew to make a detailed study, a coloured film was made both from the Medmenham model and others produced by 6th Airborne Division. By moving the camera over the models at various calculated heights it was possible to simulate actual tracks in from the coast to the dropping-landing zones. This method proved most effective and as there were adequate supplies of the film they could be studied in detail at some length by the crews[1].

Routeing

The principal factors influencing the choice of routes for the invading aircraft were as follows[2]:—

(i) To avoid flak especially that near Le Havre and fire from friendly naval forces.

(ii) To ensure the longest possible straight run on to the landing or dropping zones and to minimise as much as possible the number of turns to be made.

(iii) To obtain the best use of radio aid Gee and also to avoid detection by enemy radar.

(iv) To make use of ground aids in friendly territory.

(v) To co-ordinate with the other Commands operating at the same time. As the Americans were in action as well as bomber and fighter forces it meant that an enormous number of aircraft were airborne over a comparatively small area thus the tracks had to be very carefully chosen.

(vi) The routes were to be as straightforward as possible to avoid confusion, facilitate navigation and expedite briefing.

Before the problem of routeing the airborne forces was finally settled some difference of opinion existed between the Navy, Headquarters A.E.A.F. and No. 38 Group[3]. The Air Commander-in-Chief, Air Marshal Leigh-Mallory opposed routeing the large glider force on the evening of D Day (Operation Mallard) directly over the Navy and suggested that it would be less risky if it were routed over enemy territory. Air Vice-Marshal Hollinghurst Air Officer Commanding No. 38 Group disagreed on the grounds that it was not justifiable to accept casualties over enemy territory merely because it was not safe to route aircraft over our own forces, and put forward the following suggestions[4]:—

(i) The invading forces should not be routed directly over the Navy.

(ii) The time of landing should be 2100 hours, thus the aircraft would be approaching out of the sun making accurate opposition from the ground more difficult, and also sufficient daylight would be available for the fighter cover to return to base.

---

[1] 38 and 46 Group Joint Report, Operation Neptune.
[2] 38 and 46 Group Official Report Operation Neptune.
[3] Minutes, 9th Meeting, Airborne Air Planning Committee.
[4] 38 Group/T.S./62/1.

(iii) The aircraft should fly in at a low altitude (800 ft.) in order to minimise risk of anti-aircraft fire.

(iv) The aircraft should fly out at an even lower altitude (200 ft.)

The passage of the aircraft over the Navy would take approximately 17 minutes. Fifty per cent. of the tug aircraft were four-engined and thus easily recognisable by the Navy and also they could be painted if it were considered necessary. In the light of these suggestions the Air C.-in-C. held a meeting with Admiral Ramsay the Naval Commander on 2 May and as a result it was agreed that the operation be planned to take place at last light; thereupon Air Vice-Marshal Hollinghurst drafted the air route plan for addition to the Naval Operation Orders. The low altitudes as suggested above were incorporated and the force was allowed 21 minutes to pass any given point. This plan was forwarded to the Navy but no definite timings were included until Admiral Ramsay had confirmed the plan. A week later Admiral Ramsay undertook to withhold fire by naval forces within the prescribed limits of time and distance[1].

On 1 May 1944 the timing and routeing for the operation were finally decided upon but not before Admiral Ramsay in a letter to the Air C.-in-C. had pointed out that as the aircraft would be flying very low, if their passage happened to coincide with a low flying enemy attack, they would be in danger of being fired upon. He also complained that there had been alterations in the routeing since the plan had been agreed[2]. In reply to this letter Air Marshal Leigh-Mallory denied that there had been alterations made in the plan and stated that he was quite prepared to take the risks mentioned provided that Admiral Ramsay issued the orders regarding the withholding of fire in the immediate vicinity of the aircraft and during the agreed time limits. In the final route plan three rendezvous points at Worthing, Littlehampton and Bognor Regis were chosen for the aircraft operating from the No. 38 and 46 Group bases. From these points there was only one alteration in course to be made over mid-channel in order to avoid Le Havre before crossing the French coast[3].

Aids to Navigation

In addition to the normal navigation devices all aircraft of Nos. 38 and 46 Groups were fitted with Gee and Rebecca II[4], a radar device for homing on to a pinpoint and to assist in finding target areas. On all the main landing zones Eureka beacons were to be placed and these acted as the equivalent of a ground station to the Rebecca II instrument in the aircraft and were to be put into position by the independent parachute company. Eureka beacons were also placed at Group rendezvous points in addition to the coded lights and at all the base airfields for homing purposes. During the flight outwards navigators were to check their sets by testing with the home and the rendezvous beacons to ensure proper working and then switch off until within 10 miles of the target. Coding was not used on Eureka beacons[5]. Throughout the operations the use of I.F.F. was banned.

---

[1] A.E.A.F.R./M.S. 841/9544.
[2] 10th Meeting, Airborne Air Planning Committee. A.E.A.F./T.S./628.
[3] A detailed route diagram is shown at fig. 2.
[4] For further details regarding the use of radar see Appendix 8.
[5] Air Signals Report Operation Neptune. H.Q. A.E.A.F./S/25024/A.S.O. in C., July 1944. 38 and 46 Group Report on Operation Neptune.

Where possible routes were planned so that the tracks might run along the whole-number Gee lattice lines and new frequencies were introduced on D – 1 to minimise the risk of jamming.

Air-Sea Rescue

In view of the probability that some gliders could be expected to land in the sea, instructions were issued accordingly. Where possible a glider was to land in front of a friendly vessel and the tug aircraft, after fixing the position of the glider, return to base as soon as possible. Air Sea Rescue was the responsibility of No. 11 Group.

Providing the Lift

During the early months of 1944 whilst the planners were at work, the R.A.F. were experiencing difficulty in obtaining aircraft in time for the operations. Much of the responsibility of providing the lift fell upon Air Vice Marshal Hollinghurst who, as A.O.C. No. 38 Group, was having no little difficulty in bringing his Squadrons up to strength. Study of the minutes of the weekly Commanders Conferences at A.E.A.F. H.Q. shows a gradual alleviation of the fear that the establishment might not be reached in time for training and preparations to be carried out for the operations[1].

Each of the four types of aircraft to be used provided its problems; in January 1944 the formation of No. 299 Squadron and the re-equipment of Nos. 196 and 620 was held up for lack of Stirling IVs. To overcome this, the A.O.C. No. 38 Group requested permission to deal direct with the Ministry of Aircraft Production[2], and as a result of his personal contact with the Chief Overseer the Stirlings were obtained by the middle of March, although paratroop modifications on the aircraft were not completed until the end of April.

At the A.E.A.F. H.Q. Meeting on 2 February 1944 it was decided that the Halifax Squadron be re-equipped with Merlin 22s as experience had proved them to be considerably superior to the Merlin 20s; in fact, the unserviceability rate of the 22 was only about a quarter that of the 20. When Air Vice-Marshal Hollinghurst pressed for this change he was told to pursue the question with Air Member Supply & Organisation and to obtain the diversion of Merlin 22s from Bomber Command to No. 38 Group. The very next day the A.M.S.O. agreed to supply Merlin 22s to No. 298 Squadron.

However, re-equipment progressed very slowly and by 23 March only 25 Halifaxes of the Unit Establishment of 40 had been provided owing to the shortage of Merlin 22s. Although No. 41 Group had promised to bring the Squadrons up to strength by 7 April 1944 it was not until Air Vice-Marshal Hollinghurst had stated on 5 April that, unless the re-equipment was completed by 15 April it would not be possible to train crews in time for Overlord, that the A.O.C.-in-C. took up the matter personally with A.M.S.O. The reason for this was not due to any failure on the part of No. 41 Group or M.A.P. but rather to the reluctance of Bomber Command to release the

---

[1] A.E.A.F./T.L.M./Folder 17.
[2] This request was made on the suggestion of Sir William Freeman, then C.E. of M.A.P., in order to save vital time. A.M.S.O. File 10/A/17 Albemarle Production. Encl. S.85591.

Merlin 22s. The Albemarle V situation was also troublesome; by mid-March 92 aircraft out of 104 U.E. were available. Production was slow and the shortage entailed over use of those aircraft available.

The period May to July 1944 output fell below estimates by 11 aircraft despite the urgent need. This was mainly caused by a shortage of electricians, many of whom compulsorily transferred to their jobs, were bad workers and had to be released. When D-Day was over, fortunately with far less wastage than had been anticipated, production of Albemarles was reduced to 20 per month with further reductions in 1945. However, there still existed a shortage of spares and on 16 June 1944 it was decided, despite possible political repercussions, to use main-planes of 50-60 Albemarles intended for Russia which were scheduled to be produced early in 1945. The reason for this was that all Stirling IVs produced in 1945 would be required for Special Duty quotas and the Albemarles would be the only tug aircraft available, thus those intended for Russia could ill be spared[1].

Correspondence between A.M.S.O. and Washington March to May 1944 shows that of the 500 Dakotas originally asked for only 350 were forthcoming. In view of the high estimated wastage, a bid for 150 more aircraft was made to cover the continuous series of airborne operations[2]. Eventually 87 Dakotas were promised and it was suggested that the deficiency be overcome by diverting 79 others from M.A.A.F. which were on loan to India, but on 12 May C.O.S. decided that it was impossible to divert aircraft from India[3]. A.M.S.O. in a letter on 13 May wished to bring pressure to bear on the Americans for the 150 aircraft in view of the fact that IX U.S. Army Air Force had 300 more Dakotas than the amount agreed upon. However, A.C.A.S.(P) advised against this argument being used as the American plans for the subsequent maintenance of their Squadrons were not known and it might be that our reserves would eventually prove to be higher in proportion than those of the American Squadrons[4]. A revised estimate of requirements for Overlord was then produced on 22 May and this was deemed sufficient. Subsequent events thus involved much lower wastage than anticipated and the Dakota position improved, especially as by 13 June 1944 the promised allotment was completed.

American Troop Carrier Command. America proposed to send four Groups of transport aircraft to England early in 1944 to assist No. 38 Group in training airborne forces. This proposal was soon enlarged and accelerated; by December 1943 there were two Groups of American transport aircraft in the Doncaster area; four-and-a-half more Groups were due to arrive in January 1944 from N. Africa and seven Groups from the U.S.A. at the rate of one Group every 14 days starting 1 January 1944.

Available British Forces

The total number of aircraft available in Nos. 38 and 46 Groups for Overlord consisted of 15 squadrons with 362 Unit Equipment aircraft and 61 Reserves. By 16 March 1944 all the squadron moves having been completed it was possible to publish an Order of Battle for the two groups with

---
[1] Ibid. Encl. S.85593.
[2] Allocation of Transport aircraft, A.M.S.O. File 10/5.
[3] C.O.S. (W) 55.
[4] A.C.A.S. (P) File 7590, 13 May 1944.

the allocation of gliders to each squadron. By 6 June 1944, this was as follows[1]:—

Group	Station	Squadron	Aircraft	Gliders
38	Fairford	190	22 + 4 Stirling	50 Horsas
		620	22 + 4 Stirling	50 Horsas
38	Keevil	196	22 + 4 Stirling	50 Horsas
		299	22 + 4 Stirling	50 Horsas
38	Brize Norton	296	22 + 4 Albemarle	50 Horsas
		297	22 + 4 Albemarle	50 Horsas
38	Harwell	295	22 + 4 Albemarle	50 Horsas
		570	22 + 4 Albemarle	50 Horsas
38	Tarrant Rushton	298	18 + 2 Halifax	70 Hamilcars
		644	18 + 2 Halifax	50 Horsas
46	Broadwell	512	30 + 0 Dakotas	40 Horsas
		575	30 + 0 Dakotas	40 Horsas
46	Down Ampney	48	30 + 0 Dakotas	40 Horsas
		271	30 + 0 Dakotas	40 Horsas
46	Blakehill Farm	233	30 + 0 Dakotas	40 Horsas
	Reserves		25	400
	TOTAL		362 + 61	1,120 Gliders

The Final Plan

The whole airborne operation was divided into three subsidiary operations Tonga, Mallard and Rob Roy in that order. Tonga entailed the dropping of the two parachute brigade groups in the early hours of D-Day, Mallard took place on the evening of D-Day when the main airborne force in gliders was launched and Rob Roy covered the re-supply missions.

Originally the tasks of capturing the bridges over the Canal de Caen and the River Orne and the seizing of high ground at Ranville were allotted to 6th Airlanding Brigade as their heavier armour was better suited to holding the positions than were the paratroops. It was intended that the parachute brigades should carry out the more dispersed tasks and that they would follow in the second lift as there were not enough aircraft available to lift the whole division at once[2].

However it was discovered on 17 April 1944, by photographic reconnaissance that the Germans were erecting obstacles, mainly poles, as anti-landing devices on all the probable landing areas and so the plan had to be re-considered as it was no longer feasible to land the main body of gliders by night. It was then decided to land the paratroops before the main glider force in order to remove some of the obstacles and improve the chances of a safe landing for the gliders. The tasks were then allotted as follows[3]:—

5th Parachute Brigade Group, under the command of Brigadier J. H. N. Poett, D.S.O., were to

    (*a*) Seize the bridges over the River Orne and the Canal de Caen at Benouville and Ranville. This was to be accomplished by a *coup de main* using gliderborne troops. (Landing Zones "X" "Y".)[4]

---

[1] No. 38 Group Report. Appendix A, Operation Order 500. Appendix E, Operation Order 500.
[2] Minutes, 9th meeting Airborne Planning Committee. Appendix A. A.E.A.F./T.S./628.
[3] No. 38 and 46 Group Report on Neptune. No. 38 Group Operation Orders, 500, 501.
[4] See Figure 3.

(b) Secure and hold the high ground in the area Benouville—Ranville —Le bas de Ranville.

(c) Capture or destroy the battery on the river Orne opposite Ouistrehan. (Dropping Zone " W ".)[1]

(d) Clear the landing zones North of Ranville sufficiently to allow some 70 gliders to land before dawn on D-Day and 246 on the evening of D-Day. (Operation Mallard.) (Dropping Zone " N ".)

The Brigade was also responsible for protecting this landing zone.

3rd Parachute Brigade Group, under the command of Brigadier J. S. L. Hill, D.S.O., M.C., were to drop at the same time as 5th Parachute Brigade Group on the dropping zones at " K " and " V " and

(a) Capture and destroy the battery and its equipment at Merville (Salenelles) one and a half hours before the first landing craft were due to reach the beaches. (Involving the landing of three gliders.)

(b) Destroy the bridges over the river Dives at Varaville, Robehorane, Bures and Troam.

(c) Having completed the above tasks the brigade were to hamper the enemy's communications by denying them the use of the roads entering the Ranville area from the south and east.

As far as the R.A.F. were concerned the lift for Operation Tonga was to be carried out in three stages and it was in three sections that it left England, apart from the special force of three gliders intended for the Merville battery (at 0020 hours D.B.S.T. 6 June)[2].

The first stage. Six Albemarle pathfinder aircraft were to locate the main dropping zones—two to each. At the same time the *coup de main* party to attack the bridges at " X " and " Y " were to be carried in six Horsa gliders—three to each bridge—towed by Halifax aircraft from Nos. 298 and 644 squadrons. The remainder of the advance party were to be lifted in 21 Albemarles from No. 38 Group squadrons taking transport, guns and equipment to prepare for the main landings.

Second stage. At 0050 hours D.B.S.T. 6 June the main body of the two brigades was to be dropped using aircraft from both groups. 3rd Parachute Brigade were to be dropped on the D.Z.s at " K " and " V " from 108 Dakotas, and 11 Albemarles were to be used for heavy equipment; 5th Parachute Brigade were to be dropped by 21 Dakotas, 91 Stirlings and 19 Albemarles on the main zone " N ".

Third stage. At 0320 hours D.B.S.T. 6 June the Divisional H.Q. which included H.Q.'s of the R.A., R.E. and 4th Anti-Tank Battery were to be landed in 68 Horsa and 4 Hamilcar gliders, towed by Albemarle and Halifax aircraft.

The Special Glider Operation[3]

The timing of the landing of three gliders on the Merville battery was not finally agreed upon without some misgivings on the part of the Air C.-in-C. The timing as planned meant that, as the three gliders would be travelling

---
[1] See Figure 3.
[2] A.E.A.F. File OPS/T.S. 841 Airborne Ops.
[3] A.E.A.F. File T.S.841/24544.

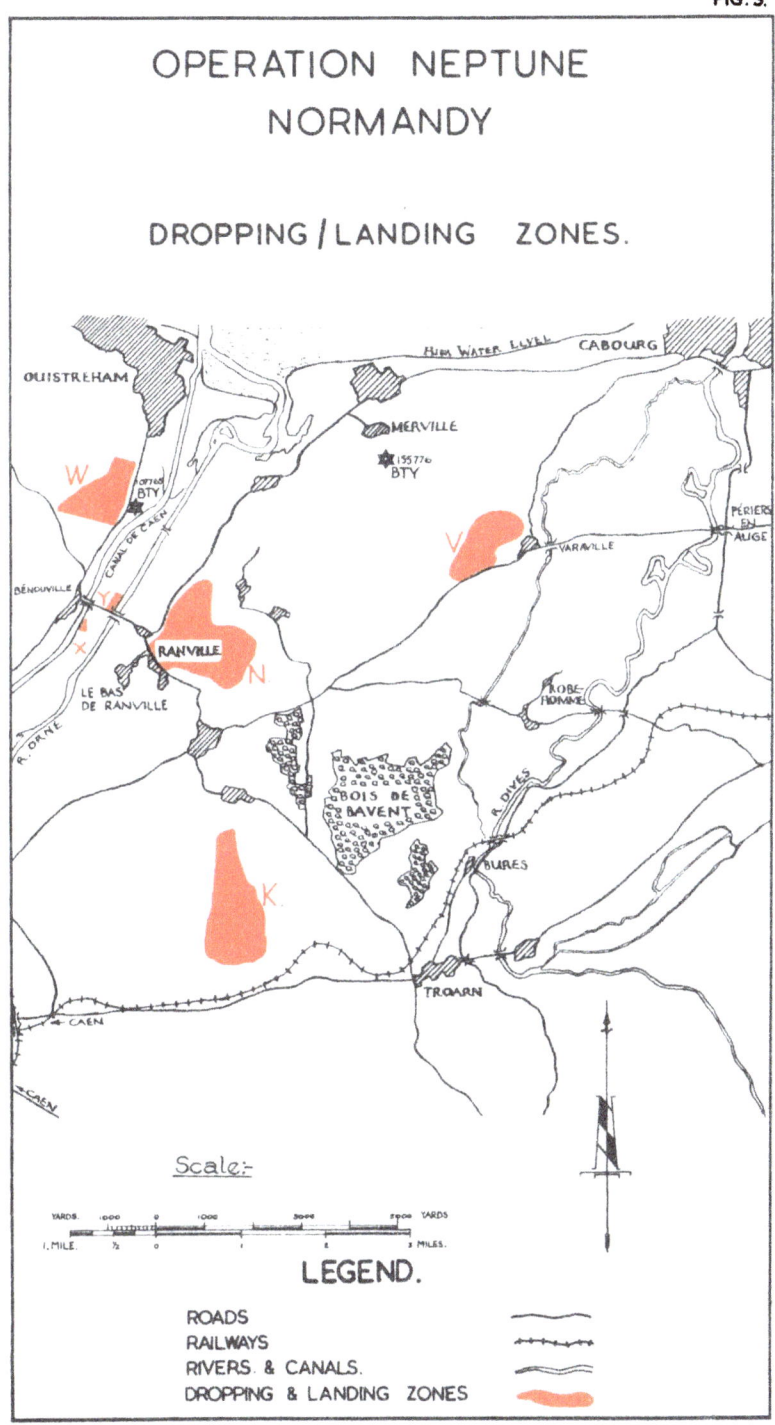

alone and forming a separate sortie, they would be liable to many risks. They would pass nearer to the Navy than the earlier sorties and, as the main operation would then have been taking place for more than four hours, they would be in greater danger from enemy opposition. The Navy had prohibited fire over the corridors and at the times when the first three columns were passing, but could not guarantee to hold fire for three gliders arriving much later. Finally, the bombing of the battery by the Lancasters, if successful, would probably render it unsuitable for glider landing. The Air C.-in-C. recommended that the bombing be postponed until immediately before the paratroop attack on the battery so that it might act as a barrage, but in his opinion the glider operation as now suggested by 6th Airborne Division was out of the question. However two days later Major-General Browning convinced the Air C.-in-C. of its absolute necessity, despite the very obvious dangers, and on 31 May the plan was altered accordingly by H.Q. A.E.A.F.

The Events of 5-6 June 1944[1]

Operation Tonga

First Stage

As darkness was falling over England on 5 June 1944, the long awaited invasion of Europe began when the first pathfinder aircraft, piloted by Squadron Leader Merrick, D.F.C., and carrying Air Vice-Marshal Hollinghurst as passenger, took off at 2303 hours from Harwell. The Pathfinder, Advance Parachute aircraft and the *coup de main* party were due over their respective target zones at 0020 hours 6 June. The weather for this initial stage was fair. Visibility was about three miles; cloud 10-10 at 4,000 ft.-6,000 ft., and wind varying from 10-30 m.p.h. from the west.

Six Albemarle aircraft of No. 38 Group carried the men of the 22nd Independent Parachute Company to the three main dropping zones " K ", " N ", and " V ". These were the Pathfinders and it was their duty to set up Eureka beacons and illuminations on the D.Z.s to guide in the main forces following behind. Two aircraft were allocated to each zone and all went well until they reached their areas when four of the aircraft were delayed owing to exit difficulties necessitating extra runs over the zone. One of the aircraft detailed for zone " K " mistook its whereabouts and dropped its men on the S.E. corner of " N " where they erected lights and beacon intended for use on " K." Although the error was soon realised and the lights and beacon switched off it was too late. Fourteen sticks of 3rd Parachute Brigade intended for zone " K " were dropped on to " N " before the " N " pathfinder party, who had unfortunately been dropped some 1,000 yards away, arrived and set up the correct signals. The outcome of this mistake was that " K " was short of equipment as several of the men wrongly dropped on " N " were taken prisoner before they were able to reach their proper zone.

---

[1] The account of operations Tonga, Mallard and Rob Roy is based upon information obtained from the following main sources: " Report on British Airborne Effort in Operation Neptune " by No. 38 and 46 Groups, R.A.F.; " No. 38 Group Operation Orders 500, 501, 502, 503 "; " Analysis of British Airborne Operations (Tonga and Mallard) No. 38 Group "; " History of No. 46 Group "; " Report of 6th Airborne Division "; " War Office Narrative of Airborne Operations "; " Glider Pilot Organisation, Training and Operations "; " O.R.B.'s Nos. 38 and 46 Groups " (and their Squadrons); " A.E.A.F. Files ".

The third zone "V" proved be an unhappy choice. Although apparently quite suitable when viewed from the air the area, being in a valley, had become extremely wet and treacherous owing to the flooding of the river. The ground was like a bog and all the equipment of one stick was lost or damaged while the other stick was dropped wide and did not arrive until the main body was due to drop. There were also many irrigation and other ditches which prevented rapid concentration. Although a later aircraft reported that Eureka beacons were working on "K" and "N" and lights were visible on all three zones there is no doubt that those on "V" were inadequate and it was this zone which had the highest proportion of scattered drops. The work of the Pathfinders can have far-reaching repercussions but the fact that zone "V" was unsuitable made it impossible for them to carry out their tasks. The mistaken choice of the ground for zone "V" might have had very serious consequences had enemy resistance been stronger.

The advance parachute parties met with mixed success, rather to be expected as they were operating without ground aids. Two Albemarles (Nos. 295 and 570 Squadrons) dropped a small party of 3rd Parachute Brigade on zone "K" but the containers in one aircraft were not dropped owing to losing sight of the D.Z. on the second run in. The second party of 3rd Parachute Brigade was carried in fourteen Albemarles—seven each from Nos. 295 and 570 Squadrons—and underwent various adventures. One aircraft, unable to find the D.Z. "V", made seven unsuccessful runs, was then hit by flak causing a paratroop to fall into and jam the exit hole. The aircraft was forced to return to base without dropping anyone. Two others dropped only three and nine men respectively while from a third six jumped far too soon near the French coast. Failure of the Gee apparatus caused another aircraft to lose time but despite these troubles 106 out of 140 troops were dropped accurately. This did not help overmuch as the lighting and Eureka equipment having been lost (in the flooded area of zone "V"), the advance party were unable to exhibit more than two green lights on the D.Z. before the main body of the brigade began dropping.

The situation on D.Z. "N" was little better; the wind had risen and the drop was scattered. Five Albemarles of Nos. 296 and 298 squadrons carried the advance party of 5th Parachute Brigade and although two of the aircraft had exit difficulties 46 out of 47 men were dropped. Fortunately the inaccurate drop did not matter because the enemy were completely surprised and the gliderborne *coup de main* troops struck so swiftly that the two bridges were easily captured. This glider operation was extraordinarily successful. Of the six Halifax-Horsa combinations three from No. 644 Squadron landed, as briefed, within a few yards of the east end of the swing bridge across the Canal de Caen, on landing zone "X".[1] The other three from No. 298 Squadron were not quite as accurate; one glider had to make a blind release on orders from the tug and landed eight miles west of the L.Z. "Y", another landed about 400 yards from the bridge and the last within 150 yards. The gliders were released at an altitude of 4,500-5,500 ft. about five to six miles from the L.Z.s. The visibility in this area was good (10 miles). The cloud was 6-9/10 at 5,000-6,000 ft. and the wind between 18-40 m.p.h., from the west at release heights.

---

[1] See Figure 3

It would appear that the Germans did not realise anything was about to happen until the gliders were over the landing zones as no flak was encountered. The defences were rapidly overcome; the bridges were seized intact and a small bridgehead was formed on the West bank of the river. The success of this part of the operation reflects great credit on the navigation and extremely accurate timing of the tug crews.

OPERATION TONGA
NORMANDY
CAEN CANAL AND RIVER ORNE

Fig. 4.

Second Stage. Subsidiary Glider and Main Paratroop Landings

Almost immediately after the landing of the advance parties Horsa gliders began to arrive carrying heavy equipment, demolition charges, guns, jeeps, etc., towed by 13 Dakotas of No. 46 Group and four Albemarles of No. 38 Group. The weather was only fair when six of the Dakotas took off from Blakehill Farm (No. 233 squadron) to release their gliders on zone " K " at 0045 hours. Five of the combinations reached the area as they thought correctly but, owing to the error with the lights on zones "K" and "N", three of the gliders landed near "N" and only two on "K". The sixth crashed some distance away.

The remaining 11 gliders scheduled to land on "V" at the same time, carrying heavy equipment for the Merville raid, were mostly unsuccessful. The weather was unfavourable with low cloud and bumpy conditions and several pilots reported that the Lancaster bombing raid on the Merville battery had caused considerable dust and smoke which obscured the landing zone. The outcome was that four gliders landed in a semi-circle $1\frac{1}{4}$ miles from the landing zone while, of the remainder, three were compelled to cast off owing to cloud over the French coast; two landed on zone "N" and two others nearby, consequently most of the equipment was not available for the attack on the battery, though as will be seen later this was not as serious as it might have been.

Close behind the gliders came the main bodies of the two parachute brigade groups. The weather was much the same except that lower cloud (2,000 ft.) was experienced over zone "V" where no ground aids were working. The bog-like nature of the ground in this zone made the landings by the main body extremely hazardous; it impeded movement and rendered the task of mustering the troops at their rendezvous points all the harder. One man lost his life, being sucked down into the bog before he could be rescued.

3rd Parachute Brigade. Zones "V" and "K"

The main body of 3rd Parachute Brigade transported in 71 Dakotas from Nos. 271, 512 and 48 Squadrons, No. 46 Group, experienced the same difficulties in finding zone "V" as had their predecessors in the gliders. No ground aids plus the after effects of the Lancaster raid still impaired the visibility and by then the enemy Flak had begun to function. The dropping was not accurate; only 17 aircraft dropped their sticks on the D.Z.; nine were within one mile and 11 within $1\frac{1}{2}$ miles. Nine sticks of the 1st Canadian Parachute battalion landed near the river Dines, five in the Breville area and the others far and wide over the countryside[1]. The lack of accuracy in this drop, including as it did two-thirds of the strength of the Brigade, was all the more unfortunate as it jeopardised the chances of what was the most vital task of the airborne forces on this night—the attack on the battery at Merville.

Dakotas from Nos. 233, 271 and 575 Squadrons provided the lift for the remainder of 3rd Parachute Brigade to drop on zone "K" to operate in the Troam-Bures area. Two aircraft were lost on the way to the zone and 35 dropped their troops but not where they should have been. The error of the Pathfinders on zone "N" again had its effect and 13 sticks fell on "N" and only eight on "K". Fortunately the objectives of the drop were attained —two bridges at Bures were destroyed by R.E. detachments and 8th Parachute Battalion, thus impeding enemy movement from the South and, at Troam, despite opposition and thanks to precipitate action by the R.E. detachment the bridge was blown up and a gap created.

---

[1] A possible contributory cause of the inaccuracy of this drop was that the No. 46 Group aircraft flew in loose formation of "vics" of three, thirty seconds separating each "vic". Keeping accurate formation was extremely difficult, especially without lights, and it is possible that if the leader of a "vic" of three made an error of navigation the other two members would also be wrong.

5th Parachute Brigade. Zone "N"

This drop, carried out by 131 aircraft, 110 from No. 38 Group and 21 from No. 46 Group, was on the whole successful. Unhampered by the vagaries of fate experienced by 3rd Parachute Brigade on their zones the crews here had the additional aid to navigation provided by signs of the fighting for the bridge over the canal and the Orne river. The lights and Eureka beacons were correctly placed. Six aircraft were lost before reaching the D.Z. and two failed to take off due to unserviceability but 123 carried out their drop accurately although a high wind did result in some being scattered more widely than expected. Most of the troops dropped wide managed to rejoin their units by daylight in time for the enemy counter-attacks which had begun to develop during the early hours. However, 7th Parachute Battalion aided by the glider force managed to repulse these attacks and enlarge the bridgehead to a depth of 800 yards. They held their position despite further counter-attacks until relieved by seaborne forces at 0300 hours, 7 June.

Meanwhile 12th and 13th Parachute battalions, although only at 60 per cent. strength when they moved to their areas managed to capture the Bas de Ranville and Ranvill le Mariquet area. Subjected to attacks by tanks and self-propelled guns (of 123rd Panzer Gren. Regt.) the position by noon was critical but due to the diversion of 1st S.S. brigade to their assistance the position was saved, until the arrival in the evening of 6th Airlanding Brigade. Out of a total of 2,125 troops carried in the first two phases 2,026 were dropped and 702 out of 755 containers.

Third Stage. Landing of Main Glider Force

As the night of D-1/D day wore on the weather deteriorated and it was in unfavourable flying conditions of rain and low stratus cloud with a rising westerly wind that the main glider force of 68 Horsas and four Hamilcars left England, towed by No. 38 Group aircraft. They were carrying the 6th Airborne Divisional H.Q. troops to landing zone "N" in the Ranville area near the site where the Divisional H.Q. was to be situated. Identification lights and Eureka beacons were functioning and 50 of the Horsas were released over the landing zone between 1500 ft. and 1600 ft., 48 of them landing on or near it between 0324 and 0334 hours. Conditions were not easy and many of the landings were made across wind—resulting in collisions with obstacles on the ground and other aircraft. Flak was active by this time and 25 of the combinations reported being hit, fortunately without causing casualties to their passengers. The Hamilcars towed by Halifaxes were more successful; two landed on the L.Z., one a mile away and one forced landed in England due to a broken tow rope. This breaking of tow ropes also caused seven of the Horsas to cast off between the French coast and Ranville, four others cast off over England, the troops joining their units in France later, and three more in cloud. Once the gliders had landed their pilots were soon involved in the fighting, digging themselves in to defend against attacks from the South West.

It could not be pretended that this part of the operation was entirely satisfactory from the air viewpoint but from the military aspect it sufficed. The arrival of the Divisional troops was most opportune as German counter attacks were developing in intensity with the coming of the light and the Airborne troops were hard put to hold their positions. That they did so, although sustaining considerable casualties, was highly creditable and contributed greatly to the wonderfully successful landing of 6th Airborne Brigade on the evening of D-Day.

The glider operation against the Merville battery

One of the most memorable operations ever accomplished by an airborne unit was the capture, by 9th Parachute Battalion, of the battery at Merville. The extreme importance of this objective to the success of Overlord has already been mentioned and to ensure its being taken many weeks of detailed and special training were spent in England[1]. In support of the attack on the battery three Horsa gliders, towed by Albemarles of No. 297 Squadron and piloted by volunteers were to undertake the highly dangerous task of landing on the battery with cargoes of anti-tank guns, jeeps and special stores; they also carried 58 officers and men of 9th Parachute Battalion and eight officers and men of the Royal Engineers.

Taking off from England in time to arrive at Merville by 0430 hours, when the assault should have reached its climax, the gliders encountered bad weather, involving almost continuous cloud flying with 10/10 at 1000 ft. The wind was still westerly but had increased to 28 m.p.h. Soon after the trio were airborne one of the tow ropes broke and the glider was compelled to force-land in England, which it did successfully. The other two were crossing the Channel when the arrester parachute gear[2], a device for retarding speed when landing, of one of them opened and caused the combination to stall and lose height. The arrester gear was jettisoned but the tail of the glider had been damaged. Both gliders were hit by flak after reaching the French coast and experienced much difficulty in identifying the battery as there were no flares or star shells to assist them, the platoon with the mortars having landed too far away to join in the attack. One glider however did manage to land about 350 yards from the battery but the tug of the other, mistaking the village of Merville for the battery, released his glider. The glider pilot having descended to 500 ft. before realising the mistake was unable to land nearer than three miles away.

The battery had to be destroyed by 0450 hours and at the time when the Commanding Officer gave the order to advance only 150 out of a battalion strength of 600 had reached the rendezvous. The majority of the heavy equipment had not arrived (owing to the failure of the glider operation) there were no jeeps or glider stores, no three inch mortars, no sappers, no mine detectors and no 6 lb. guns. Despite these tremendous handicaps and the fact also that the 100 Lancaster raid on the battery had completely missed its target, almost wiping out part of the reconnaissance party, the success signal was fired at 0445 hours. The battery had been put out of action and its garrison of 22 killed. The casualties in this operation were 70 of the 150 participants. The fact that the operation was successfully accomplished, with such seriously depleted forces and an almost complete failure of the glider operation, is a tremendous testimony to the courage and determination of the small force who took part.

This was the last of the airborne activities in the early hours of 6 June; the foundation stone of victory had been laid and the crews returned to

---

[1] See War Office "History of Airborne Forces".
[2] The arrester parachute gear was developed by Airspeeds in a commendably short time during Whitsun 1944.

England to rest prior to the briefing for operation Mallard on the afternoon of the same day. Many of the crews took part in both Tonga and Mallard with only 15 hours rest between them. By 1700 hours the tugs and gliders were marshalled ready for take-off[1].

Operation Tonga. Summary of Results

Parachute Sorties

    266 aircraft were detailed.
    264 aircraft (99.2 per cent.) took off.
    255 aircraft (95.8 per cent.) reported successful drops
       7 aircraft (2.6 per cent.) were missing.
    4,512 troops were carried.
    4,310 troops (95.5 per cent.) were dropped.
    1,315 containers were carried.
    1,214 containers (92.4 per cent.) were dropped

Glider Sorties

    98 combinations were detailed.
    98 combinations took off. (100 per cent.)
    74 gliders or (75.5 per cent.) were successfully released
    57 gliders or (58 per cent.) landed on or near L.Z.s.
    22 gliders or (22.5 per cent.) were missing. Of 196 glider pilots 125 returned to U.K., 4 were killed 14 wounded and 53 missing.
    611 troops were carried. 493 successfully released.
    59 jeeps were carried, 44 successfully released.
    69 motor-cycles were carried, 55 successfully released.
    17 guns, 6-pounders, were carried, 15 successfully released.
     4 guns, 17-pounders, were carried, 2 successfully released.
One bulldozer was successfully released.
One tank was not successfully released.

The following figures, based on plots made by H.Q. Airborne Division, give a concise if rough picture of the accuracy of the drops. The success percentages however give no indication as to the military aspect as many of the troops, dropped outside the two mile limit, contributed to the success of the operation. The percentages are based on all those dropped within one mile as being considered successful and those within two miles as 50 per cent. successful.

Tonga
Glider Landings

	Landing Zone					Battery	Total
	X	Y	N	V	K		
On L.Z.	3	1	46	0	2	0	52
Within 1 mile of L.Z.	0	1	3	1	0	1	6
Over 1 mile from L.Z.	0	0	6	5	3	1	15
Abortive	0	1	17	5	1	1	25
Detailed	3	3	72	11	6	3	98
Percentage Success	100	66	68	9	33	33	60

[1] See Appendix 3.

5th Parachute Brigade on "N"

	5 Bde. H.Q. C 13 Bn.	7 Para. Bn.	12 Para. Bn.	Total
On D.Z. ...	29	7	15	51
Within 1 mile of D.Z. ...	18	15	7	40
Over 1 mile from D.Z. ...	4	—	—	4
				95

Aircraft detailed ...	131
Missing and abortive ...	36
Percentage Success ...	71

3rd Parachute Brigade on "K" and "V"

	D.Z. "K" 8 Para. Bn.	H.Q. Para. Bn.	1 Can. Para. Bn.	9 Para. Bn.	Total
On D.Z. ...	6	1	7	8	16
Within 1 mile of D.Z. ...	2	1	5	8	14
1 to 2 miles from D.Z. ...	4	3	6	6	15
Over 2 miles from D.Z. ...	21	1	16	0	17
Missing ...	4				8
Detailed ...	37				70
Percentage Success ...	27				54

Operation Mallard

The glider operation on the evening of D-Day which transported the remainder of 6th Airborne Division to France was an almost unqualified success—246 gliders out of a total of 256 which took off landing on their correct zones. This was the first daylight glider operation of any magnitude and vindicated the opinion of those who favoured daylight to night. It was feared that a huge force of tug-glider combinations stretching over a vast distance and of necessity flying low and slowly would be an ideal, almost sitting target for ground defences. However when planning the operation it was not as though previous night operations (Husky) had created a successful precedent. Far from it—and so after considering the respective risks of day and night operations, i.e. the dangers of flak against those of collision, crashes, navigational difficulties and wide disposal, the chance was taken. The timing of the operation was most important. To ensure the element of surprise and the protection of darkness on the return journey the release was timed to take place at dusk when the sun would be in the most favourable position. (Protection against enemy fighters was arranged by No. 11 Group, Fighter Command[1].) The results exceeded all expectations and went far towards proving that, given definite air superiority and good flying conditions, the odds were in favour of daytime for this type of operation.

---

[1] (a) Close fighter escort by 15 Squadrons of No. 11 Group.
(b) Routine high and low level fighter cover over the beach-head.
(c) Escorted bomber operations and fighter sweeps to the South and South-East of the beach-head area.

OPERATION MALLARD
NORMANDY
GLIDERS ON ZONE 'N'

Fig. 5

The lift was carried out by Nos. 38 and 46 Groups using Horsa gliders for men, jeeps and trailers and Hamilcars for heavy armour and guns. All the squadrons of both groups were employed with the exception of No. 233 (which was detailed for the first re-supply mission Rob Roy I). The object of the lift was to land the full fighting force of 6th Airborne Division in support of, and in some cases to relieve, those who had landed in the early hours of D-Day. The forces transported were 6th Airlanding Brigade, the Airborne Armoured Reconnaissance Regiment and 211th Light Battery R.A. Two zones were chosen for the landing—" N " north of Ranville used in operation " Tonga " and a new one " W ", between Ouistrehan and Benouville west of the Canal de Caen.

The force was scheduled to land at 2100 hours and by evening the weather had improved so that when the time came to take off the visibility was excellent (10-15 miles) with only scattered patches of high cloud. The wind was light at the release height, 10-15 m.p.h./320. In those conditions the ground markings and Eureka beacons on the landing zones were found to be scarcely necessary and few pilots reported using them. During 6 June landing strips were cleared in readiness.

Landing Zone " N "

A total of 146 tug-glider combinations were sent to zone " N ". Of these, 74 Horsas were towed by Dakotas from No. 46 Group, and 42 Horsas and 30 Hamilcars by Albemarles and Stirlings of No. 38 Group. 142 combinations landed successfully on zone " N " between 2051 and 2123 hours. Of the remaining four—two broken tow-ropes caused forced landings in England—one combination ditched in the Channel and the fourth was missing. The only other casualty was a Dakota tug shot down by flak near the landing zone—all the other tugs safely returned to base.

Landing Zone " W "

The six remaining squadrons of No. 38 Group provided the lift for 112 Horsas on zone " W ", and although two became unserviceable prior to take off only four of the remaining 110 failed to land successfully on the zone. Two forces landed in England and two gliders cast off over the Channel, one ditching and one landing in France, but a long way from the L.Z. The operation was accomplished in 28 minutes the last glider landing at 2120 hours. There was however some confusion at the L.Z. as several of the leading gliders landed in the wrong direction with the result that the majority did the same. The concentration was very good and showed that given ample practice this standard could be improved upon. In the whole operation Mallard only ten gliders failed to reach their zone; a percentage success of 95.3 per cent.

The position on the ground by the evening of D-Day was tight though not critical nevertheless it was with considerable relief that the men of 6th Airborne Division saw their comrades arriving in, what was up to that time, the most impressive display of air power ever seen. After two days' fighting the 6th Airborne Division had gained all its objectives except for a small section on the coast near Franceville. The scattered drops had not materially affected the military outcome and despite none too favourable weather the air plan had definitely worked. Thus the main airborne effort in Overlord ended on a high note of success. The only remaining operations were those of re-supply to the forces on the ground and the S.A.S. operations which No. 38 Group had been doing throughout the early months of 1944.

Operation Rob Roy—Re-supply

The first of the re-supply missions was carried out by 50 Dakotas of No. 46 Group on the evening of D-Day. Thirty aircraft of No. 233 Squadron at Blakehill Farm which had not taken part in the earlier tasks and ten each from Broadwell and Down Ampney were detailed to drop 116 tons of supplies, consisting of food, ammunition, radio sets, explosives, medical stores, petrol and other items on the Dropping zone " N " just before midnight[1].

All the aircraft took off satisfactorily and flying in vic. formations of three reached the French coast. Unfortunately the crews had been briefed not to expect shipping on the route whereas, in fact, there were several friendly vessels anchored off the mouth of the Orne, who opened fire on the low-flying aircraft. Many were hit, two so badly that they were forced to turn back, one having to ditch in the Channel. Five other aircraft were missing from the operation. Naturally the formations were split up and the dropping suffered accordingly with the result that 6th Airborne Division Depot only received $24\frac{1}{2}$ tons of the supplies.

The reasons for this unfortunate occurrence were the same as in earlier operations, namely—inability to recognise friendly aircraft, failure of the aircraft to identify themselves immediately and the fact that the Naval forces had been bombed by the Germans shortly before and thus were rather aircraft conscious. All this was a further indication to the fact that had the operation been carried out by day the drop might have been far more successful, although night dropping did afford protection from enemy flak which might have caused equal casualties. This operation concluded the No. 46 Group contribution to Overlord and they reverted to their true role of transport. Throughout the summer months they fetched and carried in ever-increasing loads to and from Europe[2].

The remaining re-supply operations in Overlord were carried out by No. 38 Group. In the early hours of 8 June six Stirlings of No. 190 Squadron took off from Fairford and successfully dropped their loads on D.Z. " N ". All the crews recognised the D.Z. without markings or use of navigational aids and dropped from 600 ft. as the visibility was not too good owing to smoke and sea mist. Later the same day twelve Stirlings—six from No. 196 Squadron and six from No. 299—took off on a similar mission to D.Z. " N ". Unfortunately the weather had deteriorated considerably during the evening low cloud covering most of the route (as well as a possibility of fog over base airfields). A general recall signal was sent out and seven of the aircraft returned to England. The other five however being near the French coast when the signal was received decided to carry on. Recognising the dropping zone visually they dropped 112 containers and nine panniers before returning safely to their bases.

At dawn on 10 June No. 38 Group again dropped supplies on the D.Z. " N ". Six Halifaxes from Tarrant Rushton dropped containers, jeeps and six-pound guns without mishap from 1,000 ft. and nine Stirlings from Keevil were similarly successful. Little or no opposition from the ground was encountered, the weather was still cloudy but not enough to hamper

---

[1] These were carried in 18 containers, 609 panniers and 88 parcels. At a meeting at A.E.A.F. H.Q. on 28 February 1944, the airfields to be used for re-supply were chosen—Blakehill Farm, Broadwell, Down Ampney and Fairford. File 2A/A.E.A.F./778.

[2] The activities of No. 46 Group during the months prior to Arnhem are described in the " History of No. 46 Group ".

the visibility. The final operation under the code name Rob Roy took place on the evening of 10 June when three Stirlings dropped supplies on "N" and returned without difficulty. And so the great operation had been launched, the liberating armies were gradually established and daily grew stronger, thus their demands increased. By the end of June, 26 separate supply dropping missions had been successfully undertaken. The code name was changed from Rob Roy to Townhall and for the rest of the summer re-supply was carried on[1].

Conclusions

Judging by the eventual military outcome of Overlord and the fact that all the main objectives were secured, the operation was successful but from the purely air point of view there was a certain proportion of failure which, under less favourable circumstances of stronger opposition, might have resulted in severe losses and possibly the failure of the whole operation. Several of the objectives, mainly bridges captured by the *coup de main* party and the Merville battery were only possible to take with the use of airborne forces. Several factors, mainly weather, last minute re-disposition of the enemy and some technical failures made it impossible to guarantee a completely successful operation. Too much depended on circumstances beyond human control; if the conditions were favourable such as for Mallard then all was well; if they were not then the outcome was rather a gamble. However, bearing in mind that Neptune was the first airborne operation ever attempted on such a large scale and that the weather was by no means ideal, the plan very definitely justified itself and provided invaluable experience for the future.

The lessons learned from Neptune can be categorised as follows :—

(i) No operational plan should call for too great precision in time and place from the airborne forces thus no one particular airborne unit or objective allotted to it should be of a nature vital to the whole operation.

(ii) To ensure success air superiority over the whole area must have been gained. However operations may be carried out any airborne forces cannot help being a sitting target to either ground, air or sea defences.

(iii) Prior to Neptune there was much controversy as to the relative risks of day and night operations. Mallard proved beyond reasonable doubt that all circumstances being equal the odds favoured daylight for this type of operation. In other words the dangers of flak were considerably outweighed by the increased safety from collision and crashes and the simplification of navigation. From the training aspect the idea of night operations should not be discarded. If crews are trained in the difficult art of night dropping then daylight operations will seem very much simpler.

(iv) The highest proportion of failures in Neptune was amongst aircraft detailed to the unsuitable difficult zone "V" where there were no radio aids and practically no visual ones. This did not altogether excuse the failures. Radio aids were "aids" to navigation and not substitutes therefore crews should have used them as such and not relied on them to the exclusion of proficiency in ordinary

---

[1] For description of equipment carried, method of stowing and dropping, see Appendix 9.

navigation. Individual navigational skill was essential. The American airborne operations in Overlord provided excellent proof of this. It was no use relying on the leader of a formation so that on his success or failure depended that of the formation.

(v) When possible the fewer different types of aircraft used the better. In Neptune the use of four types resulted in various disadvantages —the carriage of different loads at different speeds complicated the tasks of the loaders and flight planners, which were difficult enough because of the varying speeds of parachute dropping and glider towing aircraft. Different speeds also caused "bunching" on the route, with aircraft in another's slipstream and gaps in the continuity of arrival.

(vi) There were several instances of tow rope breakages due mainly to losing position in cloud and flying in the slipstream of other aircraft. Other than by strengthening the tow ropes these were risks which had to be faced if a close formation was required and if any chance at all was to be taken with the weather. As regards other equipment there were so few failures that they could not be considered as contributory to any lack of success in the operations.

(vii) More time should in future be allowed for briefing; as it was only three days were allowed, which was not sufficient, especially in view of the shortage of models of the objectives. Only one was available for both groups whereas at least one per station should be provided to allow all the crews ample time to study it in detail.

(viii) The rehearsals for the operations which took place during training were found to be most beneficial to all concerned and when possible should always be carried out.

Special Duty Operations

The story of Special Air Service and Special Operations Executive is a long one and in the case of the latter covers the greater part of the war. It is beyond the scope of this narrative to describe these operations except in so far as they were in direct support of airborne operations. Their history has been covered in detail elsewhere[1].

In January 1944 H.Q. S.A.S. troops was formed under the command of Lieutenant General Browning[2]. The Brigade was commanded by Colonel McCloud and consisted of about 2,000 men: 1st and 2nd S.A.S. Regiment, 3rd and 4th Parachute Battalion, Belgian Independent Parachute Squadron and "F" Squadron of G.H.Q. Reconnaissance Regiment, which acted as Brigade Signals Section. In addition a special branch was formed at Headquarters from the airborne troops for the strategic and high level planning of the operations. The purposes of S.A.S. were mainly two-fold: *Strategic*: Operations in the rear of the enemy, sabotage of H.Q., dumps, transport, roads, bridges, etc.; supplying, assisting and organising resistance movements. *Tactical*: Harassing the enemy movement towards a particular battle area or during retreat—the spreading of false information or rumours, diversionary raids and small scale attacks on particular objectives.

---

[1] "History of Special Duty Operations in Europe".
[2] War Office Narrative, Chapter 18.

S.A.S. in relation to Overlord

The operations were mainly designed to hinder movement of enemy reserves into the invasion area in the early stages of battle. They were however not allowed to interfere with the vital operations of the airborne divisions and were definitely of a secondary priority. The general purpose of the operations was to destroy enemy communication in collaboration with the Maquis and assist the latter in gaining control of certain areas. From February onwards No. 38 Group took part in the Special Operations against the enemy. They were for the most part very successful and few losses were sustained in almost a score of operations. On 11 April 1944 as many as 105 aircraft took part, only two of which were lost; 88 completed their tasks satisfactorily. All these operations provided excellent training and when after D-Day it became necessary to drop S.A.S. in support of Overlord, No. 38 Group had experienced crews ready for the tasks[1].

Special S.A.S. troops in N.W. Europe were under the command of Twenty-first Army Group and their operations being strategic rather than tactical, were supervised by the G.3 (Ops.) Division of S.H.A.E.F. This supervision applied where the operations were connected with resistance groups or where they were of a purely tactical nature. These latter were not so frequent and were usually carried out by one or two Stirlings from No. 38 Group, who dropped small parties to attack objectives such as railway bridges, tunnels, airfields, etc.[2]. Normally however S.A.S. activities were directly in conjunction with resistance groups, to whom they supplied the nuclei of trained leaders and experts[3].

The first S.A.S. operations in direct support of Overlord were carried out on 5 June 1944 when two parties of three S.A.S. troops were dropped to assist in operation Titanic—the landing of dummy parachutes in support of Neptune[4]. On the same night 35 troops were dropped by a Stirling in Brittany, 18 in the N.W. (known as area Sam West) and 17 in the S.W. (known as Dingson). These troops were to contact the Maquis and prepare bases for operation Cooney which took place two nights later, when nine Albemarle aircraft from Brize Norton and Harwell dropped 56 troops in parties of three in a line across Brittany. Despite anti-aircraft fire none were lost. Their task was to sever railway lines at eighteen chosen points in order to cut off Brest and Western Brittany from the rest of France, and then to retire to bases previously prepared in Dingson and Sam West by the troops dropped two nights before.

Also on this busy night two Stirlings of No. 620 Squadron dropped S.A.S. troops and supplies south of the Loire in the area Bullbasket and another aircraft should have dropped parties on the north side, but only the first two were successful. This was known as Operation Sunflower II. On the night of 9-10 June three aircraft from No. 620 Squadron successfully dropped 50 troops of the 4th French Parachute Battalion and equipment in area Sam West, two aircraft from No. 299 Squadron and one from No. 196 Squadron dropped a similar party in Dingson. All the aircraft returned safely.

In operations of this nature a very high standard of efficiency was essential. The aircraft flew as independent units and the drop was usually done from low level, in Operation Cooney from 500 ft., and no ground aids at all were

---
[1] No. 38 Group O.R.B., February.
[2] SHAEF/17240/8 (Ops.) (a), 24 May 1944.
[3] A.E.A.F./S./806/ E.1., Appendix A.
[4] Ibid, Part I, Encl. 26.

provided. The motive behind these operations was to assist the main military plan for Overlord in which it was intended to gain control of the Atlantic ports and develop Brittany as an operational base, once the breakout from the lodgement area had been accomplished. Apart from Brittany other areas further south later became important—the Ardennes, the Vosges Mountains, the area between the Garonne and Bullbasket and the area between Lyon and Dijon. These places and others more distant were not easy to supply owing to the very short nights. Throughout the summer months following D-Day until October 1944 S.A.S. operations were carried out with a high degree of success. Each of these operations took place over several nights and although the daily effort might only involve the use of one or two aircraft it was rare indeed that No. 38 Group failed to accomplish its share of the task. The aircraft nearly always succeeded in finding the dropping zones and the fact that sometimes the operations were not completely successful could only be attributed to the innate difficulties experienced by the people on the ground.

The American Airborne Operations

Whilst the 6th Airborne Division were being landed in the Caen area the IX U.S. Troop Carrier Command were transporting the 82nd and 101st Airborne Divisions to the base of the Contentin penisular. In these operations the Americans were less successful than the British. It was true they had worse weather which, combined with inexperience, prevented their pathfinders from accurately locating the correct dropping zones but this did not entirely account for their widely scattered drops.

The principal cause of their failure can be attributed to poor navigation. The American plan was that only the formation leaders needed navigational training; the fallacy of this follow my leader principle was thoroughly demonstrated in the Normandy operations[1]. In fact General Browning, Major General Airborne Forces, signalled the Air C.-in-C., shortly after D-Day to the effect that he "considered it essential for IX Troop Carrier Command to be ordered to train and operate on the same lines as No. 38 Group, that is in navigation and map reading".

That the operation was only partially successful was not altogether unexpected—though for different reasons. In a letter on 29 May 1944 to the Supreme Commander, General Eisenhower, the Air C.-in-C. stressed the hazards involved in flying low by moonlight over the Contentin peninsular, where German troops were known to have concentrated, for a period of about three hours. He pointed out that the aircraft to be used were vulnerable, being without armour or leak-proof tanks; that the landing of gliders by night in the St. Mere Église area was dangerous; and that generally for various reasons the operation would not be justified[2]. In his reply General Eisenhower said that he was fully sensible of the risks involved but that the operation must go on[3].

The 101st Airborne Division was landed S.E. of St. Mere Église from 0130 hours 6 June 1944, and of 6,600 troops dropped only 1,100 landed near their objectives and 60 per cent. of their equipment was lost. The 82nd Airborne

---

[1] A.E.A.F. File T.L.M./M.S. 150.
[2] A.E.A.F./Ops. 3, Appendix III/10. T.S./841/Ops. 3.
[3] A.E.A.F./Ops. 3, Appendix III/12.

Division was also widely scattered west of Carentan Cherbourg road from 0230 hours. The glider landings suffered casualties but managed to reinforce the airborne units (on the night 6-7 June) who were fighting gallantly and hard in capturing the town of St. Mere Église. Once again the dispersed drop did not prevent the attainment of all objectives and as in the British sector caused confusion to the Germans as to the extent and area of the landings. The Americans were fortunate in meeting with little flak opposition and what there was proved to be ineffective. Out of 1,656 Sorties flown on D-Day and D + 1 only 46 aircraft were lost.

Invasion of Southern France

Operation Dragoon-Anvil

The purpose of this operation was to carry out an assault landing between Frejus and St. Raphael about halfway between Toulon and Cannes on the south coast of France, to be followed by an advance up the Rhone Valley. This was to coincide with the advance of the main force in Normandy[1]. Although there was little opposition in the coastal areas the German had reserves inland and to delay the movement of these to the coast an airborne force was required. Thus in June 1944 all available airborne forces in the area, which included five American Parachute Battalions, one American Air Landing Brigade and the British 2nd Independent Parachute Brigade Group, were combined into the 1st U.S. Airborne Task force under Major General Frederick. On 16 July 1944 Troop Carrier Command H.Q. was set up with the airborne forces Headquarters in the Rhone area and the lessons of previous operations were applied in wholly co-ordinated planning. An intensive training programme which stressed the use of pathfinder aids and co-operation with naval, air and ground forces was carried out. The task given to the British Brigade Group in the main operation was to capture the area between La Motte and Le Muy, prevent the enemy from reaching it and hold it for further landings later in the day.

The operation took place in the early hours of 15 August 1944 and the British 1st Independent Parachute Platoon were the first Allied parachute troops to land in Southern France. They set up Eureka beacons to guide in the main force. As a result of mist and cloud the main drops were only about 60 per cent. accurate. Out of 125 aircraft of U.S. 51st Troop Carrier Wing carrying the parachute troops, only 73 found the correct dropping zones, but, as anticipated there was little opposition and the objectives were gained without difficulty. Meanwhile the anti-airborne poles were cleared from the area in preparation for the landing by Horsa and Waco gliders later in the day. These also were carried out successfully. By the evening of 15 August approximately one Division of Allied troops were established in positions covering all enemy routes to the sea. The American forces had captured Frejus and St. Raphael by the morning of the 16th and contacted the British at Le Muy early on the 17th. The whole operation was completely successful; there were no instances of friendly fire against aircraft or gliders; the selection of routes was good as was the discipline of anti-aircraft crews. There was little enemy opposition. All objectives were captured and 2,000 prisoners were taken[2].

---

[1] War Office Narrative, Chapter 16.
[2] A.E.A.F./T.S./22607. Encl. 2A.

CHAPTER 8

DEVELOPMENT AND POLICY (June to September, 1944)

Formation of the First Allied Airborne Army

On 2 June 1944 Supreme Headquarters Allied Expeditionary Force, in a letter to the British and American Chiefs of Staff, proposed the formation of an organisation for the control by S.H.A.E.F. of airborne troops[1]. The purpose of this organisation was three-fold:—

(a) To enable the Supreme Commander to retain control of all airborne troops.

(b) To simplify the unification of British and American airborne troops if required for use as a single striking force in one or other of the Army zones.

(c) To co-ordinate planning and command with the Allied Expeditionary Air Force and the ground force Commanders.

It was also recommended that a Commanding General be selected by the Supreme Commander and that the Headquarters be formed around the already existing British Headquarters airborne forces[2]. The functions of this combined Headquarters Airborne Troops, as it was then called, were agreed upon by A.E.A.F. and S.H.A.E.F. and listed as follows:—

(a) To supervise training and to allot facilities.

(b) To study and recommend improvements in airborne equipment.

(c) To co-ordinate means of supply.

(d) To consult with the Commander-in-Chief, A.E.A.F., regarding his requirements, because an airborne operation is an air operation and thus the responsibility of the Air Commander-in-Chief.

(e) The assembling of troops, equipment, and supplies at designated air bases.

(f) The preparation and examination, in conjunction with S.H.A.E.F. Planning Staff, of the outlined plan for the use of airborne forces and the preparation of detailed plans for their use in conjunction with ground and air force Commanders.

(g) The direction and control of the execution of such plans until the ground force Commander assumes responsibility.

(h) To establish re-supply requirements, arrange for delivery to departure air bases and to supervise re-supply.

(i) Provision for the return of airborne units when released by the ground force Commander.

(j) To reconstitute airborne forces.

On 20 June, General Eisenhower, the Supreme Commander, approved the appointment of a United States Lieutenant-General, as Commanding General for the combined Headquarters.

The Supreme Commander, in a message to General Marshall[3], on 10 July 1944, stated his reasons for wishing to form the First Allied Airborne Army. He said that there was at present " no suitable agency available to the High Command to assume responsibility for combined planning between the Troop

---

[1] A.E.A.F. File T.S./22518. Encl. 1A.
[2] Ibid. Encl. 4B.
[3] T.L.M. File S. 150/8. Encl. 1.

Carrier Command and airborne forces ". This planning includes joint training, development of operational projects and logistical support until its function could be taken over by normal agencies; also co-ordination of ground and naval forces, assuring a sufficiency of supplies and equipment. Thus, General Eisenhower wanted an airborne Commander to assume these responsibilities, not necessarily to command the troops, but to provide all logistical support until the normal lines of communication be opened.

Although in general the need for unification of control of all airborne forces under one Commander was approved by Headquarters, A.E.A.F., the Air Commander-in-Chief (Air Marshal Leigh-Mallory) said he thought that including the Troop Carrier units would merely complicate planning, preparation and execution. In a letter to the Supreme Commander on 17 August 1944 he commented on each of the functions laid down for the new organisation[1].

The main points stressed in this letter by the Air Commander-in-Chief were as follows: —

The Supervision of Training and Allotment of Facilities

Basic training must necessarily be carried out on a national basis; hence, supervision by the airborne Commander can only apply to combined exercise training.

The Recommendation of Improvements in Equipment and Co-ordination of Supply

Such recommendations can only be made to higher authority, i.e. S.H.A.E.F., who would require additional staff to deal with them. Existing channels for the British Troop Carrying Units, viz. Air Ministry and M.A.P., were working satisfactorily and it would only lead to confusion if they were disturbed.

Consultation with the Air Commander-in-Chief concerning A.E.A.F. Requirements

From the time of take-off to landing, an airborne operation being purely an air operation, must be the responsibility of the Air Commander-in-Chief, who must retain the power of veto. Thus, an airborne Commander merely interposes another unnecessary unit in the chain of communications.

Preparation of Plans

Experience has proved that detailed planning must be done at a low level. Previously, this was carried out satisfactorily and since the Air Commander-in-Chief would still have to be represented from the new Headquarters, no reduction or simplification of the present procedure would result.

The Establishment of Re-supply Requirements, Arranging of Delivery and Departure Air Bases and the Supervision of Re-supply

These arrangements have always been quite efficiently carried out by existing British and American organisations, and the addition of another Headquarters to the chain between the Service Commands, War Office, Air Ministry and airborne divisions, would merely retard procedure.

---

[1] A.E.A.F. File T.S./22518/A3. Encl. 7A.

The principal criticisms of the Air Commander-in-Chief fell under two main headings:—

(a) Increase in personnel, time and labour that would be necessary, resulting in loss of efficiency.

(b) A division of responsibility on purely air problems.

Previous events e.g. Overlord—had not shown the present organisation to be a failure and therefore any re-organisation involving such division of air forces was, he suggested, illogical and unsound. In addition a general impression might be created that airborne operations were a special mysterious thing apart and as such be ignored by those outside them.

The Air Commander-in-Chief submitted that the re-organisation should include:—

Inauguration of a Corps Headquarters for the American airborne divisions, to be located near Eastcote.

The unification under one Commander of British and American airborne troops. Thus the Air Commander-in-Chief would remain responsible for all air aspects of airborne operations, while the airborne Commander would control all ground forces.

In his reply to the Air Commander-in-Chief's proposals, the Supreme Commander, although recognising the advantages proposed, felt that there was a need for the organisation as planned and that if it were to fulfil its purpose, troop carrier units must come under the operational control of the combined Headquarters. As nearly all air transport used came from troop carrier sources, the most efficient operation possible would be to place the Combined Air Transport Operation Room under control of the airborne Headquarters[1].

The formation of First Allied Airborne Army did not tally with the principle of a single theatre Air Commander, which was later stressed by Field Marshal Montgomery in his book *High Command in War*. It meant that the Commander directing the air battle did not have control over the Air Transport force, so vital to his, and the Army Commander's plans.

The final authority for the transfer of the various units to the Command of the Commanding General, First Allied Airborne Army, was issued by S.H.A.E.F. 16 August 1944. It was announced that U.S. IX Troop Carrier Command was to be transferred from the operational control of A.E.A.F. to Command of First Allied Airborne Army. The British units, including Headquarters Airborne Troops, with 52nd (" L " Division) and one airborne division, S.A.S. troops and No. 1 Polish Parachute Brigade Group, were also transferred to the command of the First Allied Airborne Army[2]. Lieutenant-General Lewis H. Brereton of the United States Army assumed command of the First Allied Airborne Army, with Lieutenant-General Browning, G.O.C., British Airborne Troops, as his deputy, on 8 August 1944.

The Headquarters for the new organisation was at Sunninghill Park, near Ascot, close to the rear Headquarters of the U.S. IX Air Force. An advanced H.Q. was later set up at Maison Laffitte, near Paris, where the planning section were able to maintain close contact with S.H.A.E.F. Headquarters at Versailles. Approval of the formation of the First Allied Airborne Army

---

[1] S.H.A.E.F. File 17281/Ops. (A).
[2] A.E.A.F. File T.S./22518. Encl. 11A.

was expressed by the Chief of Air Staff, in a letter to Air Chief Marshal Tedder, provided that the principles learned from operation Husky, and later proved by Overlord, were observed[1]. These were: —

(a) Lieutenant-General Brereton should have a British Air Deputy with suitable staff similar to any other integrated air command.

(b) The airborne operations should be under the general control of the officer responsible to the Supreme Commander for air operations as a whole.

The future of No. 46 Group was also discussed in this letter because, although the IX Troop Carrier Command was under First Allied Airborne Army, the Americans still had transport aircraft in the IX Air Service Command and the United States Air Transport Command for use in normal transport purposes between France and the United Kingdom. Therefore it was suggested that No. 46 Group should not come under the First Allied Airborne Army except when specifically required for operations or training for operations. However, the position remained unaltered, although it was by no means stabilised as will be described later. As far as possible No. 46 Group transport schedules were taken over by other units.

The effect of this fundamental change, in the organisation and control of airborne forces, upon Nos. 38 and 46 Groups, was that they came under the control of First Allied Airborne Army for airborne operations, operational training and for augmentation of resources for air lift, with the exception of aircraft required for S.A.S. or S.O.E. operations, the control of which remained with the Air Commander-in-Chief. On 3 August 1944 authority was given to the A.O.C., No. 38 Group, to use No. 46 Group aircraft (Dakotas) on S.A.S/S.O.E. missions, provided they operated only in areas where the defences were relatively weak. All planning and operational control was vested in No. 38 Group. The administrative control of these Groups still remained with their respective R.A.F. Commands[2].

As No. 38 and 46 Groups were now under the operational control of First Allied Airborne Army, it was felt in the R.A.F. that they should be represented in the new Headquarters. Air Vice-Marshal Hollinghurst, A.O.C. No. 38 Group, in a letter on 31 August 1944 to the Air Commander-in-Chief, expressed concern as to the division of responsibilities under the new organisation[3]. He quoted the fact that No. 38 Group had not been represented at the Conferences concerned with planning Linnet. He felt that as Nos. 38 and 46 Groups were to have been actively concerned in the operation they should have been represented at the Conferences. The outcome of correspondence between the Air Commander-in-Chief and Lieutenant-General Brereton on this subject, was an agreement that the Commander of an airborne operation be chosen from the force particularly interested.

Early in September, the inclusion of R.A.F. officers on the strength of the new establishment was discussed, when Group Captain Macintyre (Ops. 3 A.E.A.F.) visited Headquarters, First Allied Airborne Army. On 6 September 1944 the Americans having concurred, an establishment was drafted which included some fifteen R.A.F. officers, a General and a Brigadier.

[1] D.S.C./T.S./100/14.
[2] A.E.A.F./T.S./1317/Ops. 3. Encl. 27A.
[3] 38G./S. 18/9/Air.

Combined Air Transport Operations Room (C.A.T.O.R.)

The combined air transport operations room was established on 1 June 1944, at Stanmore, to control the whole organisation of both American and British transport aircraft[1]. Its inception arose from a scheme evolved at S.H.A.E.F. Headquarters for co-ordinating the use of aircraft for supply by air[2]. The scheme stated that all demands for either scheduled air emergency transport or supply by air, must be submitted to C.A.T.O.R. which was to be controlled by Headquarters, A.E.A.F. It was divided into two sections, an Operations Section, staffed by Headquarters A.E.A.F., and a Supply Section, staffed by personnel from War Office, E.T.O.U.S.A., IX Air Force Service Command, and R.A.F. Equipment A.E.A.F.[3]

The Operations Section was responsible for allocating aircraft to scheduled or emergency supply tasks; to inform interested parties what air lift was available, to make necessary arrangements between Supply Section and airfields, and to request fighter escort if required. The Supply Section was to arrange for emergency supply demands and to receive a detailed breakdown of demands from armies or air forces, who would arrange for the supplies to be moved to the supply loading airfields. Liaison Officers in the Supply Section of C.A.T.O.R. were also to be responsible for all packing, marking or, if necessary, despatching by alternate means of transport.

The Supreme Commander's view was that, as nearly all transport work was carried out by IX Troop Carrier Command, the most efficient operation would be to place C.A.T.O.R. under First Allied Airborne Army. Thus, control of No. 46 Group by First Allied Airborne Army would be implemented through C.A.T.O.R. As C.A.T.O.R. was formed to accept bids for transport aircraft from 2nd T.A.F., Twenty-First Army Group, and A.N.C.F., the situation was that First Allied Airborne Army would control all allocation of air lift to these Commands, and could stop it at any time, even including the air evacuation of British casualties.

When it was proposed therefore, in August 1944, to move C.A.T.O.R. to the control of the airborne forces Headquarters, concern was felt by the R.A.F. that the position of No. 46 Group might be jeopardised as regards transport work on the Continent after the Allies were well established. It seemed that the whole of the pure air transport work would fall into the hands of the U.S. Air Transport Corps[4]. However, the problem eventually solved itself because on 18 September 1944, the Air Commander-in-Chief was able to announce that control of all air transport operations on the Continent had again been placed under him and that C.A.T.O.R. was to be taken out of the First Allied Airborne Army and become a branch of A.E.A.F. It was also to be extended and a forward echelon was to be formed in A.E.A.F. (Main) alongside forward S.H.A.E.F.

---

[1] A.E.A.F./T.S. 911. Encl. 19.
[2] S.H.A.E.F. Ops. Memo. No. 29, 29 April 1944.
[3] H.Q. A.E.A.F./O.R.B. C.A.T.O.R. Branch, Appendix I.
[4] File T.C./S./300950/C.-in-C.

Operations Planned and Cancelled During the Period 13 June and 10 September 1944

The tremendous progress of the liberating armies across France and Belgium, following the breakout from the Normandy pocket, called for considerable activity from the airborne forces. Throughout the months following Overlord, S.A.S. and S.O.E. operations, vital to the advance of the armies, were carried out almost nightly by No. 38 Group aircraft. At the same time, the airborne planning staffs were continuously employed in planning airborne operations, all of which were subsequently cancelled. No less than sixteen separate operations were planned to take place at short notice by Headquarters First Allied Airborne Army and First Airborne Corps, between 13 June, and 10 September 1944.

On 20 May 1944, S.H.A.E.F. Headquarters had asked Twenty-first Army Group and First U.S. Army Group, to specify their airborne requirements subsequent to D Day, and suggested, as a basis, that three airborne divisions would require to be used every sixty days. The former replied that their possible requirements were approximately five airborne divisional operations between D Day and D+90 and after D+90, four divisional operations every sixty days. This expectation was highly optimistic and A.E.A.F. explained that the re-equipment problem of the airborne divisions used in Overlord had been fully considered and that they would not be available for a second operation until the period between D+45 and D+90, and a third operation not before 1945. Despite this, 1st Airborne Division were kept in a constant state of readiness from 6 June until 17 September, when the Arnhem operation took place. No-one was to blame for this state of affairs, but the effect on the morale of the airborne troops was unfortunate. To be in a condition of preparedness for weeks on end with the natural feeling of pre-operation tension, constantly giving way to the anti-climax of cancellation, was bound to have its effect on keen, efficient men. The most serious result, however, of this permanent state of preparation for airborne operation, was the tying-up of large numbers of aircraft. It was not possible to lay on an airborne operation at short notice unless the aircraft and crews were immediately available and prepared. Thus, the major part of the transport support force was virtually grounded. This force included the two R.A.F. Groups Nos. 38 and 46 with a total of approximately 450 aircraft. No. 46 Group, who had between 175 and 185 serviceable Dakotas (C.47) were only able to use small numbers of their aircraft each day for normal transport services between the United Kingdom and the Normandy landing fields. During the period 1 July to 10 September, No. 46 Group were required to have 130 aircraft in readiness for any of the operations which were planned and later cancelled[1]. Once No. 38 Group had ceased re-supply missions to the Normandy beaches, they were occupied with S.A.S./S.O.E. operations until 16 September 1944, but also had to stand by in readiness for airborne operations. The United States IX Troop Carrier Command, with a unit establishment of 986 Dakotas plus reserves would have been called upon to provide the major portion of the lift for any of the operations during this period, e.g. operation Swordhilt, the demand for which was IX T.C.C. 1,050, No. 46 Group 150, and No. 38 Group 300. None of these operations called for a total of less than 500 Dakotas.

---

[1] C.A.T.O.R. O.R.B., August–September 1944.

The ultimate effect of this " freezing " of transport aircraft was far reaching. Smooth deliveries of supplies and urgent daily scheduled freight to both British and U.S. Armies in the field were constantly being upset. As the armies advanced further into Europe, so their lines of communication lengthened and their need of transport aircraft grew until eventually the point was reached where they had not enough supplies to begin a new assault. When airborne operations did take place at Arnhem, it was not until an adequate reserve of air transport and supplies had been built up.

It might appear that this negative use of aircraft was the fault of insufficient co-operation between the army and the airborne forces but this was not so. The real difficulty lay in anticipating the progress of the ground forces and judging whether airborne operations might be necessary. It could not be known exactly where or when the Germans might make a determined stand, thus creating an obstacle for the overthrow of which airborne operations might be essential. Therefore, a series of planned airborne operations was maintained as nearly as possible abreast of the current military situation, in the event of one being required.

The indecision existing regarding the future use of airborne forces prompted the Air Commander-in-Chief, Air Marshal Leigh-Mallory, to write to the Supreme Commander on 3 July 1944 asking for information regarding the locality, dates, and size of force which might be required for any future operations in support of Overlord[1]. The reply on 15 July was that a definite answer was impossible but that planning was proceeding to cover eventualities in three main areas, Brittany, Normandy and the Seine crossing. The approximate dates given were during the period August to October, which shows that there was little idea in mid-July of the rapid progress about to be made by the Allied armies[2].

The first of the projected airborne operations suggested by the army for the employment of 1st Airborne Division which had taken no part in Overlord, was that the division be dropped on 13 June in an area south-west of Caen, behind the German lines, to assist in encircling the enemy in that area. A conference was called at Headquarters, A.E.A.F., on 11 June 1944 to discuss this plan[3]. It was presided over by the Air Commander-in-Chief, and attended by the airborne and air chiefs who decided that the operation was not feasible for the following reasons : —

(a) The area was too heavily defended for parachute troops to be dropped in daylight.

(b) The night of 12-13 June was not in a favourable moon period.

(c) The operation would involve flying over the Fleet for three hours and no guarantee could be given by the Allied Naval Commander, " X " Force, or by the Commanding Officers on the beaches that the aircraft would not be fired upon.

(d) An approach over the Coquentin Peninsula would involve crossing a hostile territory without navigational aids.

---

[1] T.L.M./150/M.S. Encl. 3.
[2] Ibid. Encl. 5.
[3] T.L.M./M.S. 150.

The army did not agree that the operation was impracticable but the difference of opinion was settled when, immediately prior to 13 June, the 51st Division and 7th Armoured Brigade encountered very heavy resistance and the military plans had to be revised. The operation (code name Wildoats) was cancelled on 17 June. It is of interest to consider briefly the main operations which were planned but not carried out following the cancellation of Wildoats.

Swordhilt

This operation was planned to assist in the capture of Brest during July[1]. From the air point of view, the plan was sound from all aspects. However, the successful break-through by the American Forces from the St. Lo area during the last days of July rendered the airborne operation superfluous and it was cancelled on 29 July.

Hands-up

This proposed amphibious airborne operation was to capture Quiberon Bay for use as a port. The operation was not sound from the Naval point of view, because the route lay too near convoys and U-boat bases. It was unlikely that sufficient forces would be available also three weeks preparation was necessary and operational conditions could not be forecast that far ahead. Thus, it was agreed at a Chiefs of Staff meeting on 15 July, to cancel the operation, but to file the plan for reference[2].

Beneficiary

Intended to capture St. Malo. Planning for this operation continued throughout June but Headquarters airborne forces advised against the final plan for the following reasons pointed out by General Browning in a report dated 7 July 1944. The landings would have to be made too close to enemy flak positions; the Navy would not be able to use St. Malo harbour until seven days after its capture and thus, if the weather was bad, maintenance would have to be done by air. It would also involve using the only available airborne reserves and the First United States Army Group considered that the area could be captured without difficulty by approaching from the south and south-east.

Lucky Strike/Transfigure

These were to be large-scale operations in the north of the Paris Orleans Gap. They were planned to land behind the German lines in conjunction with an attempted break-through by the Allied armies from the Leval area, to cut off main escape routes for the Germans west of the Seine. The military progress by General Patton's 3rd Army on the ground was sufficiently fast, however, not to require this operation and it was cancelled on 18 August, but 40 S.A.S. jeeps and gliders were landed and moved through the enemy lines to Auxerre (operation Wallace). This was the first operation planned by the combined airborne Headquarters (later First Allied Airborne Army)[3].

---

[1] A.E.A.F. File 22536. Encl. 21A.
[2] Ibid. File 22537. Encl. 13A.
[3] Ibid. File 22557. Encl. 42A.

Linnet I and II

Linnet I was planned to take place near Lille but was later changed to Linnet II, and involved landing in the Liege Maastricht area to seize the Meuse crossing. Planning proceeded throughout August and D Day was fixed for 3 September. The operation was cancelled on the 3rd, but warning was issued that similar arrangements might be needed in the near future[1].

Comet

The operation Comet was planned to carry out Rhine crossings in the Arnhem/Wesel area, but on 10 September the operation was cancelled and all forces including Nos. 38 and 46 Group stations were ordered to stand-by for further operations. At long last the period of waiting was nearly over. A week later, the plans for operation Comet were amplified and became operation Market, known to the world as the Arnhem operation.

Lessons

Projected operations, beginning with Lucky Strike—Transfigure, which were planned by 1st Allied Airborne Army, brought to light several lessons. Firstly, whether or not an operation took place the amount of staff work and planning to be done in preparation for it was the same. Therefore, much time and labour might have been saved on divisional and lower levels if the planners could have been informed in advance of the degree of urgency of the operation. It was essential that an Airborne Headquarters be in the closest possible touch with ground operations and that neither unnecessary time be wasted nor aircraft kept standing by which might be better employed in training or other operations. As it was, some duplication in the planning work was inevitable. This might have been avoided, if 1st Allied Airborne Army had had a similar planning staff, because, in any case all details had to be worked out at Army or Airborne Corps Headquarters.

Extension of No. 38 Group Responsibility

By the time the airborne operations in Holland were launched, the full responsibility for the development and control of airborne operations and the dissemination of information relative to them was delegated to No. 38 Group. On 16 September, 1944, a directive, detailing the policy regarding organisation of airborne operations and training, was issued by the Air Ministry[2]. The salient features of this directive as far as No. 38 Group were concerned, were as follows:—

> It was decided that the status of No. 38 Group was to remain the same, i.e. the Headquarters of airborne assault operations and training in the R.A.F.

> The A.O.C. No. 38 Group was to be responsible for supplying information both technical and tactical on airborne development to R.A.F. Commands concerned. He was to be available to advise the Air Commander-in-Chief in operational theatres of all aspects of airborne assault

---

[1] Ibid. File 22642. Encl. 45A.
[2] A.M. File G.S. 8503/2. Encls. 102A and B.

operations and training, including types of equipment and organisation. He was also responsible for training personnel for staff and Command appointments concerned with airborne assault overseas.

In order that basic training in airborne assault operations might be kept up to date, the A.O.C. No. 38 Group's advice on this matter was to be taken as a basis.

In overseas theatres, airborne assault Wings with similar functions to those of No. 38 Group, were to be formed, one in M.A.A.F. and another in A.C.S.E.A., and to consist of the minimum force required for normal airborne assault training with the Army. The A.O.C. No. 38 Group was, if desired, to advise Air Commanders-in-Chief upon the capabilities and experience of the staff of the airborne assault wing.

In view of the possibility that the majority of squadrons taking part in future airborne operations were drawn from Transport Command, it would therefore be necessary from time to time to attach units of Transport Command to No. 38 Group for advanced training. Especially would this be necessary prior to the launching of airborne operations, and in these instances the units would be temporaily transferred from Transport Command to No. 38 Group. If a very large airborne operation was contemplated, it might also be necessary to form a special transport group for the operation, similar to that already in existence in western Europe.

All aircrew joining Transport Command other than those who were over age for military operations or who had done two operational tours, were to be given basic training in the airborne assault role under Transport Command arrangements based on the technique already evolved by No. 38 Group[1].

Policy and Planning for Operation Market

General Military Situation[2]

The military situation in Western Europe by mid-September 1944 was briefly as follows:—

> The 1st United States Army had advanced as far as the Siegfried Line ; the 3rd United States Army, under General Patton, had established bridgeheads over the Moselle river, and the British Second Army had advanced from the Seine against stiff enemy resistance and was being organised on the defensive lines of the Albert and Escaut Canals from Antwerp to Maastricht. In the rear of the enemy three rivers, the Maas, the Waal and Nederijn, and the Maas-waal Canal, formed natural lines of defence against any northern thrust by Twenty-first Army Group.

The intention of Field Marshal Montgomery, Commander-in-Chief, Twenty-first Army Group, was to advance across the three rivers, secure crossings of the Rhine in the area Grave-Nijmegen-Arnhem in order to outflank the Siegfried Line and to attack towards northern Germany. The outcome of this would mean a retarding of effort along the whole front and

---

[1] See Section II, Development and Training, No. 38 Group Report.
[2] " Supreme Commanders report to combined Chiefs of Staff on operations in Europe ".

also involve freeing the port of Antwerp, as all resources would be needed. Although there were disadvantages to this plan, General Eisenhower and Field Marshal Montgomery considered that the advantages of such an operation rendered it worthwhile. There were several reasons why it was decided to attack north eastwards. Firstly, the majority of the German Army were there; secondly, if the attack was successful it would capture the area whence the flying bombs were being launched against England; also it was essential to obtain airfields in Belgium. Finally, General Eisenhower considered that the area of the lower Rhine was the best for an advance into Germany.

Object of British Second Army Plan

The plan was to position the 2nd Army across the rivers Maas-waal and Nederijn in the area Grave-Nijmegen-Arnhem, and to control the country as far as the Zuider Zee in order to cut German communications to the Low Countries. The main axis of the advance, Eindhoven-Grave-Nijmegen and Arnhem, was allotted to XXX Corps. The task of capturing and holding the main river and canal crossings on this axis, was given to the First Allied Airborne Army who were to lay " an airborne carpet " over the area. There were available for this operation 1st British Airborne Division, 82nd United States Airborne Division, 101st United States Airborne Division, 1st Polish Parachute Brigade Group, 2nd British Airlanding Light A.A. Battery, 52nd British (Lowland) Division, and 1st British Air Portable Division. The planning for the airborne operation was carried out at a Headquarters at Eastcote by a combined British and American staff.

Main Plan

The tasks for the First Allied Airborne Army were allotted as follows[1]:—

(*a*) 1st Airborne Division with 1st Polish Parachute Brigade Group to capture bridges at Arnhem and establish a bridge-head around them, to enable land forces to move northwards.

(*b*) 82nd Airborne Division to capture crossings at Nijmegen and Grave and to hold the high ground between Nijmegen and Groesbeck. The advanced headquarters of the Airborne Corps were to fly in with the first glider lift of this division.

(*c*) 101st Airborne Division were to seize the bridges and defiles between Eindhoven and Grave.

(*d*) 878th Aviation Engineer Battalion and 2nd Airlanding Light A.A. Battery, to land in gliders and to prepare and defend landing strips north of Arnhem.

(*e*) 52nd Lowland Division to be transported in Dakotas to the landing strips provided the military situation permitted.

In the Arnhem Sector the lift for the airborne forces was allotted as follows[2]:—

Nos. 38 and 46 Groups, Royal Air Force, would undertake all path finder dropping and all glider towing as well as subsequent re-supply missions. The IX United States Troop Carrier Command to undertake

---
[1] 38 Group/T.S. 10/80/Air, 12 September 1944.
[2] A.M. File C. 32058/46.

all main parachute drops and the later flying in of airfield engineer and defence units. In the Nijmegen—Grave Sector IX U.S.T.C.C. would be responsible for all tasks except the towing of the glider-borne British Airborne Corps Headquarters which would be towed in by No. 38 Group. In the Eindhoven Sector IX U.S.T.C.C. were to be responsible for the whole lift.

The Terrain

The town of Arnhem (population 100,000) lies on the rising ground which forms the northern bank of the Lower Rhine. The terrain north of the town rises to over 100 ft. above sea level and consists mainly of open heath and arable land interspersed with thick belts of pine forest. The southern bank of the Rhine opposite to the town and for some considerable distance on either side of the bridge is meadow or polder (fen) land so low lying as to be subject to flooding should the river rise more than a few feet. This was one factor that dissuaded the planners from choosing the landing and dropping zones in this area because it was feared that if the ground were flooded then landings might be both dangerous and difficult, resulting in a similar loss of effort to that caused by dropping on sodden ground in Normandy (Landing Zone " V "). This area was also very exposed and could easily be covered by fire from the slopes of the opposite bank. The other factor was the network of irrigation ditches which, it was thought, might jeopardise the safe landing of gliders and paratroops as well as hindering the concentration of men and vehicles.

Thus the main landing and dropping zones were selected on the high ground west north west of the town at distances varying from 5-8 miles from the bridge. The terrain in this area was excellent for landing both paratroops and gliders. It consisted of open clearings of heath country not dissimilar to that in the Camberley—Bagshot area of Surrey and mostly covered with heather which provided a cushioning effect for landings.

The fact that all the zones were screened on two and often three sides by thick belts of pine woods constituted a mixed blessing. From the airborne forces point of view the surrounding woods provided an effective screen for unloading and rendezvous activities and because of the clear demarcation between thick wood and open country the zones were easily discernible from the air. However, once the surprise element of the operation no longer existed the woods assumed a menacing aspect—from their obscure depths the enemy could effectively cover the open sweeps of territory.

Further disadvantages were that one of the zones lay in an enemy training area and the most easterly was within flak range of Arnhem and Deelen. Reconnaissance made a few days prior to the operation showed flak to be covering all the zones. Events were to prove that the zones selected were far too distant from the objective and that the terrain to be traversed to reach it was more difficult to advance over than to defend.

Intelligence

Information regarding enemy movements was scanty but it was known that the whole operational area was being prepared for defence and the enemy was expected to fight hard on the line of the river Rhine.[1] Information prior to June showed that the area was an important training centre,

---
[1] H.Q. 1st Parachute Brigade Intelligence Summary No. 1, 13 September 1944.

particularly for armoured and motorised troops—S.S. Herman Goering reinforcement units. It was considered that the whole area might contain some 15,000 troops—8,000 of them in the Ede and Arnhem area—also that Arnhem would be strongly defended as it was a vital centre of communication to the German defensive line on the river Waal.

The major part of the information available was from official Dutch sources, but was not up-to-date. Estimates of enemy movements in the area subsequent to June were largely based on surmise and there was no direct evidence in support. The consequences resulting from this incomplete intelligence were very serious and there is no doubt that failure to obtain an accurate appreciation of the enemy strength immediately prior to the operation largely contributed to its failure.

The problem then arose as to whether the operation should be undertaken by day or by night. It was expected that the German night fighter force would provide more effective resistance than the day fighters but, on the other hand, the flak would be much more accurate by day than by night. Lieutenant-General Brereton decided in favour of a daylight operation, in the belief that the supporting air forces could knock out flak positions in advance and destroy them during the airborne operations. A further reason for preferring to operate in daylight was the fact that the Americans, as yet inexperienced in night navigation to the high standard required and used as they were to the formation follow-my-leader principle so ineffective in Normandy, naturally preferred to operate by day. The risks involved were that the flak was known to have increased by 35 per cent. in the Market area, the troop carrying aircraft were unarmoured, were not equipped with self-sealing tanks and flew at slow speeds. This decision to operate in daylight prompted the A.O.Cs. of Nos. 38 and 46 Groups to offer the opinion that the casualties involved might reach 40 per cent. but this risk was considered to be justified[1]. The opinion of these officers was founded on the fear of a leak in security measures, for which the Americans were responsible but fortunately this did not happen. However, initial losses of aircraft en route and at the dropping zones proved to be only slight and General Brereton's contention that concentrated bombing of flak positions immediately preceding an airborne operation would greatly reduce casualties, was justified.

Air Forces Available

Lieutenant General Brereton was in command of the First Allied Airborne Army and on 11 September, Lieutenant General Browning was designated as Commander of the Initial Task Force. The United States IX Troop Carrier Command (Major General Paul L. Williams) comprised 42 Squadrons, I Path-finder School and Hadrian gliders. No. 38 Group, under Air Vice-Marshal Hollinghurst, had 10 Squadrons made up of 2 Albermarle, 2 Halifax and 6 Stirlings, also Horsa and Hamilcar gliders. No. 46 Group (Air Commodore L. Darvall) had six Dakota Squadrons and Horsas.

---

[1] T.L.M./S. 150/7 Eng. E.9, 6 September 1944.

Order of Battle and Chain of Command

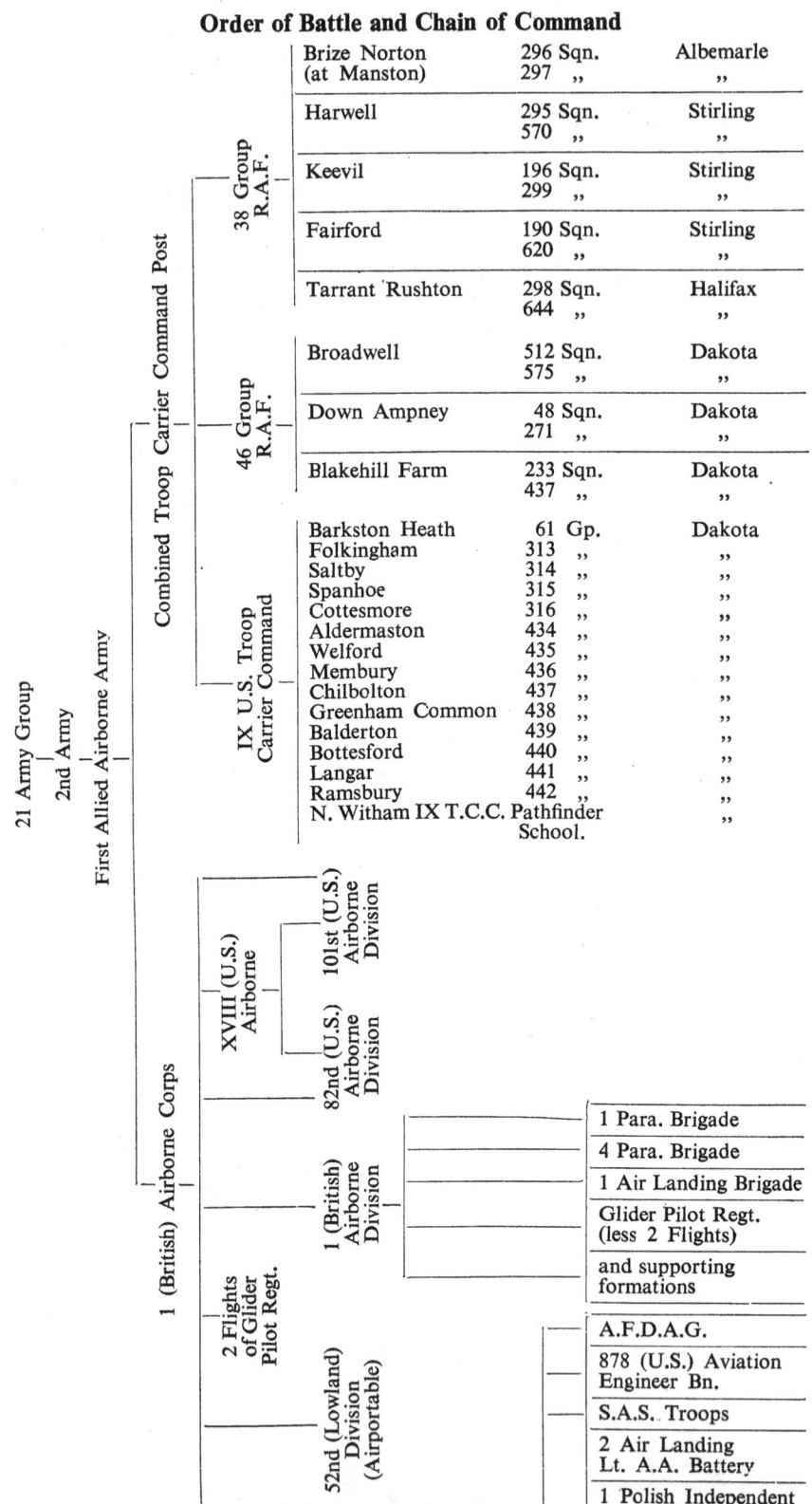

The Landing and Dropping Zones

In all, six zones were chosen[1]. Three of them, "Y", "S" and "L" lay North of the railway running West-North-West from Arnhem and two, "X" and "Z", immediately opposite on the south of the railway. A supply dropping point "V" was selected some two miles nearer to Arnhem and, as it turned out, in a most convenient position for the Germans who received all the supplies dropped on this zone. To the enemy's credit however it is now known that a large proportion of these supplies were distributed to the local Dutch inhabitants.

Once the dropping zones and landing zones had been chosen the allotment of forces to them was designed to conform as far as possible with the inevitable withdrawal towards Arnhem. Landing zones "S", "X", "Y" and "Z", could not be used after D + 1, and on D + 2, gliders would be landed only on the forced landing zone "L", and troops dropped only on dropping zone "K" immediately south of the river at Arnhem, which although unfavourable land, would be used for the sake of concentration. Another small supply dropping point "V" on the outskirts of Arnhem was chosen for use on D + 2 and it was hoped that by then, or shortly after, relieving forces from Nijmegen would have contacted the division at Arnhem[2].

The airborne movement was to be carried out in three main lifts by daylight on three successive days, followed by re-supply operations as requested. The detailed tasks in the Arnhem sector were allotted as follows:—

(i) First Lift D Day

Dropping Zone X

Six aircraft from No. 38 Group to drop marker forces of the 21st Independent Parachute Company at H - 00.20 hours Arnhem sector were allotted as follows:—

149 aircraft of the IX U.S.T.C.C. to drop the main body of 1st Parachute Brigade at H. hour.

Landing Zone S

Six aircraft of No. 38 Group to drop marker forces as above at H - 00.20 hours.

130 aircraft of No. 46 Group and 23 aircraft of No. 38 Group to tow 153 Horsa gliders, releasing them at H hour and carrying parts of 1st Air Landing Brigade Group.

Landing Zone Z

167 aircraft of No. 38 Group to tow 154 Horsa and 13 Hamilcar gliders with more elements of 1st Air Landing Brigade Group.

Total Aircraft and Gliders Employed

First Lift—161 parachute aircraft.
320 tug aircraft.
320 gliders.

Total 801

---

[1] See Figure 6.
[2] No. 38 Group Report, Operation Market, Appendix N. No. 38 Group Operation Order Market and H.Q. Troops Carrier Force, U.S. Army Air Force Field Order Market.

Also on D Day the R.A.F. were detailed to deliver H.Q. 1st British Airborne Corps in the United States sector at Nijmegen and 38 aircraft from No. 38 Group were to tow 32 Horsa and six Hadrian gliders to land at H + 00.50 - 00.58 hours on Landing Zone N.

(ii) Second Lift D + 1

Dropping Zone Y

126 aircraft of the IX U.S.T.C.C. to drop the main body of 4th Parachute Brigade.

Landing Zone X

160 aircraft of No. 38 Group and 48 aircraft of No. 46 Group to tow 189 Horsa, four Hadrian and 15 Hamilcar gliders, carrying elements of 1st Air Landing Brigade Group.

Landing Zone S

62 aircraft of No. 46 Group to tow 62 Horsa gliders carrying elements of 1st Air Landing Brigade Group.

Dropping Zone L

35 aircraft of No. 38 Group were detailed for supply dropping.

Total Second Lift—126 parachute aircraft.
270 tug aircraft.
270 gliders.
35 Supply a/c.

Total 701

(iii) Third Lift D + 2

Dropping Zone K

114 aircraft of the IX U.S.T.C.C. to drop the main body of 1st Independent Polish Parachute Brigade Group.

Landing Zone L

45 aircraft of No. 38 Group to tow 35 Horsa gliders carrying elements of 1st Polish Independent Parachute Brigade Group, and 10 Hamilcar gliders carrying elements of 878 U.S. Aviation Engineer Battalion.

Supply Dropping Point V

100 aircraft of No. 38 Group and 63 aircraft of No. 46 Group to drop 163 supply loads.

Total—277 parachute and re-supply aircraft
45 tug aircraft
45 gliders

Total 367

Subsequent re-supply of the ground forces was to be ordered as required.

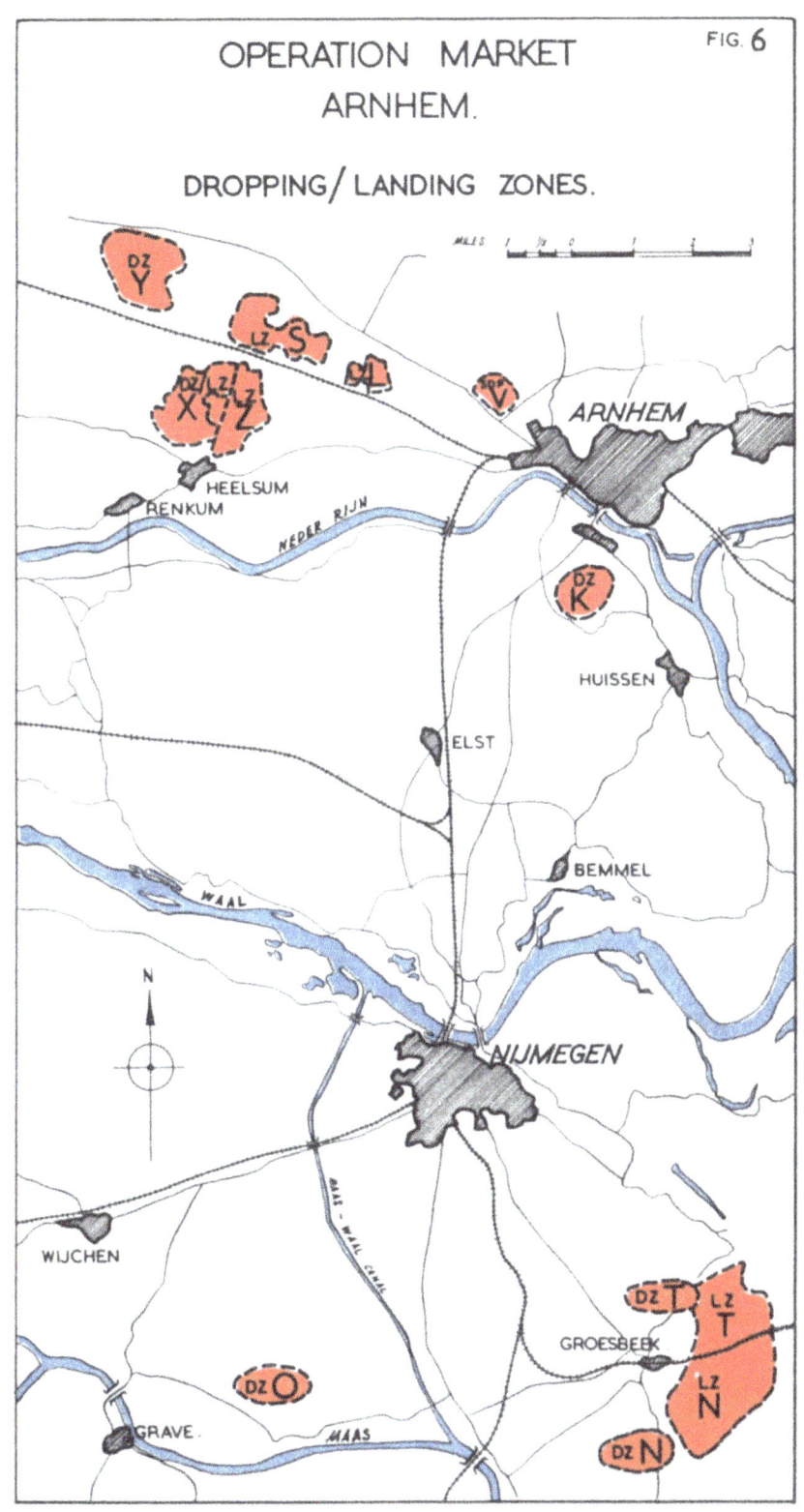

The Flight Plan

The combined flight plan for the R.A.F. and United States Air Forces was drawn up by the Joint Planning Staff of No. 38 Group and IX U.S. T.C.C., at the Troop Carrier Command Post, Eastcote. The base airfields for the complete operation formed two distinct groups—a southern group of eight British and six U.S. airfields and an eastern group of eight U.S. airfields. Aircraft from the southern group would form up over Hatfield and those from the eastern group over March. On D Day from these initial rendezvous points streams of aircraft for the Arnhem and Grave-Nijmegen sectors would form up over Aldeburgh before taking the northern route, and those for the Eindhoven sector over the North Foreland for the southern route.

The sea crossing on the northern route was from the rendezvous at Aldeburgh direct to the eastern end of Schouwen Island, thence direct to a final rendezvous at S'Hertogenbosch, thence diverging to the various dropping and landing zones at Arnhem, Grave and Nijmegen. From the initial rendezvous at Hatfield the aircraft were to fly in three parallel streams one-and-a-half miles apart. The total time length of the column on D Day would be about 65 minutes. Gliders would be towed and would release at 2,500 ft. On the second lift all aircraft would use the southern route via North Foreland, Ostend, Gheel and the Eindhoven area in similar streams. The total time length of the column on D+1 would be about 20 minutes. After release or drop all aircraft were to turn left and return on reciprocal courses at 5/7,000 ft.

The main reasons for designing this flight plan as such were to avoid as far as possible the known heavy flak areas and after D Day to provide a route along the occupied corridor from Eindhoven, but it was evident that the flight of 100 miles each way across enemy occupied territory would be dangerous. Flak in the target area was being rapidly built up in the week before the operation, and although anti-flak bombing sorties were ordered, it was expected that losses would be appreciable.

The main factors to be taken into consideration in selecting the routes were[1]:—

(*a*) The shortest distance to the target with regard to prominent land features.

(*b*) Traffic control in the air.

(*c*) Anti-aircraft and operation zones in the United Kingdom.

(*d*) Enemy anti-aircraft and search-light batteries.

(*e*) The avoidance of turns over the sea.

(*f*) Choice of prominent features on the coast for land falls.

(*g*) The shortest distance over enemy territory.

The most direct route to Arnhem was one that passed over the Dutch Islands, involving some 80 miles of flight over enemy occupied territory. The alternative was a longer route to the south over friendly Belgian territory most of the way, with the maximum of 65 miles over enemy territory. The northern route was exposed to flak from the barges in the area of the Dutch

---

[1] Air Ministry File C. 32058/46.

Islands and the southern route from the flak of the enemy front line troops. Both routes were used which avoided the necessity of having one very long column, thus exposing the rear portion to danger or having parallel columns with a necessarily wide corridor between, rendering them very vulnerable to flak.

In addition to the normal aids, Eureka beacons and Occults were to be set up at all turning points in England. Half way across the sea a Eureka beacon and a coded Holophane light were to be set up on a ship. In addition Eureka beacons were to be placed on all dropping and landing zones by 21st Independent Parachute Company. These were to be supplemented by Verey signals, ground strips and coloured smoke signals[1].

Once the basic decisions regarding landing zones and routes had been made it was necessary to arrange for air support. A conference was held at Headquarters, A.E.A.F., on 12 September 1944 followed by another meeting on 15 September, in which representatives of the VIII Air Force, IX Air Force, R.A.F. Bomber Command, Air Defence Great Britain, Coastal Command and the Allied Navies were present, in addition to General Brereton and Officers from Headquarters, First Allied Airborne Army and its subordinate Headquarters. At this meeting the assignments for attacking airfields, dive-bombing of flak positions which developed during the operation, for fighter cover along the routes and for a fighter screen east and north-east of the Market area, for diversions by Coastal Command, night fighter patrols, and dummy drops, were made.

Air Support

The following supporting air operations were ordered[2]:—

(a) On D-Day all flak positions along the route were to be attacked by VIII U.S.A.A.F. and Air Defence of Great Britain Squadrons immediately before and during the operation.

(b) Throughout the whole operation VIII U.S.A.A.F. were to provide light escort over the north-east and the heaviest cover possible over the rest of the route, both to and from the dropping zones.

(c) After the air landings, cover was to be maintained over the landing area by the IX U.S. Army Air Force in the daytime and by A.D.G.B. at night.

(d) Bomber Command aircraft were to attack enemy day fighter airfields and fixed flak positions on D - 1.

(e) Forty aircraft of Bomber Command were to drop dummy parachutes west of Utrecht, east of Arnhem and at Emmerich on the night of D/D + 1.

(f) Aircraft of No. 2 Group were to attack parks in the dropping and landing zone area, their attacks to finish by H - 25.

(g) 2nd T.A.F., R.A.F., to carry out armed reconnaissance in the dropping and landing zone area.

(h) Aircraft of Coastal Command to carry out diversionary missions outside the area of airborne operations.

---

[1] No. 38 Group Report, Operation Market. 38G/10/80/Air. Para. 34.
[2] No. 38 Group Report, Operation Market. 38G/10/80/Air. Para. 35.

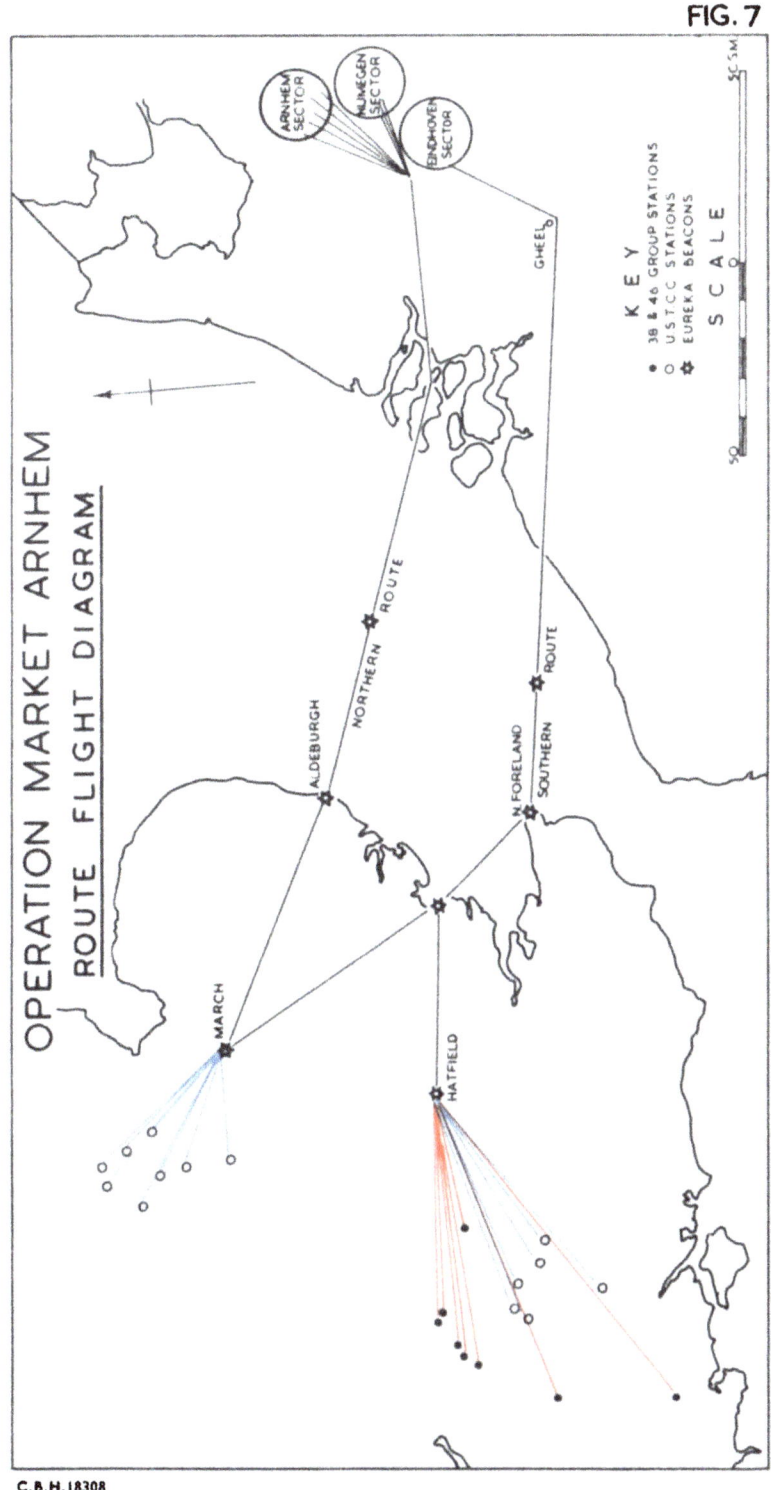

The British First Airborne Division and the Polish Parachute Brigade were located on the airfields where they had been marshalled for Operation Comet, the former in the Swindon area and the latter in the Grantham area. The 82nd U.S. Airborne Division was stationed near Nottingham, easily accessible to the aerodromes of the IX Troop Carrier Command, and the 101st U.S. Airborne Division was in the Newbury area, where the American troop carrier aerodromes were also situated. The troops began to move to their respective take-off aerodromes on 15 September 1944 and were sealed in at daylight on 16 September. In all, seven British and 17 American airfields were used in Operation Market. By the evening of 16 September, the detailed plans for the whole operation were complete; the weather was favourable and at 1900 hours Lieutenant-General Brereton gave the order for the operation to begin the next morning[1].

---

[1] No. 38 Group Report, Operation Market. 38G/10/80/A .

CHAPTER 9

OPERATION MARKET[1]

The First Lift. 17 September 1944

Early morning fog which had been forecast for D day did not delay the take off of the 358 tug glider combinations comprising the first lift of what proved to be the most historic of all airborne operations. The weather, however, was not ideal during the first two hours; many combinations encountered low cloud before reaching the English coast and this was mainly responsible for 24 gliders being compelled to force land in various parts of the countryside. However, the loads of 22 of these were recovered intact and transferred to the second lift. Visibility over the sea improved and apart from five gliders being forced down due to tow rope and tug engine failure, four of which ditched, but whose crews were subsequently rescued, the great stream of aircraft moved smoothly towards its destination. Only slight opposition was encountered over Holland—a light flak barrage was soon silenced by fighter aircraft and no enemy fighters troubled the airborne formations—but eight more gliders were lost on the way across Holland probably due to difficulties caused by the slip stream of the aircraft ahead.

Meanwhile the Stirling pathfinder aircraft which had taken off from Fairford 20 minutes before the main force, had easily located the Dropping Zones and six aircraft each on zones "S" and "X" successfully dropped elements of 21st Independent Parachute Company. Only one aircraft was damaged by flak and the ground signals were all displayed and working by the time the main force arrived. Heavy and light flak was encountered near the dropping zones but although six aircraft were damaged none were lost and the landing took place without any serious mishap. There was a tendency for the gliders to overshoot in the light wind causing close concentrations on the north end of landing zone "Z" and the west end of landing zone "S". A few gliders were damaged including two Hamilcars which overturned on zone "Z" due to the soft ground involving loss of two 17-pounder guns. Apart from scattered rifle and machine gun fire the unloading of the gliders met with little interference from the enemy. There were, however, some mechanical difficulties and the average time for unloading was about thirty minutes. Complete surprise was achieved, due, in some measure, to the time chosen—early Sunday afternoon. Apart from 38 aircraft which towed gliders to landing zone "N" in the Nijmegen sector, the remainder of the glider force towed by Royal Air Force aircraft landed on zones "S" and "Z" lying north and south respectively of the railway running west, northwest from Arnhem.

---

[1] The following principal sources were used in compiling this account of Operation Market:—
  No. 38 Group Report on Operation Market (38G/10/80/Air).
  1st Allied Airborne Army Report on Operations in Holland (Air Ministry file C. 32058/46).
  1 Airborne Division Report.
  War Office Narratives.
  A.E.A.F. Files T.S. 22650 and 35108.
  No. 46 Group Unofficial History.
  Nos. 38 and 46 Group and Squadron O.R.B's.

Landing Zone "S"

153 gliders including a complete No. 46 Group effort of 130 Dakota-Horsa combinations were detailed to land on this zone and 132 landed either on or very near it.

Landing Zone "Z"

152 gliders of 167 originally detailed made successful releases : 116 landed on the zone and 27 very close to it. In fact 25 of the near misses landed on the immediately adjoining zone at "X".

Dropping Zone "X"

The main body of 1st Parachute Group were transported in Dakotas of the U.S. IX Troop Carrier Command and dropped successfully.

Landing Zone "N"

Only three of the 38 gliders destined for this zone and carrying Headquarters 1st Airborne Corps failed to reach their objective—one was lost over England; one over the sea and one over Holland. Of the remainder it was definitely established that 28 of the 32 Horsas towed by No. 38 Group landed on the zone and that the six Hadrian gliders all landed successfully.

This first day of operation Market involved the largest number of aircraft ever to take part in any one operation with the single exception of D Day Normandy. No less than 3,887 aircraft and 500 gliders became airborne during the morning of 17 September. In addition to the 1,534 transport and tug aircraft of Nos. 38 and 46 Groups and U.S. IX Troop Carrier Command who towed the gliders and dropped the paratroops, 1,240 fighters and 1,113 bombers were used in support.

During the night and morning of 16-17 September, British and American bomber aircraft undertook tactical missions on the route from the coast of Holland inwards, attacking flak positions and enemy fighter airfields from which defensive patrols might be expected. The decision to soften flak positions on the route was justified by the lack of effective ground air interference experienced by the invading force. Dummy parachutes were dropped west of Utrecht, east of Arnhem and at Emmerich on the night of D/D+1. Other diversionary missions were undertaken by aircraft of Coastal Command, whilst 2nd Tactical Air Force carried out armed reconnaissance in the Landing Area. The fighter cover for the airborne force was provided by 371 Tempests, Spitfires and Mosquitoes from 33 Air Defence of Great Britain squadrons and 166 fighters of the IX U.S. Air Force. This fighter support was undoubtedly a deterrent to the enemy fighters for comparatively few were seen or engaged and none of these attacked the airborne formations.

The American Operations

In the Nijmegen area, the landing and dropping was carried out with a similar degree of success to that at Arnhem. The 101st U.S. Airborne Division were transported to their zones[1] by 424 U.S. aircraft and 70 gliders using the southern route. The 82nd Airborne Division were carried by 480 aircraft and 50 gliders using the northern route with the British. In all 106 gliders and over a thousand American aircraft reached their objective.

---

[1] See Figure 7.

OPERATION MARKET
ARNHEM
GLIDERS ON ZONES 'S' & 'Z'

Fig. 8

OPERATION MARKET
ARNHEM
PARATROOPS ON ZONE 'X'

Fig. 9

The Ground Situation

Arnhem

The position of the troops after landing soon became difficult, enemy resistence was stronger than anticipated and soon developed with the arrival of German reinforcements from the east, who before night fall, were already attacking the airlanding brigade defending the zone. Probably the most serious feature of the day's operations was the cutting off from the main body of the majority of the 2nd Parachute Battalion who had reached the approaches of the main bridge across the river.

Nijmegen/Eindhoven

As at Arnhem enemy resistance was considerable and the disadvantage of having a fair sized defended town lying between landing zones and the objective was at once apparent. However, the Americans took the bridges at Grave and Veghel near Eindhoven but could not prevent the Germans cutting the line of the advance in three places during the night. An attack towards the bridge at Nijmegen was stopped outside the town and generally the schedule of the whole advance was retarded.

The Second Lift. 18 September 1944

The fact that bad weather delayed the take off of the second lift for five hours was one of the major contributory causes of the failure at Arnhem. During this vital gap the position on the ground deteriorated to such an extent that it could not be redeemed. The Meteorological report for the morning of D + 1 caused a change in plan. It had originally been intended to use both routes but the rain and low cloud which was predicted would affect the southern route so it was decided by 1st Allied Airborne Army to send all troop carriers by the northern route.

By 1100 hours the weather was fit for the take-off to begin but there were still patches of low cloud in eastern England and this caused seven gliders to force land before reaching the coast. The crews, however, were all right and took off in the next lift. Weather conditions improved over the North Sea but two gliders were forced to ditch. Over Holland visibility was good and generally better than forecast; to the south could be seen low cloud over the southern route as had been predicted. Opposition along the route was heavier than on the previous day—more light flak being active as well as heavier guns at Hertogenbosch where several gliders were damaged. In all 15 gliders were lost over Holland. Only one tug aircraft was missing. Another from No. 575 squadron had an extraordinary escape. The Pilot was killed and the navigator wounded but the second navigator, after an attempt to complete the mission had been abandoned and the glider forced to cast off due to its ailerons being shot away, managed to fly the aircraft back to England and make his first ever landing a safe one. The fighter cover was again provided by Air Defence of Great Britain and the U.S. Eighth Air Force. Nineteen Spitfire, five Tempest and three Mustang Squadrons were used. Losses were light—two Tempests and four Spitfires.

The weather was fair in the area of the dropping/landing zones and despite some opposition the pathfinders set up all the ground aids. They also laid out " T's " to mark the landing direction as being different from the previous day and to utilise the remaining clear spaces. However, most of the gliders landed in the original direction but very few were damaged although there was some congestion. Trouble was experienced on the ground from the enemy using machine guns and mortar fire and thus rendering the glider unloading dangerous and difficult. Some of the gliders were damaged and some of the loads had to be destroyed to prevent them falling into enemy hands.

Landing Zone " X "

This zone had not been used on the first day and of 223 gliders despatched 189 landed on or near the zone and 12 on the adjoining zone " Z ". These two zones suffered the most from opposition after landing and almost 50 gliders were burned out although some of the loads were saved.

Landing Zone " S "

Seventy-three gliders carrying elements of 1st Air Landing Brigade were despatched to this zone on the other side of the railway. This number included 11 of those who had failed to leave England on the first day. Sixty-nine aircraft successfully released their gliders and photographic reconnaissance shows that out of 215 gliders despatched to this zone, 189 were actually on it and 13 very near.

Dropping Zone " L "

The first re-supply mission of operation Market was undertaken by 35 Stirlings from Harwell (No. 38 Group) who were detailed to drop on " L ". Approximately 85 per cent. of the supplies were dropped on the zone—the remainder drifted into enemy territory. The drop was carried out at 500 feet and of 920 panniers and containers carried, 803 were dropped. One crew dropped on zone " S " and four others failed to drop.

Dropping Zone " Y "

The main drop of 4th Parachute Brigade was successfully carried out by 127 American aircraft of IX U.S. Troop Carrier Command.

The Ground Situation

Arnhem Sector

The delay in landing reinforcements, owing to bad weather in England, allowed the Germans valuable time to build up their defence forces and thwart the attempt by the 4th Parachute Brigade to reach the high ground north-west of Arnhem and thus gain a dominating position. During the day the 1st Airborne Division was split into three parts—one at the northern end of the bridge—one on the western edge of Arnhem and one west of Oosterbeck. The situation, therefore was worsening at Arnhem and, although fierce fighting continued during the next few days, 1st Airborne Division were in a desperate situation before the British forces were able to reach the lower Rhine and assist them with artillery fire on 23 September.

Nijmegen/Eindhoven Sector

By 13.00 hours on 18 September the 101st U.S. Airborne Division had captured Eindhoven and made firm contact with the British Guards Armoured Division which had advanced north to Grave. The 82nd U.S. Airborne Division captured Grave and held the area between it and Nijmegen although the latter itself was held by the enemy. The important road bridge across the Waal was also held by the Germans until taken by the 82nd U.S. Airborne Division and British Units on 19 September.

The Third Lift. 19 September 1944

The situation on the third day was extremely serious and enemy resistance was increasing. It was decided to postpone the dropping of the Polish Parachute Brigade on zone "K", south-east of the bridge. Apart from 35 gliders carrying equipment and elements of the Polish Independent Parachute Brigade Group the day's air activity was devoted to re-supply. Although weather reports indicated that conditions might be better on the northern route it was decided to use the southern route in order to avoid using the same one on three successive days. Over England the weather was unfavourable with extensive areas of low cloud which grounded gliders detailed for the transport of the Polish units from the Grantham area by U.S. aircraft.

The take off was again delayed until after noon, and of the glider mission, seven broke from tow ropes—two in cloud over the sea. Although flak opposition was not severe, probably owing to weather, one glider was forced to ditch with a shot away tow rope and another was shot down, while both pilots of a third aircraft were hit but managed to reach the landing zones where they landed successfully. In the area of the landing zone, flak was much heavier. Because communications were so inadequate with fighter bases on the continent an error was made in the timing at the rendezvous, consequently there was no escort for the airborne missions. One hundred and twenty-seven Spitfires of Air Defence of Great Britain and one Mustang squadron of the U.S. VIII Air Force arrived at the rendezvous but, meeting no transport aircraft, assumed that the operation had been cancelled and returned to base.

Landing/Dropping Zone "L"

The last of the glider operations transported the Polish Independent Parachute Brigade Group in 35 Horsas to zone "L" and 28 released successfully. The area on the ground was heavily covered by enemy fire and some of the loads were lost when the gliders burned out. Two parachute aircraft of No. 38 Group both successfully dropped supplies on this zone.

Landing Zone "X"

Seven glider missions in addition to those already planned were flown, but only two reached the zone. Three of these gliders became available owing to failures on previous missions.

Supply Dropping Point " V "

During the afternoon of 19 September, 163 aircraft from Nos. 38 and 46 Groups flew into the area, using the southern route, on the first large scale re-supply mission. Despite intense and accurate flak they carried out the drop with commendable accuracy. One hundred and forty-five aircraft dropped their loads on the supply dropping point and five on zone " S ". The remaining thirteen aircraft were lost and no fewer than 97 others were damaged by flak.

The courage and devotion to duty of the crews of these aircraft was remarkable. They flew into the deadly zone of anti-aircraft fire at a thousand feet and, without exception, maintained accurate courses until their loads were safely released. The story of the heroism of one Dakota crew—that of Flight Lieutenant Lord (271 Squadron)—is attached at Appendix 5 and serves to exemplify the attitude of mind of the airmen who braved the perils of the flak to drop their supplies. The tragic irony of their sacrifice was revealed later when it was learned that the supply dropping point was held by the Germans. Although the forces on the ground had done their utmost to keep the point within their area, they were not able to do so. Communication with base was impossible. There were several reasons for the sometimes partial and often total failure of communications with base. The radio frequency chosen was unsatisfactory, clashing with that of a powerful British station. Early, on the first day of the operation, heavy interference as well as technical failures caused difficulty in communications. On D + 3 it was possible to receive but not to transmit, owing to the sets being surrounded by woods. This created physical interference and screening and all the low-powered sets became unserviceable. As the battle increased in intensity on subsequent days, the injuries to W/T personnel, the effect of blast and the destruction of battery charging sets, thoroughly disrupted all communications. The only method left to avert a useless sacrifice was to attempt to attract the attention of the aircraft to a new zone. This was marked with ground strips and a Eureka beacon was set up on a tower nearby but, owing to the weather, the exact time of the drop was uncertain and during this interval the enemy " strafed " the area where the ground signals were displayed. The Eureka beacon could not be left on indefinitely or the batteries would have been exhausted and although Verey lights were fired the attempt was in vain. The new supply dropping point was not distinctive from the air, being obscured by trees, and those on the ground had the mortifying experience of watching nearly all the supplies fall to the enemy[1].

The Fourth Lift (D + 3) 20 September 1944

During the late afternoon of 19 September, news of the ground situation at Arnhem was received at the Command Post at Eastcote. It was then known that supply dropping point " V " was in enemy hands and the 1st Airborne Division would require re-supply for several more days. A new supply dropping point was therefore chosen, the location of which had been signalled through during the night from Arnhem. It consisted of small fields about one mile south south-east of landing zone " L ".

---

[1] First Airborne Division Signals Report, Annexure T, Part 5.

In the American sectors of Nijmegen and Eindhoven little progress had been made; it was not until late on 20 September that the bridge at Nijmegen was captured by a brilliant feat of arms of American and British troops. The whole advance was well behind schedule and it became obvious that the problem of re-supplying and relieving 1st Airborne Division was becoming hourly more urgent.

The Airborne message of the 19 September also stated that landing zone "Z" was still being held and so it was arranged for a supply drop to take place there in addition to that on the new supply dropping point 691785. Similar weather conditions persisted over England to those of the previous day, whilst over the sea visibility was down to one to two miles with six to eight-tenths cloud and haze which increased in the afternoon. Fighter cover was again provided by Air Defence of Great Britain squadrons and U.S. VIII Air Force and no enemy fighters were encountered. The southern route was used for the fly-in in order to fly over the area of Eindhoven and Nijmegen which was occupied by the Allies.

Dropping Zone "Z"

Thirty-three Stirling aircraft of No. 38 Group were detailed to drop supplies on this zone and all but three found the zone and dropped successfully. Once again the supplies fell into enemy hands because in the 18 hours elapsing since the message had been sent to England concerning the tenure of the zone it had been retaken by the Germans.

Supply Dropping Point 691785

One hundred and twenty-two out of 131 aircraft dropped their supplies successfully but, unfortunately, in vain. Seven aircraft were lost. The enemy soon realised the location of this new zone and attacked, with the result that the Divisional line was pushed back and many of the supplies failed to reach the British although a certain amount was salvaged after dark. Flak in the target area was again severe and great difficulty was experienced on the ground in marking out the new zone. Each time a ground signal was laid out it attracted heavy mortar fire and the men were fired upon by snipers. Despite the bad visibility, fierce opposition from the ground and lack of aids, the drop was reasonably accurate but in the day's operations nine aircraft were lost and 62 damaged.

The Fifth Lift (D+4) 21 September 1944

In the early hours of 21 September, the portion of the 1st Parachute Brigade (Lieut.-Colonel Frost) who had been holding out on the northern approaches to the bridge at Arnhem against strong opposition and without any re-supply, were finally overcome. All were either captured or casualties. Further to the west the remainder of 1st Airborne Division was being forced into an ever diminishing area and their plight was desperate. It was hoped that the Polish Parachute Brigade might be dropped south of the river and thus help to relieve the situation but, although about a quarter of the force were successfully dropped by U.S. IX Troop Carrier Command, they were unable to break through to the Rhine. Meanwhile, further south, the Guards Armoured Division endeavoured to advance along the nine-mile road from Nijmegen to Arnhem but were held up by strong enemy anti-tank defences. The country adjacent to the road was not suitable for the passage of armour.

A variation in the flight plan for the re-supply was introduced; instead of one long wave the 117 aircraft were despatched in four waves in the hope of reducing flak damage to the aircraft. The southern route was used. Weather conditions were still unfavourable, with haze and low cloud over England. U.S. aircraft in the Grantham area were again delayed, but the R.A.F. transports were able to take off on time. For the first time weather adversely affected the fighter force and, although the first wave of transports was covered and the second partly so, the last two were not and the enemy took full advantage. No less than seven out of ten aircraft of No. 190 Squadron and 23 transports altogether were lost. This was the first time the enemy fighter force had really been in evidence.

Supply Dropping Point 693785

This new point was selected 200 yards east of the one in use on the previous day, making the task of recognising it even more difficult for the aircraft. On the ground, it became impossible to put out markers and, although the Eureka beacon was still functioning and Aldis lamps were used, they proved of little assistance to the aircrews, few of whom reported seeing them. Ninety-one aircraft reported successful drops, but few of the supplies reached the desperate men on the ground. In all 61 re-supply aircraft (52 per cent.) were lost or damaged in yet another vain effort.

When considering the results of these three days' re-supply operations, two outstanding conclusions became apparent. First—lack of communications—resulting in inability to obtain up-to-date tactical information of the ground situation at Arnhem. Secondly, the high rate of casualties to aircraft caused by transport aircraft and fighter cover not flying from within the same weather zone. With these two problems in mind, Air Commodore Darvall, Air Officer Commanding No. 46 Group, who had witnessed part of the unfortunate re-supply effort on D+4, conferred with the Air Officer Commanding No. 38 Group and then flew to Europe. After visiting the Air Marshal Commanding 2nd Tactical Air Force, and No. 83 Fighter Group, he went to Nijmegen to consult with the Commanders of the Airborne Corps and XXX Corps. As a result of these meetings No. 575 Squadron, No. 46 Group was sent to Brussels to undertake re-supply operations under control of No. 83 Group. This plan had the following advantages:—

(a) The latest information regarding the tactical situation would be available.

(b) Close support by fighters and fighter bombers would be possible.

(c) Shorter flights would enable a quicker turn-around and therefore more sorties to be made.

(d) Last-minute alterations to the supplies carried could be effected.

No. 575 Squadron arrived in Brussels on 23 September and carried out the remaining re-supply operations for Arnhem on the two following days.

The Sixth Lift (D+6) 23 September 1944

The weather on 22 September (D+5) had been so bad with very low stratus cloud over England, most of the route and the target area that no transport operations were possible. There was little change in the ground situation at Arnhem—the weary troops fought on bravely with the Germans calling for surrender over loudspeakers. Favourable progress had been made between the Waal and lower Rhine on the previous night, and during the day a Guards Brigade, with assault boats, fought its way to the Rhine. Although the line was at first cut, by nightfall contact had been made south of the Rhine with units of 1st Polish Parachute Brigade which had been dropped on the previous day. At 20.20 hours the Second Army gave permission to withdraw the 1st Airborne Division from Arnhem if conditions permitted.

Meanwhile, in England, preparations for the last re-supply from the United Kingdom were being made. The weather forecast was more promising and better conditions were expected over the target area in the afternoon. For the first time since 19 September, gliders of the IX U.S. Troop Carrier Command were able to take off for the Nijmegen and Eindhoven sectors. The R.A.F. re-supply mission flew over the southern route in column with U.S. aircraft, giving a time-length of one and a half hours. A very large fighter escort of 854 aircraft provided an effective cover and very little fighter opposition was encountered in the area. Flak, however, was again severe and more than half of the R.A.F. transports were damaged or lost.

The Drop

One hundred and twenty-three aircraft were despatched with the difficult task of dropping the supplies in the right place. By then the situation on the ground was such that it was no longer possible to use Eureka beacons, as the batteries were dry, or to lay out ground signals. The only method of identifying the zone was by visual signals and, as the enemy were aware of this and also used similar signals to confuse the issue, it was not surprising that the dropping was inaccurate and most of the supplies fell into enemy hands. Sixty-three aircraft were damaged by flak and six lost.

The Seventh Lift (D+7) 24 September 1944

No re-supply operations were flown from England, but 21 aircraft based at Brussels were despatched to the Arnhem area. Four of these went to the west of Arnhem, but two did not drop and the other two saw no signals in the dropping zone. All four were damaged by flak but managed to return to base. The remaining seventeen aircraft re-supplied the U.S. 82nd Airborne Division—fifteen dropped successfully and two landed on an airstrip west of Grave. None of the aircraft was lost and 36 Spitfires provided escort without incident.

The Eighth Lift (D+8) 25 September 1944

The last re-supply mission to Arnhem was undertaken by seven aircraft of No. 575 Squadron at Brussels. Six of these dropped medical supplies and food on to a dropping zone west of Arnhem at Heaveadorp 682768. One aircraft was destroyed and three damaged by flak.

On this day it was finally decided to evacuate 1st Airborne Division across the river because it was not possible for the Allies to cross it in force; the enemy were too strong below the Rhine and the Allied supply corridor had been cut. During the afternoon 1st Airborne Division were told of the plan to evacuate them. At 21.40 hours the operation began and was completed as far as was possible by 06.00 hours on 26 September. The exhausted remnants of 1st Airborne Division made their way from their perimeter across an enemy-held stretch to the river whilst covering fire was given from the south bank. Assault boats, barges and rafts were used and, in the cover of rainy darkness, the survivors made their way to safety, many of them swimming the fast flowing Rhine. The following numbers were evacuated on this night—1,741 men of 1st Airborne Division, 160 of the Polish Parachute Brigade, 75th Dorset Regiment and 422 glider pilots. A few more crossed the river on the following night. 6,400 did not return.

On 28 September 1944 the 1st Allied Airborne Army informed Twenty-first Army Group that, as the link-up had been made between Airborne forces and ground troops, the operation was considered completed and no further re-supply was to be scheduled as an operation in support of Market. In future, supply of Airborne forces was to be considered as supplying ground forces and handled through C.A.T.O.R. This decision released the U.S. VIII and IX Air Forces, 2nd T.A.F. and Air Defence of Great Britain from fighter escort duties for re-supply operations[1].

Thus ended the Battle of Arnhem, the story of which will live always as one of the most gallant undertakings in the annals of British military history.

Operation Market

Air Movement Summary (R.A.F.)

	Despatched	Successful	Unsuccessful	Casualties	Lost
"D" Day:					
Pathfinders	12	12	—	—	—
Gliders	358	319	39	6	—
"D" + 1:					
Re-supply	33	30	3	14	—
Gliders	296	272	24	30	8
"D" + 2:					
Re-supply	165	147	18	97	13
Gliders	44	30	14	9	11
"D" + 3:					
Re-supply	164	152	12	62	9
"D" + 4:					
Re-supply	117	91	26	38	23
"D" + 6:					
Re-supply	123	115	8	63	6
"D" + 7:					
Re-supply	21	21	—	4	—
"D" + 8:					
Re-supply	7	6	1	3	1
Totals:					
Pathfinders	12	12	—	—	—
Gliders	698	621	77	45	19
Re-supply	630	562	68	281	52
	1,340	1,195	145	326	71

Glider Failures not due to Enemy action

Towing failure	28
Tug failure	13
Glider failure	5
Navigation failure	2
Total	48

[1] A.E.A.F. File T.S. 35108. Encl. 124A.

Total British and American Aircraft and Gliders

	Despatched	Lost
Aircraft	12,997	238
Gliders	2,598	139

Conclusions[1]

An analysis of the results and execution of operation Market revealed the following principal points:—

(a) Whenever possible operational control of the Air Forces in support of an Airborne operation should be vested in the Air Officer Commanding of the Tactical Air Force in whose area the force is to be landed. Generally he was in the best position to assess the air situation and organise supporting operations. In the subsequent crossings of the Rhine (Varsity) the operation was planned by S.H.A.E.F. and executed by 2nd T.A.F., who provided all necessary fighter cover, escorts and anti-flak operations as well as offensive air support. These operations were completely successful.

In operation Market, however, air support was first arranged through First Allied Airborne Army and later directly with No. 11 Group. It is doubtful whether, in view of the large numbers of aircraft involved and the slowness of communications between Belgium and the U.K., control by 2nd T.A.F. of air support for the air operations would have improved the position. The fact that in Market the re-supply aircraft suffered heavy casualties was due not so much to any failure in the control system for supporting operations but rather to the unavoidable dangers of flying into a small area which was bound to be well guarded by an already forewarned enemy.

(b) As much time as possible should be allowed for making preparations for the operation. Seven days were allowed for the planning, issuing orders, briefing, etc., for operation Market. Although this was an adequate time interval for 1st Airborne Division, who were well practised in these methods, it would not have been sufficient for a division inexperienced in Airborne operations, rapid planning and issuing orders.

(c) *Importance of dropping in one lift*

Owing to the lift being split, the effective strength was reduced to that of a brigade because part of the first lift had to be used to protect the landing of the second lift. Therefore, all troops and supplies essential to the success of the mission must be landed on the first lift. Complete surprise must also be gained and, to achieve this, swift progress is essential on the first day and if this is not maintained then the enemy has time to recover. Had it

---

[1] A.M. File C/32058/46. 38 G File 10/80/7. War Office Narrative. No. 46 Group History.

been possible to carry out the first lift before dawn and the second at midday, then the surprise element would probably have been maintained, and the landing zones held long enough to be consolidated.

(d) *Dropping and landing zones always to be selected as near as possible to the objectives*

Subsequent examination of the terrain in the vicinity of the bridge, together with information obtained from the Dutch, indicated that it might have been possible to land gliders and/or paratroops on the south side of the river within one mile of the bridge. Although the ground in this area—known as Polder Land—was subject to flooding when the fast-moving Rhine was at high level, it appeared that during the few days immediately preceding the operation there was no flooding. The real disadvantage of this plan, however, lay in the existence of networks of irrigation ditches[1] which would have jeopardised safe glider landings. These might have been possible if the glider undercarriages had been jettisoned but this always involved the possibility of not being able to swing the glider tail open to unload vehicles. Because of this and also the difficulties of concentrating troops and moving vehicles, due to the ditches, the glider pilot regiment decided against taking the risk.

In previous operations the maximum dropping distance from the objectives was five miles; in operation Market it was seven to eight miles. The choice of landing zones as far from the objective as they were detracted to a certain extent from one advantage to be gained from Airborne operations—that of surprise. Although in the case of Market the surprise element was limited by reason of the approach of the Airborne forces in daylight over a considerable stretch of enemy occupied territory.

In view of the terrain to be traversed between the landing zones and the bridge—involving fighting through dense pine woods, easily defended by the enemy, and the suburban areas of Oosterbeck, it was extremely difficult for the attacking forces to reach the bridge in sufficient numbers and within a short enough time to capture a point which naturally would be the first concern of the defending forces.

(e) *Intelligence*

Intelligence appreciation of the flak defences around Arnhem was extremely pessimistic. It was both thin and inaccurate and there was little information concerning enemy troops in the area. There was no knowledge of the presence of II S.S. Panzer Corps, consisting of IX and X Panzer Divisions, who were refitting in the neighbourhood[2].

---

[1] The land here is divided by ditches into areas of 50 to 100 metres in width and 100–200 metres long. The ditches are 2–3 metres wide and 1½ deep with usually ¼ metre of water in them.

[2] Subsequent information from Dutch sources also revealed that at the time of the operation there were three German battalions in the town.

(f) Offensive Air Support

There was a lack of close offensive air support, especially during the first day, and also when the airborne troops were moving in towards Arnhem[1].

(g) Operation Market again confirmed the lesson that all personnel of Airborne Divisions must have maximum infantry and weapon training.

(h) Re-supply

There were many aspects of this problem. Firstly, lack of information regarding the flight plans of the re-supply aircraft adversely affected the provision of fighter cover. 2nd T.A.F. were unaware of the plans due to inadequate communications, thus quite frequently immediate air support was lacking for periods of three to four hours. In spite of this, whenever the weather was at all favourable the re-supply mission had to go on in view of the critical position of the ground troops. Although some support was given by No. 11 Group it was not sufficient, whereas more complete cover might have been able to silence to some extent, the light anti-aircraft fire which was responsible for most of the casualties. Secondly, the question of air defence by day; lack of information again affected fighter support and the proximity of enemy airfields also aggravated the situation. As regards air defence by night, Fighter Command was responsible for the night defence of the dropping and landing zones for the period $D+1$ to $D+4$. After this No. 85 Group took over. The method employed by Fighter Command was to fly in a G.C.I. unit which, when set up, would enable the aircraft to revert to "close control with the ground". This method clashed with No. 85 Group night defence organisation which could easily have absorbed the dropping/landing zone commitment and could have undertaken to provide close control from the first night on. This became obvious when, owing to the ground situation, it was apparent that the G.C.I. unit was unable to operate.

It was recommended that when future Airborne operations were planned a T.A.F. representative be present to advise and make provision for the very close liaison necessary between First Allied Airborne Army and the Tactical Air Force prior to and during an operation. It was agreed by S.H.A.E.F., First Allied Airborne Army and 2nd T.A.F. that future plans were to include the establishment of a small liaison co-ordinating group on the staff level of the First Allied Airborne Army with the Army and Tactical Air Commanders of the zone, and a single plan agreed upon between the Troop carrier Command, the Area Air Commander, the Airborne Forces Commander and the Army[2].

---

[1] One of the major reasons for the failure of Market was that the Germans were able to bring up reinforcements, including tanks, to Arnhem without undue interference.
[2] File 2nd T.A.F./30317/Sigs. Ops., 6 January 1945.

No arrangements were made in advance for emergency re-supply from the continent in the event of non-operational weather in the United Kingdom until it was too late due to lack of equipment, trained packing personnel and adequate supplies. At Arnhem there were instances where the supply dropping points could have been changed at the last moment had it been possible to notify the aircraft and also to confirm the exact location of the dropping points. It will be seen, therefore, that one of the principal lessons arising out of Arnhem was that adequate and well organised communications were a fundamental necessity to success in an Airborne operation. Information received after the war from the Dutch Underground Movement revealed the fact that a complete and efficient secret communication system was in operation prior to the battle and the use of it was offered to the allied forces. This system provided a direct contact to Nijmegen and thus to the allied headquarters. In view of the extreme poverty of communications, especially with regard to re-supply, it might seem that some use could have been made of it, but for reasons of security it was decided not to use it.

There were several other factors which contributed to the failure of the re-supply at Arnhem. The anti-aircraft defences were strong causing losses to the aircraft and the consequent evasive action resulted in scattered dropping. An elaborate anti-flak plan is, therefore, necessary if re-supply is to be carried out under unfavourable conditions such as those prevailing for operation Market. Generally, however, low level re-supply into an area heavily defended by A.A. is not a practicable risk[1]. No. 46 Group lost 30 per cent. of their aircraft engaged in re-supply and 80 of the remainder were damaged.

The size of the perimeter in which the ground forces were contained was very small and flying into such an area against strong enemy opposition was not satisfactory, but if it had to be done then the latest tactical and topographical information should be available and perfect co-ordination with Fighter escorts and Fighter Bomber or low firing aircraft maintained. This was scarcely feasible in operation Market where the participating air forces had to operate from scattered areas—France, Belgium and various parts of England—and where communications were slow and inadequate.

When possible the re-supply aircraft should be stationed as near as practicable to the Airborne Forces in order that advantage may be taken of changing weather conditions which may become more suitable for re-supply work and less suitable from the view-point of the enemy defences. Another advantage of basing re-supply aircraft as near as possible to the operational area was that of speed. It enabled a quicker turn-round to be made facilitating rapid concentration of dropping. This again was not possible in Market where the problem of intensive urgent re-supply was not envisaged.

---

[1] See Appendix 7.

To have done so would have been tantamount to planning for failure. On the ground, constant shelling and mortaring of the perimeter by the enemy as well as the lack of available vehicles made collection and distribution impossible in the later stages.

(i) *Height of Fly In*

It might be that the aircraft would be less vulnerable against flak if they were to fly at low level, climbing to dropping height only when near to the dropping zone. The disadvantages of this were the difficulty of map reading at low level and the reduction in effective range of radio visual aids.

(j) It was noticed that when fighter cover was lacking losses due to flak were higher than the average, also, of course, fighter cover kept off the enemy fighters. The air losses sustained during one lift and part of another were due in the first instance to lack of air cover caused by the breakdown in communications with fighter bases on the continent, and in the second case by the fact that it was not known that bad weather had grounded the fighter force, otherwise the re-supply aircraft probably would not have been despatched.

(k) *Towropes*

Some trouble was again experienced with broken towropes caused mainly by cloud conditions and the slipstream effect of the tug aircraft. There did not seem to be any antidote for this unless the problem of co-ordinating tug and glider movement could be perfected by the production of a composite aircraft.

(l) *Glider becoming redundant*

As heavy equipment could be dropped by parachute the use of the glider became less. Parachute aircraft were less dependent on weather and light; they were faster, more manœuvrable and more economical of equipment and crews. Only the Hamilcar really retained its value because of its size and the weight of cargo it was able to carry.

(m) Once more the value of the Dakota as an all-round aircraft was demonstrated. It could be used either for transport or for Airborne tasks, thus it did not need to lie idle between operations as was the case with some of the Bomber type aircraft in No. 38 Group. The ideal aircraft for Airborne operations would appear to be the four-engined Bomber type, able to carry and drop heavy loads and also to tow the Hamilcar. In order to simplify maintenance and administration, this aircraft should be of a similar type to those employed in Bomber Command.

(n) The ground aids to navigation were satisfactory but not necessarily reliable. Visual aids could not be too distinctive. Ground signals should be as large as possible and smoke dense and lasting.

From the No. 38 and 46 Group viewpoints, operation Market was undoubtedly successful. Of the 1,340 sorties flown during the eight days, almost 1,200 carried out their tasks successfully despite the severe opposition encountered by the re-supply missions. On the first three days R.A.F. aircraft carried 4,500 men, 95 guns and 544 jeeps or larger vehicles across 200 miles of sea and enemy territory, dropping them distances of up to 60 miles behind the Front line.

The following message was sent by the G.O.C., 1st Airborne Division, Major-General Urquhart to the Air Officer Commanding, No. 38 Group:—

> "We were given a very good start by the R.A.F. The result of the dropping of the paratroops and glider landings was quite first-class, it was easily the most successful and accurate of any previously achieved, either in operations or in exercises. All units were able to move on to their tasks directly at full strength, and in a very short time after landing. We must thank you also for the efforts made to re-supply us during our nine days' battle on the ground. We are full of admiration for the way in which aircraft faced the initial flak, which thickened up considerably after the initial stage. The Division was by then occupying a very small area, which was thickly covered over by trees and houses, and this made the re-supply task extremely difficult and hazardous".

German Reaction to Operation Market[1]

The Germans admitted surprise and thought that the attacks against anti-aircraft positions were an attempt to destroy the bridges. They considered that we used too much of the Air Force to protect Airborne landings instead of interfering with movements of German reinforcements.

They attributed the failure of the Arnhem operation mainly to:

(a) Time interval of the landings, caused by weather conditions.

(b) The landing places being too far from the objectives, resulting in the loss of the surprise element.

The Germans assumed that with the future Allied Airborne Operations therefore, a stronger, more timely strong-point build-up must be reckoned with—and in connection therewith, a stronger attacking ability by the Allied Air Force against the A.A. defences of the objectives must also be expected. (It is revealed from captured documents that the Allies were well informed regarding the strength and disposition of German A.A. defences.)

---

[1] Translation from German documents. No. 38 Group Report, Appendix O.

CHAPTER 10

FURTHER OPERATIONS IN EUROPE

Developments Prior to Operation Varsity

Control of No. 46 Group

Shortly after Operation Market had been completed, the question of qualifying the operational relationship between the First Allied Airborne Army and Nos. 38 and 46 Groups was again raised by General Brereton in a signal to S.H.A.E.F. Forward Headquarters, on 30 September 1944[1]. It was desired to have a permanently clear relationship to facilitate the training and planning for future projected airborne operations. The available resources of Nos. 38 and 46 Groups were, therefore, placed under the control of the First Allied Airborne Army, after allowing for the demands on No. 38 Group by SAS/SOE commitments and on No. 46 Group by transport work. The latter group screened two aircraft per squadron from transport operations to carry out airborne training.

Naples II

During September 1944 the outlined plan for Operation Naples II was produced by First Allied Airborne Army[2]. The object of this operation was to assist the advance of the central group of Armies by seizing a bridgehead on the East Bank of the Rhine in the general area Koln/Bonn and to achieve this the use of airborne troops was considered necessary. It was intended to use 6th Airborne Division, which would be ready for combat during October and the XVII U.S. Airborne Division, which had arrived from the U.S.A. in September. For the purpose of Operation Naples II, all No. 38 Group aircraft, except 25 which were to be retained for SAS/SOE operations, were made available and, with the exception of 40 serviceable aircraft for transport purposes, all No. 46 Group aircraft as well[3].

It was originally intended to launch Naples II in November, but in view of the strategic situation it was decided at S.H.A.E.F. Chiefs of Staff Conference, on 20 November 1944, that Varsity and Naples II should take place on 1 January 1945 and be operated from the U.K.[4]. For operations beyond the Rhine, however, airfields on the continent would be required, but the earliest date by which these would be available was 1 February 1945.

The whole situation was altered by the German offensive in the Ardennes in December, after which it became apparent that the assault over the Rhine could not be undertaken until the Spring of 1945. When the operation for

---

[1] A.E.A.F. File T.S. 22518/A.3. Encl. 26A.
[2] H.Q. F.A.A.A., File A.P.O. 740, 21 September 1944.
[3] The 25 aircraft of No. 38 Group might be available for the initial lift of Naples II, but not the 40 aircraft of No. 46 Group. It was the intention to maintain all scheduled air services to 2nd T.A.F. and Twenty-first Army Group at all times, but this did not preclude the possibility of No. 46 Group aircraft being required for an airborne operation if it were deemed important enough. Thus all No. 46 Group air and glider crews were kept fully trained and available. A.E.A.F. File T.S. 22518/A.3. Encl. 32A.
[4] D.S.C./T.S./100/9, Part III, Encl. 18A.

crossing the Rhine assumed reality, the First Allied Airborne Army requested operational control of the total strength of the two R.A.F. Groups, dating from 1 March 1945. This was granted, with the exception of one squadron (25 aircraft) of No. 46 Group, which was to be retained for air transport work. A further 25 of the 125 remaining aircraft were retained on transport work until three days before the operation.

As the operations in Europe moved further to the east, the range for aircraft based in Britain greatly increased and, at a meeting of the A.E.A.F. Airfield Committee on 23 September 1944 it was decided to move No. 38 Group and its squadrons to East Anglia, in order to facilitate flying for any future operations[1].

The moves took place during the early part of October and were as follows:—

H.Q. No. 38 Group to Marks Hall.

All No. 38 Group Units at Brize Norton to Earls Colne.

All No. 38 Group Units at Fairford to Gt. Dunmow.

All No. 38 Group Units at Harwell to Rivenhall (including the satellite at Hampstead Norris).

All No. 38 Group Units at Keevil to Wethersfield (later to Shepherd's Grove due to unserviceable runways).

All these stations were in Essex.

Pre-Crew Training for SAS/SOE Operations

During July 1944 an attempt was made by the Director of Operational Training, Air Ministry, to alter the Training Syllabus of No. 38 Group to conform to that in use at a Bomber Command Wellington Operational Training Unit[2]. Air Vice-Marshal Hollinghurst, A.O.C. No. 38 Group, strongly opposed this suggestion and in a letter dated 29 July 1944 expressed the absolute necessity for a high standard of training, which was in no way diminished by the use of No. 38 Group crews in SAS/SOE operations. This lesson, he said, had been outstanding from previous airborne operations. The A.O.C. pointed out that the problems confronting No. 38 Group were different from those of Bomber Command and that there was no point, therefore, in standardising the training. The very nature of the work involved in SAS/SOE operations rendered individual pre-crew training of the highest standard to be more essential than in any other phase of air activity[3]. The emphatic defence by the A.O.C. No. 38 Group of the training method then in use had the desired effect. H.Q. A.E.A.F. supported his view that no economy in pre-crew training could be effected in No. 38 Group without considerable detriment to the future operational success of the Group, and no deviation from the high standard then maintained was permitted[4].

---

[1] A.M.S.O. File L.M. 273/D.D.O. (P).
[2] Section II, 38 Group Report.
[3] No. 38G/T.S. 3/Air, Part II, Encl. 67A.
[4] Ibid, Encl. 69A.

All training in No. 38 Group was now being carried out in order to fit aircrews to complete their duties as laid down in the Standard Operational Procedure[1] and training became more or less static[2]. On 18 October 1944 Air Vice-Marshal J. R. Scarlett-Streatfield was appointed A.O.C. No. 38 Group in place of Air Vice-Marshal L. N. Hollinghurst, who was due to be posted to South-East Asia. Previously, however, Air Vice-Marshal Hollinghurst had foreseen the necessity of revising the method of supply dropping. It had been demonstrated in Operation Market that low level supply dropping could prove extremely costly. Therefore he ordered experiments to be made in dropping supplies from medium altitudes[3].

Throughout the winter months of 1944-1945, No. 38 Group continued to carry out SAS/SOE operations, although bad weather caused many cancellations. Normal training in large scale glider and parachute exercises took place, designed in preparation for any operations which might be called for in crossing the Rhine.

It was decided by the A.O.C. No. 38 Group and the Commanding General IX Troop Carrier Command that at least one wing of the IX T.C.C. would have to be available for lifting any British airborne division from the United Kingdom to Europe. A large scale combined exercise was therefore planned in which both British and American aircraft would come under the control and command of the A.O.C. No. 38 Group. Exercise Eve was carried out on 21 November 1944, and comprised a large scale parachute landing by day from both British and American aircraft together with a glider landing, the gliders being towed by British aircraft. Although there was some delay in take off, the exercise was fairly successful and was used as a basis for the planning of Operation Varsity. Exercises in D.R. Navigation were also held under the code name Quiver as it was apparent that many crews were relying too much on radar as a means of, rather than an aid to, navigation.

Re-Organisation of Training Units

On 12 December 1944 the Director of Operational Training, Air Ministry, wrote a letter on the re-organisation of No. 38 Group Training Units. In the proposed re-organisation, No. 81 O.T.U. was to expand in order to reach the output of 26 trained crews per month. It was also to be equipped with Wellington X aircraft. The re-equipment of the O.T.U. with the Wellington X, fitted with radar and other specialist equipment and capable of carrying pre-crew navigators doubled up with the crew doing advanced training, was intended to dispense with a certain proportion of the pre-crew training then being carried out on Anson and Oxford aircraft. It was also thought that the pilots' flying time on the Service type at the O.T.U.s could be reduced to nearer 80-85 hours instead of the 102 already in existence[4]. The Director of Operational Training also ordered a revised Training Syllabus for the re-organisation of No. 81 O.T.U. to be prepared. On 5 January 1945 H.Q. A.E.A.F. agreed to this proposal. The new syllabus was drawn up and remained in force until after the end of the war[5].

---

[1] See Appendix 3.
[2] No. 38 Group Report, Section II, Paras. 76-80.
[3] A full description of this is attached in Appendix 7.
[4] A.M. File S. 95943/11/T.O. 3 dated 12 December 1944.
[5] File S.H.A.E.F. A.R.S./72081.

Crossing the Rhine—Operation Varsity

General Situation

During the autumn of 1944 while the Allied Armies moved inexorably towards Germany the Planning Staff of the First Allied Airborne Army were engaged in preparing plans for the potential use of Airborne Forces in support of the ground advance. On 15 October 1944 General Eisenhower stated that the First Allied Airborne Army would operate in support of the Central Group of Armies for the crossing of the Rhine[1]. Meanwhile six airborne operations were planned—three to breach the Siegfried line and three to assist the Rhine crossing—before the first outline plan for operation Varsity was produced on 7 November 1944[2].

The area chosen for the operation was the general one of Emmerich-Wesel, as it was found to be most suitable for airborne landings. It consisted of a flat plain some five to ten miles wide, similar to Dutch " polder " land but, unlike Arnhem, the banks of the Rhine were high and reinforced against flooding. In order to establish a bridgehead, two Airborne Divisions would be required and the bridgehead would have to be five to ten miles wide and approximately five miles deep to avoid hindrance by enemy artillery. On 17 October, the United States IX Army had been moved to the left flank of the U.S. Army Group in order to be in readiness for a crossing of the Rhine. However, many months were to pass before the last great airborne operation of the European war could be launched.

The German counter attack in the Ardennes in December effectively destroyed any hopes of a Rhine crossing before the Spring of 1945. By mid-February 1945 the plan for operation Plunder (the ground assault across the Rhine) began to take shape. The main Allied effort involved the use of three Allied Armies under the command of Field-Marshal Montgomery. The U.S. IX Army on the right flank and the British Second Army on the left were to attack between Rheinberg and Rees, capture the communication centre of Wesel and then expand southwards to seize the roads through Wesel and northwards to secure a firm bridgehead for future operations. The U.S. IX Army with its bridging area at Rheinberg were to attack south of Wesel and the British Second Army north of Wesel. The latter, in addition to capturing the town, so that the IX Army could create bridgeheads there, were also to bridge the river at Xanteen and Rees. To assist the Second Army advance the First Allied Airborne Army was to drop the U.S. XVIII Airborne Corps, comprising the U.S. XVII and the British Sixth Airborne Divisions—north and north-west of Wesel in order to seize key terrain in that area[3].

Airborne Planning

The plan for this Airborne operation was promulgated on 10 February 1945, and differed from the original plan of 7 November 1944, in that the Airborne Forces were to operate a few hours after the ground assault across the Rhine, whereas in the original plan a simultaneous attack by ground and airborne forces had been proposed. This change of plan was caused by the

---
[1] Dep. Sup. Cmdr. File T.S. 100/14, Part I, Encl. 13A.
[2] See Appendix 10.
[3] Supreme Commander's report on operations in Europe, 6 June 1944 to 8 May 1945.

discovery of strongly established enemy positions a few miles east of the Rhine from which counter attacks and artillery opposition might be expected. It was also feared that a night attack would expose the airborne forces to opposition by German night fighter aircraft without the chance of protection by Allied aircraft. On the suggestion of the British Second Army the revised plan provided for a one-lift simultaneous drop by two airborne divisions east of the Rhine during daylight, a few hours after the assault across the river had been made under cover of darkness by ground forces[1].

The British 6th Airborne Division were to secure the northern part of the assault area; seize high ground east of Bergen and bridges over the Issel river; capture the town of Hamminkeln, protect the northern flank of the U.S. XVIII Corps (Airborne) and establish contact with the British XII Corps and the U.S. XVII Airborne Division.

The U.S. XVII Airborne Division were to land on the southern part of the area, seize the high ground east of Diersfordt and bridges over the Issel river, protect the southern flank of the U.S. XVIII Corps and establish contact with 1st Commando Brigade, British XII Corps and 6th Airborne Division. The Commanding General U.S. XVIII Corps, Major-General M. B. Ridgeway, was ordered to be prepared to marshal airborne troops for this operation to take place by 24 March 1945.

The *modus operandi* of the airborne operations involved in crossing the Rhine differed essentially from those in Neptune and Market. In these operations airborne forces played a strategic role in advance of the main military effort: the success of the whole operation in each case depended upon the airborne troops being able to obtain their objectives. In operation Varsity the airborne forces were ancillary to the main assault; their use was tactical rather than strategic. The airborne tasks were sub-divided and allotted to smaller groups and units which were to be landed as near as possible to the objectives. Unlike any previous airborne operation the forces arrived after the ground assault had been joined.

The decision to use airborne troops in this manner was made by the General Officer Commanding 6th Airborne Division and the Air Officer Commanding No. 38 Group after detailed study of the terrain around Hamminkeln had been made by the Commander of the Glider Pilot Regiment. He was of the opinion that units of the airborne division could be landed in gliders close enough to their objectives to accomplish their tasks immediately after landing. This was taking full advantage of the lesson so drastically learnt at Arnhem that to land airborne troops a considerable distance from their objectives was to court disaster.

The advantages of the method used for operation Varsity were that the enemy would be less likely to anticipate the points of landing and even if they did, would be unable to organise any large scale counter attack because of the scattered nature of the opposition. Subsequent events justified the plan. The enemy were confused and unable to co-ordinate their defences, with the result that the objectives were taken before they could organise effective opposition.

---

[1] Revised outline Plan for operation Varsity. First Allied Airborne Army APO. 740. A.M. File D.S.C./T.S./100/14, Part 2, Encl. 11A.

Detailed Airborne Planning

The detailed airborne planning was jointly assigned to the Commanding General XVIII U.S. Corps (Airborne) who was in control of the U.S. XVII and the British 6th Airborne Divisions and Major-General Paul Williams, Commanding U.S. IX Troop Carrier Command, who controlled the British and American Troop Carrier units. Further division of planning was necessary for the air lift as the U.S. XVII Airborne Division were based on the Continent and were to be lifted from there by U.S. XI Troop Carrier Command, whereas the British 6th Airborne Division were stationed in the United Kingdom and were to be lifted by the R.A.F. Groups, Nos. 38 and 46 and 52 Wing of U.S. IX Troop Carrier Command[1]. As in former operations, the control of the R.A.F. share of the lift was vested in the Air Officer Commanding, No. 38 Group. Each of the troop carrier formations was, therefore, responsible for issuing its own operational orders[2]. The British 6th Airborne Division in the United Kingdom comprised 3rd and 5th Parachute Brigade and the 6th Air Landing Brigade Group. All glider towing was to be undertaken by Nos. 38 and 46 Groups and all parachute dropping by three groups of No. 52 Wing U.S. IX Troop Carrier Command, which was also stationed in England. Early in March, the final decision as to where and when the operation was to take place was made, and the operational staffs of the formations concerned began their task of preparing for the largest airborne operation of the war[3].

Providing Aircraft and Crews for the Lift

The provision of sufficient transport support aircraft and crews to accomplish the movement of 6th Airborne Division in one lift provided a considerable problem for the Commanders of Nos. 38 and 46 Groups[4]. The production of transport aircraft had, for some time, been allocated a low priority, so to find 500 serviceable aircraft for the operation strained the Group resources to the limit.

The Air Officer Commanding, No. 38 Group, in a letter to the Air Ministry on 1 March 1945, requested an additional 50 Halifax IIIs and 54 Stirling IVs to increase squadron establishment to 34 aircraft. Although the Director General of Organisation, Air Ministry, was not able to fulfil this request completely, his promise that 35 Halifaxes and 32 Stirlings would be available by 15 March 1945, and that the remainder would be forthcoming as soon as possible but probably not quite in time for the operation, was accepted by the Air Officer Commanding, No. 38 Group[5]. The aircrew shortage was overcome by retaining tour expired crews in the squadrons and using every crew within the limits of the Group, by this means 320 crews became available for the operation.

---

[1] No. 38 Group Report, Operation Varsity, Section 3, Appendix S.
[2] It is not proposed to detail the American Troop Carrier share of Operation Varsity except in so far as it directly concerns the lift of British forces. The overall military and air tasks of Varsity were largely interdependent but it is beyond the scope of this narrative to describe fully the American operations. For information on this phase of Varsity, reference should be made to " Air Operations in support of Rhine Crossing ", the H.Q's. First Allied Airborne report on Operation Varsity, etc.
[3] Narrative. Operation Varsity, H.Q. First Allied Airborne Army, page 3.
[4] No. 38 Group Report, Operation Varsity, Section 3, Appendix S.
[5] No. 38 Group T.S./10/94/1/Air.

FIG. 10

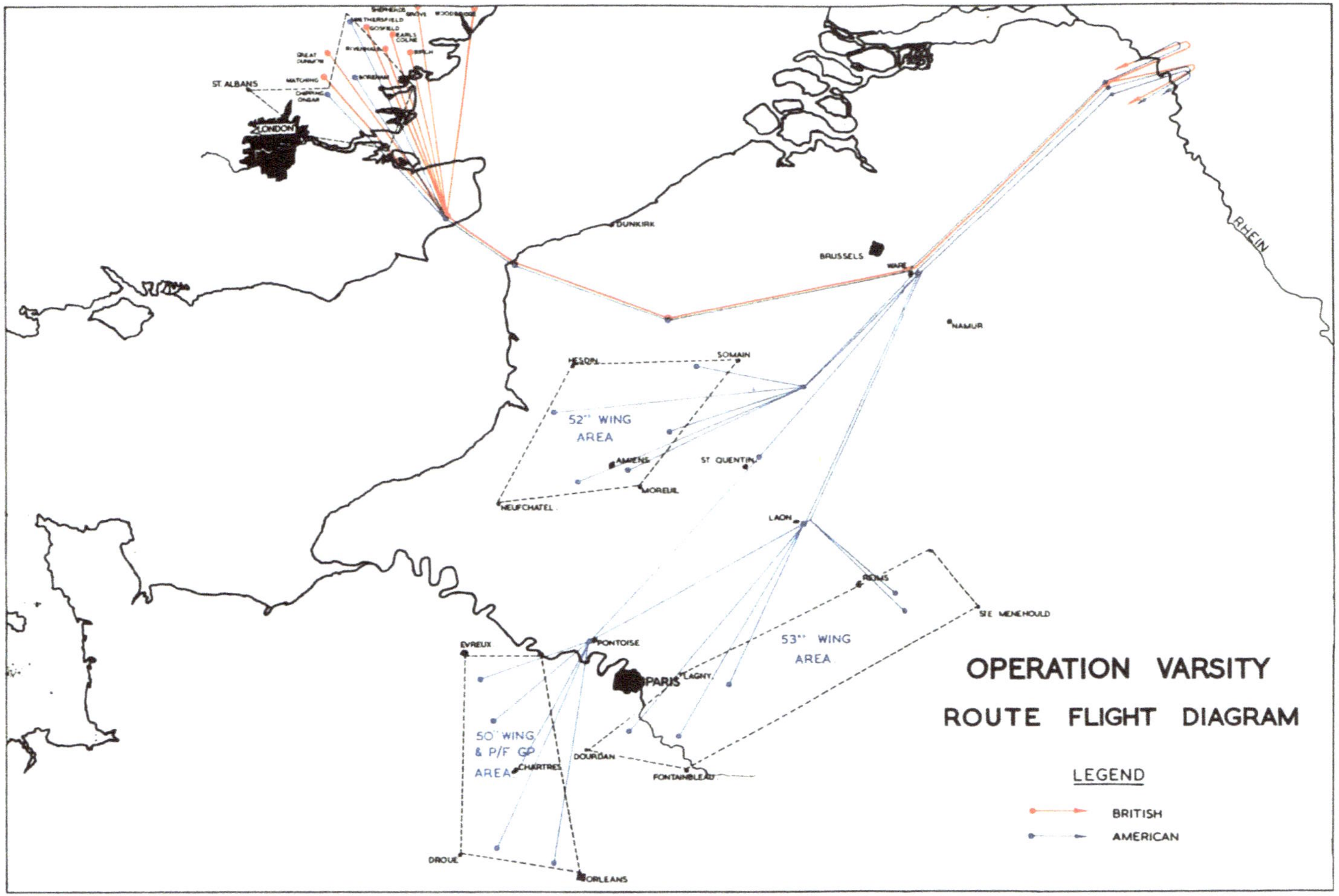

OPERATION VARSITY
ROUTE FLIGHT DIAGRAM

LEGEND
BRITISH
AMERICAN

Facing page 184

No. 46 Group also had its problem[1]. In addition to having to maintain essential transport schedules, the Group was committed to provide 120 Dakotas for the Airborne Operation[2], and approximately 60 for possible resupply on the same day. In order to increase the availability, crews and aircraft from the Operational Training Unit had to be called in. The R.A.F. contingent was thus finally able to provide 440 aircraft and crews for a simultaneous lift of 6th Airborne Division.

After the Arnhem Operation only 48 officers and 666 other ranks remained in the Glider Pilot Regiment and as approximately 1,000 crews were required for the British Airborne effort in Varsity, the deficiency had to be made up from R.A.F. reserve of aircrew[3]. These pilots were given glider refresher courses—First pilots on Horsas and Second pilots on Hotspurs—and a military course at the Glider Pilot Depot. Although the R.A.F. element were operationally inexperienced this was overcome by judicious mixing of Army and R.A.F. personnel in the squadrons and excellent results were achieved.

ORDER OF BATTLE (AIR FORCES)

6th British Airborne Division Lift

Glider Towing

(a) *No. 38 Group (R.A.F.)*

Airfield	Squadron	Aircraft	
(i) Rivenhall	295	Stirlings	60
	570	Stirlings	
(ii) Shepherds Grove	196	Stirlings	60
	299	Stirlings	
(iii) Great Dunmow	190	Stirlings	60
	620	Stirlings	
(iv) Earls Colne	296	Halifaxes	60
	297	Halifaxes	
(v) Woodbridge[4]	298	Halifaxes	12
	644	Halifaxes	48
(vi) Matching	O.R.T.U.	Stirlings	20

(b) *No. 46 Group (R.A.F.)*

Airfield	Squadron	Aircraft	
(i) Gosfield	512	C-47	60
	575	C-47	
	271	C-47	
(ii) Birch	233	C-47	60
	437	C-47	
	48	C-47	

---

[1] No. 46 Group History, page 88.
[2] S.H.A.E.F. (forward) H.Q.'s meeting, 28 February 1945.
[3] Glider Pilot Regiment Report on Operation Varsity, pages 42–43.
[4] Woodbridge was used by Tarrant Rushton to enable Tug/Glider Combinations to reach their objective.

Paratroop Carrying

(c) 52nd Wing IX U.S.T.C.C.

Airfield	Group	Aircraft	
Boreham	315	C–47	81
Wethersfield	316	C–47	81
Chipping Ongar	61	C–47	81

Supporting Air Effort

The overall air planning was initiated on 28 February 1945, at a conference at S.H.A.E.F. H.Q. attended by representatives of Twenty-first Army Group, British Second Army and First Allied Airborne Army. The basic air tasks were allotted to the various American and British formations, and Second Tactical Air Force was given the responsibility of making detailed air plans and controlling all co-operating air forces. The final plan was completed by Second T.A.F. and submitted to S.H.A.E.F. H.Q. on 20 March 1945[1].

The fact that the control of all air operations in connection with airborne assault was again vested in the theatre air commander, Commander-in-Chief Second T.A.F., Air Marshal Sir Arthur Coningham, was another instance of a lesson learned at Arnhem. This principle of theatre air commander being in control of all activity in support of an airborne operation was adhered to in subsequent operations in the Far East.

The two main objectives of the supporting air effort were the neutralisation of enemy air forces and flak positions. Special attention was to be given to the latter, both by artillery fire and by fighter and fighter bomber operations. A special anti-flak committee was set up to study all flak problems and collect up-to-date information in the area. Artillery fire against flak positions was to be continued until the first elements of the troop carrier stream crossed the Rhine. At the same time, fighter bombers and fighters were to attack all flak positions which were then known. During the landings a continuous patrol of anti-flak fighters was to be maintained in the area to deal with any flak positions which might provide opposition against the troop carrier aircraft.

Fighter Cover

Operation Market showed that with overwhelming fighter cover airborne landings could be made with little or no interference from the German Air Force[2]. Up-to-date appreciations of the German fighter strength led to the following conclusions:—

(i) The German Air Force was not strong enough to offer effective opposition to Operation Varsity.

(ii) Jet propelled aircraft, although technically superior to our own, were not in sufficient numbers seriously to affect the position.

(iii) The German Air Force would be better able to interfere if the operation were to be mounted at night.

---

[1] H.Q. First Allied Airborne Army Report on Varsity, A.P.O. 757, page 10.
[2] Dep. Sup. Cdr. T.S. 100/14, Part II, Appendix E.

Air Defence of the Dropping Zones

It was thought that the Germans might employ about 600 aircraft to oppose the operation. Therefore, a fighter screen would be necessary east of the dropping zones as well as heavy bombers to attack airfields from which jet aircraft would operate. The Second T.A.F. were responsible for the defence of the dropping and landing zones by day and night, and were also to provide squadrons to be employed on ground strafing of enemy troop movements[1].

Allocation of the Tasks

The various tasks in support of the Operation were allocated as follows[2]:—

Fighter

(a) The U.S. VIII Air Force were to provide a fighter screen east of the landing area during the period of the landings.

(b) R.A.F. squadrons were to provide air escort of Troop Carrier Command columns from the United Kingdom until they were relieved by Second T.A.F.

(c) The IX U.S. Air Force were responsible for the air escort of the Troop Carrier Formations from the French airfields until it was taken over by Second T.A.F.

Second T.A.F. were responsible for fighter cover during the final stages of the fly in.

Bomber

(a) The U.S. VIII Air Force were to attack jet airfields prior to the operation, flak positions near the area, communication targets east of the battle area, and also carry out diversionary attacks. R.A.F. Bomber Command were to bomb other targets and attack communications not already undertaken by the U.S. VIII Air Force.

(b) Radar counter-measures.

(c) Coastal Command were also to provide day and night diversionary operations.

Two major diversionary operations were conducted on 24 March. Berlin was bombed by U.S. XIV Air Force based in Italy and R.A.F. Bomber Command attacked the rail centre of Sterkrade as well as oil targets in the Ruhr.

The Flight Plan

The combined flight plan was drawn up by the Joint Planning Staff of No. 38 Group and IX U.S. Troop Carrier Command at the latter Headquarters, Maison Lafitte, near Paris[3]. Two groups of base airfields for the operation were to be used; in the United Kingdom eight British and three American airfields and, on the continent, fifteen American airfields. The Troop Carrier Formation based in the United Kingdom were to assemble

---
[1] This was the result of a lesson learnt from German comments on the Arnhem operation criticising over-concentration of defence against air attack and ignoring the danger of ground attack.
[2] A.M. File C.M.S. 754/D. Ops./TAC.
[3] No. 38 Group Report, Varsity, paras. 45–46.

north and east of London, converge to cross the channel near Folkestone to Cap Gris Nez, turn south-east to Bethune, then east-north-east to Wavre, where it would join the U.S. XVII Airborne Division from their bases in France. The whole stream would then proceed north-east to Weeze. It was decided in this operation that American and British aircraft should fly in on parallel streams. These streams were kept respectively one mile north and one mile south of the route, maintaining a space of two miles between the columns until the target rendezvous was reached. From this point the columns were to diverge on to their respective dropping and landing zones and turn left or right respectively after their release or drop[1]. The American paratroop aircraft were to fly in formations of 81, nine formations of nine, and their glider towing aircraft in formations of three. The British aircraft towing gliders were to fly in pairs at ten second intervals.

Navigational Aids

In addition to the usual navigational aids, the Eureka beacons and Compass beacons were to be set up at the various turning points, with additional beacons mid-way between Wavre and the target area. There were no ground markings to be put on the dropping/landing zones, but immediately prior to crossing the Rhine the Eureka beacons and coloured strips with distinctive letter pannels were to be set up for the guidance of all formations. This was considered to be sufficient in view of the close proximity of the Rhine to the zones.

The Choice of Dropping/Landing Zones

Once the decision to use the airborne forces in a tactical manner had been made, the next step was to select areas for landing near to the objectives. Photographic reconnaissance had shown that suitable areas existed[2]. Below the town of Bonn the Rhine flows through a flat almost featureless plain, averaging 45-80 feet above sea level, and closely resembling Dutch polderland. The immediate terrain was firm farm land consisting of meadows 2-300 yards in length and of combined farming areas from 5-600 yards in length, highly suitable for glider landing. For the dropping and landing of 6th Airborne Division, six zones were chosen—" A ", " B ", " P ", " O ", " U " and " R "[3]. Of these, dropping zones " A " and " B " were for the two Parachute Brigades, 3rd and 5th, and the other four landing zones for the air landing Brigade gliders[4]. The zones presented little difficulty for identification from the air. The towns of Hamminkeln and Wesel, the Issel canal, the double track railway from Emmerich to Wesel, a large woodland area and the main road running north from Hamminkeln all provided excellent land marks.

The Lift of 6th Airborne Division

The tasks of the 6th Airborne Division were sub-divided as follows[5]:—

(a) The first stage of the operation was to be the dropping of 3rd and 5th Parachute Brigades on landing zones " A " and " B " from aircraft of 52 Wing U.S. IX Troop Carrier Command. Their task

---

[1] See figure 10.
[2] H.Q. No. 38 Group, Varsity Report, paras. 25–26.
[3] See Figure 11.
[4] U.S. IX T.C.C. Field Order No. 5, Reg. No. A85.
[5] H.Q. No. 38 Group Report, Varsity, para. 21. 6th Airborne Division Report, Varsity.

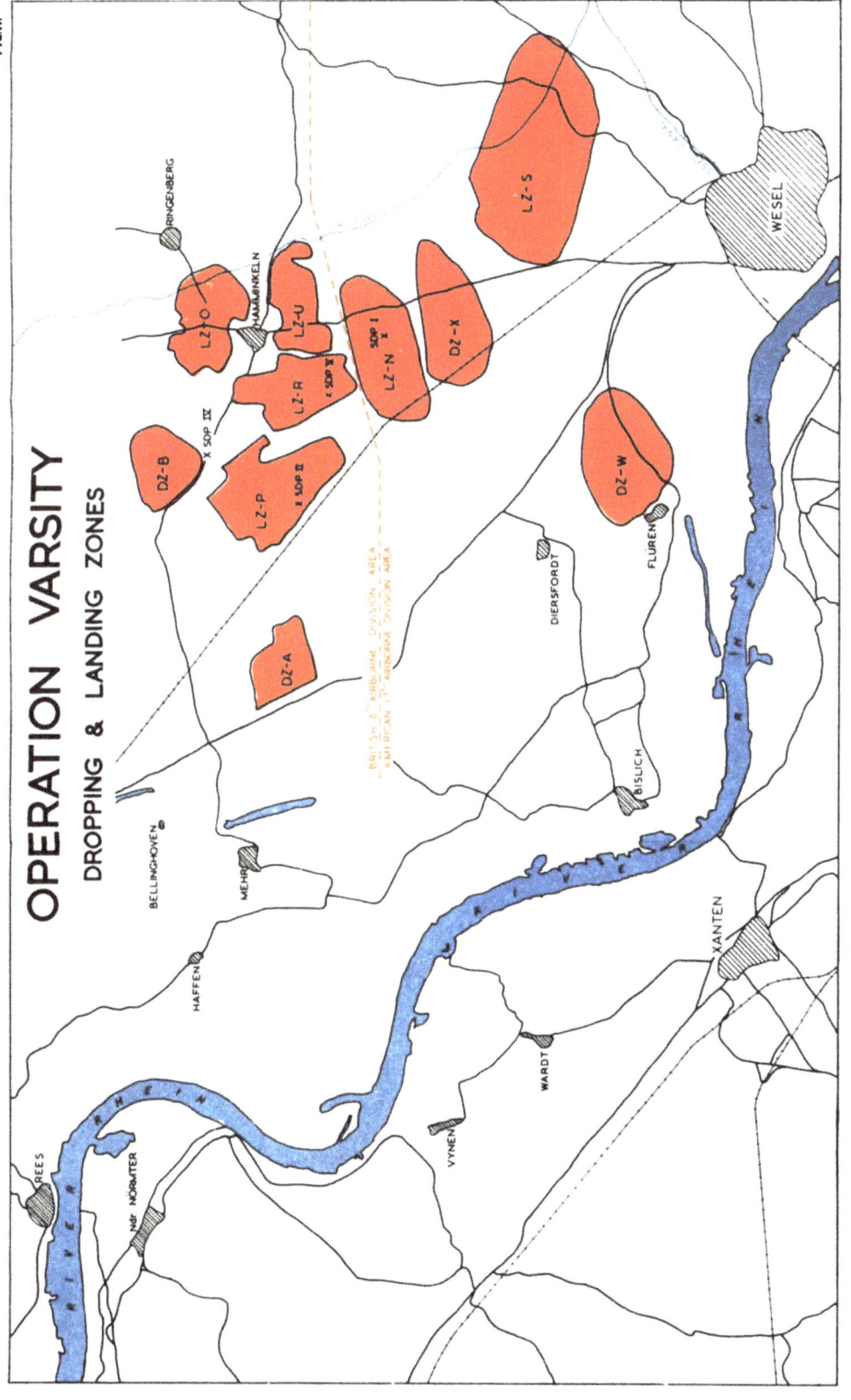

was to hold road crossings, patrol the general area and capture the high ground overlooking the river crossing. This drop was to begin at 1000 hours.

(b) Prior to the main glider landing of the 6th Air Landing Brigade Group, two *coup de main* parties were to be landed on zones "O" and "U" to capture one road bridge over the river Issel at Ringenberg and another about one mile east of Hamminkeln.

(c) The main glider landings on zones "P", "O", "U" and "R" involved the carrying of elements of 6th Air Landing Brigade Group. These troops were to be carried in 321 Horsa gliders and 34 Hamilcars and released immediately following the paratroop drop. Their task was to capture Hamminkeln and road and rail bridges over Issel river also to secure D.Z. on which the 6th Division H.Q. would land.

(d) At 1057 hours, 46 minutes after the last paratroop drop on dropping zone "B", the remainder of the remaining elements of 3rd and 5th Parachute Brigade Groups and 6th Air Landing Brigade Group were to be transported to dropping zones "A" and "B" in 56 Horsa and 14 Hamilcar gliders.

Re-supply

As in previous airborne operations, plans for re-supply were made as part of the original plan. Again, a lesson of Arnhem influenced the planners to change the method of supply dropping. Instead of having one supply dropping point as at Arnhem, six were chosen and their positions were given to all crews of the supply dropping aircraft. On the day of the operation, however, only one supply dropping point would be used for both British and American lifts, and it was intended that this point be detailed at the briefing. As an emergency measure, the aircrews were instructed to carry the pin-points of all six supply dropping points so that, if necessary, the main one could be changed even as late as after the aircraft were airborne. Arrangements were also made for a Master Supply aircraft to direct aircrews by means of R/T to their correct dropping zone. Three Master Supply Halifax aircraft were fitted for this purpose and the procedure was laid down that the leader of the supply aircraft, when within 50 miles of the target area, was to call up the Forward Visual Control Post[1], which was to be flown in with the airborne force, and verify the supply dropping point; when within ten minutes from the target the Forward Visual Control Post would broadcast by VHF to the re-supply aircraft the location of the supply dropping point.

The Re-supply Tasks

The first re-supply immediately following the landings was to be carried out by 240 Liberators of the Second Bomb Division, VIII U.S. Army Air Force, who were to drop 24 hours supply of food and ammunition equally to each airborne division.

---

[1] Forward Visual Control Posts were R.A.F. Units consisting of one Squadron Leader controller and two wireless operator mechanics with a jeep and trailer fitted with three radio sets and generators. One Forward Visual Control Post was allocated to each airborne division, and that attached to H.Q. 6th Airborne Division was set up within an hour and a half of landing. Forward Visual Control Posts could also be used for directing Second T.A.F. aircraft on to targets selected by the forward troops of the Airborne Division. (For full report on F.V.C.P., see Appendix A, 38 Group Report, Varsity).

Further re-supply, if required, was to be carried out by six Halifax aircraft of No. 38 Group, who were to load six jeeps and six-pounder guns, and all other serviceable aircraft in the Group were to load containers and stand-by at one-and-a-half-hours call from 0700 hours on D + 1. Three squadrons of No. 46 Group aircraft, after the airborne lift, were to land at Nevelles and load supply panniers. These aircraft were for emergency re-supply only and were to be at two hours call from dawn on D+1. If after D+1 emergency re-supply was required, it was to be carried out by 100 aircraft of No. 38 Group[1].

The Master Supply aircraft were to be Stirlings from No. 570 Squadron, fitted with the necessary Rebecca sets capable of making R/T contact with the special Eureka sets carried by the Independent Paratroop Brigade. The remainder of No. 570 Squadron, which was the only one fitted with the necessary GH equipment, was scheduled for medium altitude supply dropping, details of which are given in Appendix 7.

The Final Stages of Preparation

Weather: Owing to the nature of the operation the final decision as to the suitability of the weather could not be made until about 1700 hours on D – 1. The Commander, Twenty-first Army Group, was prepared, if necessary on account of bad weather, to postpone the Rhine crossing up to seven days in order to ensure support of the airborne forces. The decision as to whether the operation would take place was made by the Commanding General First Allied Airborne Army and Air Officer Commanding Second Tactical Air Force. It was then the responsibility of the Commander of the Troop Carrier Formations to decide the timing of the operation in the light of the weather forecast[2]. No difficulty arose on this score as a very favourable forecast was issued for 24 March 1945, and no alterations were necessary. Everything was in readiness for the spearhead of the airborne assault to begin dropping at the originally chosen " P " hour (10.00) 24 March 1945.

Briefing: The briefing of Station and Squadron Commanders by the Air Officer Commanding No. 38 Group took place on 19 March 1945, at Headquarters No. 38 Group, Marks Hall. Individual aircrew briefing followed on 21 March 1945. Once briefing had started all stations were sealed[3].

In view of the possibility that the visibility might be bad in the battle area, all glider pilots were individually briefed as to their own landing point. This was no small task as each pilot had to know the air plan, their own glide plan and any alternatives, as well as the exact tasks of the troops they were carrying in the event of them themselves being called upon to assist. This meticulous briefing was undoubtedly justified because, on the actual day, although the area was largely obscured with smoke and haze, accuracy of the landings was remarkable. Many glider pilots landed within 20-30 yards of their objectives despite not seeing the ground until they were within a few hundred feet of it[4].

---

[1] No. 38 Group Operation Order, Varsity. 38G/T.S. 10/94/Air.
[2] Lecture on Varsity to School of Air Support by A.O.C. No. 38 Group (A.M.W. 13), p. 5. H.Q. F.A.A.A. Report, A.P.O. 740.
[3] The weight of maps, photographs and briefing material involved was in the vicinity of five tons. No. 46 Group O.R.B., No. 38 Group O.R.B., 19 March 1945.
[4] Glider Pilot Regiment Report on Varsity, page 7.

Operation Varsity[1]

The Air Offensive, preparatory to the launching of Operation Plunder, the crossing of the Rhine, began on 21 February 1945, when the plan to isolate the Ruhr area was put into operation. From that day until D Day large scale heavy and medium bomber attacks were made on rail bridges and viaducts, road and rail traffic and marshalling and repair yards along a line from Bremen southward to Coblenz. Fighter-bombers carried out extensive armed reconnaissance and attacks on bridges and trains west of this line. In the first 20 days of March 1945 Allied Air Forces flew 3,966 sorties[2]. This air onslaught, unsurpassed since the Invasion of Normandy, culminated during the three days prior to D Day in tremendous attacks on rail and road communications, airfields, enemy troop concentrations and targets inside the Tactical Zone. The town of Wesel was smashed and, by the dawn of D Day, the whole area had been effectively " softened ". The result of this air preparation was shown on D Day by the fact that, although Allied Air Forces flew more than 8,000 sorties and over 1,300 gliders were airborne over Germany, less than 100 enemy aircraft were seen. An indication of the comprehensive nature of the air cover provided can be obtained from the following account by 2nd Tactical Air Force of the day's operations[3]:—

" The very large total of 2,100 sorties by fighters and fighter-bombers of Nos. 83 and 84 Groups, and Mitchells and Bostons of No. 2 Group, during the day concentrated on supporting and hastening Twenty-first Army Group crossing of the Rhine. In the morning 71 Mitchells and Bostons attacked four flak positions under M.R.C.P. control and claimed good results on two of them. They were followed by fighter-bombers attacking similar flak concentrations in the area of the airborne landings. Others flew immediate support missions from the Cab Rank and under F.C.P. control against gun positions, factories and centres of enemy resistance. Previous to this three headquarters behind the battle area had been attacked by Typhoons with good results, and Tempests had swept the North German airfields without finding any activity to deal with. On the turn round the Bostons attacked three medium gun positions and the Mitchells bombed a troop concentration at Raesfeld and Brunen with good results. All the time relays of four Typhoons kept attacking flak positions, guns and hutted camps, and fighters flew free lance and defensive patrols in the battle area. Reconnaissance aircraft also put in a full day on Tac R, artillery reconnaissance, contact reconnaissance and photo reconnaissance.

---

[1] Principal sources of material:—
    O.R.B. Appendices to Nos. 38 and 46 Groups.
    No. 38 Group Weekly Intelligence Summaries.
    No. 38 Group Report on Operation Varsity.
    Glider Pilot Regiment Report on Varsity.
    No. 46 Group Unofficial History.
    6th Airborne Division Report.
    Headquarters 1st Allied Airborne Army Report on Varsity, A.P.O. 740.
    IX Troop Carrier Command Report, A.P.O. 133.
    IX Troop Carrier Command Field Order No. 5.
    Deputy Supreme Commander's Airborne Operation Files.
    Miscellaneous 2nd T.A.F.
    Nos. 38 and 46 Group Files.
[2] For detailed description of Air Preparations, see " Air Operations in connection with Rhine Crossing ". (Prepared in A.H.B.)
[3] File 2 T.A.F./S. 74/10/Ops.

Total sorties divided as follows:—

Nos. 83 and 84 Groups
- Armed Reconnaissances 212
- Immediate support 254
- Pre-arranged support (Mitchells, Bostons and escorts) 550

Nos. 83 and 84 Groups
- Reconnaissance 180
- Fighter operations 904

The following message was sent by A.O.C. No. 38 Group to A.O.C. No. 83 Group on the evening of 24 March:—

'Thank you and your chaps for the magnificent cover we had today. No enemy fighters and little flak.'"

The Airborne Operation

The weather was perfect on the morning of 24 March 1945, and everything was in readiness for the greatest airborne offensive in history to begin. Gliders had been marshalled overnight and the launching of the force proceeded without hitch or delay. The efficiency and well-timed control of the ground organisation on the eight Royal Air Force airfields will be appreciated when it is realised that, out of 440 tug glider combinations scheduled to operate, all but one were on their way within one hour of the first glider being towed off at 06.00 hours. In addition, No. 46 Group were compelled to operate from two strange airfields at Gosfield and Birch, from each of which 60 gliders had to be towed. Simultaneously, from their three airfields—Boreham, Wethersfield and Chipping Ongar, 242, out of 243 scheduled aircraft of 52 Wing U.S. IX Troop Carrier Command, were airborne, carrying the main paratroop elements of the division.

The long journey to the Rhine was uneventful. The weather remained excellent with clear visibility and no enemy fighters were encountered—so effective was the huge fighter umbrella that protected the whole route, which lay over British occupied territory—hence there was no flak opposition until the area of the Dropping/Landing Zones was reached. When the stream of aircraft from Britain reached Wavre it was joined by that carrying the 17th U.S. Airborne Division from Continental bases and the huge mass of more than 1,500 aircraft and 1,300 gliders flew on in parallel streams to the target. It took $2\frac{1}{2}$ hours to pass one given point.

The Paratroop Lift

Three Groups, Nos. 61, 315 and 316 of 52 Wing, IX U.S. Troop Carrier Command were used to carry out the lift of 3rd and 5th Parachute Brigade Groups and also to make the jettison supply drop. Two hundred and forty-two C-47 and C-53 aircraft took off from East Anglia on schedule and successfully dropped 3rd Parachute Brigade Group on Dropping Zone "A" and 5th Parachute Brigade Group on Dropping Zone "B". Both these drops were extremely accurate and the supply containers fell to hand and were retrieved without difficulty. Although only eight aircraft were lost in this phase of the operation, 115 were damaged by flak from defence positions in the target area, especially heavy gun batteries North of Rees and Ringenberg.

The Glider Lift

Of the 439 tug glider combinations that took off, 34 failed to carry out their mission. Eight of these were due to technical failures, 16 to slip stream trouble and nine to broken tow ropes. The slip stream failures were not altogether unexpected in view of the extremely close concentration of the flight. Two of the gliders ditched in the North Sea but were picked up by Air/Sea Rescue. No interference from the enemy was experienced until the target zone was reached, when considerable opposition from the ground was encountered; the enemy were using 88 m.m. and S.P. guns as well as anti-aircraft.

Although the weather was still perfect over the target area, the smoke from the enemy guns in addition to that caused by the Allies anti flak barrage and also by the general fighting on the ground, created a thick haze. This proved to be a mixed blessing for, although the smoke had the advantage of confusing the enemy gunners who were unable to see where the landings were taking place, it created some difficulty for the glider pilots in finding their Landing Zones after they had been released and tended to spoil what would have otherwise been an almost flawless performance. Notwithstanding this handicap and the unenviable task of being raked with fire from the ground whilst slowly gliding earthwards, the landings showed a remarkable percentage of accuracy. Almost 300 of the gliders suffered damage from fire from the ground, although only 10 were actually shot down.

The Coup de Main Landing Zones—" O " and " U "

The 15 aircraft responsible for towing the gliders carrying the *coup de main* parties achieved 100 per cent successfully released. The landings were accurate, complete surprise was achieved and the two road bridges over the Issel were easily captured.

Dropping Zones " A " and " B "

In addition to the paratroop landings, 24 gliders were detailed to land on Dropping Zone A and 46 on Dropping Zone B. These 56 Horsas and 14 Hamilcars carried the remaining element of 3rd and 5th Parachute Brigade Groups and a portion of 6th Air Landing Brigade Group. On Dropping Zone " A " 22 gliders were successfully released, but on " B " some flak was encountered—two aircraft were shot down and five others damaged. Thirty-eight gliders were correctly released. The landings on these zones, especially on " A ", were perfectly concentrated.

Landing Zones, " O ", " U ", " R " and " P "

A high percentage of successful releases was also achieved on the other four zones where elements of 6th Air Landing Brigade Group and 6th Airborne Division Headquarters (Zone " P ") were landed. Out of 354 aircraft detailed to these zones, all but 27 reported successful releases. Photographic reconnaissance on D Day shows the excellent concentration achieved which resulted in all objectives being captured within two hours of landing. Seventy aircraft of No. 46 Group returned, after fulfilling their missions, to bases on the Continent to prepare for the resupply should the need arise.

THE RHINE CROSSING
GERMAN CHILDREN WATCHING DAKOTAS PASSING OVERHEAD ON 24 MARCH 1945

FIG. 12

THE RHINE CROSSING
HALIFAX A/C TOWING HORSA GLIDERS OVER THE FRENCH COAST ON 24 MARCH 1945

Fig. 13

17th U.S. Airborne Division

Simultaneously with the dropping of 6th Airborne Division, the 17th U.S. Airborne Division were being dropped on their four zones of the Southern Sector by U.S. IX Troop Carrier Command. This lift was carried out by 298 paratroop aircraft and 908 Waco (C.G./4A) gliders towed in single and double tow by 610 tug aircraft. Of this number, over 200 were damaged and 32 shot down by enemy action. These losses were entirely due to opposition from the ground as considerably less than a score of enemy aircraft were seen.

Resupply

Almost immediately following the landing of the last glider, the automatic resupply aircraft began dropping their cargoes on the Supply Dropping Point. This mission was carried out by 239 Liberators of U.S. VIII Air Force. By using heavy bombers for resupply, advantage was taken of another lesson learned in previous operations—that as many men and as much equipment and supplies should be landed in the shortest possible time. If the Liberators had not been used, delay would have been caused whilst aircraft employed in the actual operation returned to their bases and loaded with supplies. The resupply, in this instance, cost 15 Liberators shot down and many others damaged by flak, but as approximately 85 per cent. of the 600 tons of supplies dropped fell in the areas of the two airborne divisions, the result more than justified casualties.

Further resupply was not found to be necessary, owing to the extremely favourable progress on the ground and the arrangements which had been made for air resupply to both airborne divisions were cancelled on D Day and D + 1 by the General Officer Commanding the Second Army. It was possible to undertake the supply by normal surface transport. By the evening of D+1 the operation was complete. The Germans had been overwhelmed and both airborne divisions joined in the advance to North East Germany.

Enemy Opposition

Although enemy opposition from the air had been completely negatived by the magnificent work of the Allied Supporting Air Forces, there was appreciable opposition from flak. This was not as bad as had been anticipated but a considerable amount of damage was done to gliders and aircraft by small arms fire as well as flak weapons. One lesson was apparent. Aircraft flying at low level (600 feet) were liable to suffer as much damage from these small arms as from heavier guns. This was the case in Varsity. The U.S. IX Troop Carrier Command, flying well below 1,000 feet, lost 46 aircraft shot down by ground fire and 348 damaged, whereas the R.A.F. Groups, flying at 2,500 feet, lost only four aircraft through flak and 32 suffered damage[1].

Glider Loading and Unloading

Apart from the difficulties experienced in carrying out the loading on schedule due to the aircraft from Tarrant Rushton and No. 46 Group having to move to staging airfields, trouble was again encountered with lashings for the Hamilcar loads[2]. This was due to three factors:—
> (i) Types of loads were constantly being changed, requiring different types of lashings.

---

[1] No. 38 Group O.R.B. Weekly Intelligence Summary, Appendix 77.
[2] No. 38 Group W.I.S., Appendix 77.

(ii) Old types of loads underwent modifications which were not notified.

(iii) Modifications to loads were made without notification of the new lashing requirements.

A great deal of delay and unnecessary work could have been avoided were it possible to decide, on standard loads for Hamilcars, the responsibility for ensuring that these standards were adhered to and also that changes in load were notified in order that new lashings might be designed.

In Operation Varsity the Horsas Mark II were used principally for all vehicle loads and the Mark I for troops. The advantage of using Mark II for equipment was that it could be unloaded through the nose as well as the tail and side. This saved valuable seconds after landing.

Glider and Glider Pilot Casualties

A distinct disparity between the glider pilot casualties in the British sector of 27 per cent. and in the American section of approximately 11 per cent. was apparent[1]. This was probably due to the fact that the British gliders were released from 2,500 feet or above and the Americans from about 600 feet, thus the former were exposed to fire from the ground for a much longer period. Conversely the Americans suffered a much greater proportion of parachute and tug aircraft damage than did the British. The conclusion to be drawn from this was that a low release height exposed the tug aircraft to damage as opposed to the gliders. Whereas a high release had the opposite effect. However, one reason for the heavier casualties to the British gliders and pilots was that owing to the shortage of glider crew available, many inexperienced men had been pressed into service and thus the standard of training was not up to the high level of the previous operations. Three additional factors also contributed to the high casualties:—

(i) The difficulties of attempting a tactical landing in conditions of bad visibility and a more severe concentration of enemy fire than the Americans experienced.

(ii) Several of the tug glider combinations arrived at the target area at 3,500 feet instead of 2,500 feet; the gliders were released too high causing a tendency to overshoot.

(iii) Damage to gliders also caused on the ground by landing too fast due to lack of experience.

The success of this Transport Support Group, in spite of the fact that all its squadrons had to move from their home stations on to two unoccupied airfields whence they launched their quota of the lift and that the Group carried out all its transport commitments until D – 2 indicates that, provided facilities are always available for glider training, the launching of even a large scale airborne operation such as Varsity does not present so many fearsome problems of organisation for air transport as had been previously experienced[2].

This last of the great airborne operations to take place in the European war was, undoubtedly, the most successful. The glider landings and parachute drops were carried out with great accuracy and almost 100 per cent.

---

[1] Glider Pilot Regiment's Report on Varsity. No. 38 Group Report on Varsity, para. 130.
[2] No. 46 Group Unofficial History, page 94.

of the supplies dropped were recovered. The timing of the airborne attack achieved the surprise as planned and the rapidity with which the force reformed and established positions after landing resulted in the objectives being taken without delay and casualties being extremely low[1]. In the words of the Supreme Commander himself, General Eisenhower, " The great operation of forcing the Lower Rhine proved successful to the fullest extent of my desire ".

Conclusions

The planning and execution of the operation was an outstanding example of profiting from experience gained in earlier operations and attention being paid to enemy criticism of these operations. It can be stated, without fear of contradiction, that it was completely successful and this can be entirely attributed to the adherence, by the planners, to certain principles now fundamental to airborne operations. The main conclusions drawn from the operation were as follows :—

(a) *Air Commander*

The importance of the appointment as Air Commander for the operation of the Tactical Air Force Commander of the theatre was most emphatically illustrated. The highly effective air operation during the month preceding the operation over the whole area and the huge cover provided for the actual flying completely negatived any attempt at air defence by the enemy.

(b) *One Lift*

The operation was carried out in one highly concentrated lift, the whole force being landed in one hour. The enemy were thus unable to recover from the initial surprise and prepare for any subsequent landings as at Arnhem, but were overwhelmed almost before they were aware of what was happening.

(c) *Resupply*

Resupply followed immediately after landing and was carried out within one hour. Results indicated that one day's resupply should always be flown in as soon as possible after the landing.

(d) *Tactical Landings*

Possibly the outstanding feature of Varsity was the landing of the airborne forces in a tactical manner. The tasks of the division were sub-divided and allotted to units within the Brigades and these units were landed as close as possible to their objectives. In previous operations the troops had been landed all together at one or more zones and divided after landing. The speed with which 6th Airborne Division captured its objectives, within two hours of landing, can be attributed largely to the tactical landings causing completed confusion to the enemy who had anticipated a concentrated landing in the vicinity of an aerodrome near Hamminkeln.

---

[1] Supreme Commander's Report to Combined Chiefs of Staff on Operations in Europe of A.E.F.

(e) *Artillery Support*

For the first time an airborne landing area was within allied artillery range. This was of valuable assistance until the actual landings began, when it had to be withheld. If resupply had been needed, an awkward position might have arisen as to which was most important, resupply or artillery support. Fortunately, resupply was not needed because of the success of the operation.

(f) *Communications*

No difficulties were presented by communications and the whole system operated most efficiently despite the distances between the Commands and the number of Headquarters and Control Posts involved. Three factors were mainly responsible :—

(i) The operation was carried out in a very short time, thus there was no widely fluctuating ground position as at Arnhem.

(ii) The weather was very good.

(iii) A large practice communication exercise Token had been held on 16 March 1945.

Minor Airborne Operations

Amherst and Keystone[1]

As the Canadian First Army advanced into Holland, Twenty-first Army Group proposed to use S.A.S. troops to create confusion in enemy rear areas, stimulate local resistance and generally assist the Canadian First Army. S.H.A.E.F. did not consider that the operation could be launched before 5 April 1945 and preliminary planning conferences were held on 2 April and 3 April 1945. The first of these conferences was between No. 38 Group and Headquarters, S.A.S. Troops and the second was held at the Canadian First Army Headquarters between representatives of all formations concerned, including No. 84 Group R.A.F., who were the controlling Tactical Air Force in the area. The plan was finalised at a further meeting between No. 38 Group and S.A.S. Headquarters, Essex, and, on 5 April 1945, operational instructions were issued by Headquarters, First Canadian Army[2].

The Plan

Amherst

Forty-seven Stirlings of No. 38 Group, R.A.F., were to drop 2nd and 3rd Regiments de Chasseurs Parachutistes on 20 selected Dropping Points with the task of securing airfields at Steenwijk, Helve and Leeuwarden, 15 road and 3 railway bridges. Simultaneously 18 Halifaxes of No. 38 Group were to drop the same number of jeeps on six of these Dropping Zones.

Keystone

Seven Stirlings of No. 38 Group were to convey troops of the 2nd S.A.S. Regiment, with two Jedburgh wireless teams and three jeeps carried in three Halifaxes to four previously selected Dropping Zones. Their task was to take the airfield at Teure and seven road bridges. The area of the

---
[1] 2nd T.A.F./File 30317/86 Ops., Encl. 2A. No. 38 Group Report.
[2] Ibid, Encl. 27A.

Dropping Zones was that east of the Zuider Zee, south of Groningen and north of Zwolle, and was chosen by planning staffs of S.A.S. Headquarters and No. 38 Group[1].

Control

A combined Headquarters, with representatives of Nos. 38 and 84 Groups and the Commander S.A.S. Troops was established at Headquarters, First Canadian Army on 5 April 1945. Decisions regarding the air force rested with the Air Officer Commanding No. 38 Group, Air Vice-Marshal J. R. Scarlett-Streatfeild at his Headquarters, Marks Hall, Essex[2].

Cover Plan

In order to exaggerate the size of the operation in the mind of the enemy, it was decided to drop simulators (dummies) from the parachute carrying aircraft and for Bomber Command and No. 100 Group to operate in the areas as they would in the event of a normal airborne landing. In this connection, permission for direct contact between No. 38 Group and Bomber Command was granted. A special bomb-line was agreed upon, beyond which the First Canadian Army would not advance between the hours of 2100 and 0600 on the night of the operation[3].

Route

The flight plan, drawn up by No. 38 Group, routed the aircraft in from a southerly direction via Dungeness and Cape Grisnez, over friendly territory returning direct from Holland to their bases in East Anglia. Allied anti-aircraft defences en route were restricted for the night and prohibited within a corridor 10 miles wide of a line Brussels/Goch/Enselde/Emmen for 45 minutes before and after certain fixed times.

Re-supply

Although S.A.S. Headquarters did not wish to plan for re-supply, the R.A.F. representative stated that, as aircraft were available, provision for re-supply should be made. Daylight re-supply by fighter aircraft of No. 84 Group was agreed upon[4].

The final decision as to the date of the operation was made on 7 April 1945, for it to take place on the same night—the operation having been postponed 24 hours due to the rapid advance of the Canadian First Army.

Execution—Amherst

The weather was poor on the night of the operation with low stratus cloud and fog over the Dropping Area. No. 38 Group accordingly warned the Canadian First Army, No. 84 Group and 2nd T.A.F. that the drop would have to be made " blind " from 1,500 feet above the cloud and fog, using Gee fixes and that dropping errors up to three miles might be expected. In view of ground reception lights for dropping the jeeps from the Halifaxes not being visible from the air, it was decided to cancel this part of the operation and drop only the troops.

---

[1] For details and map references of the Dropping Zones, see No. 38 Group Report on Operation Amherst/Keystone. Reference 38G File S. 10/114/Air.
[2] Ibid, Encl. 4 and 13.
[3] Ibid, Encl. 24A.
[4] Ibid, Encl. 3A.

Forty-six of the 47 Stirlings dropped their loads of troops successfully on the night of 7-8 April 1945, and the remaining aircraft carried out its mission on the following night. No interference was encountered and all aircraft returned safely to their bases. Subsequent analysis of the drops by Brigadier J. M. Calvert, Commanding S.A.S. Troops, showed an average error in drop of slightly more than three miles, which was not unsatisfactory in view of the fact that there was insufficient time for special deployment of Gee stations and that there was poor Gee cover in the area. The 18 jeeps were flown to an airfield in the Canadian section on the following day and driven overland to the operational area[1].

Keystone

Operation Keystone was postponed until the night of 11-12 April 1945. Five Stirlings and three Halifaxes were detailed. The aircraft took off as arranged but, owing to bad weather and consequent inability to make contact with the Amherst ground parties, the operation had to be abandoned. Similar conditions on the following night again prevented the operation being carried out. On the ground the situation progressed favourably; casualties were not high and reports from the S.A.S. Headquarters indicated that the operation was successful. There were no casualties in No. 38 Group, R.A.F.

Conclusions

Operation Amherst proved that it was possible to plan and execute an airborne operation of this nature within three days, provided the Army and Air Force were co-ordinated in one Headquarters.

Although, at the time of planning, resupply might not appear to be necessary, it was always advisable to plan for it. In this case it was found to be necessary.

Selection of Dropping Zones in an operation of this nature may not always be possible in time to brief crews without a last minute rush. It was recommended that a small committee of Army and Air Force personnel should continually be reconnoitring for suitable Dropping Zones ahead of the advancing armies, so that an immediate decision might be taken, thus expediting the launching of the operation and simplifying the problem of briefing.

The jeep dropping part of the operation had to be cancelled owing to bad weather preventing the ground reception being visible to the aircraft. This could have been avoided had parachute teams been dropped simultaneously with the jeeps.

In order to facilitate linking up on the ground without delay, paratroops, when dropping at night, should always be dropped in as short a stick as possible. The reason for this was that it was impossible, at night—and possibly under unfavourable weather conditions, for the aircraft to guarantee to drop two separate sticks of drops in the same place. Even in the event of the drops being made " blind " on a Gee fix, it would be almost impossible to make the two drops in the same place. Lastly the safety of the aircraft was jeopardised by having to make more than one run over the Dropping Zone.

---

[1] Ibid, Encl. 39A. No. 38 Group Report on Amherst, Ref. 38G/S. 10/114/Air. No. 38 Group O.R.B., Appendix 86.

"Blind" Paratroop Dropping

Operation Amherst proved that, when it was necessary to drop paratroops "blind", with no assistance from the ground, use of Gee fixes was probably the most effective navigational aid. In view of the fact that the target area was badly placed for Gee coverage and as the angle of cut of the lattice lines were 16 degrees, the error of drop of three miles was not unexpected. However, even although it were possible to create the best possible conditions for the use of Gee—resulting in an accuracy of drop of approximately 100 yards, this would be scarcely practical, as it would involve setting up a special Gee chain which would take anything from one to six months, according to the area.

Operation Schnapps

On 8 May 1945, personnel and equipment of 1st Airborne Division were landed in Copenhagen by 33 Stirlings, nine Halifaxes and 10 C-46s of U.S. IX T.C.C. The operation was carried out without undue incident and subsequently re-supply was maintained at intervals during the remainder of the month[1].

Operation Doomsday

Although hostilities had ceased in Europe on 8 May 1945, and Operation Doomsday did not take place until the following day, thus scarcely coming under the category of operations against the enemy, it is worthy of mention in view of the fact that more than 7,000 troops and over 2,000 tons of equipment and supplies were transported by aircraft of No. 38 Group across several hundred miles of sea.

The object of the operation was to land Allied troops in Norway as soon as possible after the German surrender. The purpose of this was to provide support for the Norwegian Resistance Movement and to provide for the arrival of the main forces. It was also possible that minor operations might have to be performed against stray elements of Germans or Norwegians. From the political view point it was necessary to establish Allied control in Norway without delay in view of the fact that Sweden and Soviet Russia might also have aims in this direction[2].

Planning

The first suggestion of the air landing of a force in Norway, after the German surrender, was made at a conference held at Headquarters, Scottish Command on 21 November 1944. Arising out of this meeting, a Special Planning Committee was formed and a draft plan was prepared[3]. On 23 April 1945, a conference at 1st British Airborne Corps decided that, as S.A.S. troops were fully engaged at that time, it would be better to employ one of the British airborne divisions in the landing. Final orders to carry out Operation Doomsday were received by First Allied Airborne Army from the Supreme Command on 5 May 1945 and, on the following day, No. 38 Group were ordered to furnish the lift, assisted by C-46 aircraft from IX Troop Carrier Command.

---

[1] No. 38 Group O.R.B., Appendix 109.
[2] No. 38 Group O.R.B., Appendix 152. No. 38 Group Report, Operation Doomsday.
[3] Ibid. paras. 15–20.

The Air Officer Commanding No. 88 Group, R.A.F., was appointed Air Commander to co-ordinate and control all Air Forces for the operation. The Air Officer Commanding No. 38 Group was appointed Commander of the troop carrier forces.

The main objectives of the operation were as follows[1]:—

(i) Oslo, capital of Norway and centre of administration—both German and Norwegian.

(ii) Stavanger, because of its good airfields and having one of the nearest good harbours to the United Kingdom. It was also suitable for the operation of fighter aircraft.

(iii) Kristiansands, because of its importance as a mine-sweeping base in the Skagerrak. After detailed study had been made of the airfields chosen for these objectives, it was decided to use only Gardermoen, near Oslo, and Sola, near Stavanger, because they were the only suitable airfields on which four-engine transport aircraft might safely be landed. Any troops intended for the Kristiansands area were to be landed at Sola and make the rest of the journey by road.

It was not considered that there would be any enemy fighter opposition to the operation, but, as a precaution, 12 Mustangs were to cover Gardermoen airfield and six Mustangs Sola airfield, during the initial landings.

Execution

The operation was carried out in four phases between the 9 and 13 May. Delay was caused by unfavourable weather conditions and the operation took 36 hours longer than had been intended. As no enemy opposition was expected, the shortest possible route was taken by the aircraft and the landings were successfully accomplished. Three aircraft were lost, one containing the Air Officer Commanding No. 38 Group, Air Vice-Marshal J. R. Scarlett-Streatfeild, on 10 May 1945. Despite an intensive search and special air-sea rescue being carried out throughout the whole period of the operation, no trace of the missing aircraft was ever found[2]. The fly-in of maintenance and S.A.S. troops, in addition to supplies, was carried out by Stirlings, Halifaxes and C-46 aircraft when the weather permitted on the subsequent days during the month. The operation was completed and the last maintenance was flown into Norway on 27 May 1945.

Conclusions

Although No. 38 Group had had little experience in transport operations, it proved itself capable of carrying them out[3]. Using Halifax Mk III and VII and Stirling Mk. IV, in addition to C-46 aircraft of U.S. IX Troop Carrier Command, it was found possible to make the return flight from the bases of the United Kingdom direct to the Norwegian aerodromes without having to refuel.

The Halifax and Stirling bomber aircraft were not entirely suitable for a transport role. They were not designed to land with a heavy petrol and freight load, therefore the all-up landing weight had to be carefully con-

---

[1] No. 38 Group Report, Operation Doomsday, paras. 25–35.
[2] Ibid., Paras. 43–67. [3] Ibid., Paras. 68–96.

sidered when planning, so that, after landing at their destinations in Norway, the aircraft had enough petrol for the return journey. Some of the freight was carried in parachute containers in the bomb bays and jettisoned before landing, thus overcoming the danger of landing with an excessive all-up weight.

Summary

Aircraft	Destination	Number of Aircraft Detailed	Number of Aircraft Airborne	Number Successful	Number Un-successful
No. 38 Group	Gardermoen	815	714	613	100 abortive 1 lost
U.S. 52nd Wing	Gardermoen	77	50	50	0
No. 38 Group	Sola	84	83	83	0
U.S. 52nd Wing	Sola	322	322	322	0
Total	—	1,298	1,169	1,068	100 abortive 1 lost

It will be seen from these figures that the C-46 aircraft, employed by U.S. 52 Wing, was more successful than the Halifaxes and Stirlings in an operation of this nature.

Loads Carried

Between the 9 and 27 May 1945 the loads carried to Norway included 7,139 troops, 654 jeeps, 503 trailers, 234 motor cycles and 710 tons of supplies.

CHAPTER 11

DOMINION AND ALLIED AIRBORNE FORCES

Australia[1]

In September 1942 the Australian Army H.Q. acting in conjunction with the Royal Australian Air Force decided to raise an independent Parachute Company for use in jungle operations. However the difficulties of carrying out parachute training under jungle conditions led to the project being transferred to Australia itself. In October the United Kingdom was asked to provide instructors for the new Parachute Training Centre which was formed on 3 November 1942, at Leverton, Victoria.

In April 1943 Wing Commander W. H. Wetton, R.A.F., arrived from England to take command of the training centre. The weather conditions and training facilities were not adequate and on his recommendation the Centre was moved to Richmond, New South Wales on the 13 April; from then onwards the training Centre was organised on similar lines to No. 1 P.T.S. at Ringway. Also in April 1943 it was decided to raise a parachute battalion less one Company and a Parachute Troop Royal Australian Engineers and on the 15 August the first Australian Parachute Battalion was formed while No. 1 Parachute Troop was raised at the same time.

By December 1943 770 officers and men had been trained for the 1st Australian Parachute Battalion whilst output of the training scale was 50 Parachute Troops a month as reinforcements for the battalion plus additional personnel for other arms and special agents. By May 1944 the battalion and the parachute troop had been completely formed with their first reinforcements and carried out operational training wherever possible until September 1945.

The 1st Australian Parachute Battalion consisted of a Battalion Headquarters, a Headquarters Company and three Rifle Companies. Each Rifle Company consisted of Company H.Q. and Anti-Tank section, a Mortar Detachment and three Rifle Platoons, the total strength being 637. The Parachute Troop consisted of Troop H.Q. and three Sections, a total strength of 40. Although none of these units ever went into action they provided a large number of trained parachutists for operations with the " E " Force (special agents) which was used in the South West Pacific area. Throughout their history these Australian Parachute Units were an essential part of the airborne forces and wore a maroon beret and the airborne forces sign.

Canada[2]

It was early in the war—November 1940—that Canada first considered the possibility of raising airborne troops and the suggsetion was forwarded to the Canadian Military Headquarters in London. However at this time the general use of airborne forces was not envisaged by the War Office and it

---
[1] Australian Army H.Q., Canberra.
[2] Canadian Army H.Q., Ottawa.

was not until August 1941 that the question of raising Parachute troops in Canada was again considered.

Several months elapsed before the final decision to form a Canadian parachute battalion was taken. In November 1942 the War Establishment was published. It was to consist of a battalion H.Q. Company and three Rifle Companies with a total strength of 616. The original members of Canadian airborne forces were volunteers who between August and September 1942 had attended a parachute course at No. 1 P.T.S. Ringway, and these officers formed the nucleus of the 1st Canadian Parachute Battalion in Canada. By 22 March 1943, the battalion had completed training at the U.S. Parachute Training School, Fort Benning, and 97 per cent. had qualified for their parachute wings.

In April 1943, after discussions between the Canadian Military Headquarters and the War Office, it was decided that the 1st Canadian Parachute Battalion was to be placed under command of the 6th Airborne Division at the same time remaining part of the Canadian Army in Britain. The battalion arrived in the United Kingdom on 28 July 1943, and on 11 August became part of No. 3 Parachute Brigade under the command of Brigadier S. J. L. Hill. Their training continued, by detachments, at No. 1 P.T.S. to familiarise them with British methods, as their original training had been by American methods.

In October 1943 it was decided to provide a Parachute Training Company for reinforcements for Canadian Units in Britain. The 1st Canadian Parachute Battalion took part in all the operations of 6th Airborne Division and served with considerable distinction. After taking part in the Rhine crossing they returned to Canada and were the first unit to return there from overseas. Field Marshal Lord Alan Brooke, Chief of the Imperial General Staff, in a message to the Canadian General Chief of Staff, paid high tribute to the distiguished part which the battalion had played in its operations with 6th Airborne Division right up to the end of hostilities.

New Zealand

Owing to the very limited manpower resources of New Zealand and also to the fact that the country was in danger of Japanese invasion, it was not found possible for them to raise any airborne forces, but individual New Zealanders did serve with British and Indian airborne units in various parts of the world.

South Africa

South Africa, like New Zealand, was also short of manpower and did not therefore raise any airborne forces. However in 1944 the 2nd British Independent Parachute Brigade Group was short of officers whilst serving in Italy. Volunteers from South African forces were called for and between 30 and 40 officers joined the Brigade Group. They served in operations in Italy, France and Greece and some accompanied the Brigade on its return to England and then joined the 6th Airborne Division in Palestine. Individual S. African officers and other ranks served with airborne forces in other theatres.

United States of America[1]

In view of the fact that, in North Africa and in many of the subsequent phases of the war, the American Airborne Forces were very closely allied to the British it is of interest to regard briefly their history. The 82nd All American Division, after service in the First World War, returned to the U.S.A. where it remained until 5 August 1942. On that date it was converted into 82nd Airborne Division and motivated as such. Ten days later on 15 August one element was discarded to form 101st Airborne Division, which remained in the U.S.A. until August 1943. It then moved to England and went into camp near Newbury close to where 6th Airborne Division were training. The 82nd Division went to North Africa in August 1943 and joined 1st Airborne Division in training for the operation against Sicily.

The camps for the reception and training of 101st Airborne Division were prepared by parties from the 6th Airborne Division. From then until the Normandy invasion in June 1944 a very close liaison between the two divisions was maintained and an almost identical similarity of training was achieved. Everything possible was done to promote friendship and understanding between the two Divisions by means of inter-unit exchanges and visits to each others' messes.

By December 1943 there were four more airborne divisions training in the U.S.A. and it was generally anticipated that they would be operational one year after their formation. These divisions were:—

11th Airborne Division formed 25 February 1943.

17th Airborne Division formed 15 April 1943.

13th Airborne Division formed August 1943.

15th Airborne Division formed September 1943.

During 1943 48,276 Airborne Troops started training and 29,719 graduated.

Other Allied Airborne Forces[2]

By the end of 1943 there were several Allied Airborne contingents in Britain. The strongest of these was the Polish Parachute Brigade, consisting of an Headquarters, a parachute squadron of Engineers, a parachute field ambulance, a signals section and four parachute battalions, three of which were formed initially, the fourth being formed with recruits from the Middle East. There were two French parachute battalions of the Special Air Service Brigade, a Norwegian, a Belgian, a Dutch and a Czechoslovakian parachute company. Until Headquarters Major General Airborne Forces was established it was impossible for these contingents to obtain the assistance they required. However they did accomplish much useful work—for example the Belgian company volunteered for and assisted with experiments for the Airborne Forces Experimental Establishment.

The Polish Brigade were rather inaccessible, being stationed in Scotland with no transport aircraft available, their own bombers being employed in Bomber Command. A solution was found to most of these problems when, late in 1943, Headquarters Airborne Forces was formed and training facilities were provided.

---

[1] Information from Major-General J. N. Gavin, A.C. of S. G.I., 82nd American Airborne Division.
[2] W.O. File/20/Gen./597

CHAPTER 12

AIRBORNE FORCES IN INDIA AND FAR EAST

The story of Airborne Forces in India and Burma covers a long period 1940-45 and although no airborne operations took place in Eastern theatres of war in any way comparable in magnitude or significance to those in Europe, it is of interest to examine the events leading to the formation of airborne units in India and to review the difficulties with which the pioneers, both Royal Air Force and Army, had to contend.

It is necessary at the outset to define Airborne Forces as such because during the campaigns in Burma thousands of men were transported by air as distinct from being airborne troops. The account of the great part played by R.A.F. transport support squadrons in the conquest of Burma is told elsewhere[1]; this narrative is concerned only with the training, development and operation of airborne forces and the means to lift them.

As early in the war as Autumn 1940 the Commander-in-Chief, India, General Sir Archibald Wavell, authorised the formation of a nucleus of parachute troops with the intention of expanding it later to brigade status. On 22 January 1941 a telegram from the Defence Department of India notified the Secretary of State, that this plan was being put into operation subject to approval from the War Office and the Air Ministry. Subsequently Lieutenant Colonel W. G. H. Gough, who was to command the establishment, was attached to Ringway to study methods at No. 1 Parachute Training School. On his return he asked for a limited number of personnel to be sent to India to form a training nucleus[2].

High level approval was not immediately forthcoming. The question of whether aircraft, equipment and trained personnel could be spared from the slender resources then available in the United Kingdom required careful consideration. The delay proved irksome to those in India who were anxious to proceed with the development. Accordingly on 16 April 1941 an Airborne Troops Committee was formed at Air Headquarters, India, to "draw up proposals on all points affecting the formation, organisation, equipment, location and training of an airborne brigade and an airlanding school" also to "work out details and further procedure of the scheme when it was approved." On 15 May 1941 General Wavell decided to proceed with the formation of the brigade[3].

It was not until 13 June 1941 that the Chiefs of Staff approved in principle the formation of an airborne brigade in India and also the despatch to that country of two R.A.F. officers, two Sergeant instructors and two parachute packers[4]. On 8 July 1941, these personnel were posted to India. Later in the same month approval was given by Air Ministry for the establishment of a Wing Commander, as Officer Commanding, a chief ground instructor, a chief landing instructor, two more sergeants as landing instructors and one airman[5].

---
[1] A.H.B. Monograph Air Transport Support Operations in the Campaigns in Burma, 1942–1945.
[2] A.M. File CS. 7725, Part I, Encl. 7B.
[3] Ibid., Encl. 61C. Letter from A.H.Q. India to V.C.A.S.
[4] A.M. File CS. 7725, Part I, Encl. 66B.
[5] A.M. File CS. 7725, Part I, Encl. 98A.

As regards aircraft and gliders an Air Staff memorandum in August 1941 stated that airborne training in India would have to depend on its own aircraft as none could be spared from the United Kingdom for any parachute or glider operations. The 400 gliders estimated as being necessary to transport an airborne brigade were to be produced by the Tata Company of India, but production could not start until 1943[1]. An order was also placed with the Hindustan Aircraft Co. for 10 ten-seater gliders but owing to shortage of timber the prototype was not ready until May 1942 when the first tests were made[2].

In view of this unsatisfactory outlook as regards gliders, the Ministry of Aircraft Production in a wire to Washington on 3 July 1942 asked if the United States would supply 200 sets of Waco glider parts for assembly in India and also technicians to assist in this and to inspect the layout of the Tata Company as to the possibility of their manufacturing Wacos at a later date. Washington replied that no gliders could be made available until January 1943 but that it might be possible to allocate 200 to India in the period January to April 1943.

A programme was then arranged allowing for 20 Waco gliders and 10 pilots to arrive in India in January 1943; for 200 gliders to be despatched from the U.S.A. in June and a further 470 gliders to be held as reserve in America. As this plan appeared to ensure an adequate supply, the contract with the Tata Company was cancelled. However, the general shipping situation became so serious that the shipment of gliders had to be postponed[3].

In October 1941 No. 50 Indian Parachute Brigade was formed at Delhi[4] and authority was given by Air Headquarters, India, to set up an Airlanding school at the Willingdon Airport, New Delhi. The school was to be an R.A.F. responsibility, as at No. 1 Parachute Training School, Ringway. Wing Commander F. M. Benito was appointed to command but owing to his Hudson crashing en route to India, he did not arrive in Delhi until March 1942. The staff of the school consisted of eight R.A.F. officers, five Army officers, four fabric workers from Ringway, who acted as jumping instructors, and some N.C.O. airmen instructors. The parachute packers were British and Indian Army personnel who were trained by the fabric workers[5].

The purpose of the Air Landing School was:—

(a) The technical training of parachute troops.

(b) To carry out experiments and tests of equipment used for:—
    (i) Parachute troops.
    (ii) Their maintenance by air.

(c) The training of glider troops.

Air Headquarters, India, selected the Valencia aircraft, modified with a jumping hole in the floor of the fuselage, for the school but when it opened only one aircraft of an establishment of six was available[6]. It had been

---

[1] A.M. File CS. 7725, Part I, Encl. 119c.
[2] A.M. File CS. 7725, Part I, Encl. 182A.
[3] A.M. File CS. 7725, Part I, Encls. 66B and 67A.
[4] Under command of Brigadier W. H. G. Gough.
[5] A.M. File CS. 7725, Part II, Encl. 52c. O.R.B. Air Landing School, 22 September 1941.
[6] A.M. File CS. 7725, Part II, Encl. 151A.

intended to use Hudson III aircraft but it was not until October 1941 that the first one was modified at Ringway[1].

Owing to accidents and bad weather their arrival was delayed until May. In the interim the school struggled on with what Valencias were available ; at one time there were none as the only five modified for parachute work had been used in the evacuation of Burma. Progress was also very slow at this time owing to lack of statichutes and gliders as well as aircraft. So short were supplies in the United Kingdom where 1st Airborne Division was in the embryo stage, that the diversion of any to India was out of the question.

On 3 February 1942, the Prime Minister, in reply to a letter from Mr. Amery urging the development of an airborne force in India stated "there ought to be an extra airborne division—or better its equivalent—raised in India as soon as possible. Pray consider this and let me have some proposals". To which the Chief of Air Staff replied that to form a second division in India was not possible without jeopardising the overall plans already in operation. The idea was then abandoned[2].

The vital shortage of aircraft and gliders, as well as parachutes (only 200 had arrived from the United Kingdom against an order of 2,200) prompted a telegram on 31 March 1942 from the Defence Department to the War Office complaining that unless supplies improved it would be "useless to continue the effort to provide airborne forces in present atmosphere of lethargy and indifference. Forces can be provided if we receive help and guidance asked for but both must be available as soon as possible". General Wavell also signalled the Chief of Imperial General Staff that "I am now planning possible operations in Burma in the Autumn and essential to know whether any prospect of being able to use parachutists or airborne troops. We have now been waiting 15 months for definite policy[3]".

The outcome of these signals was summarised by the Secretary of State for India on 5 April 1942 under the following main headings[4]:—

(a) *Parachutes*

4,500 man-dropping statichutes had been ordered for India. Of these 250 left the United Kingdom in mid-February 1942—700 were awaiting shipment—and the remainder were being produced at the rate of 100 per week. In addition 2,250 containers with statichutes were ordered of which 80 were awaiting shipment, the remainder to be delivered at 50 per week.

---

[1] A wooden slide leading from the centre of the fuselage through the under gun hatch was fitted and trials were carried out. This slide method was not very satisfactory, except for agent and supply dropping, as it only accommodated five men, the remainder having to scramble on to the slide after the first five had gone. An aperture modification was tried, but only the first two men could sit fore and aft of it owing to the centre of gravity of the aircraft; the remainder had to drop from the forward side of the aperture, making a very slow stick. Thus this method was only suitable for training singles and pairs drops. These modifications were not completed until February 1942.
[2] A.M. File CS. 7725, Part I, Encl. 163B.
[3] Ibid., Part II, Encls. 3A and 6A.
[4] Ibid., Encl. 11A.

(b) *Aircraft*

The promised six Hudson IIIs had been delayed by altered priorities due to the entry of Japan into the war, bad weather and accidents. The supply of parachute operational aircraft was to be confined to the medium and heavy bomber squadrons in India—any balance that might be required would have to come from the Middle East.

(c) *Gliders*

The shipment of Horsas would not be possible as they could only be transported as deck cargo. The output of glider pilots in the United Kingdom was insufficient to meet demands there, let alone to send any to India.

The letter emphasised that the training of an airborne division must for these reasons be a long term project.

On 3 June 1942 General Wavell admitted the difficulties of forming and training a glider borne force in India and recommended that airborne forces there consist mainly of parachute troops[1]. The first live jumps to be carried out in India were made in October 1941 using a small number of parachutes of the " X " type in use at the Airborne Establishment at Ringway which were available to start training. The first course started on 10 November 1941—another course followed a fortnight later—during the month 208 live jumps were made and parachute training in India was launched. The first Indians to train in the school were included in the fourth course after which the intake was increased to 30 per course. By June 1942 the aircraft position had improved—four Hudsons had arrived and four Valencias were serviceable for training. In addition a Lodestar, modified for door jumping and supply ejection was being used for special duties and a small parachute operation was carried out from Dinjan. A party of 10 men, including seven Gurkhas from 153rd Gurkha Parachute Battalion, led by one British officer were dropped in the area of Myitkina on 3 July 1942 to reconnoitre suspected Japanese troop movements. The party remained in enemy territory for 42 days and gained much useful information[2].

Also in July five Valencias and one Hudson were used to drop one company of 152nd Indian Parachute Battalion to co-operate with other forces in the area of the Sind desert against the Hurs—a fanatical Moslem tribe—which had been terrorising the local inhabitants. The drop was successful but no contact was made with the Hurs. For some time prior to August 1942 a detachment had been maintained at Fort Hertz. Completely isolated, they were dependent on supplies dropped by aircraft of No. 31 Squadron. On 13 August a small detachment of 12 paratroops, including three British officers, was successfully dropped at Fort Hertz to prepare the landing ground there so that an Infantry Company could be flown in later to act as garrison troops[3].

Training continued throughout the summer months without undue incident ; the length of the Course was shortened but the number of live drops had

---

[1] A.M. File C.S. 7725, Part I, Encl. 28A.
[2] O.R.B. Air Landing School.
[3] W.O. Narrative. Hist. of Airborne Forces, Chapter XXIV. O.R.B. 31 Sqdn.

increased to 700 per month. The Indian Parachute Factory, Cawnpore, had started production and 305 were received in August 1942. By then 30 courses had passed through basic training.

In October 1942 owing to the Willingdon airfield becoming overcrowded the school was moved to Chaklala in the Punjab. This airfield was not used to any extent by extraneous aircraft, there was good accommodation for the troops, a spare hangar for ground training and good dropping zones nearby. Immediately following this move No. 215 Wellington Squadron moved in to co-operate in the operational training of No. 50 Indian Parachute Brigade. Paratroops were flown for air experience and did single jumps to give the Squadron experience in parachute dropping whilst it was doing low level and map reading training.

During this early period at Chaklala several fatal accidents occurred due mainly to faulty parachutes with the result that Wing Commander Newnham, Commanding Officer, No. 1 P.T.S. Ringway, arrived on 18 February 1943, to investigate the problem. The trouble was found to be in parachute maintenance where there was a lack of technical experience. To remedy this, two Flight Sergeants were sent out from Ringway with up-to-date training instructions to take over maintenance. The Wing Commander also revised the training syllabus and took over the duties of Chief Instructor for a short period as it was evident that a considerable improvement in ground training methods was necessary. He recommended that more experienced instructors were essential[1]. By this time—13 March 1943—the school had trained 2,206 British and Indian officers and other ranks involving a total of 15,861 live jumps. Good progress had been made with basic training of No. 50 Indian Parachute Brigade despite the shortage of instructors and equipment.

As a result of a Conference held at Headquarters, No. 223 Group on 19 April 1943, between the Commanding Officers of the school, No. 223 Group and No. 99 Squadron, it was decided that the latter be trained for parachute dropping. This was carried out during the next month and followed by No. 62 Squadron (Hudsons). In each case all the Wireless Operator/Air Gunners underwent basic training as jumpmasters in readiness for possible operations[2].

In June 1943, the Air Landing School was allotted its first Dakota and modifications to make the aircraft suitable for parachuting were begun. During July the possibility of a conversion course to door dropping from Dakotas was considered. Dummy drop trials were made and on 28 July the Dakota was passed for live drops. The first descents were made by instructors of the Air Landing School on 7 August, the syllabus was finalised and four days later No. 1 Conversion Course began jumping from Dakotas.

On 13 September 1943, Group Captain Donaldson assumed command of Chaklala in place of Wing Commander Benito, who had been in command of both the Station and the Air Landing School. Also during this month No. 177 (Airborne Forces) Wing was formed, consisting of a Headquarters and Nos. 31, 62, 117 and 194 Transport Squadrons. It also administered No. 5 Mobile Parachute Servicing Unit. The Headquarters of the new

---
[1] Report by W/Cdr. Newnham on visit to India.
[2] O.R.B. Air Landing School, Appendix 'A'.

Wing was at Rawalpindi until 16 February 1944, when it moved to Agartala. On 14 October, Group Captain Donaldson took command of the Wing and Group Captain Ommaney, R.A.F., Chaklala.

Visit of Major General Airborne Forces to India

The most important event at this time was the visit to India of Major General Browning, who arrived in New Delhi on 17 September 1943. The purpose of his visit, as outlined by the Vice-Chief Imperial General Staff, was[1]:—

(a) To report on the progress of No. 50 Indian Parachute Brigade.

(b) To advise on the plans for the operational use of the Brigade during 1943-44.

(c) To arrive at an agreement with the Supreme Commander, S.E. Asia Command, as to the requirement for airborne forces against Japan when Germany had been defeated.

(d) To advise the Commander-in-Chief, India, and the Supreme Allied Commander as to the necessary requirements of formations, depots and operational bases.

During the next few weeks as a result of several meetings of the various Commanders[2] the following main conclusions were agreed:—

(a) One Mobile Parachute Servicing Unit was to be despatched from North Africa to Chaklala to augment parachute maintenance facilities.

(b) A few experienced R.A.F. officers from No. 38 Group were to be posted to Chaklala to assist in forming an airborne wing[3].

(c) An airborne staff officer was to be appointed at Air H.Q. India, plus an R.A.F. staff officer with airborne experience.

(d) The provision of R.A.F. equipment for airborne operations during 1943-44.

(e) The formation of an airborne forces depot at Rawalpindi.

(f) The formation of an Indian Army Air Corps, as in England.

(g) The formation of an Indian airborne division for operations during the winter 1944-45 with a British parachute brigade, when available, to arrive in India by July 1944.

Regarding future operations[4], the Supreme Commander proposed the use of four airborne divisions in his theatre during the winter 1944-45, and of these one was to be formed in India[5]. This division was to consist of 50th Indian Parachute Brigade then being trained, No. 2 Parachute Brigade from the Middle East and an Air Landing Brigade. The divisional troops were to

---

[1] War Office Narrative. Hist. of Airborne Forces, Chapter XXIII.

[2] Major General Wingate on the use of airborne troops in Burma; General Sir Claude Auchinleck, Commander-in-Chief, India; Air Chief Marshal Sir Richard Peirse, Air Officer Commanding-in-Chief; Admiral Lord Louis Mountbatten, Supreme Commander; Lt. Gen. E. L. Morris, Chief of General Staff, India, and General Sir George Gifford, General Officer Commanding-in-Chief, Eastern Army.

[3] Refer correspondence between Air Ministry, No. 38 Group and India on this subject (A.M. File C.S. 7725) resulting in four officers being sent to India in September 1944 to assist in the formation of No. 238 Group.

[4] The most important of these projected operations was "Zipper", the re-conquest of Malaya and the capture of Singapore. This would have involved the use of two Airborne Divisions—44th Indian and 6th Airborne.

[5] A.M. File, C.S. 7725/Pt. III, Encl. 10A.

be raised and trained before 1 October 1944. The position as to aircraft would depend entirely on the progress in other theatres; it was probable that none would be available for the additional flying involved in training the divisional troops.

The immediate result of Major General Browning's visit was the expansion of the 50th Indian Parachute Brigade and the subsequent formation of the 9th Indian Airborne Division (later on 16 March 1944 the 44th Indian Airborne Division) under the command of Major General E. E. Down of 1st Airborne Division[1]. Although S.E.A.C. were of the opinion that operations in Burma would not necessitate the use of a whole airborne division, it was decided to proceed with the formation of 44th Indian Airborne Division[2].

Training continued throughout the winter 1943-44. On 21 October 1943 the largest formation drop of parachutists ever carried out in India was made at Campbellpur dropping zone when 140 pupils were dropped from three Dakotas of the Air Landing School and four of No. 62 Squadron. More Instructors arrived in December and courses passed through the school uneventfully, save for three fatal jumping accidents, until 21 January 1944 when heavy rain flooded much of the accommodation at the aerodrome and hindered training. On 16 February the first live jump was made from a specially modified long range Liberator aircraft. This aircraft had been modified locally to meet the requirements of organisations for infiltrating agents into enemy occupied territory[3].

On 28 February 1944 Mr. L. L. Irvin and representatives of the Ministry of Aircraft Production visited Chaklala to carry out drop testing of modified Indian " X " type parachutes[4] and a few days later, after watching the tests, Wing Commander Benito and Squadron Leader Shields made descents using this new type. Wing Commander Benito then signed a certificate stating that parachutes made to the new specifications were satisfactory and that production could go ahead without delay.

This question of parachutes was the cause of much high level correspondence in the early months of 1944[5]. Commitments for operation Overlord naturally received priority over all other theatres, but the Supreme Commander S.E. Asia was concerned at the shortage and emphasised the necessity for parachutes to maintain the then limited operational progress in India. On 22 January 1944 he stated the requirements for the period January to September as being 769,500. At that time there were only 20 days reserve of parachutes in hand. As a result, the initial shipment of Canadian parachutes started in the following month. Canadian parachute production for the period January to July 1944 was 100,000 18 ft. parachutes—these were to be sent to S.E.A.C. The Supreme Commander also pressed for the best possible delivery rate of equipment to increase Indian production, which was 61,000 in January 1944, to 200,000 per month by September[6].

---

[1] A.M. File C.S. 7725, Part IV, Encls. 100A, 107A.
[2] For detailed information on the developments in the formation and training of 44th Indian Airborne Division, its move to Bilaspur and the conditions there, refer to War Office Narrative " History of Airborne Forces ", Chapter XXIV. Being of a purely Army nature reiteration of these facts in this account would be superfluous.
[3] O.R.B. Air Landing School, Chaklala.
[4] The " X " type parachute was the ordinary statichute as used in U.K. Tests were necessary in India owing to different climatic conditions.
[5] A.M. File A.M.S.O./Equip/I.
[6] C.O.S. File 62001.

In the two months ending 31 January 1944, 121,800 British and American parachutes had been shipped to S.E.A.C. in addition to the 100,000 Canadian already promised. By 24 May 1944 it was expected that requirements would necessitate continued supplies from Canada, and it was arranged to send 15,000 per month from July onwards[1]. However, once the major operations in Normandy and Arnhem were over, it was found that the demand for parachutes had not been as great as was expected[2], and a reserve of 40,000 was created in addition to all requirements being met. A reduction in monthly production from 26,700 to 23,250 was then effected[3].

The smooth running programme of the past months received a setback because on 26 February 1944 all five Dakotas of the Air Landing School with crews and ground staff were detached for approximately two months to assist in operations in Burma. Training ceased forthwith but by this time the whole of No. 50 Indian Parachute Brigade and its reinforcements had completed their basic training on Dakota aircraft. The output of trained parachutists had increased and continued to do so. By December 1944 the output per course was 160 and by August 1945 450. The total trained by then was about 20,000 with 31 fatal accidents. The following figures indicate the high standard of the men who passed the course and give an interesting comparison between British and Indian personnel:—

	Passed Basic Course Per cent.	Refusals Per cent.
British	85.5	5.3
Indian	90.8	4.9
Gurkha	89.9	4.5

Early in April 1944 the aircraft and crews of the Dakotas which had been detached to Burma returned to the Air Landing School and in May parachute training restarted. Dakota conversion courses, involving 40 hours flying per crew, were also begun. Meanwhile, R.A.F. Chaklala had been transferred from the control of No. 223 Group to No. 229 Group and re-organised on a new war establishment as No. 1333 Transport Support Training Unit with the following policy:—

(a) Conversion of aircrews to Dakota aircraft.

(b) Training of parachute troops.

(c) Advanced training of glider crews.

(d) Training aircrews in supply and parachute dropping and glider towing.

This new policy involved almost too many activities on the one station. There were insufficient training facilities and accommodation for incoming crews for conversion, and it was only by most careful planning, rigorous economy in the allotment of aircraft, and the utmost exertion on the part of the training staffs concerned that the programme was fulfilled. Later, on 19 June the Carlton Hotel, Rawalpindi, was taken over to relieve the accommodation problem. The aircraft strength at Chaklala had by this time increased to 14 Dakotas[4].

---

[1] A.M. File Admin. Plans 2/Para./1.
[2] It was estimated in September 1944 that a deficiency of 38,000 parachutes was probable.
[3] A.M. File D/AMSO/135/2.
[4] Statement by Wg. Cdr. Benito, O.C. A.L.S., Chaklala.

On 20 August 1944 a No. 229 Group conference held at Headquarters Delhi decided that two Royal Canadian Air Force Squadrons Nos. 435 and 436 were to be trained by the Transport Support Training Unit in supply and paratroop dropping, glider towing[1] and conversion on to Dakota aircraft. This began on 15 September 1944. Although by then there were 25 Dakotas available, the training programme was so heavy that the working period had to be increased by 14 hours per week. During the month of September 1,464 hours were flown.

Glider Training

As the gliders were assembled at an airfield in Bengal and then had to be towed to Chaklala, in addition to a shortage of tow ropes, glider maintenance personnel and tractors or jeeps for ground towing, the training programme was fraught with difficulties. Two hundred and forty glider pilots had to be converted to the Waco glider in readiness for operations in Burma by February 1945. Waco C.G.4 gliders had been arriving in India during the early summer at the rate of 100 per month and, although there was at first a shortage of manpower to use them, by August a further 650 were demanded for India[2].

Although the glider supply difficulties were diminishing there was still the question of pilots to fly them. On 3 January 1944 the Commander-in-Chief India asked the War Office for sufficient glider pilots to bring the total up to 80, including second pilots, otherwise training would be very restricted. There were between 20 and 40 Dakotas then available for training. Meanwhile, 30 glider pilots were sent from North Africa to carry out initial tests on the gliders at Chaklala, 20 Wacos having been received from the United States and two Hamilcars and four Horsas from the United Kingdom for trial purposes. It was not possible to release more glider pilots from the United Kingdom in view of the operations pending in Europe[3].

Glider training was carried out during the summer months of 1944 and in August the detachment at Chaklala was established as No. 10 Independent Glider Pilot Squadron, but there were still not sufficient glider pilots. However, when the major operations in Europe were over (Overlord and Market) many more became available and in the two months ending 6 January 1945 740 R.A.F. and 231 Army glider pilots were despatched to India[4]. Two Glider Pilot Wings, Nos. 343 and 344, comprising three squadrons each 668-673 were then formed under R.A.F. commanders with Army officers as second in command.

Training facilities were also available for 40 Army glider pilot-crews per month and if the war had not ended all R.A.F. crews would have been superseded by Army personnel by September 1946. The Supreme Commander

---

[1] O.R.B. 229 Group.
[2] A.M. File C.S. 7725/Pt. III, Encl. 119A.
[3] A.M. File C.S. 7725/Pt. III, Encls. 57B and 57C.
[4] A.M. File D.A.T.P.O., Folder AVF/24.

South East Asia agreed on 10 July 1945 to reduce the number of glider pilots required to 600 crews in all, to be available plus a 10 per cent. reserve by December 1945[1].

Before leaving England the glider pilots were told that they would be required on operations soon after arriving in India; that the glider squadrons were to be entirely controlled by the R.A.F. and that there would be no Army training other than the normal R.A.F. small arms drill; also that no pilot would be on gliders for more than 18 months[2]. As most of these promises did not transpire, some dissatisfaction arose and many complaints and applications to return to powered aircraft were received by No. 229 Group. This situation had been foreseen earlier by Air Marshal Hollinghurst, commanding Base Air Forces South East Asia, who had protested against large numbers of pilots being sent out before there were sufficient aircraft available to train them. There was no antidote except to devise means of occupying the pilots, but this state of affairs was fortunately cut short by the disbandment of No. 10 Independent Glider Pilot Squadron. All pilots were then transferred to No. 670 Glider Pilot Squadron and training continued for the remainder of the war. It was hampered to an extent by the Dakota/Horsa combination proving unsuitable owing to climatic conditions. Tests proved that four engined aircraft were necessary and as these were not readily available large scale exercises were not possible[3].

Formation of No. 238 Group

When operations in the European theatre ended the demand for airborne operations in the Far East was expected to be greatly increased[4], and in a message to the War Office on 31 July 1944 A.C.S.E.A. pointed out the desirability of building up a controlling formation for the planning and execution of them. It was therefore necessary that a nucleus of experienced officers be sent to India to study and advise on airborne problems and to plan the development of an R.A.F. Airborne Forces Group Headquarters with an organisation resembling that of Nos. 38 and 46 Groups in the United Kingdom[5].

On 13 September 1944 Air Ministry approved the establishment of one Group Captain, one Wing Commander and two Squadron Leaders to form a nucleus of a planning and executive staff for airborne operations in A.C.S.E.A. Later, on the 24 September, the Group, which was to be a Transport Command formation, was allotted to Eastern Asia Command but obtained its doctrine and policy from No. 229 Group. Similarly, the R.A.F. elements of the Combat Cargo Task Force, although a Transport Command formation, were controlled for the purpose of operations by Headquarters A.C.S.E.A. and for training and administration by No. 229 Group[6].

---

[1] A.M. File C.S. 7725, Part V, Encl. 197A.
[2] War Office Narrative, Chapter XXIV.
[3] A.M. File C.S. 7725, Part IV, Encl. 111A.
[4] The first large-scale airborne operation in the Far East was to have been a two divisional assault to recapture Singapore between December 1945 and March 1946. In all, six divisional airborne operations were envisaged before December 1946. The planning at this time as to disposition of forces and equipment was influenced by the assumption that the Japanese war would outlast that in Europe by some considerable time.
[5] A.M. File C.S. 7725, Part III, Encl. 141A.
[6] A.M. File C.S. 7725, Part III, Encls. 26A and 53A.

Whilst the R.A.F. formations were being developed the Supreme Commander South East Asia formed in his Headquarters a small airborne operations division to (a) study airborne operations technique with reference to S.E.A.C. (b) to advise on airborne training policy and (c) to advise the Joint Planning Staff in airborne operational planning. A Wing Commander R.A.F. joined the Unit for airborne operations staff duties. Although it had been desired to keep the R.A.F. airborne formations separate, as in the case of No. 38 Group in the United Kingdom, this was not feasible in A.C.S.E.A. due to local conditions involving the necessity of immediately following up any airborne operation by air supply and transport of Army and R.A.F. Units into the operational area. To ensure flexibility of control it was, therefore, essential to place the whole transport force under one head. The Combat Cargo Task Force thus had an American Commander and an integrated British-American Headquarters Staff to control operations of all transport units both British and American for Airborne assault and transport support operations in Burma.

The Supreme Commander, in a letter of 15 February 1945, stressed the necessity of sending out elements of No. 38 Group to assist in developing airborne forces. Also an Airborne Corps Headquarters would be required to control the two airborne divisions (one of these divisions was scheduled to arrive later from the United Kingdom), together with one air transported division. It was estimated that to lift the minimum force necessary would involve the use of 800 aircraft and 1,600 gliders[1].

This R.A.F. nucleus of a composite R.A.F. Air Corps Headquarters was to be entitled No. 238 Group. Approval for the formation of the Group was given by Vice Chief of Air Staff on 10 April 1945, and the Group was formed on 20 April under Headquarters B.A.F.S.E.A. It was found that all officer posts which required filling immediately could be done from A.C.S.E.A. thus it was not necessary to transfer No. 38 Group personnel. By the end of May it became evident that the complete formation of No. 238 Group was necessary without further delay. The 44th Indian Airborne Division were ready to support combined training and some 500 glider crews with more arriving had to be maintained in flying practice. Both Nos. 229 and 232 Groups were too occupied in troop transport and air supply, therefore unless Nos. 238 Group were formed it was feared that the training programme might suffer. At a meeting held on 19 June 1945, by the Director-General of Organisation Air Ministry, the following points regarding No. 238 Group were agreed[2]:—

(a) No. 238 Group was to have full group status under A.C.S.E.A. and be built up according to the discretion of the Air Officer Commanding-in-Chief.

(b) The Air Officer Commanding was to be an Air Vice-Marshal.

(c) The Group was to be placed under control of B.A.F.S.E.A. because it was responsible for the training programme under A.C.S.E.A. and it was feared that flexibility of control would be jeopardised if all posting and personnel questions had to be referred to Transport Command in the United Kingdom.

---

[1] A.M. File C.S. 7725, Part V, Encl. 60B. Paper by Supreme Commander on use of Airborne Forces Ibid., Encl. 88A.
[2] Ibid., Part VI, Encl. 145B.

(d) No. 238 Group was to control all glider forces in South East Asia belonging to Transport Command.

(e) The Group was to remain under A.C.S.E.A. for operational control.

The Purposes of No. 238 Group[1]

(a) Training air and airborne forces for airborne operations.

(b) Planning airborne assault operations as directed by Headquarters A.C.S.E.A.

(c) Liaison with Headquarters 44th Indian Airborne Division on airborne matters.

(d) Operational, functional and administrative control of any Units which might be assigned to the Group Headquarters from time to time.

The Group, with effect from 1 June 1945, was also to take functional control of the Parachute Training School, Chaklala, in conjunction with No. 223 Group. It was also to take operational control of Glider Wings Nos. 343 and 344, Nos. 668 to 673 Glider Squadrons and the Glider Servicing Echelons. In addition No. 1,577 Special Duty Flight, Nos. 96 and 215 Squadrons and other Transport Squadrons were also to come under the operational control of the Group.

The Headquarters of the Group was located in Kashmir House, New Delhi. Training of Nos. 215 and 96 Squadrons continued throughout July and August until on 13 August an advance Headquarters was ordered to be located at Bilaspur. Meanwhile, No. 5 Mobile Parachute Servicing Unit had moved to Kargi Road from Raipur and by 9 August 1945, parachute packing arrangements were completed and practice live dropping was carried out by No. 96 Squadron in conjunction with 44th Indian Airborne Division. All this activity proved to be in vain for with the announcement of V-J Day all training ceased and most of the Squadrons were stood by for the evacuation of prisoners of war and the lift of urgent freight. In September A.C.S.E.A. decided that No. 238 Group be disbanded and No. 238 Wing formed in its stead: this was carried out on 15 October 1945[2]. At the same time 14 Glider Servicing Echelons, Nos. 344 Glider Wing and 668, 669, 671 and 673 Glider Squadrons were also disbanded.

Arrangements had been made for the transfer of Nos. 38 and 46 Group Squadrons to A.C.S.E.A. following the conclusion of the European war. No. 298 Halifax Squadron of No. 38 Group was to be despatched to India for training, following the operations in Norway in May 1945. The Squadron began arriving at Raipur in July. It was to be used for glider towing, parachute dropping and the dropping of heavy equipment by use of cluster parachutes. Meanwhile, in the United Kingdom the preparation of new Halifax Mk. VII aircraft was being made by No. 41 Group as No. 38 Group commitments did not permit their releasing any of their aircraft for tropicalisation. It was anticipated that by December 1945 Nos. 620 (Stirling) and 644 (Halifax) Squadrons would be available for India but owing to the abrupt end of the war in August only No. 298 Squadron was sent. For the same reason only Nos. 48 and 233 of the five No. 46 Group Dakota Squadrons,

---

[1] O.R.B. No. 238 Group.
[2] A.C.S.E.A. File S. 33791/Org.

originally scheduled to arrive in India by early October 1945, were sent there. On arrival in India the activities of these three squadrons consisted mainly of general transport work, supply dropping to isolated outposts and the evacuation of prisoners of war[1].

Although not having any specific policy No. 238 Wing continued to act in an advisory capacity to Headquarters B.A.F.S.E.A. and undertook various duties including operation Pilgrim. This operation involved dropping six months' supplies to each of seven posts on the north-east frontier of India, using Dakotas from the Parachute Training School at Chaklala. The dropping zones were ill situated, some in very narrow valleys, and considerable skill and courage was necessary to fly low enough to drop accurately. The operation was successfully carried out by flying 28 sorties, only one of which was abortive, between 30 October and 5 November 1945. The Wing continued to function until its disbandment in November 1946, carrying out supply by air missions and airborne training.

Plans were made for the use of 44th Indian Airborne Division in Burma and Malaya and Headquarters I Airborne Corps moved to Gwalior under Lieut.-General R. N. Gale who took command of the division in August 1945. However, in the same month the Japanese surrendered and the Airborne Corps became redundant. It was disbanded on 23 October 1945. The Division continued training and carried out numerous operations in connection with the relief of prisoners of war and internees. The glider pilot training ceased as the R.A.F. Glider Pilot Squadrons were disbanded. The name of the Division was changed to the 2nd Indian Airborne Division and as such it continued training and carrying out various operations in India until with the partition of India in August 1947 the whole division became dispersed and no longer existed as a Unit[2].

Operations

There were very few operations in the Far East which could be strictly categorised as airborne. Apart from the minor ones, already referred to in this chapter, there remain only two of note, and although they were carried out entirely by American gliders, tugs and parachute dropping aircraft, it is of interest to examine them briefly. Both of these operations have been described in detail elsewhere[3].

The operation in connection with the second Wingate expedition in March 1944 involved the flying-in of Long Range Penetration Groups behind the enemy lines in the area Wuntho-Bhamo in northern Burma. The object of the operation was to hinder communications of the enemy opposing General Stilwell's United States Forces advancing towards Myitkina. In order to carry out this plan troops had to be transported by air to enemy territory, and air strips maintained therein for their reception and eventual re-supply Originally three sites for the air strips were chosen—one, sixty miles north of Katha and two, twenty miles south of Katha. These were 100 miles inside

---
[1] O.R.B. 38 and 46 Group Squadrons. A.M. File C.S. 7725, Part VI, Encl. 209.
[2] War Office Narrative. History of Airborne Forces, Chapter XXIV.
[3] R.A.F. Monograph, Air Transport Support Operations in the campaigns in Burma 1942–45, also War Office Monograph, History of Airborne Forces, Chapter XXIV.

enemy territory, 260 miles from the transport base, and within 50 miles of Indaw. The two sites to the north-east of Indaw were known as Broadway and Piccadilly, and the third, south-east across the Irrawaddy, as Chowringee[1].

From the airborne aspect, only the first phase of the operation is of particular interest—the transport by glider of the troops and engineers to prepare the landing grounds for the fly-in of the main force of 77th and 111th Brigades by Dakotas of the Troop Carrier Command. The airborne movement of the operation was a fully integrated effort using both R.A.F. and U.S.A.A.F. Squadrons. Forty-four Dakotas (C.47) from Nos. 31, 62, 117 and 194 R.A.F. Transport Squadrons and 39 Dakotas from Nos. 27 and 315 Troop Carrier Squadrons and the Troop Carrier Squadron of No. 5318 Air Unit (Prov.). The R.A.F. Dakotas were used only for the fly-in and were based at Tulihal in the Imphal Valley. The United States Squadrons were based in the area of Lalaghat. The glider part of the operation was carried out by No. 5318 Air Unit (Prov.) towing Waco (C.G.4A) gliders from the Lalaghat air strip[2]. The operation took place on the night of 5 March 1944, but shortly before the squadrons were due to take off photographic reconnaissance of Piccadilly showed that the site there had been completely obstructed by the Japanese and glider landings would be impossible. It was decided, therefore, to put all the gliders into Broadway and land the whole of 77th Brigade there.

Conditions were excellent, from the Allies point of view, with bright moonlight, when the squadrons took off, but out of a total of 61 gliders only 35 arrived at Broadway. There were several reasons for this high failure rate. Firstly, gliders were towed over mountains 7,000 feet high, and difficulties with air currents as well as with the tug engines overheating, due to the long climb, resulted in several gliders being prematurely released. Also, as the gliders had to be towed in pairs, due to the shortage of tug aircraft, the weight factor was considerable, as most of the gliders were laden with heavy equipment such as bulldozers, scrapers and other tools. Two of the gliders released early landed near a Japanese Divisional Headquarters and three near a Regimental Headquarters, creating an unrehearsed diversion effect. Lastly the nylon tow ropes for the gliders had been laid out on the airfield at Lalaghat for two weeks prior to the operation to allow them to unkink. During this period numerous trucks had been driven over them which had weakened their threads.

Unforeseen difficulties arose at Broadway. The surface of the ground was uneven causing some gliders to crash, and as the timing programme was very rapid, many of those following piled up. Landing speeds were also high due to the heavily loaded gliders. Eventually no more could be received at Broadway and the last flight was returned to base. Despite these difficulties, and some loss of equipment and personnel, the American engineers, assisted by British and Gurkha troops, prepared the landing strip in time for the main fly-in to take place on the following night. Sixty-two U.S. and R.A.F. Dakotas landed—only two of which were damaged. During the next six days over 9,000 men, 1,100 mules and 225 tons of stores were flown into Broadway. Meanwhile, at Chowringee, 12 gliders towed singly had been

---
[1] A.M. File C.S. 15345, Encl. 109A.
[2] Despatch on Air Operations in E.A.C. by Lt. Gen. Stratemeyer, p. 99 *et seq.*

landed on the night of 6-7 March and, although work on the strip was held up by the loss of a bulldozer, on the night 8-9 March, 78 Dakotas were landed and 40 more on the following morning. On 10 March, 111th Brigade left the area, abandoned the strip, and crossed the Irrawaddy to move towards Bhamo[1].

In the words of Lieut.-General Stratemeyer, " The operation had been no mean achievement. The 3rd Indian Division[2] had been flown in behind the enemy line fully equipped and supplied and, after deploying in the area against the surprised Japanese, had succeeded in disrupting their north-south communications in Burma upon which they depended to fight the Chinese forces in the north. The surprise operation had resulted too, in establishing a definite airfield, in Broadway, in the vicinity of Indaw, Katha and Bhamo, a situation most inconvenient to the enemy." This was alone made possible in the time by the use of an airborne operation in the shape of the gliders landing at Broadway and Chowringee. As a result, General Wingate's troops were able to join up with 16th Brigade and provide a total force of 12,000 to operate against the Japanese within a radius of 60 miles of Indaw.

The Capture of Rangoon

Although the use of airborne forces in support of several major operations had been contemplated[3] it was not until the events leading up to the capture of Rangoon that they were required. American glider-borne engineer units were again used to prepare landing strips for supplies and troops during the advance of IV Corps towards Rangoon. Fifty-five American C.G.4.A. gliders based at Meiktila airfield were used to carry runway equipment, bulldozers, tractors, etc. As the ground forces pushed forward and when the airfields were captured and found to be necessary for future use the gliders were towed in and the airfield prepared for the main forces to be flown in later. These operations, which were used at Lewe, Tennant and Zayathwin airfields were known as Gumptions. All these operations in support of the advance on Rangoon, including the Gumptions were carried out by United States aircraft of the C.C.T.F. There was little opposition from the Japanese and the operations were performed most efficiently despite bad weather and the necessity for speed[4].

Operation Dracula

There was much conjecture both before and after the launching of operation Dracula as to its necessity. The arguments for and against it are a matter of higher strategy and beyond the scope of this narrative. The fact remains that it did take place and airborne forces were used[5]. Dracula was put into operation on the recommendation of Lieut.-General Sir Oliver Leese, Commander-in-Chief Allied Land Forces, S.E.A., who thought that an overland advance might not accomplish the capture of Rangoon before the monsoon period began. To make this task more certain operation Dracula was modified to a combined sea and air attack. The original plan

---

[1] Despatch by Earl Mountbatten on operations in S.E.A.C. 1943–46.
[2] The 3rd Indian Division was the over-all name for 77th and 111th Brigades and the other forces taking part.
[3] Operation Capital calling for airborne operations against Kalewa and the Mandalay Plain was cancelled in December 1944. See " Air Transport Support Operations in Burma ".
[4] IIJ50/47/63, C.C.T.F. Intelligence Extract No. 16.
[5] Despatch on Air Operations in A.C.S.E.A. by A.V.M. Sir Keith Parke, Air C.-in-C.

for Dracula (1944) had provided for the use of 900 aircraft and 650 gliders involving a fly-in of 480 miles, but owing to the demands of the European theatre, it was not practicable and as such was postponed in October 1944. Planning for the revised version had to be accomplished at a high speed, faced as it was with a deadline of five weeks before the monsoon was due to break about 15 May 1945[1].

In order that the invasion force might be free from opposition by guns at the entrance of the Rangoon River it was decided to drop a parachute battalion on the day preceding the main assault in order to neutralise them. A Gurkha Parachute Battalian comprised of units of 2nd and 3rd Gurkha Parachute Battalions from 50th Indian Parachute Brigade was concentrated at Chaklala were it was joined by Engineer, Ambulance, Intelligence and Signal detachments and expanded to a Battalian Group. Three training exercises were carried out at Chaklala before the Group moved to Midnapore to collect equipment and carry out a rehearsal. On 29 April 1945 the Group moved to Akyab, together with a reserve party of 200 all ranks from 1st Indian Parachute Battalion and 2nd and 3rd Gurkha Battalions[2].

The lift was provided by 40 C-47 Dakota aircraft of Nos. 317 and 319 U.S. Troop Carrier Squadrons of 1st and 2nd Air Commando Groups under the command of Colonel A. L. McCullough[3]. The American crews of these aircraft had had no previous experience of paratroop dropping and jump masters experienced in the handling of Gurkha and Indian troops were obtained from Nos. 435 and 436 Royal Canadian Air Force Squadrons. Parachute racks from Nos. 31 and 117 R.A.F. Squadrons, modified for British containers, were fitted to the aircraft. The force was to be dropped in two lifts at a dropping zone five miles south-west of Elephant Point.

On 1 May 1945, at 0230 hours, two Pathfinder aircraft, containing special radar equipment, took off from Akyab. They located the dropping zone without difficulty and dropped an advance parachute detachment to mark the zone and set up a Eureka beacon to guide in the main forces in addition to the one 10 miles off shore. At 0300 hours the main force transported in 38 Dakotas began to take off. Despite some rain and no light all the aircraft were airborne in 11 minutes. The flight to the dropping zone was uneventful and the drop was carried out with precision. Some 700 troops as well as containers were landed on the zone, dropping from an altitude of 600 to 800 feet. Only one aircraft failed to make the return journey, landing at Kyaukpyu on Ramree Island with engine trouble. Immediately after landing at base eight aircraft were serviced and took off again at 1130 hours carrying 160 Gurkha reinforcements and despite monsoon weather dropped successfully at 1445. Another aircraft landed at Kyaukpyu on the return journey with engine trouble. Supplies were flown in later the same afternoon by 10 Dakotas. The day's operations involved a total of 58 transport sorties; no aircraft were lost and only five minor casualties were sustained in the actual dropping. The operation was successful as might be expected in view of the fact that there was no enemy opposition. Possibly the most creditable aspect of the airborne part of Dracula was the fact that the planning, training and staging of the operation was perfectly carried out at very short notice.

---

[1] Despatch by Lt. Gen. Sir Oliver Leese on Operations in Burma, November 1944–August 1945. O.R.B. H.Q. A.C.S.E.A., Appendix C. F/Air/9.
[2] War Office Monograph History Airborne Forces, Chapter XXIV.
[3] O.R.B. H.Q. A.C.S.E.A., Appendix C, F/Air/9.

CHAPTER 13

ENEMY AIRBORNE FORCES

German Airborne Forces[1]

Inception. Early in 1936 an experimental staff of about 15 officers and 60 to 80 other ranks under the command of a Major Immanns was formed in Stendal to review the question of future parachute operations and what form of exercises and practice jumps were to be employed. By the spring of 1937 it had been decided definitely to use an automatic parachute and a system of training was evolved. A parachute training school was then formed in Stendal and in the spring of 1937 Generalmajor Bassenge was put in command. Also about this time Goering gave orders for an S.S. Platoon of about 35 men to be trained as paratroops at Stendal.

The first suggestions as to the future use of parachute troops were made by Generalmajor Bassenge as follows:—

(a) The parachute battalion was to be trained as a special demolition unit and to be used against objectives such as railways, bridges, power lines, high tension lines, etc. The purpose of this proposal was that objectives of this nature could normally only be destroyed by employing strong bomber forces whereas by dropping the demolition troops, usually under the cover of darkness, the destruction could be carried out with greater economy.

(b) A parachute battalion of the Army was to be formed consisting of a Headquarters, a Signals Platoon, three Rifle Companies and one Heavy Company; then two parachute battalions were to be set up with the object of forming a Parachute Infantry Regiment and finally a Parachute Infantry Division. These forces were to be used in conjunction with Army operations and were to form part of the Army which would control their training, equipment and organisation.

(c) A Transport Group was to be formed consisting of three squadrons, each of 36 aircraft, and it was proposed that this Group remained exclusively at the disposal of the Army Parachute Units for peacetime training. In the event of mobilisation, it was to be reinforced with transport planes up to the strength of a Transport Division.

Probably because of rivalry between the German Air Force and the Army, Generalmajor Bassenge received no conclusive answer or decision on his proposals. Nevertheless, the Parachute School at Stendal was confirmed in its status and had the right to make agreements with the German Air Force and Army Authorities. It was also permitted to create an experimental department and to give orders to industry on behalf of the Army and Air Force.

---

[1] Most of the information contained in this section was obtained from interrogation reports of Generaloberst Student and Generalmajor Bassenge who, as will be seen in the following pages, played a major part in the development, training and control of airborne forces in Germany. Both of these reports are believed to be reliable. Additional material on the invasion of Crete has been obtained from Headquarters R.A.F. Middle East Intelligence Report on that operation. Copies of these reports are held by the Air Historical Branch.

First use of Airborne Forces

Parachute forces were used for the first time in Germany at the Army manoeuvres in the autumn of 1937 and were employed as follows:—

A Parachute Demolition Force of 14 squads were used in night operations against railway lines and communications in West Prussia and Pomerania. They carried out their tasks successfully and were unobserved by the " enemy ".

The second unit to be employed in these manoeuvres was a Parachute Infantry Company but little useful information was derived from their part of the exercise because it was carried out as a demonstration for Hitler.

Towards the end of 1937 the development of cargo gliders was sufficiently advanced for experiments to be undertaken. It seemed that the cargo glider would supply the answer to one of the main problems confronting the Parachute Infantry Units which was the transportation of the heavy weapons. Experiments were conducted at Stendal without, however, producing any definite high level decision as to their introduction as an essential part of Army air transport. The Training School in Stendal was expanded by the summer of 1938 to a strength of 12 training companies with about 180 parachute instructors. Courses lasted normally for two months and the peace-time capacity of the School was over 4,000 per year. The eventual war time capacity was more than twice this number.

Planned Operation for Sudetenland

On 29 May 1938, a conference with Hitler took place in Berlin in which the military situation and intentions were discussed in view of forthcoming operations in the Sudetenland, and Generalmajor Bassenge was ordered to equip, organise and train an airborne force to be employed in the autumn against Czechoslovakia. He was also ordered to train the parachute forces of the Air Force in addition to that of the Army to the highest possible standard. Air Transport Units also were to be reinforced, equipped and trained. Generaloberst Student was made Tactical Commander of this Airborne Force although up to then he had had no connection with Airborne Units. The Airborne Unit was given a new title of 7th Flieger Division[1] and although

---

[1] *Original Composition of 7th Flieger Division*
  The Division was composed of the following Units:—
    Parachute Units:
      Para-jager Battalion of 5 Companies.
      Signals Platoon and Engineer Platoon.
      Para-infantry Battalion with 4 Companies.
      Signals Platoon and Engineer Platoon.
    Airborne Units:
      Airborne Battalion " Hermann Goering ", 3 Companies.
      Signals Platoon.
      16 Infantry Regiment.
      S.A. Stanarte. " Feldheronhelle ", 3 Battalions.
      1 Airborne Artillery Troop with 4 Skoda guns.
      1 Airborne Medical Company.
      German Air Force Flying Units.
      1 Reconnaissance Echelon.
      1 Combat Squadron of He. 123s.
      1 Fighter Squadron with He. 51s. and Ar. 68s.
      8 Transport Groups totalling about 250 Junkers 52s.
      1 Glider Echelon with 12 Dfs. 230s.
  The total strength of the Parachute and Airborne Troops was approximately 9,000 men and was ready for action on 1 September 1938.

it was not required in the annexation of the Sudetenland one battalion took part in a demonstration drop into a field in the occupied zone. Goering witnessed this drop and was so impressed that he informed Student that he would form an Airborne Corps. This promise was never fulfilled. When the Division returned to Germany, it was dispersed and eventually all that was left was one Parachute Battalion of the German Air Force.

Czechoslovakia

The next task allotted to 7th Flieger Division which was to be organised as for the Sudetenland operation was the capture of airports, north, north-east and north-west of Prague, and it appeared that Generaloberst Student was anxious not only to capture the airfield but also to penetrate Prague itself. It seemed that he wished to justify Airborne Forces as being capable of carrying out difficult tasks more quickly than normal units. Although the operation as staged against Prague was unnecessary the intended airborne landings were carried out in the area of Freudenthel in order to test the plan. This took place on 1 October 1938 when approximately 250 Ju. 52s landed on the selected small strips of territory in fields and hillsides and in the valleys. Only 12 aircraft were damaged. This exercise provided much useful experience and knowledge for the future.

Command

The command of all Parachute and Airborne Forces was transferred to the German Air Force at the end of 1938. 7th Flieger Division was to be set up as a real Parachute Division. 22nd Infantry Division was to be equipped and trained as an airborne Division. Hitler ordered that as far as large airborne operations were concerned the German Air Force would remain in command of the Airborne Forces until such time as contact had been established between larger Army formations and the airborne units which had been landed in the enemy's rear. This order remained in force until the end of the war.

Tactics

The most important and difficult task was to lay down principles for the commitment of parachute and airborne troops. There was no previous experience on which to build; and the Russians maintained the strictest silence about their experiments. Two methods were considered at this time.

> The direct method consisting of a parachute or airborne landing as near as possible to the objective. In this way the enemy could be overpowered and destroyed in the shortest time.
>
> The indirect method consisting of a parachute and/or airborne landing outside the reach of enemy weapons, followed by the approach to the objective and the attack. The disadvantage of this method was that the important factor of surprise—the main asset of any parachute attack—was lost to a great extent. The enemy could find time for defence and the attacking paratroops then suffer losses which they could have avoided by landing on top of their objective.

The German paratroops used the first of these methods in almost all their operations. During this period a large number of airborne exercises were carried out. The largest took place in July 1939 at Bergen, when nearly

1,000 men jumped. Dummy parachutes were also used as a diversionary measure with success.

Polish Campaign

7th Flieger Division was to have been employed in the Polish Campaign but the ground operations developed so favourably that they became unnecessary and Hitler wished to keep his parachute forces intact for use in the Western campaign.

The Western campaign

At the end of October 1939 Generaloberst Student was ordered to prepare 7th Flieger Division and 22nd Infantry Division for tasks in Belgium. It was intended to begin the Western offensive with these operations, for which some 400 Ju. 52 aircraft were available. During the winter 1939-40 special training in Germany was carried out. Paratroops were dropped on to frozen fields and one Company was flown at a temperature of minus 15 degrees Centigrade for $2\frac{1}{2}$ hours and then had to jump; this was necessary because the Ju. 52s had no heating apparatus. This was typical of German thoroughness. During this period night jumps also were made.

On 10 January 1940 a German parachute officer landed in error on Belgian territory. He had with him documents relating to the intended airborne operations in Belgium and this mishap led to their abandonment. Hitler ordered that an airborne operation should take place in Holland to capture the large bridges in the Rotterdam area. Meanwhile, the occupation of Norway and Denmark was begun on 9 April 1940. A Parachute Regiment of 7th Flieger Division took part in this operation. In the early morning of 9 April one Company jumped on to the airfield of Stavengar and took it by surprise. Another Company jumped in Denmark and occupied the crossings near Aalborg.

At the end of April, the 7th Flieger Division and 22nd Infantry Division were assembled in preparation for the operations in the west. Their tasks were as follows:—

> (a) 7th Flieger Division was to capture bridges at Moerdijk, Dordrecht and Rotterdam and hold them until the ground troops arrived. The only landing field available for these operations was at Waalhaven, near Rotterdam.
>
> (b) 22nd Infantry Division were to occupy the Hague and take prisoner the Royal Family, the Army High Command and the Government. Three favourable airfields were available for this task on the three open sides of the city. Landings in the open country were not possible in the area of Rotterdam and the Hague because of the numerous dykes. For emergency purposes Student had designated certain motor roads and had practised landings on these in Germany.

Operations in Holland

The operations began early on 10 May 1940. 22nd Infantry Division met with no success at all, but 7th Flieger Division captured the bridges near Rotterdam and the airfield at Waalhaven in a very short time. In the ensuing four days approximately 7,000 men with heavy weapons and artillery were landed at Waalhaven despite the fact that the airfield was under heavy artillery fire and subjected to bombing by the R.A.F. Large scale allied counter-attacks were beaten off and although losses to the personnel of 7th Flieger Division were comparatively light, approximately 170 Ju.52s were lost or very badly damaged.

Also on 10 May 1940 airborne attacks were made on Fort Eben Emael and the bridges over the Albert Canal. Fifty gliders were used, but as these were not sufficient, approximately 150 men were parachuted. In all, about 600 men took part. Elaborate training, using exact models of the fort and bridges, and practical exercises in demolition work, glider landings, etc. had been carried out in preparation for this assault. The operation was mounted from airfields near Cologne and the take-off was made whilst it was still dark. Parachute engineers were landed on the roof of the fort and stormed and blasted the casements with charges. The Belgian defences were completely surprised and only six paratroops were lost. The remainder of the airborne force occupied the three bridges across the Albert Canal. The Belgians were able to blow up one, but the other two fell intact into German hands. Heavy battles developed for these bridges but the airborne troops held them until advanced German ground units arrived.

As a result of these successful operations in Holland, it was realised by the German High Command that there was a future for parachute and airborne forces and the formation of 7th Flieger Division as a purely parachute unit was carried out with vigour. The XI Flieger Korps with korps troops was set up as a commanding unit for parachute and airborne troops and Generaloberst Student was put in command. In order to fulfil the glider programme, rapid construction of 1,000 gliders (D.F.S. 230) was required. The *Luftlandegeschwader* was newly formed as a glider unit consisting of three squadrons each equipped with 53 tug aircraft and gliders.

Proposed Attack on England

During the summer of 1940 an airborne attack was planned to form a deep bridgehead on the south-east coast of England (operation Seelowe). In order to transport as strong a force as possible with the first wave, the aircraft towing gliders were also to carry parachutists. The bridgehead area was surveyed and photographed from the air. It was considered that the area was being made impracticable for airborne landings by the systematic and skilful use of obstacles of all kinds, digging of ditches, ploughing of tracts of land and erecting high obstacles. The eventual conclusion from these observations was that a successful execution of the operation was doubtful, though from an English viewpoint this opinion seems to be unnecessarily pessimistic. Hitler eventually abandoned the plan late in the summer. Meanwhile the problem of dropping heavy loads was tackled and a solution was found. As a result, parachute troops could then be supplied immediately with their light anti-aircraft guns and motorcycles. A special lightweight gun had been developed.

The Operations in Crete

The decision to attack Crete by parachute and airborne forces was made on the suggestion of Student early in April during the beginning of the campaign in Greece. He considered that he had adequate forces to carry out this task and that they represented the best means for an eventual attack on the Suez Canal. In his opinion, Crete was the first step and Cyprus the second to this end. Hitler's sanction to the Crete operation was given at a conference on 21 April 1941.

At that time XI Flieger Korps was stationed in Central Germany and was transported by rail and air to the Athens area. This move to Greece was carried out with considerable difficulty owing to roads and railways being impassable in many places. The bulk of the ammunition and supplies, therefore, had to be brought by ship which caused considerable delay. By the capture of Greece the Germans had obtained airfields suitable for long range bombers and transport aircraft in Northern Greece and in the Athens area. For short range fighters and dive bombers it was necessary to have bases nearer to Crete. With this in mind reconnaissances for suitable sites in the Peloponnese were carried out. By the middle of April the Germans had three airfields—Mulaoi, Melos and Scarpanto—ready for use within 100-120 miles of Crete. On these aerodromes dive bombers and single engined fighters were concentrated. The transport, bomber and reconnaissance aircraft were based mainly in the Athens area and during the first half of May German aircraft reconnoitred Crete daily. Attacks were also concentrated against allied shipping, for the most part by Ju.88s operating from Greece. Of 27,000 tons of supplies sent to Crete at this time, 21,000 tons were turned back, 3,400 tons were sunk and only 2,700 tons were delivered; this made the allies supply position extremely acute.

There were available for the operation about 530 Ju.52s. Although there were more gliders available, Student decided to use only about 100, mainly because of a lack of highly trained glider personnel. The glider troops all belonged to No. 1 Storm Regiment. The gliders were used for combat assignments and the transport of the airborne staff and heavy equipment. The German intelligence as to the position in Crete before the attack was very limited, and the presence on the Island of the whole of the 2nd New Zealand Division and a large part of the 6th Australian Division was unknown to them. The Germans realised that allied troops were probably installed in very well camouflaged positions. The airfields at Malemi, Heraklion and Retimo, as well as a new one under construction near Castelli, were kept under constant observation.

The plan for the attack was as follows. The important towns, as well as the existing airfields, were on the north coast of the Island[1]. The airfields were small and landings in open country with transport planes were only possible on the few isolated plateaux in the interior of the Island. There was, however, limited landing space for single aircraft on the beaches, but insufficient for a large scale undertaking. Therefore, it was decided to capture the three airfields by landing parachute troops directly on them. A further parachute regiment was to jump south of Canea in order to pin down the allied reserves. Concentrated bombing attacks were to soften the allied positions prior to the jumping. Owing to insufficiency of aircraft to support all four tasks simultaneously, it was necessary to carry out the attack in two waves, thus partially losing the advantage of surprise.

---

[1] See figure 14.

FIG. 14.

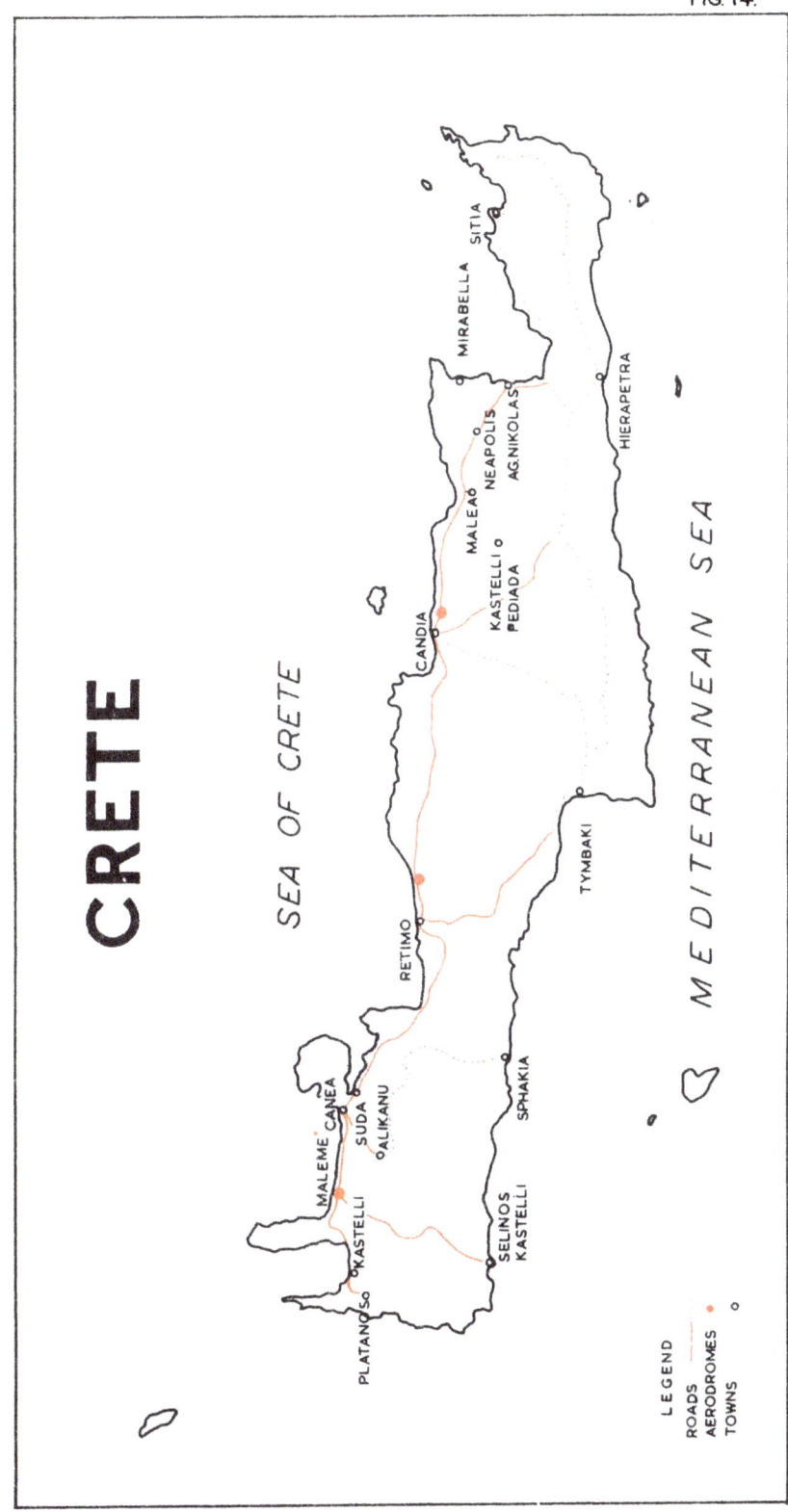

The attack on the Island began in the early morning of 20 May 1941. Visibility was moderate but there was a heavy ground haze. After a short but very heavy bombing attack in the vicinity of Malemi airfield and the Canea area, two companies using gliders successfully attacked anti-aircraft positions in this area. Further attacks by gliders south of Malemi and on the Akrotiri peninsula were complete failures owing to faulty dropping and poor navigation. The gliders were followed, according to plan, 15 minutes later by the arrival of parachutists but in many cases, owing to the thick haze, aircraft dropped the paratroops inaccurately, particularly at Malemi and Canea. In many cases paratroops were dropped right amongst Allied troops, although this was not intended, and at other places landings were dispersed. Because of heavy initial losses due to these reasons, neither unit could fulfil its task. After a time the survivors regrouped and attacks were carried out towards the Malemi airfield. It was not possible, however, to capture it and the landings planned for the following morning could not take place.

It had been intended for the second wave of the attack to follow as soon as possible in the afternoon of 20 May, but due to delay in refuelling of the transport planes the take-off was retarded. In an effort to make up for lost time the original starting order was not maintained and some units arrived in the wrong order and others did not take off at all. The second wave were not successful in capturing their objectives at Retimo and Heraklion and suffered high casualties.

At the end of the first day the position was that some 750 glider troops and 8,000 parachutists had been landed. At Malemi some success had been achieved and the western side of the airfield was in German hands. In the other areas the parachute landings had failed to achieve their objective and heavy casualties had been sustained.

On the morning of 21 May further parachute attacks were carried out west of Malemi airfield and bitter fighting ensued, but it was not until two further companies had been dropped during the afternoon that the airfield was finally captured and was available for use by the Germans. Immediately after this had been accomplished Ju. 52s began to arrive, bringing in further airborne elements and supplies during the following days. It had been arranged for supplies to be brought by sea in small ships and during the night 21-22 May attempts were made to bring these boats in at Malemi. They were attacked by British naval units and dispersed. The airfield, however, although under intermittent fire from allied artillery, remained in constant use by the Germans. During the battle on the Island, up to 30 May 1941, approximately 15,000 men and about 750 vehicles of all kinds were landed on this airfield. After 22 May 1941, operations went more or less according to plan for the Germans and on 30 May the allies evacuated their forces by sea from Heraklion. The casualties in the fighting for Crete were very heavy; about 4,000 men were killed or missing, amongst them a large proportion of officers. Of the 530 Ju. 52s employed some 170 were lost or heavily damaged.

The following summary from the German view-point of the airborne operation on Crete is of interest:—

(a) In Crete gliders were employed for the following purposes:—

(i) To destroy anti-aircraft gun positions in the line of approaching troop carrying aircraft.

(ii) To seize positions and give covering fire to the arrival of parachutists.

(iii) To cut communications, seize wireless stations and cut telephone lines.

(iv) To provide heavily armed Storm troops for the capture of key points.

(b) Gliders were used only in the first wave of the attack and attempted to achieve surprise. The sequence of attack was—gliders, parachutists, air landing troops, seaborne troops.

(c) Advantages of gliders over parachutists as demonstrated at Crete were:—

(i) Silent approach.

(ii) Spot landings close to target.

(iii) Concentrated fire power. A glider landed men, munitions and supplies together. In the case of parachutists, they were dropped separately.

(iv) Immediate action. A glider crew could go into action within two minutes of landing.

(d) Gliders approaching a target were very vulnerable but could land successfully under cover of air protection. Where air protection was missing the attack failed.

Generaloberst Student considered that the airborne success in Crete brought home to the allies the importance and possibilities of airborne forces and they then started forming them on a large scale. He said, however, that the German High Command was impressed less by the success of the operation than by the high losses suffered. Hitler's view was that parachutists were essentially a surprise weapon and therefore only effective once. He considered that as the allies had been surprised by it once, they would now take defensive measures and that the time for large airborne operations was over. He did not believe that the allies would form strong airborne forces and was confirmed in this view by the fact that they were not used during 1942. It was not until much later that he realised his mistake.

Generaloberst Student, however, continued to press for an increase in German airborne forces. His theory was that the presence in Germany of large forces of airborne troops would force the allies to keep large formations available in rear areas as a defensive measure. It was known that the airborne operations in Holland and Crete had caused a general psychological effect. However, no extension or development was allowed in Germany after Crete, whilst it was just at this time that the allies really started to develop their airborne forces. The German paratroop force was preserved as it stood and XI Flieger Korps remained in existance as a mobile reserve. 22nd Infantry Division, however, was sent to the Russian front. From then on parachutists were used in ground operations.

Training

Experience had shown the Germans that mistakes in dropping had always been made at the actual moment of dropping, especially at Crete. It was, therefore, decided that in every aircraft there should be one man who would be responsible for the correct approach to the dropping point and for the orderly jumping of the parachutists. These men were chosen from old parachutists and were trained at the para-training school. They were called paratroop observers and a minimum of 600 of these trained officers and N.C.O.s was maintained.

Aircraft

Until after Crete the Ju. 52 had been exclusively used for parachutists. Now the Heinkel III was added. This aircraft, like the Ju. 52, had room for 12 parachutists but had the additional advantage of higher speed, greater range in armament and fire-proof fuel tanks.

Gliders

The operation in Crete had demonstrated the value of cargo gliders, even though the D.F.S. 230, which was used there, was obsolete. Student therefore concentrated on the improvement of the D.F.S. 230 as his demands for a new battle glider had been turned down. They were equipped with machine guns and parachute brakes, and later on, a rocket brake developed at Peenemunde was incorporated which could bring them to a halt within a few metres.

Proposed Operations

During 1942 German paratroops were not used in airborne operations at all but a number of operations were planned. The most important of these was an attack on Malta, decided upon at a conference between Hitler and Mussolini early in 1942. August was the date fixed for the operation and it was intended that strong paratroop forces should land first on Malta and establish a bridgehead through which further airborne forces could be brought to the island. The Italians, too, were expected to contribute to this operation and their Paratroop Division was to take part. 500 Ju. 52s and He. IIIs, in addition to 80 Italian Savoias 82, were to be available. However, during the summer Hitler decided to cancel the operation. The actual reason for this is not known, but it is probable that Hitler had no great opinion of the Italian forces and did not wish to sacrifice his highly trained German paratroops on what might prove to be a forlorn venture. Another operation which was planned but did not take place was an attack on Gibraltar, but it was eventually decided that the defences would probably be too strong and this was abandoned.

Shortly afterwards Hitler decided to carry out an airborne operation on the Eastern front, using 7th Flieger Division to open up a coastal road along the Black Sea in the rear of the Russians near the town of Adler. It was intended to use gliders in strength for this operation. However, the situation from the German viewpoint deteriorated badly and 7th Flieger Division was committed to ground operations near Smolensk.

New German Airborne Formations

Early in 1943 Hitler realised that the allies were developing airborne forces on a large scale and reconsidered his decision made after Crete. He ordered Generaloberst Student to train airborne troops for use in the West against possible allied airborne operations. XI Flieger Korps was then moved to Brittany and a new division, 2nd Paratroop Division, was set up.

In the Spring of 1943 1st Paratroop Division was transferred from the Eastern front to Normandy. Training schools were set up and both divisions, combined under XI Flieger Korps, were trained and ready for employment in France by the summer of 1943.

Operations in Italy

The next airborne operation of interest was the rescue from Campo Imperatore of Mussolini by a company which was landed in gliders. The operation was successful and Mussolini was evacuated in a Storch aircraft to Vienna. The Germans also used airborne forces to capture the island of Elba and this was carried out by one battalion of the 2nd Paratroop Division.

Expansion of Paratroop Forces

At the end of 1943 it was found that large numbers of German Air Force ground personnel could be released to the paratroops. Goering, therefore, decided on several increases. The formation of I and II Paratroop Corps and 3rd, 4th, 5th and 6th Paratroop Divisions was ordered. Generaloberst Student was made Commander-in-Chief of a newly formed Paratroop High Command, which was set up from XI Flieger Korps Headquarters. It was found that the German Air Force personnel were of good quality. In spite of the sudden increase in numbers the volunteer system was adhered to until the middle of 1944. These volunteers had to pass through the main testing unit of the parachute forces at Gardelegen, where they were medically examined and given intelligence tests. Training in jumping was continued but shortage of time and aircraft fuel made it impossible for everyone to receive this training. The following schools were active at this time—Wittstock, Freiburgh and Druex. The capacity of these schools was from 12,500 pupils at a time and the course lasted three weeks. In all, about 30 per cent. of the new formations received jumping training.

The Final Phase

Early in 1944 considerable reorganisation took place within the airborne units; new divisions and training establishments were formed. The main object of this was as a defensive measure against the invasion of France. By June 1944 the estimated strength of the paratroop army was 160,000 men. Shortly after the invasion in Normandy, Student was ordered to prepare an airborne counter-attack against the allied bridge-head. Transport planes and gliders and 15,000 paratroops were put at his disposal, but the allied advance was so rapid that the plan had to be cancelled.

Meanwhile, in the middle of July 1944 owing to the severe defeats in the east and west, the Paratroop High Command was ordered to establish in Germany further new paratroop divisions for ground operations. Great difficulties were encountered, but eventually five independent paratroop regiments were formed. On 3 September Student was ordered to occupy a sector on the Albert Canal between Antwerp and Maastricht. At about this time the training regiments, which had suffered severely on the Western Front, were returned to Germany and re-formed; these regiments were combined into a paratroop training division and in the autumn of 1944 the following divisions were also re-formed—2nd, 3rd, 5th and 6th Paratroop Divisions.

The Ardennes Offensive

The last parachute operation of the German Army took place during the Ardennes offensive. A battalion of about 1,000 men was given the task of jumping on the morning of 16 December at Mont Rigi and of occupying an important road network there. 100 Junkers 52 aircraft were available for this task, but their crews had little experience of night flying or dropping paratroops. The start of the operation was delayed by 24 hours but the offensive had already begun and the German High Command, therefore, decided on a night operation in spite of the inadequate training of the aircrews. As a result the dropping was poorly carried out and casualties were high. Only about 300 men assembled at Mont Rigi and these were unable to carry out their tasks; with very few exceptions the battalion was destroyed. A further airborne operation was contemplated to establish a bridge-head over the Meuse as a continuation of the Ardennes offensive, but was never carried out. This was the end for German airborne forces as such, although further reorganisation was attempted, and the paratroop army took part in ground operations as the Allies drove into Germany in the closing weeks of the war.

Japanese Airborne Forces[1]

The Japanese parachute training organisation started in 1940 when four training centres were set up at Shimoneseki, Shizueka, Hiroshima and Himeji. Courses lasted for six months. By the autumn of 1941 100 German instructors were in Japan and by this time there were nine training centres and approximately 15,000 men under training. The Army and Navy had their own separate forces of paratroops; the Naval training period was much shorter than that of the Army. By 1 November 1941, the Naval parachute force was 2,000 strong comprising the Yokosuko 1st and 3rd Special Naval Landing Forces; all these were ready by 7 December 1941.

The Army Parachute Units were part of the Air Forces and were called Raiding Units which were split into formations, the largest of which was a Raiding Group. A Group was the equivalent of a Division consisting of a Headquarters, a Raiding Flying Brigade, a Raiding Brigade, two Glider Infantry Regiments, a Raiding Machine Cannon Unit, a Raiding Signal Unit, and a Raiding Engineer Unit. The total strength of a Group was about 6,000 men and was commanded by a Major General. The Raiding Brigade was composed entirely of paratroops with a strength of about 1,500 all ranks.

Transport aircraft were attached to a Group and controlled by a Raiding Flying Brigade consisting of two Raiding Flying Regiments, one Glider Flying Regiment, a Brigade Signal Unit, a Headquarters and an Air Raiding Regiment, the latter consisting of about 20 transport aircraft and crews. The Raiding Flying Regiments undertook the transport of gliders and paratroops and had 35 aircraft and about 500 men. Each transport aircraft carried between 10 and 13 men. The regular Navy and Army Airborne Forces had available some 125 aircraft but, had a large operation been planned, the Regular Raiding Special Landing Units would have been supplemented by trained air landing and parachute troops transported in aircraft from other Units. This was also the case in Germany where several hundred transport aircraft could be mustered from Flying Schools. The majority of airborne

---

[1] Air Publication 3146, " Organisation of Japanese Army, Navy and Air Forces ", pp. 56, 57.

troops were normally retained in the Infantry and other ground units and called upon when a specific airborne operation was planned. However, no large scale operations took place; throughout the whole war only five airborne operations were carried out by the Japanese.

Gliders

There were several types of gliders and an elaborate scheme was evolved for training youths in glider flying as a preliminary to power flying. It was estimated that in 1944 over 70,000 students were being instructed on gliders by some 1,250 instructors, using over 2,000 gliders. The Japanese claimed to have trained about 25,000 troops for parachuting or air landing since 1940.

Operations

The first Japanese parachute operation was the capture after a few hours' fighting, of Menado airfield on Celebes Island by paratroops on 11 January 1942. Three companies were dropped from 900 feet by Nell transport aircraft escorted by fighters and preceded by bombers. This was the only operation in which the Japanese Naval Airborne Force took part. It was later wiped out at Saipan[1]. The only parachute operation carried out by the Japanese of any real importance was during the campaign against Java and Sumatra early in 1942. In an attempt to prevent the British and Dutch destroying oil refineries at Palembang, the Japanese dropped paratroops on 14 February 1942. According to a Japanese account[2] the operation consisted of two separate attacks, both part of the overall plan to destroy allied air forces in Sumatra and neutralize them in Java. The first attack was to capture the airfield at Palembang, but it is the second which is of particular interest because, if the Japanese account is to be believed, it illustrates an extremely effective airborne operation which took the defenders by surprise. The operation was carried out by the 1st Raiding Group and it took off from Kluang and Kahang Airfields at 0830 hours on 14 February 1942. Dropping began at 1120 and was completed by 1130. Bomber and fighter cover was provided and 15 allied fighters were driven off. The oil refinery raiding unit, part of the 2nd Raiding Regiment, consisted of one Infantry Raiding Company, a number of technicians, a portion of the Signals Section, and totalled 130 men. This unit was landed in the vicinity of the oil refineries and was successful in capturing almost immediately the nearby firing positions. Sixty allied troops with machine guns were overcome and the central derrick of the refinery was captured by 1330. Demolition was in progress and oil gushing from the tanks. Allied troops continued firing on the tanks with trench mortars, setting fire to them. Fierce fighting continued throughout the afternoon and the Japanese suffered casualties. At 2300 hours the Japanese launched a night attack and the refinery was captured. Counter-attacks became less and, after further attacks by the Japanese, all the derricks were taken by 1000 hours on 15 February. By the afternoon the mopping-up of the defenders was complete. Although one refinery was blown up by a time fuse, the Japanese claimed to have captured 250,000 tons of oil in the refineries. The refineries were defended by 550 allied troops with 10 anti-aircraft machine guns and, in the words of the Japanese report,

---

[1] Maltby Report, Operations in Malaya and N.E.I., paras. 455 to 462.
[2] Vol. XXVII, Aerial Activities Java Campaign, No. 72, Air Operations in Java and Sumatra. (Copy held by A.H.B.)

" the enemy airfield and oil refineries had been occupied before their destruction, after overcoming various obstacles. The operation contributed greatly to future operations." According to the Japanese, their losses were 28 killed (three due to parachute failures) and a few aircraft.

Exactly a week later another operation took place at Timor in conjunction with the main attack on Koepang. Some 25 Douglas type transport aircraft were used to drop about 350 troops near the allied forward positions. There was no opposition and the operations were successful, thus the position was easily taken by the seaborne forces who landed on 22 February 1942.

During the remaining three years a few minor operations were carried out. Two in particular were designed to sabotage American aircraft in Leyte in November and December 1944. The first operation was completely abortive, all the troops carried in the three aircraft being destroyed. The second on 6 December was larger, 300 paratroops were dropped from about 40 Topsy land based transport aircraft, 18 of which were shot down. The object of this drop was to seize airstrips and to paralyse Allied main bases, but in the main most of these attacks were unsuccessful and little damage was done to important installations although the Japanese had trained specially for the operation. Within a week all the parachutists had been liquidated and the enemy had achieved none of his major objectives.

Italian Airborne Forces

As early as 1927 training for about 250 airborne troops was started but nothing was heard of them again until 1937 when manoeuvres and training for parachutists were carried out in Libya. By 1939 there were two trained parachute battalions in Libya and a further two battalions of native troops were ready in the following year, making a total of some 700 trained men. Throughout the war the Italians carried out only one parachute operation, and that a small one, to capture the Island of Cephalonia off the west coast of Greece. Otherwise the airborne troops were used in ground roles, although a large training centre was maintained at Tarquinia. The total strength was one Division, comprising about 5,000 men. In March 1942 an airborne attack on Malta was contemplated by Hitler and Mussolini and the Italian airborne division trained for it but the operation never took place.

CHAPTER 14

CONCLUSIONS

This concluding chapter has been written to summarise as succinctly as possible the principal lessons and conclusions from the air viewpoint arising out of the development and operation of airborne forces in the Second World War. As the narrative only covers the period of hostilities, it should be borne in mind that the contents of this chapter are related solely to the 1939-45 period. It may be that subsequent development and research on the subject of airborne forces has materially altered or revised the conclusions expressed herein.

The following three major factors indigenous to the employment of airborne forces should always be taken into account before contemplating a large scale operation:—

Air Superiority

To ensure a successful airborne operation local air supremacy must be established and maintained. Airborne forces at any time provide an easy target for ground, sea or air attack. It is necessary also to neutralise as far as possible enemy ground defences before, during and immediately following the operation. Thus a detailed anti-flak plan must be prepared. In operation Varsity considerable damage was sustained by aircraft flying at low level from small arms fire. During the North African campaign the Germans learned the danger of transport operations without air supremacy—losing many of their aircraft crossing the Mediterranean.

Moral effect on the enemy

The dropping of airborne forces in the rear of the enemy lines has a moral effect out of all proportion to the size of force employed. This factor should be utilised to the fullest extent by the planners of an airborne operation. The timing of an operation may have a considerable psychological impact on the enemy in addition to the direct military effects. The use of airborne forces against an area where the enemy population is unprepared or where defence measures are disorganised, greatly enhances its chances of success. The German operations in Crete and Norway, and the Japanese at Penambang, Sumatra, took full advantage of this fact.

The " freezing " of transport aircraft

Probably the main drawback to the launching of a large scale airborne operation is the fact that, both for training purposes and when airborne forces are being maintained at readiness for sudden demands, large numbers of transport aircraft may be tied up when they might be better employed elsewhere on normal transport duties[1].

---

[1] See Chapter 8.

The above conclusions are mainly of a strategic nature; it remains now to deal with the tactical aspect of the air transport of airborne forces. In general the narrative as a whole has not dealt at length with the fate of paratroops once they have left the aircraft or gliders after being released from their tugs. Thus unnecessary duplication of the War Office monograph on the same subject has been avoided wherever possible[1].

Command

The overall command of the air operations should be vested in one air commander at the highest possible level, to act as adviser on airborne matters to group or Army commanders and through whom all requests for airborne forces should be made. If possible he should be the Tactical Air Force commander of the theatre. This lesson was put into practice for the Rhine crossing with successful results.

As regards the control of the transport operations, including the airborne tasks, experience indicated that a central authority responsible for the overall transport commitments should be created on the principle of an Allied Combat Cargo Task Force which would function under the direct control of the Supreme Commander of the theatre, who would be best qualified to estimate long and short term priorities for air-lift. The diversified control to which No. 46 Group was subjected during the last year of the war—under S.H.A.E.F. for operational direction, First Allied Airborne Army for Airborne tasks and 2nd T.A.F. for the transport role—could not make for cohesive and economical action.

Planning

A high degree of co-ordination between the commanders concerned is essential and, in order to facilitate the rapid mounting of an airborne operation, which may become necessary as a result of the fluctuations of battle, it is necessary to establish a *modus operandi* for combined planning between the staffs of the services concerned. Overlord exemplified this necessity for co-ordination when minute timing arrangements had to be made with the Navy. The planning staff should be informed as early as possible to cut down time factor.

Training

Training of aircrews must be of a high standard. They should have had previous operational experience and special training in low flying, navigation over the sea, judging distances by moonlight and precise accurate flying. Deficiencies in this direction were most apparent in the Sicily operations. The Airborne Force and Air Force Headquarters should be located as near as possible to one another for planning and training.

Intelligence and Briefing

Complete and, wherever possible, up to the minute intelligence of the operational area and enemy movements within and in the vicinity of the area is vital. The lack of intelligence available for the Arnhem operation proved

---

[1] For a more detailed study of the organisation, problems and lessons arising out of Airborne operations from the Army viewpoint, reference should be made to the War Office monograph, " The History of Airborne Forces ".

very costly. Adequate time must be allowed for briefing. In Overlord insufficient time was allowed and there was a shortage of briefing equipment. There must always be a good supply of maps, photographic intelligence of the area and models of the objectives.

Day or Night

Opinions varied as to the relative advantages and disadvantages of operating by day or night. Both were carried out on a large scale. Night operations for paratroops were found to be practicable—especially under favourable conditions—half moon, no cloud. Paratroops should be dropped in short sticks at night to facilitate linking up on the ground. They increased the surprise element for the enemy and were less liable to interference from enemy air and ground attack.

Experience seemed to show (at that time) that large scale glider operations by night were not practicable, as in Sicily, but small numbers as in the *coup de main* landings in Normandy, were possible. Daylight operations were generally regarded as being more favourable. Given a high degree of air supremacy over the area, the risk from flak and other opposition was outweighed by freedom from collision, simplification of navigation and ease of forming-up for the troops after landing.

Navigation

In any airborne operation it is vital that the Air Forces deliver the troops at the right time and in the right place; thus a very high standard of navigational training is required. Experience in Normandy and Sicily proved that it is essential for each crew to be capable of its own navigation. The follow-my-leader principle so ineffective in the American operations in Normandy, is not feasible. Although in the future, with rapid development of radio aids, it may be possible to employ a master navigator who can guide the transport aircraft to the dropping zone on a similar principle to the Master Bomber. Radio aids (Eureka, Gee, etc.) should be used wherever possible though crews should be instructed that they are aids to navigation and not the sole means of navigation.

Type of Aircraft

A standard type of aircraft is desirable—one capable of carrying paratroops towing gliders and transport of equipment. The use of several different types, carrying different loads at varying speeds, complicates the task of the flight planners and aircraft loaders.

Tow Ropes

Breakages of tow ropes in flight caused trouble in most operations which involved flying in close formation or through cloud. Other than strengthening the tow ropes, no satisfactory solution to this problem presented itself. Possibly tug-glider co-ordination may be perfected by the production of a composite type aircraft, or the adoption of the "automatic pilot" in the glider.

Launching an Airborne Operation

An accurate and detailed Army-Air Force base organisation is essential to ensure any number of aircraft being airborne in the shortest possible time[1]. All airborne personnel (Air Force and Army) should be trained in loading and unloading aircraft and gliders, packing, stowing and lashing crates and containers. Where possible loads should be standardised to simplify lashing arrangements. Much delay was caused by late modifications to the loads for the gliders in operation Varsity[2].

Gliders and Glider Pilots

Standard type gliders are essential. Glider pilots, whether they be Army or Air Force, require highly specialised training and, although expected to fight on the ground after landing, should be withdrawn from the fighting as soon as possible. Glider pilots should be stationed on the airfields from which their tug pilots are operating in order that a close liaison be maintained, and to simplify training.

Air Support for Airborne Operations

Direct air support is essential for all major airborne operations undertaken when enemy opposition is expected. It should be maintained for re-supply and until the airborne force is relieved. This should include fighter cover for the fly-in; offensive support ahead of the first wave of airborne forces, continuing after the landing; bombing and tactical air force attacks on enemy defensive positions; also, when possible, especially at night, diversionary attacks employing dummy parachutists and noise simulators were found to be most effective. Very close liaison is essential between the Airborne Army Headquarters, the Tactical Air Commander of the theatre, the Troop Carrier Command, the Army and the Air Commander of the area, in order to agree and implement a unified plan for air support.

Communications

All phases of communications are of vital importance to a successful airborne operation. Nowhere was this more emphatically proved than at Arnhem, where communication between the airborne forces—the re-supply units and the air supporting forces—was inadequate. Good communication is also essential between airborne troops and re-supply aircraft so that supply dropping plans may be changed at short notice.

Re-supply

Provision should always be made for supply by air even if, at the time of planning, it does not appear necessary, and, if possible, emergency re-supply from alternative bases should be arranged in the event of non-operational weather at the original ones. Automatic re-supply should be planned as soon as possible after the drop on D Day in the event of unfavourable weather on the following day or days or in case ground formations do not link up as planned. Initial re-supply is an integral part of planning for airborne operations. Bases for re-supply aircraft should be obtained as near as is practicable and, where possible, in the same weather area as

---

[1] See Appendix 3.
[2] See Appendix 9.

that in which the airborne forces are operating. Thus advantage of unforeseen changes in weather conditions may be taken. In the Arnhem operation the difference in weather between the United Kingdom and Arnhem greatly complicated the task of the re-supply forces.

The following conclusions have a more general bearing on the operation of airborne forces and concern mainly the airborne elements as distinct from the Air Forces. Their significance is such, however, that they are of interest.

Dropping an airborne force in one lift

It is always desirable to transport the part of an airborne force most essential to the early stages of the operation in one lift provided that there is an adequate supply of transport aircraft. When the lift is split, as at Arnhem, the effective strength of the force is greatly reduced. Part of the first lift has to be used to protect the landing of the second, and the enemy may have time to recover from the initial surprise, which is one of the salient advantages of airborne operations. There is, however, a possible advantage which may result from splitting the lift in that it may disorganise the enemy defence plans and confuse them as to the main objectives of the landing. It was found that a diversionary effort need not necessarily be large—a few paratroops can cause considerable consternation. All troops and supplies essential to the initial success of the operation should be landed on the first lift, or if this is not possible, at least on the same day. In the Rhine crossing the whole force was dropped within an hour—one of the main reasons for the success of this operation.

Dropping/Landing Zones

These should always be chosen as near as possible to the objectives. Their selection is a joint Army/R.A.F. task. The risk of ignoring this principle is sometimes justified in the case of small operations, such as the landing of *coup de main* parties in the early stages of an operation. The fact that they were not, was a major contributory cause to the failure of operation Market. From the air view point the zones should be easily recognisable. It is advisable to reconnoitre for suitable sites for dropping zones in advance of ground operations in order to save time should an airborne operation be requested at short notice. Care should be taken, however, to avoid drawing unnecessary attention of the enemy to any intended dropping zones. Whenever possible the leaders of airborne formations should, prior to the actual operation, be flown over the areas of the dropping zones to familiarise them with topographical features, thus simplifying identification under the stress of operational conditions.

The experience gained and the results of airborne operations in the Second World War give sufficient indication of their value in modern warfare. Examples of every kind of operation were carried out in various parts of the world. Gliders were towed by night and by day over vast areas of sea, jungle and enemy-held territory, with degrees of success varying from the ill-fated attack on the heavy water plant in Norway and the mistakes at Sicily, to the model operations of Normandy and the Rhine. The part played by paratroops ranged from the individual dropping of agents in numerous countries to the large scale lifts in Normandy and Holland.

APPENDIX 1
THE GLIDER

A. Introduction

1. This Appendix contains descriptions of the main types of gliders used by airborne forces during the war—Hotspur, Horsa, Hamilcar, Hadrian—but does not deal with those types such as the Hengist, which were not used. Detailed specifications are given at Annexure I.

B. Hotspur

2. The original conception of the Hotspur was for an eight seater glider capable of a very long approach, the idea in those days being to cast off at a considerable altitude and glide in, so that the sound of the tug aircraft would not give warning of the attack. A best gliding angle not steeper than 1 in 24 was required for this purpose, and it was intended that each aircraft should be used for one flight only. Thus an aircraft of considerable aerodynamic refinement was required, but it also had to be cheap and simple to construct. These requirements were put to the designers, The General Aircraft Company Ltd. in June, 1940, during the Dunkirk evacuation and the Hotspur Mark I was produced to meet them. This had a wing span of sixty-two feet and an aspect ratio[1] of 12, a fuselage of the best known shape, a jettisonable undercarriage, and a gliding angle very little inferior to a high performance sailplane. The first flight of this aircraft took place on 5 November 1940 a little over four months from its original conception.

3. The Hotspur Mark I had a "lid" type fuselage. The whole of the fuselage top, or lid, could be thrown off in a few seconds by the troops, who then jumped out over the sides of the boat shaped lower half. However, in October, 1940, the official view had changed somewhat, and it was thought that parachute troops might be dropped from gliders. A new type of fuselage was therefore introduced, of more conventional type, with two side doors for jumping.

4. At about the same time, there was another most important change in policy, and it was decided that the tug aircraft would go right in to the landing zone at low altitude and that a very steep approach would be made. This was of course a complete reversal of the original requirements, necessitating a more robust aircraft, with little emphasis on good gliding qualities. The Mark II glider was therefore introduced, having a reduced wing span of forty-six feet, which raised the strength factors by fifty per cent. and caused a twenty per cent. increase in the minimum gliding angle. The second type of fuselage was used on this mark. A further increase in angle of glide was obtained by using a brake parachute, but this method did not get beyond the experimental stage.

5. As far as is known, no operational flights were made with Hotspurs, as the Horsa came along soon after, and the Hotspur was relegated to training. This represented a further change of the original policy as the aircraft had been designed for a very short flying life. There was a scheme to use Hotspurs as freighters on a quick turn round basis using pre-packed freight trays for the Normandy invasion, but this did not take place.

---

[1] The ratio between the wing-span and the width of the wing.

6. When work was started on the Hotspur, little was known about multiple towing, but the aircraft were originally fitted with nose and tail hooks, for towing in trains. This was soon found impracticable, as there was no known solution to the dynamic stability problem[1]. They were sometimes towed in threes, each glider having a separate tow rope to the tug.

7. In 1942, an attempt was made to introduce an interim fifteen seater glider by joining two Hotspur fuselages, twelve feet apart, by means of a new wing centre section, the outer wings being standard Hotspur. A prototype was built but the project was dropped, largely owing to the unpopularity of the arrangement with pilots.

8. In all, one thousand Hotspur gliders were built.

C. Horsa

9. The first Horsa glider was the Horsa Mark I which was originally developed as a means of increasing the capacity of bomber aircraft to carry parachute troops. Evidence of this is to be seen in the two passenger doors, one in either side of the fuselage, which was widely separated for simultaneous exits and which are designed to be opened in flight by being slid round the inside of the fuselage. A further tactical use of this arrangement was the ability to fire guns at attacking aircraft. Other such firing points were the aperture in the roof aft of the main spar and a trap-door in the tail. The firing points were never used in action. The method of attachment of the parachutist's static line to the fuselage was to be a short rail just over each parachute door. The parachutist was to hook his line to this rail on approaching the door just before making his exit. Supporting arms and supplies were to be dropped by containers and panniers.

10. Originally six containers could be carried in wing cells. As four of these were located over the undercarriage it was necessary to drop two first, but this was to be the normal technique, as it would decrease the glider's drag and so increase the radius of action. The undercarriage was to drop soon after take-off, on parachutes. On the return to base the glider was to land on its skids. Later, when the undercarriage was normally retained, the use of these four cells was discontinued and the bomb-releases removed from them. For discharging the panniers from the parachuting doors a double roller conveyor was designed but was not a great success and was not used.

11. The means of access to the Horsa I, apart from the two passenger doors was by means of a rectangular loading door in the port side just aft of the nose. This measured 7 ft. $9\frac{1}{2}$ ins. × 5 ft. and was hinged at the bottom edge so that it provided an unloading platform when dropped on to the separate light-weight unloading trestle. A pair of troughs 11 ft. 8 ins. × 6 ins. were used as ramps to ground level. These troughs were used in flight under the wheels of heavy equipment to spread the weight over the lightly constructed floor. The use of the door as a platform was restricted to unloading when it was of little consequence if it was damaged slightly in the process. For loading, however, a large, heavy and robust loading ramp was used which spanned the complete path from the ground to the glider floor.

---

[1] Stability of the aircraft in flight.

12. Originally the only vehicles required to be carried with the airlanded troops were solo and combination motorcycles: it was a remarkable piece of luck that the jeep could be loaded with so little modification. With the necessity to manœuvre heavy equipment round the corner of the loading door from the interior which was barely wide enough the unloading time was lengthy and means were sought to reduce it. Experiments were carried out by Messrs. Airspeeds Ltd. in early 1944 to remove the tail by means of a band of cordtex explosive round the fuselage at the rear of the load carrying compartment. This was successful and this surcingle, as it was termed, was carried on the Normandy operations. It was not however used, which was as well in view of the loud noise it made on explosion. This might have proved disastrous on night operations where as much time as possible was necessary between landing and detection. Meanwhile the R.A.F. Air Transport Technical Development Unit, devised a means of making the tail as a separate unit which was bolted to the main fuselage by eight bolts with ingenious quick-release nuts. A pair of powerful wire-cutters was carried to sever the control cables. A large number of Horsa Mark I gliders were modified in this manner and used in Normandy, the surcingles being carried for emergency use. To distinguish between the modified and unmodified Horsas Mark I they were termed " Red " and " White " Horsas respectively.

13. A development of this quick method of unloading was the design of the Horsa Mark II glider—at first termed the " Blue " Horsa, which would carry 29 passengers and two glider pilots. It had a hinged nose to give straight access for both loading and unloading, the controls to the pilot's cockpit in the nose being ingeniously coupled together by pairs of push rods butting together so that no lock was required. The nose is, of course, a part of any glider which is particularly vulnerable to damage on landing under difficult conditions and the loading door may therefore become jammed. To provide against this eventuality the detachable tail feature of the Red Horsa Mark I was retained in the Horsa Mark II.

14. With the use of the Horsa glider as a means of landing men and heavy equipment, rather than dropping them by parachute, it became normal technique to retain the undercarriage where the range permitted and to land on the wheels. This lengthened the landing run but gave greater control of the glider and enabled a large number of gliders to be parked fairly compactly to avoid obstructing the landing zone. An endeavour was made to shorten the landing run required by developing an arrester parachute system. This system used a pair of 14 foot parachutes which were released from a stowage under the tail just before touch-down. A fully-laden Horsa could be stopped in less than 100 yards with this device. Twelve Horsas were fitted with it and used for *coup de main* assaults on the River Orne bridges and the Merville battery on the night before D Day of the Normandy operation.

15. Another device carried for the coastal battery assault was a Rebecca position indicator, but it is believed that this was not used due to the loss of the Eureka beacon on the ground. Altogether 600 of these Horsa Mark I Rebecca sets were produced but only a few were fitted in gliders.

16. The speed with which the Horsa was originally produced is interesting. Mock-up conferences were held on 15 and 30 January 1941. The first official prototype flight was on 10 September 1941, piloted by Wing Commander

Wilson of the Royal Aircraft Establishment. The development flying was done by Mr. G. B. S. Errington of Messrs. Airspeeds. The first production model was made in June 1942 and in all, about 5,000 Horsa Mark I gliders were made. Some of these were flown in North Africa and in India. As the wood shrank in tropical countries renovation kits were produced. On 17 April 1942, Mr. Errington, at a demonstration flight at Netheravon, flew a "Very Important Personage" load which included Admiral Lord Mountbatten, General Marshall, Major-General Browning, Major-General Sir Hastings Ismay, Wing Commander Sir Nigel Norman, Sir James Grigg, then Secretary of State for War, Sir Arthur Street, Captain Harold Balfour, Mr. Duncan Sandys with Sir Archibald Sinclair as second pilot—a responsible load.

17. The Horsa glider was largely built by furniture manufacturers all over the country and the parts were assembled by No. 41 Group R.A.F. storage units. It is of interest to note that the Horsa chain lashings were developed by Airspeeds Ltd. at the same time as the glider and seven years later were still the standard cargo lashing gear for aircraft and gliders.

D. Hamilcar

18. The Hamilcar glider was the second contribution made by General Aircraft Ltd. during the war period to meet the requirements of airborne troops. It was preceded by the Hotspur which had an all-up weight of 3,600 pounds. The Hamilcar which weighed 36,000 pounds fully loaded, therefore constituted a major development in design.

19. After preliminary conferences and design studies the general lay-out for the Hamilcar was finalised early in 1941. It was considered advisable to design and construct a half-scale flying model. A design team of over 100 draughtsmen and 20 technicians was allocated to the complete task and the resources of the Royal Aircraft Establishment and the National Physical Laboratory were made available to provide structural and wind tunnel test data. The prototype was designed and built in 12 months and successful test flights were made in the early spring of 1942. Flight trials were completed in three weeks.

20. The Hamilcar was the largest wooden aircraft ever constructed during the war. It was designed to carry heavy armoured vehicles, or combinations of vehicle equipments. For this to be done with structural and aerodynamic efficiency, it was necessary to select a wing loading much greater than anything previously contemplated for a glider—21.7 lbs./sq. ft.—and the aircraft took on itself more the character of an aircraft without engines as opposed to the popular conception of the lightly loaded sailplane of pre-war years. With it was developed the technique now so well appreciated in airborne operations—that the time taken to land after release from the tug aircraft should be a minimum, so that the glider is exposed to fire from the enemy ground defences for as short a time as possible. One noteworthy feature of the Hamilcar design was, therefore, the large and powerful wing flaps, operated by servo-pneumatic means, which enabled the pilot to control at will the angle of glide, and to effect a landing in a confined space.

21. Because of its great size, the Hamilcar needed the largest and most powerful four-engined bombers available to act as tug aircraft, and the Halifax had an excellent operational record in this capacity. Apart from the engine

power available in the tug, the successful take-off of a heavily loaded glider depends on the total weight on the tug-glider combination. Consequently every effort had to be made during the design to keep the Hamilcar structure weight within strict limits. This was done with such effect that the aircraft came out eight hundred pounds lighter than the original estimate. The Hamilcar was able to carry almost its own weight in the form of military load.

22. The decision to design the Hamilcar as a high wing monoplane with a nose-opening door was to ensure that, with the aircraft lowered on to its skids, armoured track vehicles could be driven straight out without needing special ramps. They could, therefore, be in action in as little as fifteen seconds after the aircraft had come to rest. To assist in this rapid exit, the vehicle engine was started up in the air before landing, the exhaust pipes having temporary extension pipes to the outside of the aircraft, which disengaged as the vehicle moved forward. In the case of tank and bren gun carrier loads the anchorages, which held the vehicles securely in place in the aircraft, could be discarded instantaneously by pulling a lanyard from inside the vehicle. The forward movement of the vehicle then operated a mechanical device which freed the nose-door lock and automatically opened the door.

23. Originally the Hamilcar was intended to make skid landings when used for military operations. For this purpose it had a special chassis for take-off which could be dropped by parachute (the chassis weighed three quarters of a ton). For more normal purpose the aircraft was fitted with a permanent undercarriage. Developments in the tactics of airborne landings, however, caused a change in technique. The possible landing sites during an operation are usually very restricted, and, in order that they may be used by the maximum number of gliders, they must be kept clear. It was, therefore desirable that the aircraft should land on its normal chassis and use its speed, combined with separate wheel brake operation to steer itself clear of the landing strip. Immediately it came to rest, high pressure oil in the chassis shock absorber struts was released, causing them to telescope and permit the aircraft to sink on to its skids for the vehicle inside to drive out.

24. The variety of equipment which the Hamilcar could carry presented a formidable list and was continually being augmented. Up to a military load of seventeen thousand five hundred pounds (7.8 tons) it included:—

(a) Tetrarch Mark IV tank.
(b) Locust T.9 tank.
(c) Two Bren gun universal carriers.
(d) Three Rota Trailers.
(e) Two armoured scout cars.
(f) 17-pounder anti-tank gun with tractor.
(g) 25-pounder gun with tractor.
(h) Self-propelled Bofors guns.
(i) Jeep and universal carrier with slave batteries.
(j) Universal carrier for 3 inch mortars and eight motor cycles.
(k) Bailey pontoon bridge equipment.
(l) Forty-eight panniers containing equipment and ammunition.

(m) D. 4. tractor with angledozer.
(n) Scraper with Fordson tractor.
(o) Grader.
(p) H.D. 10. bulldozer (carried in three Hamilcars).
(q) H.D. 14. bulldozer (carried in three Hamilcars).

The design and construction of the basic aircraft was only part of the whole problem. Each variation of load required special study in respect to anchorage equipment, as with heavy loads there could be no movement during flight.

25. Special praise is due to the expert team of works personnel who operated up and down the country on the various aerodromes to which Hamilcars were allotted. It was their task to install the formidable series of modifications entailed by the variety of military loads and to be on hand at all times, to advise and instruct the R.A.F. and airborne personnel. During the period prior to Normandy they played a considerable part in the final preparations.

E. Hamilcar Mark X

26. The Hamilcar Mark X Air Freighter was a development of the Hamilcar tank-carrying glider. It was a twin engine, high wing monoplane of wooden construction, having a fixed under-carriage. It owed its existence to the necessity for an increase in the operational range and an improvement in the take-off performance of the tug-glider combination, to enable operations to be undertaken in conditions less favourable than those afforded in England. At the time of the Japanese surrender the prototype powered Hamilcars were undergoing exhaustive tests in the hands of the Airborne Forces Experimental Establishment and quantity production of the aircraft had commenced.

27. The reports of the machines' performances and flying qualities were favourable in all respects. Carefully balanced control surfaces and the provision of servo-trimmers[1] ensured that the aircraft was comfortable to fly throughout its speed range. The Hamilcar's stability was such that its easy flying qualities were maintained either empty or fully loaded and at various centre of gravity positions. The pilot's cockpit was arranged in tandem and was above the cargo cabin ahead of the main plane. All controls were duplicated, the rudder bars being adjustable. Trimmer controls for elevator, rudder, and ailerons were combined in a single unit. Engine controls were grouped on the starboard side. The high-lift flaps were pneumatically operated: the control was progressive, it being possible to stop the movement of the flap in any desired position. The air system was fed by engine driven compressors which supplied air reservoirs capable of storing enough to operate all air services in the event of it being desired to use them with the engines stopped.

28. Access to the cargo space was through the front of the fuselage. The streamlined nose, which had transparent plastic windows was hinged on the starboard side of the fuselage. The entrance so formed was the full height and width of the cargo space, and was 6 ft. 8 ins. high by 8 ft. wide.

---

[1] Mechanically assisted trimmers.

The stowage space was 27 ft. 2 ins. long giving an area of 1,440 cu. ft. The maximum weight carried was seventeen thousand five hundred pounds, when in towed flight, or three thousand pounds with full fuel tanks when operating under the aircraft's own engine power.

29. To facilitate the loading of vehicles and heavy cargo, the undercarriage oleo struts were used as hydraulic jacks which, when deflated, allowed the fuselage to come in contact with the ground where it rested on skids which were permanently attached to the underside of the fuselage. When loading operations had been completed the aircraft was raised to its normal position by recharging the oleo struts by means of hand pumps which were permanently fitted to the axle struts. When not in use the pumps were isolated by stopcocks.

30. The materials used were, for the most part, highest grade spruce timbers and birch plywood joined with waterproof synthetic resin cement. The plywood skin was covered with cotton fabric and protected with a doping scheme suitable for tropical conditions. Highly stressed metal parts were of stainless steel. Mild steel parts were protected against corrosion. All the materials of construction conformed to the specifications adopted by the Ministry of Aircraft Production.

F. Hadrian (U.S.C.G.—4A)

31. The Hadrian was the standard medium glider for American airborne forces, and was used on a number of occasions by British airlanding troops as a result of the close co-operation between them and the pooling of resources which was treated as a matter of course throughout the war. The name Hadrian, applied to it by British airborne forces, was in keeping with the existing series of names for British gliders—Hotspur, Hengist, Horsa and Hamilcar—but it was known by its owners, the Americans, as the C.G.—4A (Waco), being made by the Waco Aircraft Co., U.S.A. It was a fifteen seater troop and cargo carrying high-wing monoplane with rectangular wings, manually operated flaps to assist landing and conventional landing gear. Two types of undercarriage were designed. The first, known as the "training" gear, was fitted with pneumatic-tyred wheels equipped with hydraulic brakes and a spring oleo shock absorber. The second type, the "tactical" landing gear could be jettisoned after take-off in the same manner as that fitted to the early Horsa glider.

32. The pilot's compartment and the cargo compartment were hinged together along the roof, so that the nose of the glider could be raised up, and locked in the open position. In addition the tail could be supported on a jack, so that two hinged loading ramps at the front of the cargo compartment were tipped forward and touched the ground. By this means the cargo compartment could be loaded to full capacity, and jeeps, artillery and motorcycles could be easily run into it. To unload a jeep after landing, a cable and pulley system from the nose of the glider was attached to the rear bumper of the vehicle. On driving the jeep forward this cable pulled the nose up, and was then automatically uncoupled as the jeep moved on. Apart from this device, the nose could be opened and closed by hand.

ANNEXURE I

Glider Mark	Wing Span	Length	Passengers	Internal Dimensions of Fuselage	All-up Weight	Military Load
Hotspur I	61 ft. 11 ins.	39 ft. 3 ins.	8	—	3,600 lbs. (1·6 tons)	
Hotspur II	45 ft. 11 ins.					
Hadrian (U.S.C.G.-4A)	83 ft. 8 ins.	48 ft. 4 ins.	15	13 ft. 2 ins. 5 ft. 10 ins. 5 ft. 6 ins.	7,500 lbs. (3·3 tons)	3,750 lbs. (1·7 tons)
Horsa I	88 ft.	67 ft.	29	34 ft. 4 ft. 6 ins.	15,500 lbs. (6·9 tons)	6,900 lbs. (3·1 tons)
Horsa II					15,750 lbs. (7·0 tons)	
Hamilcar	110 ft.	68 ft.	40	27 ft.	36,000 lbs. (16·1 tons)	17,400 lbs. (7·8 tons)
Hamilcar X: Towed flight				8 ft.	47,000 lbs. (21 tons)	
Solo flight				6 ft. 8 ins.	32,000 lbs. (14·5 tons)	3,000 lbs. (1·3 tons)

APPENDIX 2

THE PARACHUTE

1. The Germans were quick to realise the possibilities of parachute troops after they had seen the Russian demonstration in 1936. By the spring of 1937 they had decided to use an automatic parachute for their new parachute forces. By the outbreak of war, this type of equipment had been produced by both American and British manufacturers. Previous R.A.F. parachutes, required only for emergency use, were operated by the wearer, pulling a rip cord after he had jumped out of the aircraft. He had to estimate when to open his parachute and needed his hands free to operate it. Such a method was used in the summer of 1940 by the Central Landing School, but was found to be unsuitable for army parachute troops, who would be required to jump in groups instead of singly, and from the lowest height consistent with safety carrying heavy equipment. So the school soon changed to a parachute of American design.

2. This parachute was securely attached to a strong point on the aircraft by a length of material known as a static line. The other end of this line was attached to the apex or top of the parachute canopy by a weak link, the slack or lazy cord. As the jumper fell from the aircraft, the parachute was pulled from the pack on his back, canopy first, followed by the rigging lines, the cords connecting the canopy to the harness. The jumper's weight then broke the lazy cord, and he was left with a fully developed canopy over him, the static line remaining attached to the aircraft.

3. This method had many advantages over the rip cord type, as the parachute opened automatically at the correct moment without any action on the man's part, thus eliminating the possibilities of failure through the

human factor. As it developed more rapidly, a lower jumping height was possible, making the drop on to a pin pointed area more accurate and leaving the parachutist exposed to small arms fire for a shorter time. But after only fifty-seven descents had been made with this type, a fatal accident showed that, although the method was good, the inherent fault lay in the ballistic instability of the human being. A man jumping from an aircraft twists and somersaults in a peculiar manner. If, as the canopy emerged, the man were twisting, it could catch under his arm, or if he were somersaulting, on his leg, and the resulting friction would break the lazy cord, before the canopy was withdrawn from its pack. The man and tangled parachute would soon hurtle the short distance to the ground.

4. The remedy for this was found by Mr. Raymond Quilter of the G.Q. Parachute Co., Woking. He had produced a static line parachute named the " X " type, which reversed the process. When the man jumped, the parachute pack containing the canopy and rigging lines was broken from his back by a series of progressively stronger ties, and hung from the aircraft. As he fell, the rigging lines were dragged from this pack and by the time the canopy appeared, the man was the length of the rigging lines, twenty-two feet, below. A final tie, holding the apex of the canopy to the pack, then broke and the parachute was fully extended leaving the pack and static line attached to the aircraft. This method of deployment was an improvement upon that of the American pattern being more controlled and simpler, and giving approximately only a fifth of the shock previously experienced.

5. The device was immediately adopted, and despite the somewhat haphazard but extremely keen methods of servicing and the lack of technical knowledge on the part of the parachute troops, twenty-four thousand drops were made without a single accident. It was then found that such was the confidence in the apparatus, that the parachutes were being packed with the rigging line loops broken and in a damp condition, because of the previous continued success under apparently any conditions, and were therefore in a thoroughly unserviceable condition.

6. This excellent start proved that, as the parachute troops were working from a very low altitude, and only wearing one parachute, the system employed was good and worth while perfecting and as the quantity of parachutists was increased from the small numbers originally required, a very determined and methodical approach was made to the problem both at the Airborne Forces Experimental Establishment under Group Captain L. G. Harvey and at the Royal Aircraft Establishment, Farnborough, under Mr. W. D. Brown, both parties working in the closest co-operation with Mr. Quilter. It was found that a number of trained observers to each descent was essential. These observers noticed that whereas a parachutist leaving the hole beneath an aircraft from the front edge always turned round and round, the man jumping from the rear side always tended to somersault. Two reasons have been advanced to explain the first case. It may have been that when the static strop came out of the pack on the man's back it hit his shoulder, and so started him twisting, or possibly it was due to the effect of the slipstream on him. In the second case, the man from the rear side was struck in the shins by the airstream, which made him somersault.

7. Both of these failings were remedied by a new design of pack. In this the strop emerged at the back of the man's neck instead of from waist level, and so was well clear of his shoulder. This strop too required more tension to pull it out, and so counteracted the somersaulting tendencies previously experienced. The methods of jumping and landing were improved, and accidents were reduced to a minimum. There were accidents, however, caused by faulty canopy fabrics, particularly noticeable with silk, and this material was largely superseded by nylon and finally by ramex which proved very satisfactory. In addition, tests were introduced to detect material which was too porous.

8. In the original pack, the rigging lines were carried on a flap at its mouth. A second design and the one used after the end of the war, was produced in which they were on one side, but for a time a combination of old and new was used—the strop in the high position with the rigging lines on the flap.

9. The "X" type of parachute, or statichute, was the standard type employed by British airborne forces throughout the war, and apart from its role as a man dropping parachute it was used in clusters of up to twelve for dropping heavy equipment. Though statistics may often be misleading, out of over half a million descents made in training at No. 1 Parachute Training School with this statichute up to August 1948, only forty-two fatal accidents have occurred, an average of under one in twelve thousand.

APPENDIX 3

STANDARD OPERATING PROCEDURE FOR AIRBORNE AND TROOP CARRIER UNITS

SUPREME HEADQUARTERS
ALLIED EXPEDITIONARY FORCE

| Operation Number | Memorandum 12 | 13 March, 1944 (amended 8 June, 1944 and 4 November, 1944) |

Standard Operating Procedure for Airborne and Troop Carrier Units

Section I. Liaison.
Section II. Staff Procedure.
Section III. Operating Procedure.
Section IV. Joint Responsibilities of Airborne and Troop Carrier Commanders.
Section V. Responsibilities of Troop Carrier Units.
Section VI. Responsibilities of Airborne Units.
Annexure I. Schedule of Planning for Airborne Operations.
Annexure II. Navigation and Employment of Pathfinder Units.

1. Object

The object of this memorandum is to provide a common basis upon which the training and operations of allied airborne and troop carrier units can be conducted, and to define the responsibilities of the First Allied Airborne Army and the Airborne and Troop Carrier commanders.

Section I

Liaison

2. General

Upon receipt of directives or orders to participate in training or combat missions, the commanding officers of the airborne and troop carrier units concerned will immediately exchange experienced and competent liaison officers to act as advisors and co-ordinators on all matters of common interest. Such exchange of liaison officers will prevail through all echelons as soon as assignments are issued down through the commands.

3. Duties

(a) Duties of the liaison officer will be:—

(1) To represent his unit commander at the Headquarters to which he is assigned.

(2) To act as advisor to the commanding officer to whom he is assigned on matters pertaining to his own command.

(3) To co-ordinate all matters involving dual responsibility such as

(a) Joint staff meetings.

(b) Joint briefings.

(c) Availability of equipment.

(d) Provision and implementation of plans, marshalling, and parking and loading diagrams.

(e) Examination of all parallel orders to insure complete agreement of plans and arrangements.

(f) Procurement of equipment and facilities belonging to his own command which are required by the command to which he is assigned.

(g) In the case of lower echelons, to act as airfield co-ordinator in conjunction with his opposite number.

(h) Preparation of joint reports.

Section II

Staff Procedure

4. Planning

(a) The sequence of planning and detail of matters requiring decision are set out in the Schedule of Planning attached at Annexure I. *This Schedule will be adhered to throughout all stages of planning.*

(b) At the earliest possible date after receipt of directives or orders to participate in joint training or combat mission, the commanding officers involved will meet in a joint planning conference, accompanied by such staff officers, unit commanders and liaison officers as are necessary, and will arrive at complete agreement on all matters pertaining to the mission and its accomplishment.

5. Air Movement Table

The issuing of the completed Air Movement Table with the associated assignments of transporting and transported units to airfields must be accomplished at this stage in order that detailed planning and arrangements of lower echelons may be completed at the earliest possible date.

6. Planning and Conference Centre

A combined planning and conference centre will be established with the necessary communications to units concerned.

7. Forms

(a) Common forms for air movement tables, loading tables, and load manifests will be employed. Additional forms for internal and domestic procedures may be used at the discretion of the Formation/Unit commanders concerned.

(b) Standard Forms to be employed are listed below:—

(1) Form A—Air Movement Table.
(2) Form B—(Parachutes)—Load Manifest for Parachute Units.
(3) Form B—(Glider)—Load Manifest for Glider Units.

(c) An inspection form listing the points to be checked will be posted in each airplane.

Section III

Operating Procedure

8. Airfield Organisation

(a) An airfield command post, plainly marked, will be established at each airfield for the use of the commanders involved. It will normally be in close proximity to the flying control building. Both liaison officers and two airforce despatch riders will be located at this command post.

(b) The command post will be connected by telephone with the troop billeting areas, the loading areas, the traffic control officer, and the airfield Private Branch Exchange.

(c) The Command post will be provided from air force sources with a radio equipped vehicle, tuned on Flying control channels, for the use of the troop carrier commander or his liaison officer.

9. Loading of Aircraft

(a) The troop carrier unit commander will provide the airborne unit commander, through the liaison officer, with a parking diagram of all aircraft, including gliders, which will show by number the location of aircraft and the sequence of take-off.

(b) All aircraft, including gliders, will be numbered on both sides of the fuselage.

(*c*) Guides will be provided from airborne units and will be posted at a convenient place, on or near each airfield, under the control of the airborne liaison officer, to direct each truck load of airborne troops to its respective aircraft. Each truck will be numbered to correspond with the aircraft for which it is intended.

(*d*) A reserve of planes and gliders will be maintained at each airfield. Priority allotment will be made by the airborne liaison officer. The time of take-off of allotted reserve aircraft is dependent on the situation at the moment and is the responsibility of the troop carrier unit commander.

10. Tug Glider Marshalling

(*a*) Airfields from which gliders will be launched will be predesignated and will be equipped with additional working and marshalling areas.

(*b*) Marshalling and take-off procedures will be standardised for all airfields in order to provide for complete interchangeability of equipment and crews.

11. Dispatching Arrangements

(*a*) Each airfield will adopt the standard dispatching system outlined in the following paragraphs:—

(*b*) *Para-dropping operations*

(1) The Control Officer will be positioned to the port side and forward of the aircraft so as to be plainly visible to the pilot. The Control Officer will give the executive signals to the pilot to taxi and take-off. Light or flag signals will be given by day and light signals by night (white—taxi, green—take-off, red—stop).

(2) An Assistant Control Officer will be stationed along the runway at a position estimated to be that at which the aircraft will become airborne. The Assistant Control Officer will signal to the Control Officer by white light as each aircraft becomes airborne.

(*c*) *Glider operations*

(1) The Control Officer and Assistant Control Officer will be stationed as for para-dropping operations and will use the same signals.

(2) The Assistant Control Officer will have telephone communication with the Control Officer and the Control Officer with the airfield command post.

(3) A towmaster will be stationed at the position of glider "hook-up". He will signal to the Control Officer by pre-arranged flag signal or white light as each glider is prepared for take-off. As soon as the runway is clear the Control Officer will give the white signal to taxi forward. The towmaster will give a green signal to the Control Officer when the rope slack has been taken up. When the Control Officer has received this green signal from the towmaster and the signal from the Assistant Control Officer that the preceding combination has become airborne, he will give the green

signal to the pilot to take-off. Thereafter the Control Officer stands clear and moves to the next combination, takes up position, and repeats the process.

(*d*) All Control Officers will be operationally qualified officers. They will be furnished with the necessary enlisted or other rank assistants.

12. Pathfinding and Navigation

Navigation and pathfinding activities will be in accordance with Annexure II to this memorandum.

13. Formation

(*a*) Standard formations are prescribed in order to expedite training and to simplify procedures. However, it is recognised that special situations may demand a variation from the standard. Such variations will be mutually agreed to by airborne and troop carrier commanders concerned and approved by the next higher headquarters.

(*b*) *Parachute dropping formation*

(1) British aircraft, by day, will fly in a column of three ship Vs. British aircraft, by night, will fly by single ships on concentrated accurate timing.

(2) American aircraft will fly four ship Vs in V, day and night.

(*c*) Jump altitudes will be not less than 400 feet by day and 500 feet by night above the highest terrain in the drop zone. During the drop, the C-47 aircraft will fly in the " tail-up " position.

(*d*) *Glider tug formation*

(1) British combinations, by day, will fly in three " streams " aircraft line astern. British combinations, by night, will fly in single units on concentrated accurate timing.

(2) American combinations will fly in a column of two to four units echeloned to the right or left, both day and night.

14. Troop Procedure Aboard Aircraft, including Signals

(*a*) *C.47 type troop carrier*

(1) Twenty (20) minutes from the DZ, pilot will alert the jump-master (U.S.)/stick commander (BR), who will make an initial check of men and equipment.

(2) Four (4) minutes from the DZ, pilot will turn on red light.

(3) When over the DZ with the aircraft in the proper attitude the pilot will turn on the green light as the " go " signal. The flashing on of the green light is a command to " go " at that instant.

(4) The jump will be made on the green light unless some condition in the aircraft precludes a safe exit.

(5) Prior to take-off, the jumpmaster (U.S.)/stick-commander (Br.) will instruct the crew chief (U.S.)/bomb-aimer or navigator (Br.) in the correct procedure for the release of the parapacks. When the red light is flashed on, the crew chief (U.S.)/bomb-aimer or navigator (Br.) will take his position forward of the door, wearing his interphone helmet, so as to provide alternative means of communication in the event of failure of the green light.

(b) *British bomber type troop carrier*

For troops jumping from British bomber type aircraft there will be a twenty minute warning as in 14a (1) above. A final warning will be given when there are five minutes to go. The red light will be turned on fifteen (15) seconds before reaching the DZ. Troops will jump upon the green light being turned on.

15. Procedure for Signalling to Glider

(a) Ten (10) minutes warning of cast-off will be given to the glider pilot by the tug pilot.

(b) Command to cast-off will be given by the tug pilot when at appropriate position on the approach leg.

(c) Warning and order to cast-off will be given over the intercom system and confirmed by Aldis lamp. In the absence of intercom facilities, complete reliance will be placed in the Aldis lamp.

(d) If, in the opinion of the tug pilot, the glider pilot has not released when he should have done so, the tug pilot will release the glider so that it will land in the landing area.

Section IV

Joint Responsibilities of Airborne and Troop Carrier Commanders

16. General

Unit commanders will be jointly responsible for reaching complete agreement and understanding on all points contained in the Planning Schedule (Annexure I) and will issue the necessary orders in such detail as to enable commanders of lower units to proceed to training and arrangements with the fullest understanding of the problems involved.

17. Requirements

Commanding officers of units on battalion and group level will require that:—

(a) Pilots and troop commanders understand and prepare the appropriate parts of all forms.

(b) Each pilot signs his copy of Form B and has it available upon the arrival of the airborne troops. Each troop commander will have his copy of the form completed upon arrival at the aircraft and will compare with the pilot for correctness of assignment.

(c) Pilot and jumpmaster (U.S.)/stick-commander (Br.) carry out the prescribed inspection of aircraft and equipment and complete Form B by signing in the proper place certifying that the inspection has been made.

(d) Upon completion of the Form B, two copies are left with the Airborne Liaison Officer, one for air records, and one for ground records. Additional copies will be furnished as required by higher headquarters in each situation. One copy will be retained by the troop commander in order that he may make a check of his personnel after landing on the D.Z. or L.Z.

Section V

Responsibilities of the Troop Carrier Commander

18. Troop Carrier Commanders

A troop carrier commander will be responsible for the execution of all items contained in the check list of the planning Schedule (Annexure I attached) in so far as they apply to his level. He will reach a complete agreement with his opposite airborne commander on all matters.

19. Group and Squadron Commanders

Commanding officers of groups and squadrons will be responsible for:—

(a) Taping of doorway and projections.

(b) Proper functioning of lights, accessories, bundle or bomb racks, radio, R/E. intercom, visual signals, etc.

(c) Providing all air force accessories and special equipment required by an airborne unit for a particular operation, e.g. R/E. equipment.

(d) Providing emergency equipment including air/sea rescue equipment.

(e) Conducting air/sea rescue drills and ditching procedure.

(f) Completion of all forms applicable to their units.

20. Prior to Emplaning

(a) The first pilot will accompany the jumpmaster (U.S.)/stick-commander (Br.) in the inspection of the aircraft as outlined on the aircraft inspection card posted in the aircraft. He will also be present during the loading of the containers.

(b) The crew chief (U.S.)/bomb-aimer or navigator (Br.) will check the correct functioning of the container release mechanism and will be present when the containers are loaded by the parachute troops, to ensure correct loading. He will receive detailed instructions from the jumpmaster (U.S.)/stick-commander (Br.) regarding the time of release of the containers.

(c) The pilot will make final mechanical check of the aircraft thirty (30) minutes prior to time of emplaning.

(d) The pilot will immediately advise his commanding officer and the airborne liaison officer if his aircraft will not be able to take off on schedule, and will assist in the transfer of the load to the spare aircraft assigned.

21. During the Drop

(a) The pilot will maintain the prescribed altitude, attitude and speed prescribed for each type of aircraft.

(b) The pilot in C-47 aircraft, bomb-aimer in British bomber type aircraft, will give the warning and jump signals.

(c) The crew chief (U.S.), bomb-aimer or navigator (Br.), will comply with instructions concerning the release of containers and will determine that containers have been released. He will notify the pilot when all men have jumped and when the containers have been dropped. The pilot will then release the automatic salvo switch.

(d) The crew chief (U.S.), bomb-aimer or navigator (Br.), assisted by the radio operator or other designated crew member, will pull in static lines and will turn them and any equipment left in the aircraft over to the parachute unit upon landing.

22. Gliders

The loading, inspection and handling of gliders will be accomplished as outlined for the airplane in so far as it applies.

Section VI

Responsibilities of the Airborne Commander

23. Airborne Commanders

The Airborne commander will be responsible for the execution of all items contained in the check list of the Planning Schedule (Annexure I attached) in so far as they apply to his level. He will reach complete agreement with his opposite troop carrier commander on all matters.

24. Parachute Battalion Commanders

Commanding officers of parachute battalions will be responsible for:

(a) Packing of equipment containers, and loading to prevent incorrect distribution of weight and improper balance of the aircraft.

(b) Loading of the aircraft and container racks in the presence of the pilot and crew chief (U.S.), bomb-aimer or navigator (Br.).

(c) Completion of airborne portion of Form B—(Parachute).

(d) Procuring and fitting of parachutes for both troops and containers.

(e) Briefing of parachute troops.

(f) Movement of troops to take-off airfields.

25. Glider Unit Commanders

Commanding officers of glider units will be responsible for:

- (*a*) Preparation of loads for gliders in accordance with approved published practices.
- (*b*) Loading of gliders in the presence of the glider crew.
- (*c*) Completion of the Form B—(Glider).
- (*d*) Briefing of glider troops.
- (*e*) Movement of troops to take-off airfields.

By command of General Eisenhower.

SCHEDULE OF PLANNING FOR AIRBORNE OPERATION

ANNEXURE 1 TO APPENDIX 3
to SHAEF Op. Memo. No. 12
dated 13th March, 1944
(Issued 4th November, 1944)

	A.1 INITIAL PLANNING CONFERENCE by FAAA with Airborne and Air Commanders involved	B.1 INITIAL STUDIES—AIRBORNE COMMANDER	C.1 CONFERENCE BETWEEN THE AIRBORNE AND TROOP CARRIER COMMANDER	D.1 PLANS AND ORDERS OF AIRBORNE COMMANDER
DIRECTIVE FROM SHAEF — CONFERENCE FAAA WITH APPROPRIATE ARMY GROUP ON OUTLINE PLAN — ISSUANCE AND DISTRIBUTION OF A PLANNING STUDY BY FAAA	(a) General plan of whole operation.	(a) Mission and plan of action of Unit upon landing.	(a) Number and types of available aircraft.	(a) Training programme.
	(b) Mission of the Airborne units to include general destination date and approximate hour of landing.	(b) Strength and composition of Unit.	(b) Load capacity of each type of aircraft.	(b) Rehearsal plans.
	(c) Command and composition of airborne units.	(c) Equipment and weapons to be taken within weight limitations.	(c) Definite selection of L.Z.s and D.Z.s.	(c) Initiation of steps necessary to obtain special equipment required.
	(d) Command of and composition and equipment of Air Force units to provide lift.	(d) Composition and equipment of all subordinate Units and their commitment priority.	(d) Pathfinder methods and requirements.	(d) Movement to departure bases and occupation of base bivouacs.
	(e) Operational control.	(e) Lift requirements of subordinate Units.	(e) Size and shape of serial formations.	(e) Loading plans.
	(f) Outline plan for supply and re-supply.	(f) Training and rehearsal requirements.	(f) Order of arrival at D.Z.s and L.Z.s.	(f) Air Movement table.
	(g) Air support plan for convoy and for ground operations.	(g) Supply and re-supply requirements.	(g) Air Movement Tables.	(g) Field orders for operation to be conducted immediately upon landing.
	(h) Airfields available for operation and route limitations.	(h) Amphibious lift requirements.	(h) Allotment of aircraft and airfields to each Airborne Unit.	(h) Supply and re-supply plan.
	(i) Plan for co-ordination with other forces.	(i) Intelligence requirements, reconnaissance.	(j) Communications arrangements in departure areas.	(j) Final briefing, issue countersign, exact destination made known to all ranks.
	(j) Cover plan.	(k) Movements and bivouac requirements.	(k) Supply and re-supply plans.	
	(k) Security plan.		(l) Plans for movements to and billeting at airfields.	
	(l) Planning and responsibility for rehearsal.			
	(m) Intelligence and sources of intelligence including photographs, maps, models and priorities for obtaining them.	B.2 INITIAL STUDIES—TROOP CARRIER COMMANDER		D.2 PLANS AND ORDERS OF TROOP CARRIER COMMANDER
	(n) Signals and communications arrangements.	(a) Availability and status of aircraft, equipment and crews.	(m) Plans for loading to include parking diagrams, timing, and motor transport traffic control.	(a) Training programme.
	(o) Special equipment and administration arrangements including Air/Sea rescue equipment.	(b) Condition and equipment of available airfields.	(n) Disposition of glider pilots, parachutes and containers after landing in combat zone.	(b) Rehearsal programme.
	(p) Navigational aids.	(c) Intelligence information and further intelligence requirements reconnaissance.	(o) Training and rehearsals.	(c) Procurement of rehearsal facilities.
	(q) Arrangements for altering or cancelling operation.	(d) Meteorological astronomical information.	(p) Briefing arrangements.	(d) Procurement of additional service facilities.
		(e) Restrictions imposed by plans for co-ordinating with other Services.	(q) Reconnaissance arrangements.	(e) Loading plans.
		(f) Tentative flight plans.	(r) Signals arrangements.	(f) Movement Table.
		(g) Air support plan and requirements.	(s) Security arrangements.	(g) Intelligence.
		(h) Arrangements at departure airfields to include traffic control and service facilities.		(h) Flight plan.
		(j) Provision of pathfinder aircraft to include system for marking landing, and dropping grounds.		(j) Preliminary briefing of key personnel.
				(k) Traffic control, air and ground.
				(l) Plan for servicing and replacement.
				(m) Field Orders.
				(n) Security arrangements.
				(o) Final briefing.
				(p) Forced landing and air/sea rescue procedure.
				(q) Escape procedure.

ANNEXURE II TO APPENDIX 3

NAVIGATION AND EMPLOYMENT OF PATHFINDER UNITS

1. Organisation

(a) *Ground*

(1) Each Airborne Division will constitute, train and maintain:

British : Eighteen (18) Parachute Pathfinder teams.

U.S. : One (1) Parachute Pathfinder team per battalion.

(2) Teams will consist of one (1) or two (2) officers and nine (9) to fourteen (14) men, and will be reinforced by such protective personnel as the division commander may deem necessary under the circumstances. The teams will be equipped with radar and other navigational ground aids as may be specified from time to time for a particular operation.

(b) *Air*

(1) No. 38 Group R.A.F. will have all crews trained for Pathfinder Operations and approximately seventy-five per cent. of its aircraft equipped with the necessary navigational aids.

(2) IX Troop Carrier Command will constitute, train and maintain a Pathfinder Force on the basis of six crews per Group and three aircraft per Group.

2. Procedure

(*a*) Two (2) or three (3) aircraft with two (2) or three (3) identical pathfinder teams for each D.Z. or L.Z. will precede the first Serial of the main effort, the exact time interval being established by both airborne and air commanders. The leading group of the 1st serial of the main effort into each D.Z. or L.Z. will be prepared to drop as scheduled even though the Pathfinder teams may have been neutralised, and will, in addition, be prepared to re-establish Pathfinder aids for subsequent groups.

(b) *Marking of Drop Zones*

(1) *By Day* :—The standard day marking for each D.Z. will consist of a panel " T ", a code letter, and smoke signals. Both the " T " and the code letter (which letter is to identify the D.Z. and distinguish it from others in the same area) will be constructed from panels or ground strips, each panel measuring three (3) feet by about fifteen (15) feet. The colour and size of the " T " and of the letter will be dependent upon the size of the cleared area, vegetation, and any trees obstructing vision, and will be agreed upon by the airborne and air commanders. White smoke will be employed to indicate the position of the " T ". The " T " will be positioned with due regard to wind speed and direction, shape and size of D.Z., the formation being flown, so as readily to be observed from aircraft running in from Target R.V. to D.Z. The identifying letter will be placed in any suitable position in close proximity to the " T ". The Eureka will be placed within a radius of 100 yards from the head of the " T ". Smoke signals will be placed near the base of the stem of the " T ", with due regard to the wind so that smoke

will not obscure the "T" or the identifying letter. The axis of the "T" will be parallel to the line of flight, with approach, up the stem. The jump signal will be given when the leader of the formation is over or level with the head of the "T". Six panel strips will be used, three (3) across the top of the "T", and three (3) forming the stem. Panels will be spaced one panel length apart (see A below):

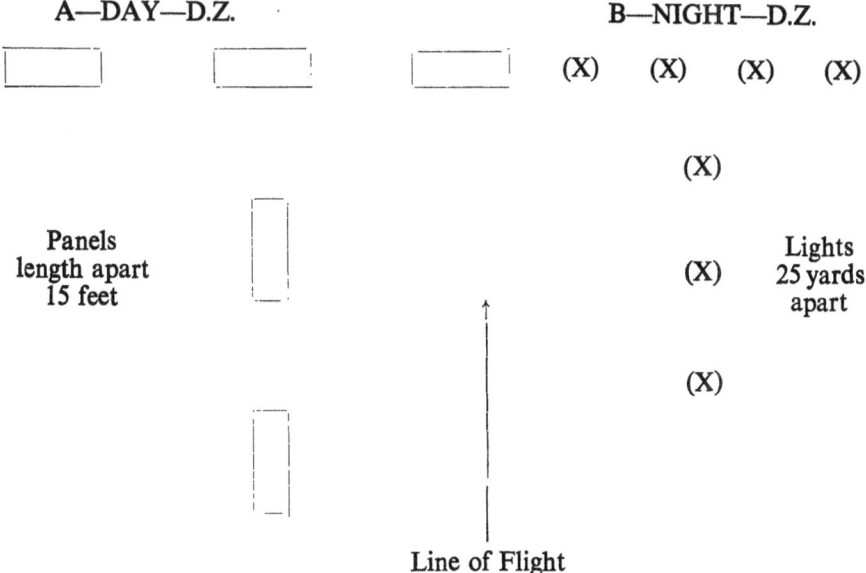

Line of Flight

(2) *By Night* :—The standard night marking for each D.Z. will consist of lights forming a "T", with at least four (4) Holophane lights across the top and at least three (3) Holophane lights forming the stem, all lights being twenty-five (25) yards apart. Lights to be red, green or amber, and with 180° screening. The number and colour of the lights in the "T" at each D.Z. to be agreed between the airborne and air commanders, to meet conditions encountered. The tail light of the "T" will be the code light. The Eureka will be placed within a radius of 100 yards from the head of the "T" (see B above).

(c) *Marking of Landing Zones*

(1) *By Day* :—The day marking of glider L.Zs. will be by panel "Ts", panel code letters and coloured smoke. Panels will measure twelve (12) to fifteen (15) feet by three (3) feet. The "T" for L.Zs. will be laid with the stem parallel to the line of glider landing, and so as to be readily observed from aircraft running in from Target R.V. to L.Z. The direction of landing so indicated will be not more than 90° out of wind, the amount depending on wind strength and on configuration and shape of L.Z. the best compromise being adopted. White smoke will be placed in the same manner as for a D.Z. The Eureka will be placed in such a position relative to the direction of run in of aircraft from Target R.V. to L.Z. that gliders can be brought in to a point where they can execute

a 90° (or not more than 180°) turn, preferably left hand to land into the wind. Code letters marking L.Zs. will be prepared from panels similar to those used for marking "Ts" (see C below).

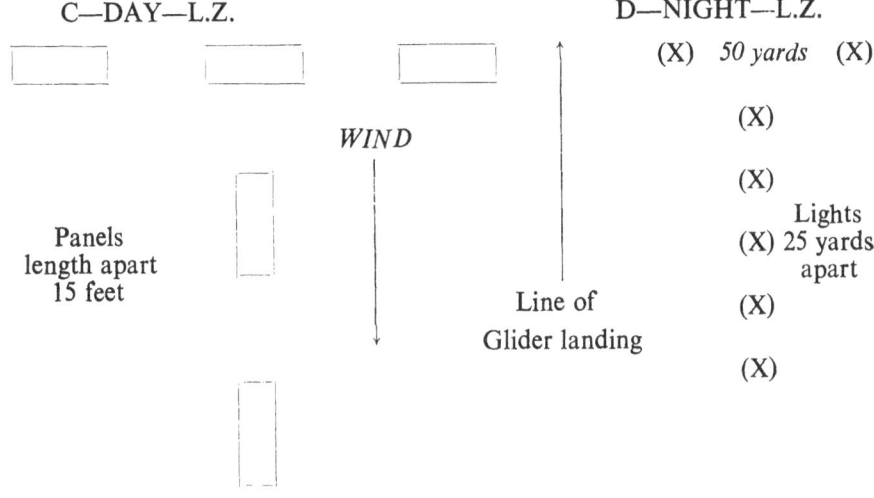

(2) *By Night* :—(The following marking system for glider L.Zs. by night presupposes sufficient light for glider pilots to distinguish individual fields for landing as briefed.) Night marking of glider L.Zs. will be a "T" formed of Holophane lights, two (2) across the top fifty (50) yards apart and at least five (5) lights forming the stem, twenty-five (25) yards apart. The tail light of the stem to be the code light. Lights to be red, green or amber and with 180° screening. The position of the "T" and of the Eureka will be the same as in the marking of L.Zs. by day (see D above).

(d) *Marking for subsequent Group*

It will be the responsibility of the Airborne Unit Commander to make provision for maintaining and securing Pathfinder teams and their equipment in operation until all serials have arrived.

3. Methods of Navigation

(a) Initial Pathfinder aircraft will employ accurate dead reckoning (D.R.) and map reading closely checked by Radar aids and the use of special D.Z. maps for the location of Drop Zones and Landing Zones.

(b) Main serials will be led to the Drop Zones and Landing Zones by accurate D.R. and Radar aids, and utilise Rebecca-Eureka for the exact location of the areas.

4. Airborne Re-supply Dropping Zones

Re-supply D.Zs. will normally be marked in the same way as paratroop D.Zs. Where correct equipment is not available, the same configuration will be used with improvised equipment.

APPENDIX 4

THE AIRCRAFT

During the period 1940-1945 many different types of aircraft were employed in connection with airborne forces. It is not the purpose of this appendix to include technical details of these aircraft but merely to give a brief general description of those most widely used and to list others, some of which were not used, although modified for various purposes. The brunt of the airlift for airborne forces was borne by the following five types of aircraft.

Albemarle (Armstrong-Whitworth)

The Albemarle was designed as a medium bomber and was first delivered to the R.A.F. in January 1943. From that date onwards it played a major role in airborne training and operations being employed by 38 Group as a glider-tug, normally towing Horsas or Hadrians, and as a paratroop carrier. Marks I and II of this aircraft were used primarily as tugs and had an all up weight of 35,000 lb. The practical range of the combination varied between 850-900 miles and radius of action was 345 miles. It would tow either a Hadrian (7,800 lb.) or a Horsa (15,500 lb.).

The Mark V was used mainly as a paratroop carrier, ten of whom could be carried. They were stationed forward of a large dropping hole in the floor of the rear fuselage. Rails were fitted to the sides of the fuselage for the parachute static strops. The extreme practical range at which troops could be dropped varied between 360-820 miles according to weight of equipment carried by the troops, whether or not a beam gun was fitted to the aircraft and climatic conditions. The radius of action was 290-520 miles. Normal cruising speed 130 knots. The Mark VI Albemarle was introduced into 38 Group in June 1944 and differed only from its predecessors in having a large pair of cargo doors on the starboard side.

Dakota

The Dakota (made by the Douglas Co. of America) proved itself to be the outstanding all-purpose transport aircraft of the war and was widely used in all theatres. Although designed as a civil air transport it was easily modified for paratroop dropping (side door) and glider towing. When No. 46 Group was formed in January 1944 it was decided to equip with Dakotas completely and the five squadrons, subsequently formed, contributed enormously to the success of the airborne operations from then onwards. Three Marks I, III and IV were the most used by the R.A.F. and U.S. IX Troop Carrier Command for their operations in Europe. Principally used for re-supply duties and for the carriage of paratroops the Dakota also towed gliders —Horsa (operation Varsity) with radii of action as follows—325 miles Horsa, 350 Hadrian and 450 as paratroop carrier.

Halifax (Handley-Page)

From February 1943 when No. 295 Squadron 38 Group began to re-equip with the Halifax Mk. V in place of the Whitley V until the cessation of hostilities this aircraft took part in all major operations. One year later a second Halifax squadron (644) was formed. The first airborne operation in which

Halifaxes were used was the ill-fated Freshman in November 1942. The Halifax undertook the first long range ferry of gliders in July 1943 when Horsas were towed to North Africa from the U.K. It was also the only aircraft available capable of towing the Hamilcar glider. Owing to its internal design the Halifax was unsuitable for the carriage of paratroop in any degree commensurate to its proportions.

The Mark A III, A VII and A IX were designed and modified to be the airborne forces versions of the original heavy bomber. Instead of the Merlin engines used in the Mark V Hercules VI and XVI were fitted. Marks III and VII were similar and used in the operations in Europe but the Mark IX with an extended wing span, re-designed fuel system and larger dropping apertures was not in service until after the war. The radius of action when towing a Hamilcar was 400 miles, Horsa 600 and as paratroop carrier 710.

Stirling (Short)

The Stirling towards the end of 1943 tended to become obsolete for its intended purpose as a heavy night bomber and although the transfer involved much wrangling at the time between Bomber Command and Transport Command many of them were transferred to 38 Group early in 1944. On all aircraft produced from then on a glider towing hook and remote control release were fitted. Larger and more powerful than the Albemarle the Stirling IV gradually superseded the former until in 1945 six squadrons were operating. The Stirling was used both as a tug and paratroop carrier. When towing a Horsa the radius of action was 525 miles.

The Mark IV Stirling was the long range troop transport conversion from the Mark III. The nose and mid-upper turrets were removed and replaced by fairings but the four gun tail turret was retained. Paratroops were dropped through a large opening in the underside of the rear fuselage. The bomb cells were retained and used for the carriage and dropping of airborne supplies. The Stirling was used throughout 1944 for S.A.S.-S.O.E. operations with considerable success—it could carry 22 paratroops plus 12 containers; had a range of 1,500-2,000 miles and a practical radius of action of over 700 miles.

Whitley (Armstrong-Whitworth)

When the War began the Whitley was Britain's largest bomber but its slowness and vulnerability soon made it obsolescent for this purpose. But the Whitley was not finished. It was used extensively for the training of paratroops and took part in the first important airborne operation—Colossus—in Italy in February 1941. The Whitley proved very suitable for paratroop dropping and was used from the early days of No. 1 P.T.S. at Ringway—in 1940. The rear turrets were removed, a circular aperture cut in the floor of the fuselage and fitted with hinged doors. In January 1942 Nos. 296 and 297 Squadrons were formed at Netheravon as Glider and Parachute Exercise units. The Whitley was used here as a heavy tug to tow Horsas and also as the main parachute dropping aircraft. It remained in service with No. 38 Group until superseded by the Albemarle in 1943. At Ringway the Marks II and III Whitley, fitted with Tiger radial engines, were primarily used. They carried a maximum of 10 paratroops. The Mark V with Merlin engines was designed as a reconnaissance aircraft for Coastal Command and did operate as such but was also employed by 38 Group or Wing as it then was, and had a Radius of Action minimum 500 as paratroop carrier.

The following types of aircraft were all used or adapted for use in conjunction with airborne forces.

Hawker	*Hart*	... A single-engine bi-plane used in the infancy of No. 1 P.T.S. for towing civilian type elementary gliders.
Hawker	*Hector*	... A variant of the Hart used for towing Hotspur gliders at the Exercise unit when No. 38 Wing was first formed.
Hawker	*Hurricane IV* ...	... Single engine fighter capable of carrying and dropping supplies in two 300 lb. containers.
Hawker	*Typhoon F* ...	... Single engine fighter also capable of carrying and dropping a similar load to the Hurricane.
Miles	*Master II* ...	... Fast single engine trainer adapted for glider towing.
Lockheed	*Lodestar*	... Twin engine aircraft smaller than Hudson used occasionally in Far East for dropping.
Avro	*Lancaster I, II, III*	... Most successful 4-engine heavy bomber of the war, capable of carrying 6,000–7,000 lb. of supplies. Adapted for glider towing though never used as a tug on operations.
Vickers	*Wellington III and X*	... A twin engine heavy bomber—adapted for glider towing. Used as a freighter and communications a/c in Middle East 1943.
Vickers	*Valencia*	... Very early type twin engine bi-plane bomber. Used for parachute training Middle East 1941 and at Air landing School Northern India. Its very slow speed made it ideal for " ab initio " training.
Lockheed	*Ventura*	... Twin engine reconnaissance aircraft intended for use by No. 299 Squadron but replaced immediately by Stirlings in 1944.
Lockheed	*Hudson I and II*	... Twin engined reconnaissance medium bomber—it was never used in European airborne operations but took part in minor operations in Middle and Far East. Also used for experimental purposes at Ringway.
Lockheed	*Commando* ...	... D.C. 46. Transport a/c made by Curtis Co. of America, it was first used in airborne operations for Rhine crossing " Varsity " by U.S. IX T.C.C. Probably largest twin engined aircraft in the world and notable for double-door dropping.

Dimensions:
  Span: 108′—1″
  Length: 76′—4″
  Height: 21′—9″
Engines. Pratt and Whitney
    R. 2800–51 Double Wasp.
Max. Speed: 265 m.p.h.
All up weight: 45,000.
Crew: 4
Radius of action: 500 (max. load)
    1,400 (min. load)
Total load 40 paratroops—20 in two sticks from doors each side of a/c.

Westland	*Lysander*	... Single-engined. Used for Army Co-operation—Capable of flying at slow speeds. Used for towing Hotspur gliders.

Aircraft Mark		Maker	Engines	Span	Length	Height	Max. Speed	Range	Max. All up Weight	Crew
Albemarle	I, II, V, VI	Armstrong-Whitworth	2 X Hercules XI Mark I.	77 feet.	59 ft.–11 in.	15 ft.–7 in.	250 m.p.h.	1,350	36,500	4
Dakota (D.C.3)	C.47 I, C.47A III, C.47B IV	Douglas U.S.A.	2 X Twin Wasp R. 1830–92 or 90 C.	95 feet	64 ft.–5½ in.	16 ft.–11 in.	229 m.p.h.	1,500	31,000	3
Halifax	II, V	Handley-Page	4 X Merlin XX or XXII	104 ft.	71 ft.–7 in.	21 ft.–7 in.	270 m.p.h.	3,000	65,000	6
	III, VII, IX		4 X Hercules VI or XVI							
Stirling	I, III, IV, V	Short	Hercules XI Hercules VI or XVI	99 ft.–1 in.	87 ft.–3 in.	22 ft.–9 in.	280 m.p.h.	2,000	70,000	7
Whitley	I, II, III, V	Armstrong-Whitworth	2 X Tiger IX 2 X Merlin X	84 ft.	72 ft.–6 in.	15 ft.	230 m.p.h.	2,400	33,500	5

N.B.—(1) Figures relating to speeds and range are taken from Makers Specifications and bear no relation to those actually obtained under operational conditions. Too many factors—fuel load, altitude, cargo etc. have to be taken into account, therefore to give a constant figure is impossible.

(2) Further details may be found as follows:—

Albemarle ... Air Publication 1688 A. B. F. G. Pilots Notes.
Dakota ... ,, 2445 A. C. ,,
Halifax ... ,, 1719 B.C.E. Ge J. ,,
Stirling ... ,, 1660 A. C. De E. ,,
Whitley ... ,, 1522 D. E. G. ,,

APPENDIX 5

VICTORIA CROSS CITATION

"V.C.—LORD"

Tuesday, 13 November 1945

The King has been graciously pleased to confer the Victoria Cross on the under-mentioned officer in recognition of most conspicuous bravery:—

Flight Lieutenant David Samuel Anthony LORD, D.F.C. (49149), R.A.F., No. 271 Squadron (deceased).

Flight Lieutenant Lord was pilot and captain of a Dakota aircraft detailed to drop supplies at Arnhem on the afternoon of the 19th September 1944. Our airborne troops had been surrounded and were being pressed into a small area defended by a large number of anti-aircraft guns. Aircrews were warned that intense opposition would be met over the dropping zone. To ensure accuracy they were ordered to fly at 900 feet when dropping their containers.

While flying at 1,500 feet near Arnhem the starboard wing of Flight Lieutenant Lord's aircraft was twice hit by anti-aircraft fire. The starboard engine was set on fire. He would have been justified in leaving the main stream of supply aircraft and continuing at the same height or even abandoning his aircraft. But on learning that his crew were uninjured and that the dropping zone would be reached in three minutes he said he would complete his mission, as the troops were in dire need of supplies.

By now the starboard engine was burning furiously. Flight Lieutenant Lord came down to 900 feet, where he was singled out for concentrated fire of all the anti-aircraft guns. On reaching the dropping zone he kept the aircraft on a straight and level course while supplies were dropped. At the end of the run, he was told that two containers remained.

Although he must have known that the collapse of the starboard wing could not be long delayed, Flight Lieutenant Lord circled, rejoined the stream of aircraft and made a second run to drop the remaining supplies. These manœuvres took eight minutes in all, the aircraft being continuously under heavy anti-aircraft fire.

His task completed, Flight Lieutenant Lord ordered his crew to abandon the Dakota, making no attempt himself to leave the aircraft, which was down to 500 feet. A few seconds later the starboard wing collapsed and the aircraft fell in flames. There was only one survivor, who was flung out while assisting other members of the crew to put on their parachutes.

By continuing his mission in a damaged and burning aircraft, descending to drop the supplies accurately, returning to the dropping zone a second time and, finally, remaining at the controls to give his crew a chance of escape, Flight Lieutenant Lord displayed supreme valour and self-sacrifice.

N.B.—This was the only V.C. won by a member of the R.A.F. whilst operating in connection with airborne forces.

APPENDIX 6

GLIDER RECOVERY

On 10 March 1944, a minute from Administrative Planning Section of A.E.A.F. requested information regarding the possibility of recovering gliders after an operation. This had not been possible during the Mediterranean operations and had resulted in considerable wastage, if, therefore, a practical scheme could be evolved for the recovery of gliders a very useful economy might be effected[1].

In reply to this minute Group Captain McIntyre of Airborne Operations estimated that 50 per cent. of gliders used in an operation might be repairable and recovered provided the area in which they landed did not become the battle-ground, and also that they could be recovered within three weeks of landing, in view of deterioration due to weather. But if a special organisation was formed it would be at the expense of aircraft recovery, thus any recovery of gliders in the early stages of Operation Overlord was not feasible.

On 11 April 1944, the Senior Technical Staff Officer, H.Q. A.E.A.F. issued an administrative instruction for the recovery of gliders after overseas operations[2]. Whether or not recovery was to be attempted would depend on:—

(a) Condition and location of the glider.

(b) The effort required for recovery, compared with that of the construction of a new glider.

(c) The overall availability of gliders if required for further operations.

(d) The effect on other requirements of the decision to allocate sufficient priority to glider recovery to ensure that the craft would be fit for further use.

No. 38 Group were responsible for forming a glider recovery unit organised as follows:—

(a) The maximum effort to be catered for was to be 500 men.

(b) The unit was to be self-contained and the figure 500 to include all overheads as well as technical personnel.

(c) The unit must be mobile and would require approximately 90 vehicles.

Air Vice-Marshal Hollinghurst, A.O.C., No. 38 Group, in a letter to A.E.A.F. on 19 May 1944, said that experiments at Netheravon showed that a C.47 aircraft with an 8,000 lb. standard winch could pick up an unladen Horsa, or a laden Waco. Tests had also been carried out at Farnborough with 8,000 and 16,000 lb. winches[3].

It was suggested that pick-up apparatus be installed in R.A.F. Dakotas, or 12 extra aircraft with the apparatus already fitted be obtained. It was recommended that a small pick-up unit be formed in No. 1 Heavy Glider Servicing Unit, who were responsible for the salvage and repair of gliders. At this time there were no C.47s fitted with pick-up apparatus available, and there was little likelihood of obtaining Dakotas fitted with pick-up apparatus in the U.S.A. without several months' delay. It was necessary, therefore, to ask for assistance from U.S. IX T.C.C.

---

[1] A.M. File AEAF/MS/22187.
[2] Ibid Encl. 3B.
[3] Ibid Encl. 4A.

The possibility of retrieving gliders by towing them away from the landing zone was examined by the Air Force Engineer, A.E.A.F., and a landing strip was prepared in the Normandy beach-head by 7 July 1944. No. 38 Group had sent a reconnaissance party of the H.G.S.U. to France on 15 July, who worked on the repairable gliders at the various landing zones. Much of their work was spoiled by enemy shelling and bombing, which wrecked approximately 30 gliders, damage was also caused by Army personnel camped near the gliders. Recovery could not be undertaken until the area was cleared of the enemy. However, a considerable number were ready to be flown out by 17 August[1].

Meanwhile representation having been made to the Americans for assistance from IX T.C.C., approval of an exchange of 12 American C.47s fitted for glider pick-up for 12 British C.47s was received on 18 August. Six of these were allotted forthwith to No. 1 H.G.S.U. in No. 38 Group and three to No. 46 Group, the remaining three were held in reserve. No. 38 Group then issued operational instructions for the removal of gliders salvaged from the Overlord Operation, and 40 Horsas were towed out by the six Dakotas of H.G.S.U., commencing on 9 September 1944[2]. Glider pick-up following Operation Market was not feasible in view of the fluctuating military situation on the ground, but by 12 October 1944, approximately 300 gliders were available for recovery in the American area and a pick-up strip was prepared by the British Airfield Construction Group[3].

Method of Glider Pick-Up[4]

The technique employed by the United States Army for "snatching" a glider of up to 8,000 lbs. all-up weight was described in a report by an R.A.F. observer in the United States.

" American experience is that special training is necessary to teach the crews pick-up technique. The job of the winch operator is considered to demand the most skill, the tug pilot coming second and the glider pilot third. Current experience indicated that it took about three weeks to train a skilled mechanic to act as winch operator, an appreciable portion of this time being occupied with ground training apart from the actual operation of the winch.

The tug pilot was trained by a series of practice approaches and contacts with the ground station. For the first 20 or so practices no glider was used, and it was considered adequate if contact was made with the glider tow-line as laid out on the ground. When this practice had been satisfactorily completed a glider flown by an experienced pilot was introduced and the tug pilot was considered competent when he had made 15 consecutive successful pick-ups. The need for a skilled glider pilot was particularly stressed as tug pilots were often inclined to climb too steeply after making contact.

The training of the glider pilot is simple. He is merely given a short theoretical appreciation of the technique, in which stress is laid upon the need to remain in the low tow position until the pick-up sequence is complete, and also a demonstration of the best method of change from a low tow to

---

[1] A.M. File AEAF/MS/22187 Encl. 24B.
[2] Ibid Encl. 28A and B.
[3] AEAF/TS/22650.
[4] DATPO Folder ABF. 36 Encl. Appendix C(e).

a high tow position. Owing to the fact that the fair lead for the tow cable projects below the level of the tow-plane when the tug flies straight and level, it is possible for the cable to foul the tugs elevators if the glider flies too high. No guard is provided on the tug to prevent this and such precaution is not considered necessary. The average pilot is normally given three or four pick-up practices and is considered competent when he has completed five satisfactory solo contacts.

The installation of the pick-up apparatus in the tug aircraft consists of fixed fittings and removable parts. The complete installation for the 8,000 lb. unit weighs approximately 950 lb., of which about 700 lb. is removable in order to impose a minimum permanent reduction in the useful load of the tug when it is required for other roles. When installed in the C.47 the removal of the detachable unit is a comparatively simple matter owing to the lack of obstructions in the cabin of the aircraft and the consequent accessibility of the unit itself."

Emergency Release

Accidents occurred sometimes when there was no intercommunication between the tug and the glider, therefore a cartridge operated cable cutter was incorporated in the tug installation. This was mounted externally on the cable fair lead of the tug and could be fired from either the pilot's cockpit or the winch operator's station.

Ground Run

The following figures represent the length of run necessary when gliders are picked up by the 8,000 lb. winch:—

Light Horsa—C.47. Ground Run 200 ft.
Light CG.13—C.47. Ground Run 170 ft.
Light CG.4A—C.47. Ground Run 120 ft.

Nylon Ropes

Due to the shortage of nylon all unserviceable nylon ropes were collected and the nylon recovered from them re-generated and used for tow rope manufacture. This procedure came into use in June 1944, but the re-generated nylon ropes were not considered sufficiently reliable for operational use. Nylon ropes were used because they stretched one-third of their total length thereby easing the strain of the snatch.

APPENDIX 7

SUPPLY DROPPING FROM MEDIUM LEVELS[1]

After Operation Market the necessity of revising methods of re-supply by parachute to an enemy surrounded garrison became apparent. The normal procedure for supply dropping by parachute was from 500-600 ft. above ground level, and the dangers of this were obvious when it was considered that re-supply aircraft might have to return to their dropping zones more than once, flying at this very low level into an area where the enemy were fully prepared to stop the supply at all costs.

---

[1] No. 38 Group Report Paras. 127–130.

Therefore, if a method could be found of dropping supplies from medium level a far greater degree of safety for the aircraft might be obtained. In a letter from the A.O.C. No. 38 Group, to S.H.A.E.F. Main Headquarters on 21 November, the following points were stressed.

1. The cost of supply dropping by low flying aircraft was very high. The technique then employed entailed a low release from a thousand feet or below, and also reduction of air safety to the lower safety limit. (In Operation Market 630 sorties were flown by Nos. 38 and 46 Groups, and of these 335 or 53 per cent. were casualties, either missing or damaged.)

2. When the supply dropping point was changed at Arnhem there were no means of informing the despatching authority or supply dropping aircraft. Although a new supply dropping point was marked out on the ground, it was not sufficiently clear to be recognised from the air, thus the majority of the supplies were dropped on the original supply point, then held by the enemy.

3. Preliminary experiments have shown that supply containers can be released from medium altitudes with a delay fuse so that the parachute opens approximately 500 ft. above the ground. The aiming of the container is being reduced to bombing technique using the Mark IX.A Bomb Sight and a special adaptor to the height scale incorporated to allow for the slow rate of fall of the container.

   The delay fuse used for the opening of the main parachute was Type Mark III.A.2, and there was no difficulty in obtaining these. The modification to the container consists of a wire strop and an " L " shaped bracket to the container.

4. It was suggested that the probable height of release of future supplies be between 6,000 and 8,000 ft. according to weather conditions, in order to fly above the worst of the light flak. It might also be possible to release supplies blind by using radar aids. Gee H radar sets were considered to be the most suitable and delivery of two of these to No. 38 Group was requested for training purposes and also a further 38 sets to be available for the equipment for equipping No. 570 Squadron, No. 38 Group.

5. It was also essential to devise a sure method of communication between the ground receiver and the supply aircraft, and the A.O.C., No. 38 Group, proposed to introduce a scheme similar to that existing in Bomber Command. One or two master bombers would have direct communication with the supply dropping point and would issue orders and corrections to the supply scheme by means of V.H.F. radio. The communication between the master bomber and the supply dropping point would probably be done by means of a speech current on the Eureka beacon. Tests with this method had been carried out and speech range from about nine miles had been achieved. The Eureka attachment was very small and the whole beacon, together with talking sets and batteries, could be fitted into the normal Eureka basket of a parachutist.

6. No. 570 Squadron were selected to carry out tests of this new method of supply dropping using Stirling aircraft, and this development progressed during the winter months of 1944-45. On 7 March 1945, the Officer Commanding, No. 570 Squadron, made a detailed report of the subject. A full description of these tests can be found at Appendix Q to Section III, No. 38 Group Report. The conclusions arrived at as a result of the work of No. 570 Squadron were that:—

(a) Supplies could be dropped on a dropping zone of reasonable radius from heights of 7-10,000 ft. The supplies could either be aimed visually or by using Gee H., and possibly Rebecca.

(b) A team of two or three crews were required over the dropping zone for control; a master supplier and deputy to calculate the necessary data to enable the main force to drop correctly.

(c) An accurate forecast approximately four hours ahead was required of the Q.F.F. at the D.Z., and the wind velocity for the time of the drop.

(d) The personnel on the dropping zone would have to be capable of estimating surface wind. The lapse rate and obtaining the correct drift of the containers by use of tables was done in the aircraft.

APPENDIX 8

RADAR HOMING DEVICES

1. In the early days of airborne forces two of the most difficult tasks of the air forces in an airborne operation were first to locate the exact dropping zone for each unit and then to ensure that all aircraft dropped their troops on their correct areas. The R.A.F. presented this problem to their Telecommunications Research Establishment, Great Malvern, who already had equipment which, with very little modification, would solve a great many of the difficulties.

2. The first aid to direction was a navigational device named Gee, from which an aircraft could deduce its exact position. Before the formation of No. 38 Group in the autumn of 1943, this apparatus was only fitted to aircraft in Bomber and Coastal Commands, but after the group was formed, airborne forces were allowed to use it. The second aid was a homing device named Rebecca-Eureka. Eureka was a beacon, set up on the ground and set to receive on one fixed frequency, and transmit on another fixed frequency. Rebecca was carried in an aircraft and transmitted on the Eureka receiver frequency and received on the Eureka transmitter frequency. On receiving the impulse from the aircraft Rebecca set, Eureka on the ground automatically replied, which gave the captain of the aircraft his bearing to and distance from the beacon. This in outline was the Rebecca Mark I. The beacon, a rectangular box with a collapsible aerial was to be carried by the pathfinders of the independent parachute companies, and being

set up on their dropping zones would lead subsequent formations to the correct places. It had a morse key fitted to it, so that the operator could send the code letter designating his particular dropping zone to the Rebecca in the aircraft. With this arrangement however, it was found that an aircraft, approaching adjacent dropping zones where several beacons were in use, would "react to" all within range, thus making it almost impossible to identify the correct dropping zone. Rebecca Mark II and Eureka Mark II were developed to overcome this difficulty. In these equipments five separate frequencies were provided, common to both the receiver and transmitter portions of Rebecca and Eureka. It was now possible to arrange combinations of transmitter or receiver frequencies and prevent both the action of beacons one on the other at close ranges, and reaction to more than one beacon by the aircraft. The increased channels available of course gave added security. The different combinations could be selected in flight on the Rebecca, and by the operator of the Eureka on the ground, though normal practice was that the Eureka was issued pre-set and tested.

3. The original Rebecca-Eureka was sent to the United States where similar equipment working on the same frequencies was produced. This equipment, known as "AN APN2" (Rebecca) was fitted to all aircraft of United States Troop Carrier Commands. American Eureka equipment was also produced, known as "AN PPN1." The Horsa gliders carrying part of 9th Parachute Battalion to Normandy were fitted with a battery-operated Rebecca Mark III, to enable them to home onto their objective, the Merville battery. At the same time, a light-weight beacon, carried in webbing pouches, Eureka Mark III was produced for Special Forces Headquarters. The Eureka Mark II beacon, used by pathfinder companies of the airborne divisions fitted into a normal leg kit-bag; complete with battery and collapsible aerial it weighed only 28 lb., and was powered by a 12-volt battery. In an emergency any 12-volt battery, say from a jeep or civilian car, could be used. The weight of Eureka compared favourably with the 100 lb. Rebecca in the aircraft. Best results were obtained where a direct line of sight existed between the aircraft and the beacon. A hill between the two would drastically diminish the range, but a hill behind the beacon relative to the approaching aircraft acted as a "reflector" and produced a greater range forward of the hill. Wooded country or buildings close at hand resulted in fading and poor results, but with reasonable country for siting the beacon, an aircraft flying at 2,000 feet would expect to home on it from eight to 12 miles away. For a low-flying plane the range would be less.

4. The only operational use of Rebecca-Eureka Mark I was for the abortive attack on the Norwegian heavy water plant in November 1942. During the summer of 1943 the Mark II equipment was hurriedly sent to North Africa for use by No. 38 Wing in the invasion of Sicily. However, it was felt to be too difficult a task in the short time available to fit this new equipment, and it was not used. For the invasion of Normandy 90 per cent. of aircraft using Gee got satisfactory results. Eureka beacons were successfully used to mark group rendezvous, but on the dropping zones several were damaged and others were set up in the wrong areas, and a number of aircraft were misled. More successful results were obtained on the first two days of the Arnhem operations, and in March 1945, over 95 per cent. of the aircraft used it successfully on crossing the Rhine.

5. One other use was made of radar in an airborne role. This was a ground radar set produced as a result of the Arnhem operation and designed as a link between airborne forces on the ground and aircraft. The set, known as a "Dinner Wagon," was carried in three Horsa gliders, and was used by the visual control posts with complete success for the Rhine crossing. It incorporated facilities to control day and night fighter cover, and beacons to enable fighters to orbit dropping and landing zones, and could be used to give warning of the approach of enemy aircraft, as well as provide communications with our own supply planes.

APPENDIX 9

EQUIPMENT FOR DROPPING STORES FROM AIRCRAFT

A. Introduction

1. This appendix shows how the problems of delivering stores and equipment to troops were solved and the reasons why certain types of dropping equiment were produced. It does not go into the technical considerations connected with the development of the equipment.

2. In all the operations undertaken by the British airborne forces during the war, most heavy loads such as transport, artillery and engineer equipment and medical stores had to be landed by glider. But before the gliderborne airlanding battalions were formed, the original parachute battalions had to devise their own methods of dropping with their small arms and equipment, as at that time no suitable equipment existed.

B. Containers

3. At the outbreak of war, the Royal Air Force had two types of equipment for dropping stores. The first was a cylindrical metal container two and a half feet long and one foot in diameter, opening at one end. The second consisted of a wooden beam to which packing cases could be strapped. The limits for both of these types were one hundred and fifty pounds weight and an aircraft speed of one hundred and twenty miles per hour, and they were dropped from the bomb cell of an aircraft by a 10 foot or 14 foot parachute. These methods were obviously not suitable for parachute troops, as not even a rifle could be fitted into the container, and by the box method, it was impossible to unpack the equipment quickly on the ground, quite apart from the difficulties due to the restriction in weight.

4. As a result, the Central Landing Establishment experimented with various designs for dropping stores. The first, produced by the Elliot Equipment Company was a quilted mat, stiffened with bamboo rods, fitted with pockets in which rifles and other equipment were carried. The mat was rolled up, strapped to a steel bar, and had a 28 foot parachute attached to one end. This canopy, similar to that in the X type man-carrying parachute, had to be fitted into a pack the same diameter as the rolled mat, so that it could be carried in the bomb cell of an aircraft. It controlled the design of many subsequent containers, as each type has had to employ existing

pack specifications. The limitations of the roll soon became obvious. Only a very restricted range of arms could be carried, and insufficient of those. In addition, it was difficult to unpack on the ground, and did not stand up to rough usage.

5. The development of the next container, designed to fit into the bomb cell of the Whitley aircraft, was given to the G.Q. Parachute Company, who produced a number for the Special Operations Executive. The Central Landing Establishment designed containers for the Airborne Forces which were known as C.L.E. Marks I and II containers. These were six feet long and fifteen inches in diameter, and again opened at one end only. The first to be packed was stood on end between two pairs of steps. Mr. Quilter and Squadron Leader Miles then held a boy employee of Mr. Quilter's by the ankles and lowered him into the container; in this position he was handed rubber padding and the equipment to pack. When he had had enough he was hauled up for air. Despite its "Heath Robinson" aspect, the container worked in practice but showed the need for some other form of opening. Further types were made to open longitudinally, and eventually a satisfactory model of metal skinned construction was produced which was able to carry six hundred pounds.

6. However, a difficulty arose over certain stores which would not fit into a cylindrical container of fifteen inches diameter, notably wireless sets. Accordingly, two containers were designed, to fit the No. 11 and No. 22 set respectively. Due to modifications to the sets, these containers rapidly became useless, which showed very clearly the error of designing merely "one-purpose" equipment. Later, working on the principle that any container should be designed to the maximum size of the bomb cell in which it is to fit, one was constructed for the two-thousand pound bomb cell in Halifax, Stirling and Lancaster aircraft eleven feet six inches long by one foot six inches square.

7. An example of the problems of the design of containers is shown by the requirements put forward by the Special Operations Executive in one case:—

> "(1) A container which can be carried in the bomb racks of any Bomber Command aircraft.
>
> (2) To be released at approximately 1,000 feet for dropping into water.
>
> (3) To have a negative buoyance so that it will sink immediately, and remain submerged, to be capable of remaining submerged in fresh or salt water up to six months in a depth up to 15 fathoms and to have an anchorage system to withstand a two knot current.
>
> (4) The parachute to be automatically detached from the container on striking the water and to sink when detached.
>
> (5) A marker buoy to be released immediately on touching the water, or at any time up to one hour thereafter.
>
> (6) The container to be capable of being raised by the buoy cable and unpacked by one man in a small boat."

C. **Crates for Loads unsuited to Containers**

8. While the container system was the most desirable for stores and equipment dropping, certain loads could not be carried by this method. Special crates and a range of different sized parachutes were consequently produced for these. Many of these crates could be suspended from a single parachute, such as the three inch mortar base plate and camouflet sets, although certain light and bulky loads tended to somersault in the air, thus collapsing their parachute, and had to be fitted with fins to stabilise them. Use was also made of the standard cradle used for the normal container. By fitting wooden blocks of various shapes, a variety of different stores could be carried, including Bangalore torpedoes and spare barrels for the 75 mm pack howitzer. In most cases the 28-ft. canopy was sufficient but in the case of the gun barrels three 38 ft. chutes were used in a cluster.

9. More complicated crates were required for loads such as motor cycles which were not bulky but had several weak spots that had to be protected for landing. For the 350 c.c. motor cycle an overall framework was needed to prevent damage on the ground, but such a crate had to be instantly detachable. It also had to give support to various components of the cycle which could not take parachuting inertia stresses in their own structure. The motor cycle proved one of the most awkward loads to crate and carry as it had to lie flat in a bomb cell for the bomb doors to be closed, then had to be turned in mid-air to enable it to land the right way up.

10. Certain loads, by reason of their shape or size could not be stowed in the bomb cells but had to be carried inside the aircraft and dropped through the jumping hole or thrown out of the door. A good example of this was the folding bicycle, of very low weight, but inconvenient shape. It covered three bomb positions if placed in the bomb racks and also called for a special crate to be provided. To drop it through the door needed only a parachute and an attachment strap. Some experiments were needed to find the best way of landing it. The obvious way, to make use of the shock absorbing capacities of the wheel tyres, was found to be wrong. In nearly all tests the wheels were buckled, and the cycle useless. It was found that to drop it for final impact on its handlebars was the best. Normally there would be no damage, and although in bad cases, where landings were made on hard ground or in high winds there might be a bent handlebar, the cycle would still be rideable.

11. The success of this means of dropping and the coming of the Dakota aircraft, which at first had no bomb racks, led to the introduction of the pannier, a square wicker basket into which a very large variety of arms and equipment could be packed and which could be thrown from the door of the aircraft. With the introduction of the Dakota in quantities this method was standardised and roller conveyors and other means were introduced into the aircraft to enable the largest possible number of panniers to be ejected in a short time.

D. **Ancillary Equipment**

12. The growth and development of parachute dropping led to the need for several items of ancillary equipment to be used with parachute canopies and crates.

13. *Location Devices.* One of the most important of these was the need for locating equipment that had been dropped at night. Containers were at first camouflaged and even in broad daylight were difficult to locate, and though later a white finish was given, this was very little help at night. Four lamps were fitted to light up on touching the ground, so that whichever way the container lay one was showing on each side. Further, the lights had coloured discs over them, so that certain containers could be readily identified. These lights worked well on flat unobstructed ground, but undulations, however slight, bushes, walls or crops made them ineffective. Alternative methods varied from the use of illuminated jets of water to the scenting of containers and the dropping of dogs to find them. Electric bells could not always be heard in the general noise, and pyrotechnics were discarded as too dangerous in that they were a fire hazard. The final design was a collapsible frame, made up of three legs of equal length, hinged together at one end which when closed could be stowed in a two-inch tube on the container, and when open formed a pyramid with lights and flags at three of the apices, and an impact switch at the fourth. The device was also fitted with a triangular parachute between the legs, arranged so that it hung with the impact switch downward. It was connected to the container by a cord attached to the centre of the upper side of the canopy on the device. The natural springiness of the framework caused it to give when striking an obstruction and to " dance " over rough ground. Radio methods were given extensive trials before they were finally rejected, and by the end of the war, no satisfactory answer had been found, in spite of exhaustive research into the problem.

14. *Delay Devices.* Various delay devices were evolved, to facilitate dropping containers and men together on the ground. It was soon found that the best dropping order for men and equipment was for half the stick to jump, followed by the containers which were released by the action of the last man to jump in the first half. The remainder of the stick then jumped so that on the ground the containers were in the centre of the pattern. This system meant that the man jumping after the containers had to estimate the pause necessary to allow the containers to clear the aircraft. An unnecessary strain was placed on this man, and he might in his enthusiasm jump early and collide with the containers, or for safety delay too long and make a very long stick on the ground. The device adopted eventually allowed the containers to be dropped together and fall free for a period, clear of the men. Their parachutes then opened by a delay action device with an interval between each to avoid entanglement. A second type allowed equipment to be released at a high altitude, about fifteen thousand feet and to fall freely to five hundred feet from the ground when the parachute opened. The object was to allow supplies to be dropped accurately on to a point without forcing the aircraft to fly low, exposed to fire from ground weapons.

15. *Canopy Release Devices.* It had long been known that it was highly desirable for the parachute to be separated from its load immediately upon landing, to avoid dragging in the wind. No really satisfactory device was produced, but designs have been used with some success in dropping heavy standard loads like the jeep and 6-pounder anti-tank gun.

16. *Wheeled Equipment.* It is well known that the parachutist is most vulnerable directly after landing. His arms and stores may be several yards away in a container, and even when he is armed he is encumbered with heavy loaded containers to hamper his movements. Several devices have helped to minimize this weakness, the earliest being a folding trolley. This was a useful vehicle for carrying stores but was not big enough to transport loaded containers, and in any case took some minutes to assemble after it had been dropped. Accordingly, equipment was designed to fit wheels on to containers, and after teething troubles were overcome, an axle and rubber tyred wheels were produced and dropped attached to the container. It could then be manœuvred by two men over rough ground, or towed on roads at up to thirty miles per hour without overturning.

17. *Kit bags and Valises.* At this point it is worth considering the object of all these devices—to deliver a soldier on the ground armed and ready for battle. The parachutist was, up to now, dropped parted from his arms. At the worst the container holding his arms might get stuck in the aircraft, and be flown home again. It might collide with him during his descent, or at the other extreme, land miles from him. He might spend half an hour on landing looking for his rifle or his wireless set. The ideal of dropping the man with his arms was achieved with the development of the kitbag, a landmark in the early days of airborne forces. It rapidly became an indispensable part of the parachutist's equipment and the design, in various guises, was modified to take a variety of stores. The kit-bag was made of canvas reinforced with leather, two and a half feet long and a foot in diameter, opening at one end. Inside it could be packed any stores of that size, such as wireless sets, suitably padded, or a Sten gun in two sections owing to its length, up to a weight which the parachutist could lift—sixty to eighty pounds. The opening was then roped up, and the bag strapped around the man's leg or both legs depending upon the type of door or hole through which he was to jump. As soon as his parachute had opened, the leg straps were freed by the parachutist operating a quick release device, and he then lowered the bag on a twenty foot length of rope, until it dangled below him, secured to his parachute harness by the rope. The bag on hitting the ground first lessened the weight on the parachute, and enabled the man to land unencumbered with his stores, but yet attached to them by a length of rope. In the same fashion, valises to carry a rifle or bren gun were designed and proved invaluable.

18. *Percussion Heads.* Investigation was carried out to find the best type of percussion head to absorb landing shocks. Some designs used springs and rubber but both of these mediums proved unsuitable as the container tended to bounce and somersault on landing. Other designs absorbed the shock by the bending of mild steel members or using aerated plastics which broke and crumbled, thereby dispersing the shock.

E. Heavy dropping

19. The dropping of loads heavier than the standard container, at that time three hundred and fifty pounds, started with the airborne lifeboat, a collapsible boat weighing eight hundred pounds. On account of the fragile nature of the boat, three 32 ft. canopies joined together in a cluster were

used. After development in this field, including the dropping of a six thousand pound midget submarine with a crew of one, it was found that a cluster of twelve 32 ft. canopies could be satisfactorily released. This system was used for the first jeeps dropped in operations. In dropping the jeep it was found that the chassis itself could not possibly take the landing shocks. To obviate this, a sub-frame was fitted under the vehicle and a top frame above, the two connected by rods so that the jeep was sandwiched between two strong structures, which supported it at many points, holding the various heavy units such as engine and axles in relation to each other, a function the normal chassis could not perform under parachute strain. Under this sub-frame were fitted crash pans.

20. The six-pounder gun was fitted with extra supports to hold up certain heavy items, but the whole design was simpler owing to the gun's very robust construction. In the case of both jeep and gun, all projections were faired off by metal fittings or wire rope guards so that in the event of somersaulting any rigging line that became wrapped around the load would slip off. To reduce the somersaulting, both jeep and gun were tilted forward as they fell from the bomb cell of the aircraft; this caused each to somersault against the force of the slipstream, which gave the opposite effect. It also positioned the load at right angles to the parachute rigging lines and produced more satisfactory results.

F. Free Dropping

21. A certain amount of work was also done on the dropping of stores from aircraft without the use of parachutes. The first method tried was free dropping—in general not found to be a successful system, being applicable to only a restricted range of loads such as bundles of blankets, and sacks of rice double sacked with tins of food in among the grain. Liquids were free dropped, but a flexible double container, complicated and expensive was needed. The inner container was almost invariably broken and the whole useless for further work. Attempts to fit " wings " to boxes, resulting in a " sycamore seed " effect were made, but proved to be a complete failure, and this method was not pursued.

G. Summary

22. The development of supply dropping equipment through the war was unfortunately carried on almost entirely on a " trial and error " basis. This was because of the almost complete lack of any knowledge on the subject at the outbreak of hostilities and also because the need to produce equipment under the pressure of operational requirements precluded any long term basic research. In general the system produced good results as equipment was ready as needed but it resulted in a lack of planned development, and the information obtained was largely in the form of trial reports in development files, not an easy form of reference.

23. The various items of ancillary equipment, releases, lighting sets and time lag devices were produced as needed and were capable of almost infinite variety to suit special conditions. Work on other methods of dropping showed that free dropping was of very limited application, that vanes provided

suitable retardation for small loads but were difficult to launch and that rocket decelleration was possible but much work was needed to bring it to a state of development fit for service use.

24. All the work was carried out at the Royal Aircraft Establishment, Farnborough, or the Airborne Forces Experimental Establishment, Beaulieu, these units either testing equipment put forward by contractors or designing and testing their own items.

APPENDIX 10

CANCELLED OPERATIONS, 1945

The following large scale operations were planned by the First Allied Airborne Army to assist the advance of the Allied Armies towards Germany but, owing to the rapid progress made during the early months of 1945, none were considered necessary, with the exception of Operation Varsity[1].

Tripod

This operation was planned to outflank the Siegfried Line North of Karlsrue and assist the advance of the Southern Group of Armies.

Wildfire

Owing to the priority of the preparations for Varsity, this operation was cancelled on 11 February 1945; it had been intended to assist the central group of Armies in their advance to the Rhine[2].

Choker II

The final plan was produced on 9 March 1945 for an airborne operation between Mannheim and Minz to assist the U.S. 7th Army in crossing the Rhine[3].

Effective

This was the last main airborne operation in the European war to reach the final planning stage. It was intended to be launched in the U.S. 7th Army area of Eisingen, near the Black Forest, after 7 April 1945, but was unnecessary owing to the rapid progress of the Sixth Army Group.

Talisman

In the event of a collapse of German resistance or the surrender of the greater part of their armed forces, operations, under the code name Eclipse, were planned to cover this eventuality. Eclipse embraced the whole of Europe, with the exception of Norway and the Channel Islands. To assist the motivation of this plan, airborne forces might have been required to operate in the areas of Berlin and Kiel, seize important targets and contact the Russian forces[4]. With this aim in view the First Allied Airborne Army produced plans. The operations were cancelled on 31 March 1945, when it became apparent that the enemy intended to fight on until the end[5].

---

[1] File DSC/TS. 100/14 Part II Encl. 4A.
[2] Ibid. Encl. 12A.
[3] Ibid, Part III Encl. 6A.
[4] S.H.A.E.F./GCT/370.43/Plans 29/10/44.
[5] 2nd T.A.F./301402/1/Plans, Encl. 28A.

APPENDIX 11

DIAGRAM OF COMMUNICATIONS FROM H.Q. I AIRBORNE CORPS

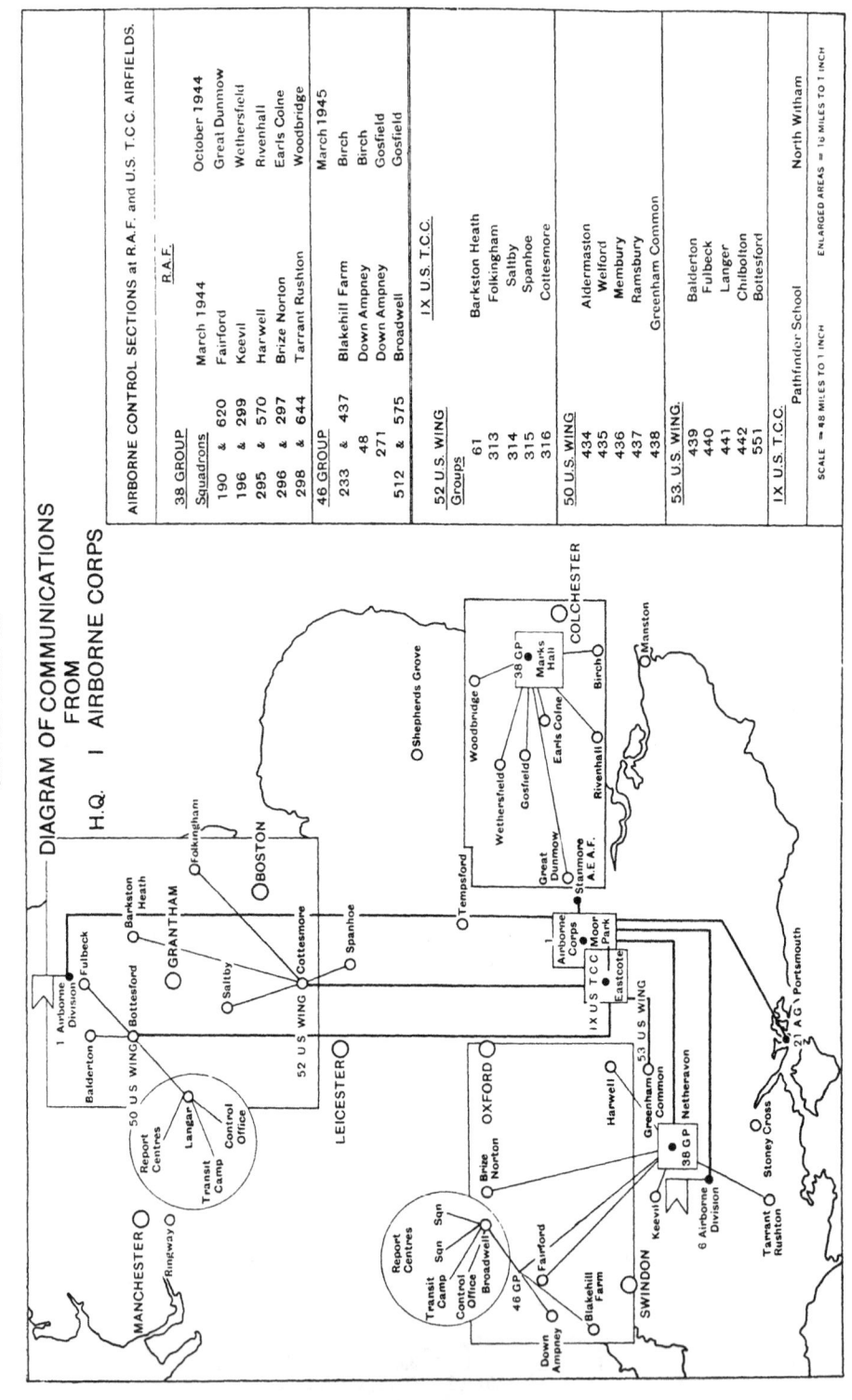

AIRBORNE CONTROL SECTIONS at R.A.F. and U.S. T.C.C. AIRFIELDS.			
		R.A.F.	
38 GROUP			
Squadrons		March 1944	October 1944
190 & 620		Fairford	Great Dunmow
196 & 299		Keevil	Wethersfield
295 & 570		Harwell	Rivenhall
296 & 297		Brize Norton	Earls Colne
298 & 644		Tarrant Rushton	Woodbridge
46 GROUP			March 1945
233 & 437		Blakehill Farm	Birch
48		Down Ampney	Birch
271		Down Ampney	Gosfield
512 & 575		Broadwell	Gosfield
		IX U.S. T.C.C.	
52 U.S. WING			
Groups			
61		Barkston Heath	
313		Folkingham	
314		Saltby	
315		Spanhoe	
316		Cottesmore	
50 U.S. WING			
434		Aldermaston	
435		Welford	
436		Membury	
437		Ramsbury	
438		Greenham Common	
53. U.S. WING.			
439		Balderton	
440		Fulbeck	
441		Langer	
442		Chilbolton	
551		Bottesford	
IX U.S. T.C.C.			
		Pathfinder School	North Witham
SCALE = 48 MILES TO 1 INCH			ENLARGED AREAS = 16 MILES TO 1 INCH

APPENDIX 12

OPERATIONAL CHANNELS
HEADQUARTERS FIRST ALLIED AIRBORNE ARMY

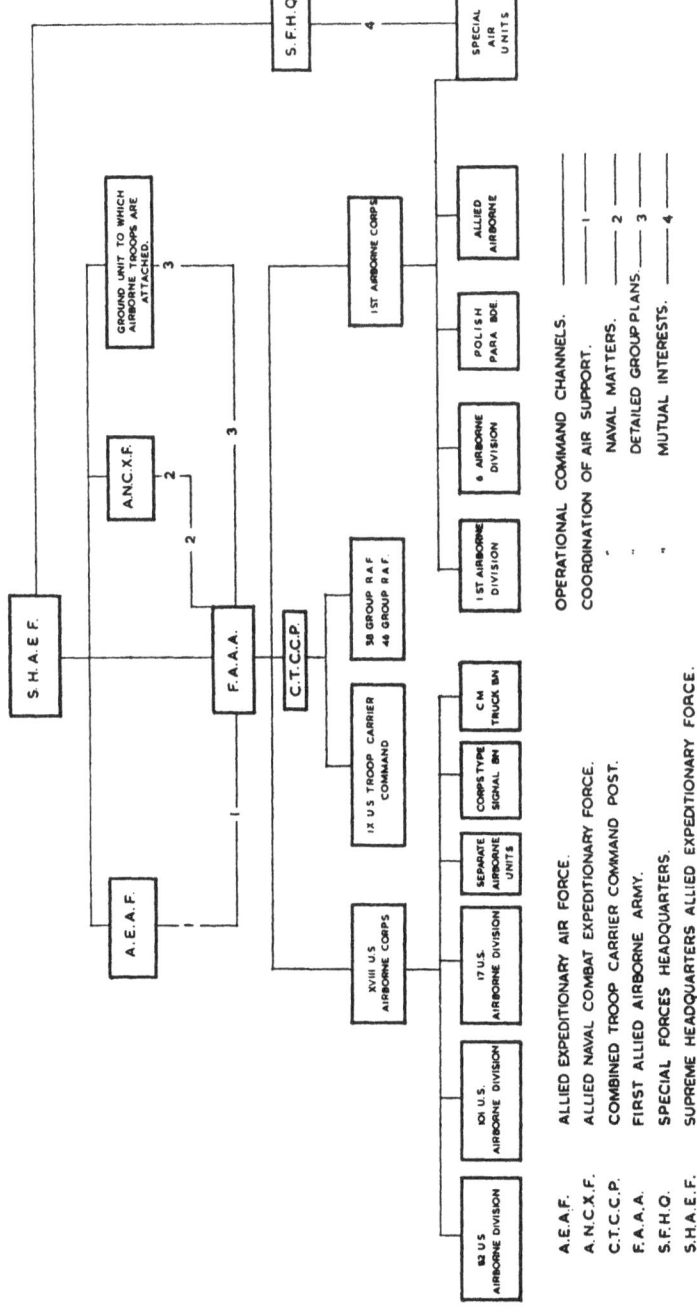

A.E.A.F.   ALLIED EXPEDITIONARY AIR FORCE.
A.N.C.X.F.   ALLIED NAVAL COMBAT EXPEDITIONARY FORCE.
C.T.C.C.P.   COMBINED TROOP CARRIER COMMAND POST.
F.A.A.A.   FIRST ALLIED AIRBORNE ARMY.
S.F.H.Q.   SPECIAL FORCES HEADQUARTERS.
S.H.A.E.F.   SUPREME HEADQUARTERS ALLIED EXPEDITIONARY FORCE.

THE HANDLEY PAGE HALIFAX

Fig. 15

THE ARMSTRONG WHITWORTH ALBEMARLE

Fig. 16

THE SHORT STIRLING

Fig. 17

THE ARMSTRONG WHITWORTH WHITLEY

Fig. 18

THE DOUGLAS DAKOTA

Fig. 19

GLIDER MARSHALLING AT WOODBRIDGE

Fig. 20

THE HORSA GLIDER

Fig. 21

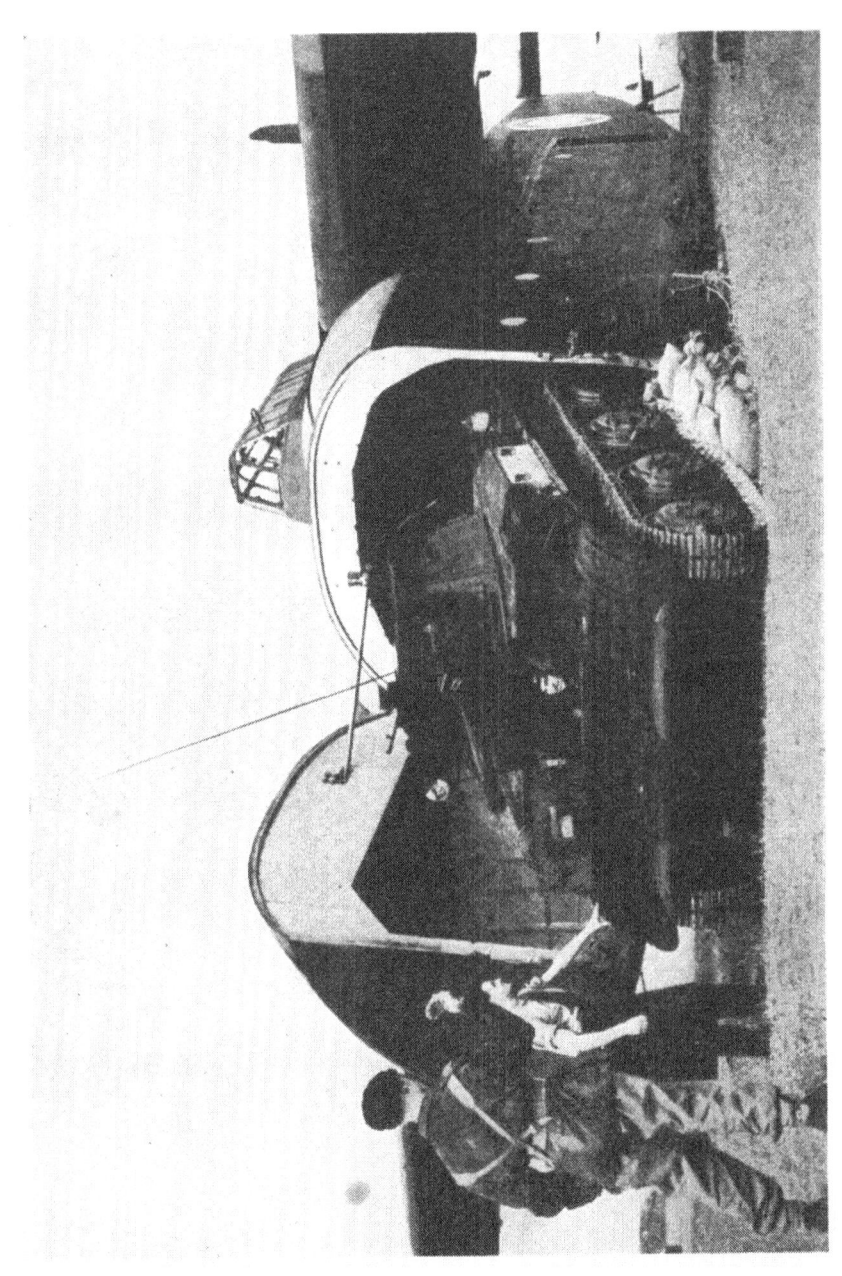

UNLOADING TANK FROM HAMILCAR GLIDER

Fig. 22

www.ingramcontent.com/pod-product-compliance
Lightning Source LLC
Chambersburg PA
CBHW082030300426
44117CB00015B/2419